Beethoven
The Last Decade 1817–1827

BEETHOVEN

An engraving after a crayon drawing done by the French pastel-artist, Louis Letronne, in 1814. The whereabouts of the original drawing are not known. Beethoven gave Letronne two sittings of an hour each, and the portrait was said by contemporaries to be an excellent likeness, if slightly idealized. Beethoven's approval of the engraving is suggested by the fact that he signed it, although this was contrary to his usual practice.

MARTIN COOPER

BEETHOVEN

The Last Decade
1817—1827

With a medical appendix by
Edward Larkin

London
OXFORD UNIVERSITY PRESS
New York Toronto

Oxford University Press, Ely House, London W.1

GLASGOW NEW YORK TORONTO MELBOURNE WELLINGTON
CAPE TOWN SALISBURY IBADAN NAIROBI DAR ES SALAAM LUSAKA ADDIS ABABA
BOMBAY CALCUTTA MADRAS KARACHI LAHORE DACCA
KUALA LUMPUR SINGAPORE HONG KONG TOKYO

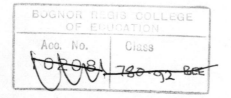

Printed in Great Britain by
The Camelot Press Ltd., London and Southampton

Preface

'Think of a flower'—'Rose'. 'Think of a colour'—'Red'. 'Name a composer'—'Beethoven'. These are apparently the commonest stock responses; and this fact alone is perhaps, after two hundred years, sufficiently remarkable to warrant yet another study of Beethoven. It is true that the last decade of his life, which is the period that I have chosen, is not the period during which he wrote the works which have won him the reputation reflected in the common equation of his name with 'composer'. But it was during those ten years that Beethoven finally came to realize the potentialities of both his art and his nature, so that his death at fifty-six does not leave us with a sense of wasted opportunities or of powers still unused. Even his contemporaries seem to have felt this. It was not of course as uncommon in 1827 as it is today to die at fifty-six; but even so, the absence of all contemporary laments over unwritten masterpieces is remarkable in the case of a man with Beethoven's reputation. His work evidently seemed, if not yet finished, still in some sense complete.

It was certainly not felt, on the other hand, as it is today, that in the compositions of those last years Beethoven had, as it were, distilled the essence of his musical nature. The last piano works were still regarded as for connoisseurs only and the last quartets as indisputably eccentric, even if not providing evidence of actual mental derangement. One hundred years after Beethoven's death it was these 'third period' works that first spoke to me at anything but a purely superficial level. Brought up, like all my generation, on the symphonies and an unimaginative selection of the piano sonatas, for which my enthusiasm was taken for granted, I automatically rejected them (and, as I thought, the composer *in toto*) and turned to music of an entirely different type. Stravinsky was at that time leading a campaign aimed at toppling German nineteenth-century music from its all-but-undisputed domination of music and musical thinking, and I fell without a blow or a regret under the new spell of French and Russian music, of the newly appreciated Mozart and the rediscovered Verdi. My rejection of Beethoven was that of a child: the associations of his

music and personality (as presented to me) with stuffy provincialism
and academic good taste were so potent that I simply did not hear the
music. Long after I should have outgrown this childish state of
reaction I remember, to my shame, writing that the Adagio of the
Ninth Symphony simply recalled to me a wet English Sunday afternoon. How bright and bold I must have thought this at the time, and
how pathetic it looks now!

This book, then, is something in the nature of an *amende honorable*,
the belated repayment of a debt whose very existence I for long could
not acknowledge. Of course there are many people to whom my
contrition will seem as comic as my fault trivial, both arising from an
attitude to music that belongs to another age.

The cultural milieu has changed, and a fascination with new media, with more
searching methods of analysis, has replaced the older tendency to explain music
with reference to ideas and beliefs held by the composer. Just as the philosopher has lost interest in the traditional metaphysical systems and has found
a new and vital task in the mathematics of thought, so the music critic has
turned aside from the examination of meaning to a study of structure. The
question of meaning does not arise. If a work is aesthetically significant, there
is no need to use too many words about it. Its significance can be illuminated
by analysis.[1]

'Structure' is perhaps only a new word for, or a new aspect of what
used to be called 'meaning'; but it remains true that many of those
who write about music today are overwhelmingly concerned with
its mechanics. These, however, do not interest the ordinary intelligent
music-lover, and it is to him, rather than to professionals, that this
book is addressed.

I found the chief inducement to writing in the music composed by
Beethoven during the last decade of his life; but I was also attracted by
questions of Beethoven's personality, and particularly by the supposed
contradiction—universally accepted, though never really investigated
—between the composer's life and works during this period. I have
never been able to accept the doctrine, fashionable in my youth and by
no means abandoned today, that it is useless to search in an artist for
any connection between what he is and what he does, between his
personality as expressed on the one hand in human relationships and on
the other in artistic creation. This supposition has always seemed to
me quite as simple-minded as the contrary, from which it was of
course the reaction: that 'beautiful' music could only be written by a

[1] Philip Barford, 'Beethoven' in *The Music Review* August 1965.

'beautiful' character. The only real flaw in this, apparently naïve belief is the painfully restricted sense generally given to the word 'beautiful'. It seems to me irrefutable that the 'beauty'—or perhaps better 'greatness'—of a work of art does indeed argue some kind of 'beauty' (or 'greatness') in its creator; only in most cases this will not take commonly expected forms nor leap to the innocent eye, but may rather be masked, or even distorted by conflicting characteristics of a purely superficial nature or frustrated by contradictory physical circumstances. In Beethoven's case there is an exact parallel, I believe, between a 'difficult' character and the difficult nature of many things in the last works. These contain many passages—the fugal finales of the D major cello sonata op. 102 no. 2, for instance, or of op. 106, not to mention the Grosse Fuge of op. 130—which are very far from being obviously or conventionally 'beautiful'; and to discover and appreciate their 'beauty' and significance needs exactly the same patience, discernment, and humility in the listener as are needed to see past the superficial inequalities and roughness of Beethoven's character to the diamond quality which they effectively conceal from the too casual observer. Mozart, in this connection, is in many ways a more puzzling case than Beethoven. For it hardly needs more than a cursory acquaintance with Beethoven's often uncouth letters, or with the reports of his contemporaries, to discover the deep, unmistakable unity between the man's character and his work, especially during his last years. The bungling of his personal affairs—domestic, financial and, in the case of Karl, personal—can be seen to be as purely super-ficial and incidental, as little significant in estimating the real quality of the man, as (say) the fact that a composer today might drive a car badly, make bad income-tax returns or mishandle the bringing-up of a child. The notorious romantic pathos of genius half starved, exploited, quarrelsome, and more than half 'mad', yet inexplicably producing sublime music, vanishes at the first intelligent contact with the facts of Beethoven's life.

The list of books devoted to various aspects of Beethoven's music or personality occupies more than 36 columns in the catalogue of the British Museum Reading Room; and I have not been spared the pungent question whether it was in fact possible to say anything new on so voluminously discussed a topic. I have comforted myself with the reflection that portrait-painters and photographers instinctively choose different angles and lights for their studies and, by so doing, often produce fresh portraits of even the most familiar personality— 'in a new light' or 'from a new angle', as the saying goes. Choice, as well as necessity, decided me to confine myself as nearly as possible to original sources, and to avoid filling my head with other men's theories and ideas. My bibliography will reveal even to those who are not experts how much of the Beethoven literature I have in fact neglected.

In one instance, however, this book really does make a new contribution to the study of Beethoven. This does not come from me but from my friend Dr. Edward Larkin, whose painstaking and detailed investigation of the evidence has led him to formulate an entirely new hypothesis to explain the still unsolved problems of Beethoven's medical history. My warmest thanks are due to him for allowing me to include his invaluable study in an appendix, and also for the many hours during which he has generously put his wide knowledge of mental and physical medicine at my service.

I am greatly indebted to Dr. Hans Hollander and Mr. Alan Tyson for reading and commenting on my proofs; to Dr. Kurt Sluzewski, for kindly allowing me to reproduce a letter from Beethoven to his nephew Karl, never before reproduced, and also a portrait signed, contrary to his common practice, by the composer himself; to Dr. Richard Sickinger, formerly assistant-director of the Austrian Institute in London, for his elucidation of a number of linguistic and historical points; to the Revs. Lawrence Hollis and A.Sampers, CSSR, General Archivist of the Redemptorist Order; to Anna Kallin, Margery Weiner, and Roger Fulford for help over points of historical detail; to the Beethovenarchiv in Bonn; and to the staff of the British Museum Reading Room.

In quoting from Beethoven's sketches I have not added either key-signatures or clefs where the composer himself omitted them. All quotations from Beethoven's letters are taken from the English edition by Emily Anderson (3 vols., 1961).

Contents

Part One

Part Two

Plates

Beethoven. An engraving after a crayon drawing
done by the French pastel-artist Louis Letronne
in 1814. Reproduced by courtesy of Dr. C. Sluzewski.
Frontispiece

A letter to Karl, of October 1816. Reproduced by
courtesy of Dr. C. Sluzewski. *Facing page 20*

For

Egon Wellesz

teacher and friend,
with affectionate respect

'Über die Blinden, die Beethoven für einen Tauben
hielten!' (Wilhelm von Lenz)
('Shame on the blind men who took Beethoven for a
deaf man!')

'Ein gehörloser Musiker! Ist ein erblindeter Maler
zu denken? Aber den erblindeten Seher kennen
wir—Teiresias' (Richard Wagner)
('A musician without a sense of hearing! Can we
imagine a painter deprived of sight? No, but the
seer deprived of sight we know—Teiresias.')

Part One

CHAPTER 1

Introduction

Beethoven's case is unique in the history of music: there is no other instance of a composer whose works, one hundred and fifty years after his death, still form the staple basis of the repertory in the concert-hall, in chamber music, and among pianists of all degrees, from the beginner to the greatest virtuoso, satisfying in different ways the simplest, most ignorant listener and the most intellectual, most exclusively 'musical' professionals. The extraordinary position that he occupied in the imagination of his contemporaries—'one God in heaven and one Beethoven on earth,' as a young English admirer put it—he has never really lost. Even when the natural processes of artistic development and reaction shortly obscured his reputation among some musicians, it was the time-encrusted cult-image of the man and the aesthetics of his age which they rejected. No reputable musician has seriously questioned the quality of Beethoven's music, though they may, like Stravinsky, have delighted in finding flaws in a popular idol, may have resented the domination of the repertory by often unintelligent, routine performances of his music and felt that the concept of the 'Beethoven symphony' weighed like a dead hand on the further development of the art and must therefore be violently rejected. The ordinary music-lover, on the other hand, has been unswervingly loyal to the great works by which he has known Beethoven—the symphonies and the concertos in the first place, perhaps a dozen of the thirty-two piano sonatas, half a dozen chamber works, *Fidelio* and its overtures. Everyone who has even the most superficial interest in Western European music has a vague acquaintance with at least some of these works; and there are many people who would hardly claim any serious interest in 'classical' music and would certainly declare themselves uncomprehendingly indifferent to the music of Bach, Mozart, Schubert, Wagner or their successors, yet find in the Third, Fifth, or Seventh Symphonies, the op. 57 piano sonata, and the E flat major piano concerto the same kind of spontaneous, inarticulate sense of elevation and heightened awareness that they experience in the presence of imposing natural phenomena—on the top of a mountain, at the foot of a waterfall, or before a flamboyant sunset. These works of Beethoven 'speak' to quite uncultivated human sensibilities and command their attention in a way that is literally unique. It is for this reason that Beethoven is probably still unconsciously accepted by unthinking people in Europe and America as the fundamental type of the composer, vaguely identified with inarticulate longings for freedom and for something outside and above the daily round of material cares and preoccupations, with some element of nobility and fearlessness.

The quite ignorant, who know Beethoven only from his music, have, in a sense, until recently been in a better position to understand him than the half-informed who have been exposed to the legends which formed, first about the man and then about his music, almost before he was dead. This growth of legend round his name is not the only, though it is perhaps the most striking, similarity between Beethoven and those heroes of the popular imagination for whom in earlier ages their admirers demanded the semi-divine honours of canonization. Hero-worship is spontaneous in children and in simple people, who also demand that their heroes should be not, like themselves, compounded of human inconsistencies and frailties, but all of a piece and divinely consistent. If Beethoven himself has occupied the place of a kind of secular saint in the imaginations of countless admirers of his music, it is because they could not conceive that the creator of the works which they justly found sublime could himself be anything other than sublime, or be subject to the humiliating faults and pettinesses of ordinary humanity.

The first instances of this inclination to romanticize or 'heroicize' Beethoven's personality are to be found in two of the three letters which Bettina von Arnim published in the *Athenaeum für Wissenschaft, Kunst und Leben* in 1839. Of the three, ostensibly written by Beethoven to Bettina Brentano (as she then was) in 1810, 1811, and 1812, only one appears to be genuine. The other two are rambling, high-falutin, and 'romantic' in style, absolutely unlike Beethoven's other letters. They were almost certainly forged by Bettina, though possibly based on her memories of Beethoven's conversation, a 'memory' very much influenced by her preconceived ideas of the artist's role and by her own personal vanity. In these letters she represents Beethoven as a 'natural' genius, a revolutionary, a magician, and a priest; and these remained almost to the end of the nineteenth century the attributes, singly or in conjunction, of the romantic artist. It is interesting that even Beethoven's first biographer, Anton

Schindler, instinctively rejected Bettina von Arnim's letters with the comment that 'Beethoven had never been a *bel esprit* or a monstrous big talker'. Schindler in fact knew that Beethoven's personality was strongly ethical, and very little concerned with pure aesthetics. It was therefore the ethical side of the portrait that Schindler felt obliged to touch up, and he had no sympathy whatever with Bettina's aestheticizing inventions.[1] Even as late as 1911 Paul Bekker could speak of Beethoven as 'himself crucified and descending to hell and rising again', language that clearly reveals the writer's sense of something at least super-human, if not actually 'divine', in Beethoven's character.

The contrast between the man and his music was already painful to many of his contemporaries. This embarrassment may be seen in its simplest form as early as 1809, when the Baron de Trémont reported his visit to the composer:

Picture to yourself the extreme of dirt and disorder: pools of water decorating the floor, and a rather ancient grand piano on which dust competed for room with sheets of written or printed notes. Under it—I do not exaggerate—an unemptied chamber-pot. . . . Most of the chairs had straw seats and were decorated with clothes and with dishes full of the remains of the previous day's supper.[2]

It would hardly be fanciful to see in that unemptied chamber-pot a symbol of something in Beethoven's life that proved so absolutely unacceptable to the nineteenth century that its presence simply had to be denied, and with it all the other evidences of Beethoven's often primitive human personality. The twentieth century is less squeamish and even inclined to react too sharply against the well-meant but ill-judged idealizing of Beethoven by nineteenth-century biographers. It is no more reasonable to glorify Beethoven's crude or slovenly physical habits and 'uncultured' behaviour than it is to deny their existence. Instead of the superficially unappetizing truth biographers, led by Beethoven's blindly loyal but not very intelligent factotum, Anton Schindler, instinctively elaborated the kind of portrait that might have been conceived by Beethoven's contemporary, the Danish sculptor Bertel Thorwaldsen—an heroic cross between Nordic giant and Greek god, purest marble from leonine head to powerful foot, a 'noble' and imposing generalization comparable to the apostles that Thorwaldsen carved for the Vor Frue Kirke in Copenhagen. Schindler, who lived in close and almost daily communication with Beethoven

[1] The whole subject is thoroughly discussed by Arnold Schmitz in *Das romantische Beethovenbild* (1927).
[2] Published in *Guide Musical*, Nos. 11 and 12, 23 and 27 March 1892.

during the last ten years of the composer's life, was well aware that in order to present such a portrait to the world—a portrait that he himself instinctively wished to present and knew was demanded of him—a great deal more than a single unemptied chamber-pot had to be suppressed, and he had no scruple in suppressing it. Before condemning him out of hand, it is only just that we should consider first the attitude to biography in general that obtained during the first half of the nineteenth century, and then the particular circumstances of Beethoven and of Schindler.

The idea that all the intimate details of a great man's private life should automatically become public property at his death was adumbrated by Boswell but belongs really to the twentieth century.[1] Since Freud has shown that the apparently trivial, unpremeditated, and often unconscious details of everyday behaviour may provide a key to human personality, educated people have been obliged to adopt a new attitude to biography. Where earlier biographers accepted a man's statement of his motives and ideals at their face value and interpreted his actions in terms of them, the twentieth century reverses the process, examining a man's actions, including the smallest and most trivial, and interpreting his conscious statements in their light. To take a concrete instance very relevant in Beethoven's case—it is an easily observable fact that many of those who proclaim most loudly their love of the human race are in fact difficult neighbours, intolerant or suspicious in their family relationships. Their general, theoretical benevolence seems to break down the moment it is tested by the practical demands of an individual case. The nineteenth-century biographer slurred over, or tried to explain away, what seemed to him a painful and inexplicable inconsistency of this kind. What other course was possible, except to lay his subject open to the charge of hypocrisy? Schindler, and the many biographers who followed him, were perfectly right in regarding it as unthinkable to accuse Beethoven of conscious hypocrisy; and when Beethoven's practice failed to coincide with his precept, they simply drew a veil over the situation. In so doing they were certainly following the universal practice of the day, but they were flying in the face of Beethoven's own explicit wishes. 'There are papers here and papers there,' he said on his death-bed to Stephan von Breuning. 'Gather them together and make the best use of them, but the strict

---

[1] It was over precisely this principle that Schindler quarrelled with Ries. See Schindler, *Biographie von Ludwig van Beethoven* (3rd edition Münster, 1860), p. 12: 'Überhaupt vertheidigte Ries den Satz: über grosse Männer darf alles ausgesagt werden, es schadet ihnen nicht.'

truth in everything. I make you both [Breuning and Schindler] responsible for that.'[1] When, owing to death and defaulting, it finally fell to Schindler to write the first official biography of the composer, he could not bring himself to fulfil this explicit request. Indeed in 1840 it would have required a man of quite exceptional intelligence and bravery to publish all that Schindler knew of Beethoven personally, to realize that the truth could never inflict lasting damage on Beethoven's name, and to face the storm of public indignation and the accusations of disloyalty that his frankness would certainly have aroused.

Schindler's task was, in any case, made doubly difficult by the fact that Beethoven was an artist, and that any estimate of his character which failed to take his music into account was plainly worthless. Even the twentieth-century biographer, who fixes his attention on a man's actions rather than his words, has to confront the fact that by far the most important 'actions' in any artist's life are his creations. Beethoven himself was bitterly aware of this when he said (as reported by the publisher, C. F. Peters, in 1824) 'Everything I do apart from music is badly done and stupid.' The professions of idealism and philanthropy, of tenderness and nobility, religious devotion and human forbearance that are scattered throughout his letters, diaries, and conversation-books are often in the shrillest possible contrast with his everyday behaviour as we know it to have been; but they are perfectly reflected in his music, the field of activity in which Beethoven himself would have asked to be judged, and indeed the only field in which such judgement is in the last issue valid. We know far too little of the ultimate springs and determinants of human behaviour to condemn the man even when we can deplore his behaviour, as we sometimes may in the case of Beethoven; and Schindler's action in suppressing much of the evidence relating to his personal life during the years between 1819–27 is regrettable not because it leaves a serious blank in some imaginary indictment of Beethoven's character, but because no evidence is too small or too trivial to be taken into account when trying to form a true picture of the man whom Antonie Brentano could describe in 1819 as 'even greater as a human being than as an artist'. (Letter to J. M. Sailer, 22 February 1819.)

The last decade of Beethoven's life forms for several reasons a kind

[1] Schindler, p. 19. But there is no doubt that on 30 August 1826 he formally authorized Carl Holz as his biographer. Schindler pp. 681–2: 'Ich schenke ihm das volle Vertrauen, dass er das, was ich ihm zu diesem Zwecke mitgetheilt habe, nicht entstellt der Nachwelt überliefern wird'.

of separate entity, a unity which can be traced most clearly in the compositions dating from these years. Wilhelm von Lenz's division of the composer's life into three creative 'periods' was founded on real and demonstrable stylistic differences;[1] and it is valuable so long as the divisions between the three periods are not regarded as rigid and it is remembered, for example, that during the third and last period that concerns us here Beethoven interspersed his work on the Ninth Symphony and the Missa Solemnis with the revision or transcription of his own early works, in order to make money. Psychologically these last ten years were dominated by an obsessive devotion to his nephew Karl, by the bitter struggle with his sister-in-law to obtain sole legal responsibility for the boy, and by the slow and agonizing process of disillusionment, which ended with the realization that he had lost the promising child in the commonplace youth. From the biographer's point of view these ten years are unique by reason of the evidence available. Beethoven was virtually stone-deaf by 1818 and the only way of communicating with him was by writing. For this purpose he provided his visitors with pads, or notebooks, on which they could write their own questions and answer his. At his death in 1827 there were, according to Schindler, some four hundred of these 'conversation-books', which must have provided an extraordinarily complete chronicle of the composer's social and private life—the identity of his visitors, the nature of the conversations which they held with him, and his own preoccupations, which are reflected in countless jottings of every kind in his own hand. These include innumerable references to lodgings and servants, to foods and wines, to books that were recommended to him or advertisements that caught his eye in the newspaper, from new types of coffee-machine or a new swimming-belt with bladders attached, to the re-stuffing of mattresses, the provision of mousetraps and Herr Cazeneuve's 'odourless mobile lavatory'. In order to reconstruct the day-to-day character of Beethoven's life during these years we have only to turn to these conversation-books and to his letters, to the accounts left by his many visitors and to the notes made for his own purposes, sometimes in the conversation-books and sometimes on loose sheets of paper. If we still possessed this evidence as Beethoven left it at his death, we should have a unique documentation for these ten years only comparable to tape-recordings of the telephone conversations and casual table-talk of a great man. The picture of Beethoven that emerged would have been, in a sense, like the negative of a photograph, since it is mostly his visitor's answers that are recorded,

[1] See Part 2 chapter 15, pp. 133.

and his own words were only written down on the comparatively rare occasions when the conversations took place in a restaurant or some other public place and were concerned with private or controversial matters. Even this negative portrait, however, threw a shadow-likeness of Beethoven that Schindler felt it his duty to modify very extensively before he gave it to the world; and he therefore deliberately distorted (or, as he would have said, corrected) the image of the composer by destroying more than 50 per cent of the evidence, 264 of the the 400 conversation-books that he inherited from Stephan von Breuning. He justified his action by claiming that what he destroyed contained matter that was either purely trivial or else politically undesirable—what he described as 'zügellose Ausfälle gegen Allerhöchste Personen, Kaiser und Kronprinz' (unbridled ranting against people of the highest station, the Emperor and the Crown Prince).[1] What Schindler considered trivial may well have included much that seemed to him to show Beethoven in a disreputable light and must certainly have contained a priceless record of just those immediate reactions, spontaneous interjections, and unconscious revelations of character and interests to which modern psychology attaches the greatest importance. Where politics were concerned, Schindler was very much aware that Beethoven's European reputation and his many friends and admirers among the Viennese aristocracy had given him a unique immunity. Schindler himself had suffered from the unwelcome attentions of Metternich's secret police when he was a law-student at the University of Vienna in 1815, the year of the Congress when police vigilance was redoubled and private espionage developed on an enormous scale. Exactly how far Schindler was implicated (he was only twenty at the time) and the nature of the 'conspiracy' we do not know; but the fact that he belonged in 1816 to the short-lived society that demanded the abandonment of French fashions, among other things in dress, and the return to national customs (*deutsches Wesen*) suggests that he may have done no more than attend the meeting of some such nationalist club. In any case he took a post in his native Moravia, was arrested but finally released by the police and had to tell Beethoven, whom he had not known for long, the whole story. In fact Schindler, the son of a schoolmaster sympathetic with his son's musical ambitions, was by

---

[1] In the case of two of the destroyed note books Schindler was animated, on his own admission, by jealousy of Karl Holz, who replaced him from the autumn of 1825 to that of 1826 as Beethoven's factotum. According to Schindler Holz encouraged Beethoven's drinking and shared Beethoven's radical political opinions. Schindler and Holz carried on an undignified wrangle over their right to Beethoven's papers in the *Kölnische Zeitung* during 1845. For Schindler's case see op. cit., pp. 679–86.

temperament as respectful of authority, as Beethoven, who had been bullied by a father he could not even respect, was intolerant; and his early brush with the police had convinced him that radical opinions, even if not actually wicked in themselves, were at least to be kept quiet. In the conversation-books that Schindler did not destroy Beethoven's occasional outbursts against the government or the royal family are struck through with a pencil.[1]

As if Schindler's act of pious vandalism were not enough, the remaining conversation-books have suffered an extraordinary series of misfortunes. No plan to make them available to the public was initiated until after the 1914–18 war, and then the Beethoven scholar Walter Nohl died after editing a single volume.[2] This covered no more than the years 1819–20. Some twenty years later Georg Schünemann produced three volumes covering the years 1818–23, part of an edition planned to cover the whole of the conversation-books in ten volumes.[3] He died in 1945, leaving the project uncompleted; and in 1951 the autographs disappeared for some time from the Deutsche Staats-bibliothek. Although the autographs have been returned to the library, it still remains true that, for the years 1824–7, all that we now possess in published form, apart from quotations in the writings of earlier Beethoven scholars such as A. W. Thayer, Theodor Frimmel and Alfred Kalischer is the selection published in French translation by J. G. Prod'homme.[4] The process of elimination has, at least for the moment, ended in a landslide.

Of course the crucial evidence for the last decade of Beethoven's life is to be found not in any literature, but in the music that he composed. A striking negative argument in favour of distinguishing a 'third period' in Beethoven's creative life, covering roughly this last decade, is to be found in the fact that none of the works that enjoy greatest favour with the musically uninitiated were written during these years. Of the symphonies only the ninth, op. 125, belongs to this period. There are no concertos and the only other large works employing an orchestra are the Missa Solemnis and the rarely heard overture *Die Weihe des Hauses*, op. 124. The piano sonatas opp. 101, 106, 109, 110, and 111, the Diabelli Variations op. 120, and the string quartets opp. 127, 130, 131, 132, and 135 all reveal, as I shall hope to show in a later chapter, the characteristic marks of a late style,

[1] In the third edition of his biography Schindler gives a clear and reasonable account of Beethoven's hostility to the Austrian Government of his day, (op. cit., pp. 345 ff.).
[2] Walter Nohl, *Ludwig van Beethovens Konversationshefte*, Band I (Munich, 1922).
[3] Georg Schünemann, *Ludwig van Beethovens Konversationshefte* 3 vols. (1941).
[4] J. G. Prod'homme, *Les Cahiers de conversation de Beethoven* (1946).

in which nothing is conceded to the listener, no attempt is made to capture his attention or hold his interest. Instead the composer communes with himself or contemplates his vision of reality, thinking (as it were) aloud and concerned only with the pure essence of his own thoughts and with the musical processes from which that thought itself is often indistinguishable. Yet if, as has been said, Beethoven in fact bade farewell to the big public in the Ninth Symphony and the Missa Solemnis and thereafter confined himself to the introspective and austere form of the string quartet, this was far from being his conscious intention. His plans during the last two or three years of his life included a tenth symphony, for which sketches exist; another Mass, in C sharp minor, a Requiem, an oratorio, *Der Sieg des Kreuzes*; and the project which he mentions in a conversation dated from the year 1823:

I am not writing what I should most like to, but in order to earn the money that I need. That does not mean that I am writing simply for money—once this period is over I hope at last to write what is both for the art of music and for me personally the highest—'Faust'.

At the same time he was perpetually on the look-out for a new opera libretto, only abandoning with regret the plan of collaborating with the greatest Austrian playwright of the day and his personal friend, Franz Grillparzer. Beethoven was only fifty-seven when he died, and it would be a great mistake to envisage his last years as consciously dedicated to mystical contemplation or metaphysical speculation, to suppose him to have lost interest in the everyday life around him, in food and drink and human society. His never-ceasing preoccupation with money, which he was spending on or saving for his nephew Karl, witnesses to his complete awareness of everyday matters, even when his mismanagement of practical affairs suggests that his real interests were increasingly elsewhere, in the domain of spirit rather than of matter.

Misconceptions of a composer's nature are chiefly important when they lead to a serious misunderstanding of his work; for the object of any study of a composer's life and character is to obtain a clearer and more deeply penetrating insight into his music. The works of Beethoven's last years have, in fact, been surrounded in many people's minds with a kind of aura that is directly connected with the halo designed by Schindler and fitted with such difficulty to the composer's recalcitrant head. Because these last works of Beethoven's were sometimes found difficult to understand—'we can make nothing of your music', laments Grillparzer in one of the conversation-books—and their syntax certainly made new demands on listeners, it was soon believed that they possessed some extra-musical significance which could only be grasped by the learned or specially illuminated. We can find an echo of this belief, and a just resentment of it, even in so intelligent, if prejudiced, a musician as Edward Dent, who wrote in 1926: 'Beethoven's noble and visionary idealism, in its ardent insistence on the spiritual, tended more and more to suggest that the reality of music lay not so much in the actual sounds perceived by the physical ear as in the relations between them, in sounds—or rather relations between sounds—never actually heard at all, but induced in the perceptive faculty by association. The works of Beethoven's third period often seem to lead us into a metaphysical labyrinth. .   '[1]

This would have astounded Beethoven, as it astounds us. Dent was here repeating, and implicitly accepting without real investigation of its truth or falsehood, the nineteenth-century belief that some extra-musical *mana* attached to Beethoven's last works, something that removed them from the purely musical sphere and gave them quasi-religious significance. This belief was intimately and organically connected with the equally mistaken idea that Beethoven himself was some kind of superhuman being not subject to the ordinary human frailties. How untrue both these propositions are, I hope to show in the course of what follows.

[1] E. J. Dent, *Terpander or the Music of the Future* (1926), p. 71. Reprinted 1965 as *The Future of Music.*

CHAPTER 2

Beethoven's Position in 1816

B eethoven's life may be said to have entered its last phase on 15 November 1815, when his brother Carl Caspar died, leaving him joint-guardian, with the boy's mother, of his son Karl. The next four and a half years were occupied in the legal struggle to oust his sister-in-law from her part in the guardianship and in attempts first to decide on the right educational policy for the child and then to form some kind of stable domestic background for him. Karl was a boy of nine when his father died and Beethoven a bachelor of forty-four, a composer with a European reputation but almost stone-deaf, very eccentric, and irregular in his domestic habits. The seriousness with which he regarded his responsibilities as guardian, and the passionate feelings of proprietary tenderness aroused by the boy, were accompanied by an emotional revolution in Beethoven's life and a marked deterioration in his physical health, including his hearing. It is significant, too, that Beethoven finally gave up all idea of marriage at this time. He might have been expected to marry now, if only in order to provide a home for his nephew; and there was a keen candidate in the person of Fanny Giannatasio del Rio, daughter of Karl's first schoolmaster. Beethoven often confided his worries to her, and she described him in her diary as 'a man whom I so greatly prize and who, ever since we became acquainted, has become more and more dear to my heart'.[1] His attitude to women was always ambiguous, as is shown by the conflicting accounts of his contemporaries and his known abortive relationships with a series of generally aristocratic girls; but now it hardened into an unmistakable and often violent hostility. His deep fund of tenderness was all expended on the boy Karl, and jealousy of sharing his affection with a third person not only militated against Beethoven's marrying but also complicated his relationship with the housekeepers and servants who succeeded each other in his household with such rapidity and confusion.

These physical and emotional factors brought Beethoven in 1816

[1] Extracts from Fanny del Rio's diary were published by Ludwig Nohl: *Eine stille Liebe zu Beethoven* (1875), pp. 159 ff.

very near to what would today be termed a nervous breakdown. This condition is clearly reflected in the reduction of his output, for the years 1816–18 were the most unproductive of his life. Between the two sonatas for violoncello and piano op. 102 (dated by the composer '1815, towards the end of July') and the piano sonata op. 106 finished in the spring of 1819. Beethoven concerned himself to an unusual extent with trivialities—the arrangement of his trio op. 1 no. 3 as a string quintet (published as op. 104); *Six Thèmes pour le pianoforte avec accompagnement d'une flûte ou d'un violon ad libitum*, op. 105; *Dix Thèmes russes, écossais et tyroliens variés pour le piano avec accompagnement d'une flûte ou d'un violon ad libitum*, op. 107, which followed on the *25 schottische Lieder fur eine Singstimme mit Begleitung von Pianoforte, Violine und Violoncell obligat* that had occupied him during the summer of 1815 and during 1816. *An die ferne Geliebte* dates, it is true, from the April of 1816; but there are only two exceptions among these light-weight works, though they are formidable ones—the piano sonatas[1] op. 101, written in November 1816, and op. 106. This latter, which alone of the two has retained the title 'Hammerklavier' ('hammer-keyboard'), was begun in the autumn of 1817 and finished fifteen months later. This astonishing work makes it very clear that Beethoven's creative powers had been only temporarily impaired or were perhaps rather lying fallow before the unique period of activity which lasted from the summer of 1819 until the autumn of 1826.

If the disturbances in Beethoven's private life provide sufficient explanation for his comparative infertility between 1816 and 1818, there were other factors which would have accounted objectively for a certain dissatisfaction and anxiety on his part, a feeling that he had come to the end of one period of his career as a composer and should be looking for some new way of living, a more specialized field for his powers. There was in the first place his slowly but unmistakably deteriorating health, which had never recovered after the serious illness of 1794. Whatever this may have been—rheumatic fever, typhoid, or typhus (not always distinguished in those days)—one of its permanent legacies seems to have been the colitis, enteritis, or chronic diarrhoea from which Beethoven seems hardly ever to have been free for more than a few months at a time. Another was a catarrhal infection which took the form of repeated 'colds' and, either alone or in conjunction with the chronic infection of the colon or bowel, probably accounted

[1] The title 'für das Hammerklavier' which qualifies both is Beethoven's tribute to that movement for *deutsches Wesen* which also interested Schindler.

for the deafness which Beethoven first noticed in 1798.[1] The increasingly recurrent bouts of severe colitis or enteritis would account for the great majority of Beethoven's physical complaints and, continuing over a long period, for the changes and deteriorations that all his friends observed in his character—intense irritability and bouts of nervous prostration, growing suspiciousness at times almost delusional and much aggravated by his deafness, and the indecision and confusion of thought which were so marked a feature of his behaviour during the last ten years of his life, at a time when his music passed into a new and supremely powerful, well-organized phase, a dichotomy by no means uncommon. Whatever its origin, his deafness had now reached a degree that made it impossible for him to appear in public as a performer of his own works, and very difficult to conduct them. The divorce between composing and performing music being still unknown, Beethoven must have been aware that even his enormous reputation could hardly counterbalance this handicap, which had already cut him off from performance and was soon to isolate him effectively from ordinary human contacts. The future that he imagined for himself, and confided to his diary in 1815, may seem unexpectedly modest for a composer of European fame and only forty-five years of age, but it was in a way optimistic. '. . . a small Court with a small chapel for which I could write and perform music in honour of the Almighty, the Eternal and Unending, so may my last days pass!'

When it was too late, Beethoven was to nourish optimistic dreams of a great concert-tour in England, but in 1815 he had had what he may have guessed to be his last great popular success in Vienna. At the Congress, which opened in September 1814 with the solemn entry of Tsar Alexander I and King Friedrich Wilhelm III of Prussia and broke up five months later when Napoleon escaped from Elba, he received flattering attentions from royalty. Despite the fact, mentioned in a secret police report of 30 November 1814, that 'the English delegation is so pious that they won't listen to music on a Sunday and Herr van Beethoven's concert has therefore been moved to a week-day',[2] the Seventh Symphony, *Der glorreiche Augenblick* and the *Battle of Vittoria* (two of the composer's weakest works, be it noted) were performed in the presence of the Empresses of Austria and Russia and the King of Prussia and the concert was rated as a *Hoffestlichkeit* (Court festivity). The diplomatic parties at the house of his old friend

---

[1] Beethoven himself believed that his deafness was intimately connected with the state of his bowels. For a new interpretation of Beethoven's physical symptoms see Appendix A.

[2] August Fournier, *Die Geheimpolizei auf dem Wiener Kongress* (1913) p. 288.

and patron the Russian ambassador, Count Razumovsky, were Beethoven's most noticeable appearances during the months of the Congress, and he himself described how the Empress of Russia 'paid court' to him during a reception at the Archduke Rudolf's, when he behaved 'very grandly' (*sehr vornehm*). On the occasion of the same Empress's birthday (25 January 1815) there was a concert in the Rittersaal at at which Franz Wild sang *Adelaide* and the programme included the quartet from the first act of *Fidelio* ('Mir ist so wunderbar'), while Beethoven himself played for the last time at a public concert. His music was not universally admired, however. Varnhagen von Ense, writing more than twenty years later and in the light of Beethoven's posthumous fame, observed that in 1814 'his name, although famous and honoured, was by no means so universally recognized as it has since become'. The Congress, he adds, in any case 'preferred Italian grace and lightness to German seriousness'.[1] From police records we also learn that 'two factions, for and against Beethoven, are forming. In opposition to Razumovsky, Apponyi, and Kraft, who idolize Beethoven, there is a large majority of connoisseurs who don't want to hear anything composed by Herr von [sic] Beethoven.'[2] In fact the Viennese taste for light music, which a year later (November 1816) was to find ideal satisfaction in the music of Rossini, demanded, as Varnhagen von Ense suggested, nothing more serious than the dance-tunes which formed the almost uninterrupted background to a congress of which it was wittily said 'le congrès danse, mais ne marche pas'.[3]

More than twenty years of unsuccessful wars, two foreign occupations and a state of bankruptcy had in fact completely changed Vienna, and Beethoven might well complain that life there was different from when he arrived as a young man in 1792. After the treaty of Campo Formio (1797) the atmosphere in Austria was very like that in England, and many other Western European countries, in the years between 1933 and 1938, with Napoleon playing the part of Hitler. Anxiety was followed by reprieve which was in turn replaced by a new anxiety. Caroline Pichler, who was a young married woman at this time, tells in her memoirs of hunger-marches and soup-kitchens, where a concoction called 'Rumford soup' was dispensed. Already in 1802 she speaks of the great distress caused by 'long and unsuccessful

---

[1] Varnhagen von Ense, *Denkwürdigkeiten*, 1840, vol. 5, pp. 86–7.
[2] Fournier, op. cit., p. 289.
[3] This *mot* of the Prince de Ligne's was strongly resented by the Austrian chancellor Metternich, who devotes a humourless footnote in his memoirs to refuting it. Metternich, *Denkwürdigkeiten*, vol. I, p. 319.

wars, financial complications, the devaluation of paper money, the increasing luxury of the lower orders and a succession of bad harvests'.[1] Ten years later, in 1812, she noted that 'foreign occupation, the insecurity of life and the repeated crises that threatened even the most peaceful citizen had given rise to a kind of fatalism' and deplored the popularity in the theatre of 'tragedies in which a desperate man's curse makes Providence the instrument of vengeance, hatred and even of blind stupidity'.[2] Despite Metternich's policy of 'order and stability', which seemed to receive triumphant confirmation in the restoration of the Bourbons to the French throne and the final defeat of Napoleon, the Austrian crown-lands in 1815 were in a state very nearly bordering on collapse.

Beethoven, though taking no part whatever in public life, had experienced personally not only the alarms and discomforts of the two occupations and the campaigns which were fought in the neighbourhood of Vienna, but the general deterioration, both moral and financial, inseparable from so long a period of external pressure and internal disturbance. Behind the façade of suave equanimity and good-humoured paternalism which Metternich and the Emperor Franz contrived to present to the world, the face of life in Austria, and more particularly in Vienna, was changing fast. The nobility, whose position under Maria Theresa had been unquestioned and under Joseph II only superficially damaged by paternalistic measures of centralization, never wholly recovered their power after the French invasions of 1805 and 1809, when the occupying troops spread by example the democratic principles that the secret police had been desperately trying to prevent infiltrating into Austria.

As early as March 1803—two years before the first French occupation—Count Pergen, chief of the Secret Police, had warned the Emperor that 'not only France produces secret *philanthropic* societies dedicated to destroying the basic principles of Christianity and monarchical government'[3] and had obtained permission to proceed ruthlessly against all forms of revolutionaries, whether they went under the names of *illuminati*, Tugendbündler, Carbonari, Burschenschaften, or Mazzinisti. Spies were planted everywhere in society, not only in inns, restaurants, and coffee-houses, but in the private drawing-rooms and assemblies of the middle and upper classes, especially in

[1] Caroline Pichler, *Denkwürdigkeiten aus meinem Leben* (1844), vol. 2, pp. 32f. The author was a copious writer, and submitted a libretto ('Mathilde, ou les Croisades') to Beethoven.
[2] op. cit., vol. 2, pp. 236 sqq.
[3] Fournier, op. cit., p. 7.

bankers' houses, where the society was cosmopolitan and entry not difficult. These spies, known as 'Vertraute höheren Standes' (confidants of higher rank), were drawn from the upper ranks of society, and their reports often make amusing reading. During the Congress, when Vienna was filled to bursting with tourists, cranks, intriguers and adventurers of every kind, either working for themselves or in concert with one of the innumerable official delegations, the activity of the Secret Police reached an almost unimaginable pitch. *Chiffons*, or the contents of diplomatic waste-paper baskets and grates, were regularly presented to the police by cleaning-women (Castlereagh insisted on hiring women servants privately, not through the police, but his cleaners still reported the trivialities they collected) and *Rapporte* and *Interzepte* poured in from every imaginable source. The archives show that even the Austrian Empress's letters and those of the Emperor's sisters, were opened. The English couriers used by Castlereagh were reported 'unbribable', and the Russian delegation—huge in numbers and leading, as at later international conferences, a life almost entirely apart from the rest—were popularly believed to have instituted a large network of informers among the Viennese prostitutes. It is certainly true that one of the best known of the day—'die Wolters'—received a regular salary from General Volkonsky.[1]

Beethoven himself, who made no secret of his anti-feudal views (as we shall see later, this is a more correct description than 'republican') was only left unmolested by the police because of the protection that he enjoyed among the aristocracy. He certainly shared, however, with every other Viennese citizen the knowledge that the Secret Police had spies everywhere, and there are repeated references to this in the conversation-books. In 1820, for instance, there is an entry which must have been made in a restaurant or café, and consists of a single line of warning to Beethoven

> another time—just now the spy Haensl is here

Moreover by 1815 Beethoven had lost or alienated the majority of his aristocratic friends and patrons, except the Archduke Rudolf who, as brother of the Emperor, was the most influential of all. The death of

---

[1] August Fournier, op. cit., p. 21. Although the similarity between the bureaucracy and police supervision in Austria under Franz I and in Russia under Alexander I seems clear enough to us, we find Josef Karl Bernard—one of Beethoven's intimates and editor of the official *Wiener Zeitung*—countering a jeremiad of the composer's by the observation 'Well anyhow things are better here than in Russia'. Metternich, in his interesting portrait of Tsar Alexander I (*Denkwürdigkeiten*, I, pp. 281ff.) expresses almost exaggerated horror of political and social conditions in Russia.

Prince Lobkowitz at the end of 1816 left the Archduke the only remaining member of the trio who, in 1809, had kept Beethoven in Vienna by guaranteeing him a yearly allowance. Prince Kinsky had died in 1812, and the composer was obliged to negotiate with his heirs the continuance of his part of the pension; and Prince Lobkowitz had been made virtually a bankrupt. Both these events had occurred during the very worst period of Austria's financial crisis after the second French occupation, when the Finanz Patent of 1811 had introduced Redemption Bonds in place of bank-notes, at the rate of one for five. This was equivalent to depreciating paper-money to one-fifth of its nominal value, and the distress that it caused was not confined to Beethoven.[1] Vienna was at this time just becoming a modern industrial town (there were 27,000 factory workers in 1810) and the absence of all social legislation and welfare organization led to the proletarianization of a large section of the middle classes after the occupation and inflation. Grillparzer's autobiography gives a vivid picture of the desperate position of a lawyer's family, and manual workers, shopkeepers, and small officials were in many cases reduced to beggary. In June 1815 —four years, that is to say, after the Finanz Patent—a police spy reported a conversation in which the University Librarian had told him that 'even professors take on additional work in order to make enough to keep wife and children alive, while the students work less and less, realizing that no one can live by his profession, i.e. simply on his salary and the *Zuschuss*' (an additional allowance granted in the autumn of 1814). No wonder, then, that Beethoven suffered from money anxieties between 1811–15. Only the Archduke made up his allowance to pre-inflation value, and the contributions from Prince Lobkowitz after September 1811, and from Prince Kinsky after his death in November 1812 were uncertain until the spring of 1815, when the pension was restored from both sources. That he was making a livelihood by his compositions at this time is certainly true: from English sources alone he received during 1816 considerable sums from Neate and Birchall and a further sum from Thomson, while his appearances during the Congress months had brought him 4,000 silver gulden.[2] But he was not only impractical in planning his expenditure; his frequent changes of lodging and his habit of ordering a number of different dishes in a restaurant and eating only the one which most attracted him amount to the extravagances of a rich man. Moreover,

[1] There was no payment of the Kinsky annuity between December 1812 and March 1815, or of the Lobkowitz annuity between September 1811 and April 1815.
[2] Roughly £400—the gulden was worth 2 shillings (1961).

after his brother's death he was obsessed by the idea that he was 'wholly financially responsible' (as he says in a letter) for his nephew. This was not in fact the case, but the 4,000 gulden which he earned during the Congress were invested in bank-shares for Karl, and letters, diaries, and conversation-books make it clear that for the rest of his life this making and saving of money for Karl was one of his main preoccupations.

Beethoven's financial anxieties and general sense of resentment were aggravated by a number of different factors. In the first place his deafness made him pathologically suspicious of being robbed or exploited. Then his pathetic ignorance of the most elementary mathematics (seen in the conversation-books, as when he cannot multiply five and seventeen but adds five seventeens) made it almost impossible, even had he really wished, to understand either the meaning of the new financial regulations or the effect that they might have on the affairs of his patrons as well as his own. Lastly, his strong sense of what was due to him was deeply offended by the fact that he had lost contact with the aristocratic milieu which had welcomed and fêted him as a young man, and had found in its place no large appreciative public whom he could respect. He resented in no uncertain terms having to consort with the 'rabble' of servants and housekeepers and with the petty-minded or even shady characters with whom the lawsuit over his nephew Karl brought him into contact. This mood is very clearly reflected in Karl von Bursy's description of a visit that he paid Beethoven in the spring of 1816. The conversation could still be carried on by word of mouth, though Bursy had to speak loud and Beethoven often failed to understand what he said.

He told me a great deal about Vienna and his life here. Venom and rancour raged in him. He defies everything and is dissatisfied with everything, blaspheming against Austria and especially Vienna. . . . Art no longer stands so high as it once did, he said, is no longer respected, and above all no longer valued in terms of recompense. . . . 'Why do you remain here when every foreign ruler would be willing to make a place for you near his throne?' 'Circumstances keep me here', he replied [no doubt a reference to the guardianship of his nephew] 'but in Vienna things are shabby and mean. It could not be worse, from top to bottom. Everyone is a scoundrel. There is nobody one can trust. What is not down in black and white is not observed by anyone, not even by the man with whom you have made an agreement. Moreover one possesses nothing in Austria, since everything is worthless—that is to say, paper.[1]

[1] Karl von Bursy's diary—with some deletions by the Russian censor—was first published in 1854 in the *St. Petersburger Zeitung*, a German-language magazine concerned with belles lettres which only lasted from 1853 to 1855.

The truss-maker has called once already, but to no purpose. He has promised to call again, to bring you another truss and to take away the old one to have it washed. He has already been paid for everything.

All good wishes. May God enlighten your soul and your heart!

Your uncle and guardian   Beethoven'

The letters of 1816 are mostly concerned with business and addressed either to his Viennese publishers, Steiner or Haslinger, to his London admirers Charles Neate and Sir George Smart or his old pupil Ferdinand Ries, also in London. Apart from these there are three affectionate letters to the Countess Erdödy, a few to old Rhineland friends like the Brentanos and Wegelers, and the usual notes to his patron and pupil the Archduke Rudolf, in which resentment seems to struggle with gratitude, a bad conscience with a genuine affection. The rest are addressed either to his nephew Karl or to Giannatasio del Rio, Karl's schoolmaster, and they resemble nothing so much as the letters of a fussy middle-aged widow worrying about a small boy. 'You will understand that I long to hear how my beloved Karl is now progressing. When informing me please do not forget to send me your full address, so that I may write to you direct.' And to the boy himself: 'Put on a pair of under-pants, or bring them with you so that you can put them on immediately after your bath, in case the weather turns cooler again. Has the tailor been yet? when he comes, he is to measure you for linen under-pants, too, as you need them.'[1] The letter is signed 'your trouser-button L. v. Beethoven', which he explained much later by saying that he clung to Karl 'like button to trousers'. It is a strange, pathetically playful word for a man of forty-six to use to a ten-year-old boy, but Beethoven was to use it again during his last illness to the young Gerhard von Breuning. It is clear that Beethoven was obsessed at this time by the nature of his relationship to his nephew. In one letter he describes himself as the boy's physical (*leiblich*) father, and to his old friend Wegeler he wrote: 'You are a husband, a father— so am I, but without a wife'. The nature of his feelings for the boy's mother Johanna van Beethoven, whom he nicknamed the Queen of the Night, can be seen from the following passage in a letter to Giannatasio del Rio: 'Last night that Queen of the Night was at the Artists' Ball until 3 a.m. exposing not only her mental but her bodily nakedness—it was whispered that she was willing to sell herself for 20 gulden![2] Oh horror! and are we to entrust to such hands as hers, even for a moment, our precious treasure? No, certainly not.' Since we are to meet Johanna van Beethoven very often, something should be said of her background and character.

It must be admitted that Beethoven was unlucky in his sisters-in-law. The elder of his two brothers, Carl Caspar, Karl's father and Beethoven's favourite, married in 1806 Johanna Reiss, the daughter

---

[1] See *Letters of Beethoven*, trans. Emily Anderson (London 1961), II, pp. 562, 599, 602.
[2] About £2.

c

of a prosperous upholsterer. Five months later Karl was born, so there may have been a certain element of compulsion in the marriage. In any case Carl Caspar himself was a weak and rather childish man, of no great character and unscrupulous in turning Beethoven's affection for him to good financial account. The marriage, which enraged Beethoven, did not turn out very happily; Johanna was a crass muddler and during her husband's last illness she took a lover by whom she had a child after her husband's death. That she subsequently had a second illegitimate child by another man hardly justifies Beethoven's belief— already clear from this letter of 1816—that she was a professional prostitute. Viennese sexual morality has always been permissive, and it should not be forgotten that this was a typical post-war period, when all standards were relaxed. Nevertheless Carl Caspar had been quite clear that his wife was not a fit person to have sole responsibility for their son, though he was optimistic when he made his brother co-guardian and recommended 'compliance to my wife and greater moderation to my brother'. Beethoven's principles in matters of sexual morality were puritanical; and he could not fail to suspect the worst of any feckless, pleasure-loving, possibly unbalanced woman, such as Johanna seems to have been.

Nikolaus Johann, the youngest of the three brothers, was much less close than Carl Caspar to Beethoven, but he contrived to disgrace himself almost as badly in his brother's eyes. In 1812, having made a considerable profit from his Linz chemist's shop by selling to the armies during the campaigns of 1809, Johann bought a house in which he let an apartment to a doctor and his wife. The wife's sister became first his housekeeper and then his mistress, and this fact reached Beethoven's ears. He at once travelled to Linz, and when Johann naturally refused to break off the relationship, Beethoven went to the bishop, the civil authorities and finally to the police, in an attempt to get the girl removed from the town. Johann very naturally retorted by marrying her, although she already had an illegitimate daughter. This marriage, too, turned out none too happily, and the conversation-books show that Johann in a serious illness was neglected (and probably cuckolded) by his wife and treated impertinently by her daughter. By a strange irony, however, Johann's wife seems to have been the only member of the family present when Beethoven died.

CHAPTER 3

The Lawsuit (1816–1820)

The legal proceedings by which Beethoven finally obtained sole control over his nephew Karl played so large a part in his life during the years 1816, 1817, 1818, 1819, and the first half of 1820 that it is impossible to spare the reader some account of them. There were three main stages. The first opened on 28 November 1815 when Beethoven submitted an appeal to the court of Lower Austrian Landrechte, stating that 'he could produce weighty reasons for the total exclusion of the widow from the guardianship', which the same court had confirmed when Carl Caspar's will was deposited with them the previous week. The 'weighty reasons' consisted in the revelation that four years previously Johanna had been condemned to a month's house-arrest by the Vienna Landesgericht, on the ground that she had been guilty of embezzling from her own husband (who had, of course, himself brought the charge). The Landrechte were courts for the nobility, and it may well be that Beethoven persuaded some of his aristocratic friends to use their influence; but whether this was so or not, he won his case and was solemnly invested by the court with the sole guardianship of his nephew on 9 January 1816. Karl entered Giannatasio del Rio's school as a boarder on 2 February, but his mother made repeated attempts to see him; and there is possibly some indication of her character (and certainly of her appearance) in the fact that on one occasion she disguised herself as a man in order to gain admittance to the school. Beethoven returned to the court and obtained an injunction by which the mother could see the boy only with Beethoven's consent. Even so, his jealousy of Karl's affections was so strong that it soon extended itself to the del Rio family, and he wrote at the end of July to say that he meant to remove his nephew from the school and have him to live with him, though this did not in fact happen until January 1818. This unhappy position continued with various fluctuations throughout 1816 and 1817. Beethoven was intensely disturbed, found it difficult to compose and seems, from entries in his diary,[1] to have suffered from a sense of guilt towards his sister-in-law:

[1] The so-called 'Diary' is contained in the Fischoff Manuscript. This contains miscellaneous papers, jottings, memoranda copied by Jacob Hotschevar, the guardian of nephew Karl, who

My part, O Lord, I have performed. It might have been possible without hurting the widow, but it was not so. Only Thou, All-powerful One, lookest into my heart, knowing that I have neglected my own good for my dear Karl's sake. Bless my work, bless the widow! Why can I not wholly obey my heart and help her, the widow?

God, God, my refuge, my rock, O my all, Thou seest my inmost heart and knowest how it grieves me to make anyone suffer through my good work for my dear Karl! ! ! Oh! hear, ever ineffable one, hear me, Thine unhappy, unhappiest of all mortals!

Help, God! Thou seest me abandoned by all mankind, for I will not commit injustice. Hear my cry, that I may yet in the future be with my Karl, for no possibility points to it now. O hard fate! O terrible doom! No, no, my unhappy state is unending.

That he was also concerned with the impression that the rest of the world would have of his behaviour towards his sister-in-law is shown by his remark to Fanny Giannatasio 'What will people say? they will take me for a tyrant.' His despair over the adverse effect that these emotional disturbances were having on his work is clear, too.

There is only one way to save yourself—by getting away. Only thus can you soar once again to the heights of your art, instead of sinking into a commonplace existence. Only write one symphony and then away, away, away!

Instead of this escape, the inner necessity of Beethoven's nature or perhaps the gradual deterioration in his physical condition caused him to sink still further. In 1818 the uneasy truce between him and his sister-in-law in their battle for Karl came to an end, and the second stage began. Beethoven had removed the boy from Giannatasio del Rio's school in January, and in May he took him to Mödling, a village in the neighbourhood of Vienna where he often spent the summer months. Karl was now a boy of twelve, and the emotional disturbances of the past three years were making themselves felt in his behaviour. The conflict between his natural affection for his mother and the compound of fear and affection that he felt for his uncle had already begun to show itself in trivial misdemeanours. Beethoven took these very seriously, immediately attributing them to his mother's bad influence, though his diary for February 1818 contains the note 'since August 10 his mother has not seen Karl'. At Mödling the boy was sent to school with the parish priest, Father Fröhlich, but after a month he was expelled for bad behaviour. Beethoven was indignant,

---

inherited the originals, which were lost after his death in 1858. Hotschevar's copies passed to Joseph Fischoff.

and was later to accuse the priest of having 'an understanding' with
Johanna; meanwhile he sent Karl for private tuition to the Gymna-
sium. Johanna, however, who had news of her son through Beethoven's servants, determined to make another effort to regain at least
partial control of him. In September of this year (1818), therefore,
she made two petitions to the Landrechte. The first of these was
unsuccessful, but Beethoven was summoned to answer her charges
in the second. This he did in writing, and Johanna's second petition
was rejected early in October. Then on 3 December Karl, hitherto a
passive pawn in the battle of grown-ups, took matters into his hands
and ran away from Beethoven's lodging to his mother. He was
returned, after a few hours, by the police to whom, as usual, Beethoven
had appealed; but when Johanna made still another appeal to the
Landrechte, both Beethoven and Karl himself were summoned to
appear. The transcript of the evidence shows the boy nervous and
anxious to placate both his mother and his terrible uncle. Johanna
said in her evidence that she had heard that his uncle meant to send
him to boarding-school away from Vienna, and she petitioned for
him to be sent instead to the Imperial and Royal University Konvikt.
Beethoven in his evidence rejected this suggestion, on the ground that
the discipline at the Konvikt was too lax. He suggested returning Karl
to Giannatasio's and then sending him to the Konvikt at Melk 'or, if
he were only of noble birth, give him to the Theresianum'. This
casual observation, thrown in as a kind of implied (and probably
unconscious) boast—an English equivalent would be 'or I might have
sent him to Eton'—proved a gross tactical error. The Theresianum
was an academy founded by the Empress Maria Theresa for the
sons of the nobility, and open to no one else. Beethoven's admission
that Karl was not eligible thus implied that the whole case should have
been brought before another court, the Landrechte being as exclusively
reserved for the nobility as the Theresianum. Beethoven was at once
asked for a diploma or patent proving his noble birth, which he was of
course unable to produce. The Dutch 'van', which is not an aristocratic particle, had been loosely accepted in Vienna as equivalent to
the German 'von' and had (at least according to Schindler) played
some part in persuading the aristocracy to accept Beethoven when he
first arrived in 1792. Certainly it was the Viennese custom, often
followed by Beethoven himself in his letters, to be very generous with
these mildly honorific particles and not to enquire into the exact
justification for their use. On several occasions he gives a courtesy
'von' to such unmistakably bourgeois characters as the Lobkowitz's

tutor, Karl Peters, and even to real vulgarians like the Janitschiks.[1] On this occasion, however, it was not a matter of courtesy but of hard fact, of which the court was bound to take cognizance. Johanna supported her case by documents from Father Fröhlich, to whom Karl had admitted that Beethoven encouraged him to speak disrespectfully, even abusively, of his own mother; and from a legally trained relation of hers, Jacob Hotschevar, who reported that Karl was dirty, inadequately clothed and had chilblains on both hands and feet when he arrived at his mother's, adding that 'the child is forced to conceal his real feelings, to make a hypocritical pretence of feelings that he does not have, and to lie'.[2] Beethoven retorted with a long memorandum but, as was to be foreseen, on 18 December the Landrechte handed over the whole case, and all the documents connected with it, to the commoners' court or Municipal Council, which was competent to deal with political, criminal, and civil cases. Beethoven and his nephew, Johanna and Hotschevar were all summoned to appear for a hearing on 11 January 1819, of which there is no record. On 1 February Beethoven addressed an extraordinary letter to the magistrate in charge—confused in thought, often faulty in spelling and containing high-sounding references to himself as Philip of Macedon and Karl as Alexander the Great. He received no answer, and the first conversation books that we possess, which cover the months of March and April 1819, reveal the state of despair to which he was reduced. We find his friend Josef Karl Bernard, who was editor of the *Wiener Zeitung*, one of the leading Viennese newspapers, advising him: 'If you hope to have some peace, I think it would be well for you to name a guardian as you were willing to do yesterday. But if it were feasible to send the boy to Sailer at Landshut, this would be even better, for in that way your mind could be entirely at ease, as you would know that he was in the best of hands.'

Sailer was an extremely liberal-minded educationist, a priest who eventually became bishop of Regensburg but was at this time professor of moral and pastoral theology at the university of Landshut in Bavaria.[3] Beethoven was enthusiastically in favour of this suggestion; and although at the end of March he resigned the guardianship of his nephew in favour of a Councillor Tuscher, he applied for a two-year passport for Karl, who was at that time with his mother and being taught (one cannot but imagine rather sporadically) at the Kudlich

[1] There are even mentions of 'Herr von Schindler'.
[2] See *Letters*, vol. III, Appendix C.
[3] See pp. 112–14.

Institute. The magistrate, however, ruled that, although Karl should be removed from his mother's influence, there was no reason why he should be sent abroad. The passport was refused, and he was to stay at Kudlich's. In June, however, Beethoven, who had moved to summer quarters at Mödling, contrived to have Karl moved from Kudlich's to an institution run by a Swiss pupil of Pestalozzi, Josef Blöchlinger. Tuscher resigned the guardianship at the beginning of July, whereupon Beethoven at once reassumed it; but when the court had re-examined the whole question, Beethoven's right to do this was disallowed. The court very reasonably asserted that 'the boy has been subject to Beethoven's whims and has been tossed backwards and forwards from one educational institution to another'. The mother, it continued, should remain as legal guardian with a 'capable and honest man'—in the form of the Municipal Sequestrator, Leopold Nussböck. This ended the second stage of the battle, with a defeat for Beethoven.

His first reaction to this unexpected blow was a plan, mentioned in a letter written in October to Bernard, to smuggle Karl out of the country. Instead of this, however, he had recourse to a lawyer friend, Johann Baptist Bach, who at once approved the suggestion of Karl Peters as an alternative guardian to replace Nussböck. Peters was tutor to the sons of Beethoven's patron Prince Lobkowitz, and seemed in every way a suitable person to have a say in the boy's upbringing. Meanwhile Karl, who must have possessed his full share of the resilience of youth, was doing well at Blöchlinger's, though his entries in the conversation-books suggest that he was not well cared for physically:

'I don't know where all these lice come from!
'But it's healthy to have lice.'
'On each foot I have five corns.'
'He cut open my frozen [i.e. chilblained] toe today.'

His entries are well written and correctly spelt, and they are a refreshing change from the recriminations and grousings of his elders. In December 1819 an application to the court by Dr. Bach was rejected. In February 1820 the court again refused, giving reasons in full, to rescind its decision of the previous September, which excluded Beethoven from the guardianship. Thereupon Beethoven drew up with Bernard's help a memorial in which he gave a lurid account of Johanna, and then proceeded to attack first the court itself and finally, in a supplement, the Mödling priest, Father Fröhlich, whom he describes as a drunkard and a libertine. The Appellate Court, to which Beethoven had now appealed against the decision of the Municipal Magistrate, figures frequently in the conversation-books. Blöchlinger, for example, who is always anxious to please Beethoven, says: 'The magistrates are always trying to fish in troubled waters. Anyone, even with the justest cause, who does not bribe, loses his case. If you had used bribery, you would have won your case long ago.' The hearing was on 29 March 1820 and three weeks later Beethoven was informed that the court now completely excluded Karl's mother from the guardianship, which was to be shared between Beethoven himself and Karl Peters. Johanna appealed to one of the Archdukes against this ruling, but by the end of July this last attempt had failed and Beethoven's four and a half years' struggle for his nephew had finally succeeded.

The lawsuit has an absolute importance only because it engaged Beethoven so deeply, revealed or intensified many traits of character which were salient in his mature personality and in one way or another influenced the quantity or the quality of his musical production. We have spoken already of the drastic reduction in the quantity of music produced during these years. Our consideration of the effect of the case on the quality of Beethoven's output must take two, in a sense contradictory, facts into account. In the first place there is the obvious circumstance that Beethoven was too ill, harried, and emotionally disturbed, even too engaged with the sheer physical labour of writing letters, arranging visits and planning the strategy of the case, to concern himself with more than comparatively trifling works. But what are we to make of the fact that, among trivialities, we suddenly come upon op. 106—the so-called 'Hammerklavier' sonata, which is assuredly one of the least trivial of all compositions. We know in some detail when this was composed. It was begun towards the end of 1817, the period when Beethoven had won the first round in the fight but was enjoying his victory with the bad conscience that is clearly reflected in the passages from his diary quoted above. The first two movements were finished by April 1818, the month before Beethoven took his nephew to Mödling. The remaining two movements were written during the black period when Johanna was appealing against the court's decision and just before Karl ran away to her.

It is from this period onwards that we can trace most exactly the different levels at which Beethoven experienced human existence. The conversation-books and the letters show him concerned with the practical details of everyday life, with politics and economics, housekeeping and ordinary human intercourse. The Missa Solemnis and

the Diabelli Variations (both begun in 1819), the last three piano
sonatas (1820–2), and the Ninth Symphony (1822–4) continue the
process of abstraction and concentration begun in op. 106. The last
quartets (1822–6) belong to an interior world, in which the battles
and debates, the agonized questionings and triumphant affirmations
of the earlier works are seen for the most part in a kind of distant
perspective that it is tempting to equate with *sub specie aeternitatis*.
The lawsuit over his nephew brought out the worst in Beethoven's
character, and during its course he exhibited self-righteousness,
vindictiveness, unscrupulousness, lack of self-control, and a wholesale
disregard for any point of view but his own. Moreover he exhibited
these traits, which are in varying degrees common to all human beings,
in such naked, violent form that we are sometimes led momentarily
to question his sanity, in the generally accepted sense of that word.
In fact, however the primitive nakedness and immediacy of Beethoven's emotions, and his complete inability to disguise or veil them in
any way, were assets to him as an artist and form an important element
in the appeal of his music to unsophisticated music-lovers all over the
world. Those who find this music alien are for the most part complex,
disillusioned sensibilities easily offended by genuine simplicity and
directness.

CHAPTER 4

The Background of the
Lawsuit

Although the end of the lawsuit over his nephew brought us to the
summer of 1820, we must return for a moment to say something
of the exterior course of Beethoven's life after June 1816, when Karl
von Bursy visited him.

The summer months of 1816 he spent at Baden, a favourite spa
only a few miles from Vienna and much frequented by the Viennese
of all classes. Beethoven was a great believer in mineral baths, both
for his general health and for his deafness, which he was probably right
in believing to be intimately connected with the state of his bowels.
The Giannatasios spent the day at Baden with Beethoven and his
nephew during September, and Fanny noted in her diary that while
they were there he had a quarrel with a servant, returning with his
face 'scratched'; and that on their walk he had confided to her father
that he was 'unhappy in love'. 'Five years before he had made the
acquaintance of a person, a union with whom he would have considered
the greatest happiness of his life. It was not to be thought of, almost
an impossibility, a chimera—"nevertheless it is now as on the first
day" . . . It had never come to a declaration, but he could not dismiss
it from his mind.'[1]

We may connect this statement with the songs *An die ferne Geliebte*
written this year. Five years before this there is no doubt that Beethoven was very attracted to the singer Amalie Sebald, whom he met
at Teplitz in 1811 and again in 1812. She was possibly the 'Immortal
Beloved' to whom in July 1812 Beethoven wrote the letters found
among his papers after his death. It is doubtful whether in fact those
letters were ever despatched; and if they were not, this would confirm
Beethoven's remark in 1816 that 'it had never come to a declaration'.
Whoever the woman may have been of whom Beethoven was still
thinking in 1816, she was probably the last in his series of abortive

[1] L. Nohl, *Eine stille Liebe zu Beethoven*, pp. 159 ff.

loves. For the next ten years his devotion to Karl left no room in his life for any relationship with a woman, even if his deteriorating health and complete deafness had not been almost insuperable obstacles. The final footnote (and perhaps the key) to Beethoven's relationships with women may perhaps be found in two entries in his diary. One of these, undated but probably belonging to the years 1816–17, is a laconic reflection of fact, such as is prompted by an individual concrete experience, rather than a theoretical consideration. 'Sensual enjoyment without a union of souls is bestial and will always remain bestial; after it one experiences not a trace of noble sentiment but rather regret.'[1] *Omne animal post coitum triste*; and if, as we may fairly suppose from our knowledge of the man, of his upbringing and the tone of the society in which he lived, Beethoven on occasions paid this particular debt to man's animal nature in the most primitive form, he was certainly not the first bachelor of high moral principles to do so and then to vent his bad conscience on women in general, and in particular on any woman who thwarted his wishes (and perhaps aroused his desires?) as did Beethoven's sister-in-law Johanna.

The other entry, dated 'July 27 Baden', shows the reverse of the medal, the last flickering of his dream of an ideal love—its object unidentifiable. 'Only love, yes! love alone can give you a happier life. O God, grant me the grace to find her at last, the woman who will strengthen me in virtue and whom I can possess with a quiet conscience!—when M[? or R] drove past and seemed to give me a glance.' The contrast between these two entries reflects a conflict that had probably bedevilled Beethoven's life, at least from the moment he realized the full extent and seriousness of his deafness, and possibly before. Like the large majority of men in educated society at this time, Beethoven seems as a young man to have conducted his sexual life on two distinct levels. On the one hand he prosecuted 'affairs of the heart' among the women of his own circle, with in most cases a minimum of sensual gratification, and on the other he turned for purely physical relief to prostitutes. Certainly the warnings in Beethoven's letters to his brothers when they first settled in Vienna and later his letters to Zmeskall, make it clear that he spoke from personal experience of prostitutes, and extremely probable that he had contracted venereal disease of some kind—'farewell, keep away from decaying fortresses; assaulting them is more costly than assaulting well-kept ones'. This supposition is lent further colour by his interest in a French treatise, Louis-Vivant Lagneau's *Exposé des symptômes de la maladie vénérienne*,

[1] Leitzmann, *Beethoven's Persönliche Aufzeichnungen*, p. 33.

des diverses méthodes de traitement qui lui sont applicables et des modifications qu'on doit leur faire subir. This went into five editions between 1803, when it first appeared, and 1818, when Beethoven noted the title in one of the conversation-books. The details of the autopsy at his death provide no conclusive evidence of his having suffered from syphilis, and the attempt (by Ernest Newman among others)[1] to enrol him among 'les grands syphilitiques' must be considered as a symptom of that reaction against the hagiographical approach to great men, which found its most brilliant expression in Lytton Strachey's studies of nineteenth-century personalities. Newman makes much of the fact that Dr. Bertolini, with whom Beethoven quarrelled, burned notes and prescriptions relating to the composer rather than make them public. Even supposing that these documents did in fact relate to a venereal infection, it is quite possible that this was not syphilitic or, if it was, that it was taken in time and cured. Hundreds of thousands of young men have had venereal infections without dying of them, and there is absolutely no conclusive evidence that Beethoven was not one of these. The phenomenal mental activity that he showed during the last ten years of his life provides a strong argument against Newman's view, and it can now be stated categorically that Beethoven's early death was not caused by syphilis.[2]

On the other hand the 'affairs of the heart' to which Beethoven confessed proved without exception abortive; and it has been argued with some cogency[3] that Beethoven only fell in love with women whose age, rank, or circumstances made them virtually unattainable. The attraction that he felt towards his aristocratic pupils—among the most famous Therese von Brunsvik, Josephine von Deym, and Giulietta Guicciardi—often seems to have thrived in proportion as it was unrealizable in fact[4] and the letters to the Immortal Beloved, even if they were ever sent and were not simply a literary effusion, show him retreating behind vague excuses and finding reasons in advance why his passion could never be consummated. Such instinctive shyness and nervousness in a man of Beethoven's otherwise confident, even aggressive temperament are not perhaps so difficult to explain as might at first appear. He was both a commoner and extremely deaf; and his pride made him sensitive of any possible element of condescension or pity in an amorous relationship. If we add the probability of a bad

[1] *The Unconscious Beethoven* (1927), pp. 41 sqq.
[2] See Appendix A.
[3] Richard and Editha Sterba, 'Beethoven and his nephew', 1957 chapter VII.
[4] There is no hard evidence for the tale that Josephine von Deym had a child by Beethoven.

conscience—the sense of guilt bred by his relations with prostitutes and easily extending, in the case of so deeply ethical a character, to the whole sexual realm—we shall have little difficulty in understanding the situation in which Beethoven found himself. Two other considerations should be added. Beethoven was well aware of the demanding nature of his own genius and of the almost insuperable difficulty that he would find in combining his own natural way of life, in which the claims of music were absolutely paramount and every other consideration secondary, with the domestic order and stability which attracted him in marriage. The awareness of this incompatibility did not prevent Beethoven from continuing to regard the physical and emotional satisfaction of a happy marriage as one of life's greatest blessings, or from hankering after this blessing for himself.[1]

A further complication of the situation, though in itself no impediment to a happy marriage, may have been the homosexual component in Beethoven's character. This has been greatly exaggerated and unnaturally isolated by Richard and Editha Sterba, but should not for that reason be ignored. The whole tone and temper of Beethoven's life and character, and above all of his music, exclude the possibility of regarding him as anything but what is loosely called a 'normal' man, one whose whole conscious sexuality is engaged with the opposite sex. It is a singular fact, certainly, that we do not know the name of any single woman with whom Beethoven had sexual relations, but it has never been suggested that he was without sexual experience. We must take into account the homosexual component present in all human beings, in different degrees at different ages and differing widely in consciousness. In the large majority, who provide the norm, this element may well prompt no conscious physical desires and will certainly find no overtly sexual expression. It may, however, play a considerable part in determining the nature of a man's emotional life; and this was so in Beethoven's case, particularly after 1816, when ill-health must in any case have drastically reduced, if not altogether destroyed, the promptings of physical desire. We find him at this time surrounded by a circle of exclusively male friends, and suspicious of women, whom he was inclined to identify with the sisters-in-law whom he disliked or the servants whom he distrusted. All his emotions

[1] It is interesting to compare Beethoven's case with that of Franz Kafka. Deeply attracted to Felice Bauer, he noted in his diary after marriage plans were broken off 'I could not marry at that time; everything in me revolted against the idea, however much I loved Felice. It was first and foremost the consideration of my work as a writer that held me back, as such work seemed to me jeopardised by marriage.' Kafka 'Briefe an Felice', ed. Erich Heller and Jürgen Born 1968.

during these years were centred on his nephew Karl, to whom he tried to be both father and, in his clumsy way, mother. This relationship absorbed so much of the psychic energy that remained apart from that expended in musical creation, that there would have been no place for a woman, let alone a wife. We shall find Beethoven on very warm terms during these last ten years with good-looking and friendly young men and boys such as Karl Holz, Michael Krenn, and Gerhard von Breuning. On the other hand none of these ever for a moment prejudiced Karl's place in his affections, still less gained that kind of hold over him that they would certainly have exercised if the homosexual component had been dominant in his personality.

To venture in further detail into this field and to attempt a full psychological investigation of Beethoven's sexual character is no doubt fascinating, but any conclusions must by their very nature remain conjectural. All that we know for certain, and all that really matters to our understanding of the man, is that the gulf between ideal love and sensual fact was unusually wide in Beethoven's case, and that he never achieved the compromise that most men find in marriage. The reason for this failure lay partly in his deafness, but perhaps even more in his instinctive feeling that it was impossible to combine domesticity with complete devotion to his art. It is easy to see how he found in his nephew the object of a devotion in which there was no conscious physical element, but a deep fund of frustrated paternal tenderness.

In the same month of September 1816, Beethoven returned to Vienna, and in October the young Peter Joseph Simrock, of the Bonn publishing house, visited him and heard the story of his quarrel with an English visitor, which was extended to his one-time friend Neate and to the London Philharmonic Society, whom he imagined were dictating to him what sort of music he should write. The quarrel was eventually mended after a good deal of correspondence during the autumn, when his health was bad, a 'feverish cold' (or 'inflammatory catarrh') hanging on all through the winter and following spring, when he was living in the Sailerstätte but spending much time (and possibly giving lessons) at the inn 'Zum Römischen Kaiser'. A pupil, Carl Friedrich Hirsch, remembers him at this time 'working in a flowered dressing-gown. Out of doors he wore a dark green or brown coat with grey or dark trousers to match—on his head a kind of low top-hat or in warmer weather a brown or dull gold straw hat. In his whole dress Beethoven was very slovenly. In his rooms there was the greatest disorder—music, sheets of paper and books lying partly on the desk and partly on the floor. Now and then the master wore spectacles for reading, but he did not wear them continuously.'[1]

In April 1817, he moved to new lodgings in the Landstrasse suburb, but a few days before he moved he wrote another rather quarrelsome letter to Neate, to whom he had given the cello sonatas op. 102 a year before and ending 'I swear that you have done nothing for me, are doing nothing and will do nothing—summa summarum nothing! nothing! nothing!' Probably in late June he left for the country, going first to Heiligenstadt and then to Nussdorf. A letter from his old pupil Ferdinand Ries, who now acted as his agent in London, brought a commission from the Philharmonic Society for two symphonies, with the additional proviso that he should visit London himself in the following winter. Beethoven acknowledged this on 9 July, accepting the fee of 300 guineas but stipulating for a further 100 guineas for travelling expenses. In spite of this encouragement, the problem of his nephew continued to depress him during the summer, and towards the end of August he described himself to a friend as 'so often in depair that I should like to end my life, for there is never an end to these afflictions. God have mercy on me, I consider myself as good as lost.' It was during this summer that his self-pity was at its strongest, and he signed one letter 'this poor, persecuted, and despised Austrian musical drudge—Beethoven', while quarrels with a perpetually shifting stream of servants are reflected in his letters to Frau Nanette Streicher, who continued to give her good offices in this despairing matter.

how one feels when one is uncared for, without friends, without anything; left entirely to oneself and even suffering—all that can be known only by experience. . . . NB. You would do well to give the bearer of this note the laundry list, adding a few friendly words to me, but in a closed cover. Do engage immediately the man you know of, until we have considered the question of the housekeeper.[2]

Among his visitors this summer were the English musician Cipriani Potter and the young German composer Heinrich Marschner. To Potter Beethoven was full of admiration for England, declared Cherubini the greatest living composer and Handel his first choice among composers of the past. He also told him that he was composing a *Romulus* with text by Treitschke, who was responsible for the final two-act version of *Fidelio*. Marschner, who was only twenty-one, showed his music to Beethoven at this time and was very disappointed by what seems to have been a kindly but very unenthusiastic reaction— not to be wondered at, if we take into account Beethoven's first reaction

[1] See Theodor Frimmel, *Beethoven Studien* (1905–6), II, pp. 55–69.
[2] See *Letters*, II, pp. 694–702.

to the romantic extravagance of Weber's *Freischütz* and Marschner's admiration of Weber's music.

In October he returned to Vienna, to another lodging also in the Landstrasse suburb, in the Gärtnergasse, where he was near to Karl's school and to Frau Streicher. Hirsch remembered clearly his appearance at this time. This had lost the dashing character and the pretensions to elegance of his youth, but had become increasingly characteristic. He was small in stature, only five feet six inches, but very thick-set. Hirsch remembers Beethoven returning to Vienna from his summer at Baden in 1817 'his face a healthy red, his eyebrows very thick and his brow low. His nose was very big and broad, especially the nostrils, which were finely shaped. His thick, bushy hair was already partly grey and stood up from his face. His hands were coarse and thick, his fingers short, the veins on the back of his hands swollen and his nails cut short.' His clothes were generally neglected—Fanny Giannatasio speaks of a torn coat, and many witnesses remember his trailing handkerchiefs and shapeless hats. But his linen seems always to have been spotless in public (at home there were no such scruples) and he had such a mania for washing that many of his friends attributed his deafness to it. It seems that he would get up from his work-table and plunge his head into a basin of cold water, often singing at the top of his voice as he did so, and also spilling water all over the floor; and that he more often than not let his head remain wet, and the floor remain unmopped. His physical habits were coarse—we read of him spitting into his handkerchief and inspecting it, or on the floor; and his table manners left Thayer speechless. He was in fact a middle-aged bachelor with no pretensions to elegance, one doubly compelled, by his genius and deafness, to live in a world of his own. But everyone who saw him during his last years agreed that, despite all his roughness and his coarse habits, he radiated a kind of goodness. At the very end of his life it was noted that he developed a habit of looking upwards in a striking manner, and he himself mentions this *Blick nach oben* in his letters, as though it were a habit of mind rather than of body.[1] Everything now pointed to Beethoven settling down to compose the symphonies for London, as he had undertaken to be in England during the following January. But although the sketchbooks for this winter do contain sketches for the first and second movements of the Ninth Symphony, the work which chiefly concerned him at this time was the piano sonata op. 106, begun this autumn and finished in

---

[1] This was in fact the piercing, intent, questioning look common to deaf people, whose eyes must supplement the deficiencies of their ears.

the spring of 1819. The short song 'Resignation', written this autumn, is an extraordinary instance of Beethoven's ability to set a formal eighteenth-century type of poem much in the manner of his earlier works, at the time that he was exploring an entirely new world of thought and feeling in the new language of the piano sonata op. 106. He was particularly delighted with Count Haugwitz's poem, and asked the editor of the *Wiener Moden-Zeitung*, in which the song appeared, to convey his thanks to the poet for the stimulus he had provided for such a 'happy inspiration'.[1] Contrast this with Mörike's 'Verborgenheit' and Beethoven's D major 3/8 with Wolf's plangent E flat major hymn. Beethoven marked the song 'in gehender Bewegung—mit Empfindung jedoch entschlossen, wohl accentuirt und sprechend vorgetragen' (andante with feeling but determination, in a rhythmical, well accented parlando manner). This is resignation with that touch of humour, even gaiety, that argues the humility of sheer reasonableness. The D major fugue for string quintet, which appeared a month earlier, is a similar occasional piece from the composer's workshop, but without any particular significance.

In January of the following year (1818), it will be remembered, Beethoven removed Karl from Giannatasio's school. In February he wrote to thank Broadwood for the gift of the '6 octave Grand Pianoforte, no. 7362, tin and deal case' which delighted him in spite of the fact that his deafness had taken a still further turn for the worse.

---

[1] This poem suggests a very different kind of 'resignation' from that of the Romantic poets.

> Lisch aus, lisch aus, mein Licht!
> was dir gebricht,
> das ist nun fort;
> an diesem Ort
> kannst du's nicht wieder finden!
> du musst nun los dich binden.
> Sonst hast du lustig aufgebrannt,
> nun hat man dir die Luft entwandt;
> wenn diese fortgewehet,
> die Flamme irre gehet,
> sucht, sucht und findet nicht . . .
> lisch aus, lisch aus, mein Licht!

> (Out, little candle, out! your needs no more
> can here a satisfaction find
> and you must free yourself, away!
> Once you burned merrily,
> now you are robbed of air;
> when this blows otherwhere,
> the flame burns fitfully,
> seeks sustenance but nothing finds.
> Out, little candle, out!)

D

There can be no doubt that the new instrument, and especially the additional range in the highest and lowest registers,[1] stimulated Beethoven's imagination in the writing of the last sonatas, including op. 106 on which he was engaged at the time. In March he wrote to Ries excusing himself for having to postpone his promised visit to London. The move to Mödling in May was embittered by Karl's expulsion from the parish school and when Beethoven returned to the Gärtnergasse in September, he was faced with the unpleasantnesses of the revived lawsuit, Karl's escape to his mother early in December, her suing Beethoven and the case being referred to the Municipal Council. A letter written to the Archduke Rudolf in June, 1819, suggests that Beethoven himself remembered 1818 as the year of op. 106:

I enclose two pieces [first two movements of op. 106] which I wrote last year before Your Imperial Highness's name-day (17 April), but despondency and so many sad circumstances, and my bad health at the time so discouraged me that only with the greatest anxiety and embarrassment could I approach Y.I.H. From the time I moved to Mödling until nearly the end of my visit there my health improved, but how many calamities confronted me! Meanwhile many things gathered on my writing desk. . . . To the two pieces which I wrote down in MS. for Y.I.H's name-day two others have been added, the last of which is a big Fugato, so that it constitutes a Grand Sonata which will soon be published and was long ago in my heart intended for Y.I.H.

As we shall see, Beethoven's extraordinary permission to Ries[2] to print the movements in almost any order and to omit some—inexplicable in a work which he himself told Czerny was to be his greatest piano sonata—bears out the impression made in this letter that op. 106 was not perhaps originally conceived as a single unity. That his mind was already turning in a new direction is suggested by a diary entry probably made at Mödling during this summer—'In order to write true church music . . . look through all the monastic church chorals and also the strophes in the most correct translations, and perfect prosody in all Christian-Catholic psalms and hymns generally.' At the same time a more positive form of resignation than that suggested by Count Haugwitz's little poem is suggested by the following entry: 'Tranquilly will I submit myself to all vicissitudes, and place my sole confidence in Thy unalterable goodness, O God! My soul shall rejoice in Thy immutable servant. Be Thou my rock, my light, forever, my trust!' These two entries point clearly to the interests and moods which were soon to find expression in the Missa

[1] The compass was 6 octaves, from C 5 leger-lines below the bass staff.
[2] See p. 164.

Solemnis, of which Schindler reports that he 'saw the score begun late in the autumn of 1818, after the gigantic sonata in B flat major op. 106 had just been finished'. A sketchbook in the Wittgenstein Collection in Vienna, that contains sketches for the Kyrie of the Mass[1] and also for the Diabelli Variations, dates from the first months of 1819. Although the Archduke Rudolf's appointment to the archbishopric of Olmütz (Olomouc) was not announced officially until 4 June 1819, news of it had probably been circulating in Vienna since the beginning of the year.

The year 1819 was completely overshadowed for Beethoven by the lawsuit, which was not going in his favour at this time, as will be remembered. In May he took up his summer-quarters in Mödling again, and it was during this summer that Schindler reported that he had never seen the composer working in such a state of uninterrupted 'Erdenentrücktheit' (obliviousness of everything earthly). Little wonder, then, if between anxiety and despair over Karl and his creative labours on the Missa Solemnis and the Ninth Symphony, Beethoven fell even more foul than usual of his daily surroundings. When Schindler visited him at Mödling at the end of August this year, he arrived at 4 o'clock in the afternoon with a friend.

As soon as we entered we learned that in the morning both servants had left, and that there had been a quarrel after midnight which had disturbed the neighbours—both servants had gone to sleep and Beethoven found the food which they had prepared earlier uneatable. In the living-room, which was locked, we heard the master singing parts of the fugue in the 'Credo'[2]—singing, howling, stamping. After listening to this almost terrifying performance for a long time, we were about to leave when the door opened, and Beethoven stood before us, his features so distorted that it was enough to inspire fear. . . . His first utterances were confused, as if he had been disagreeably surprised by our overhearing him. Describing the events of the day he obviously controlled himself. 'Pretty doings here,' he said, 'everyone has run away and I have had nothing to eat since yesterday lunch.'[3]

The next month (September) Zelter, the Berlin musician who was Mendelssohn's teacher and Goethe's musical adviser, tried to visit Beethoven, but missed the appointment by oversleeping. What Zelter does make clear, however, is that Beethoven still enjoyed a quite extraordinary reputation in Vienna. 'Steiner (the music-publisher) had

[1] In the conversation books for March–May 1819 there is a note in Beethoven's handwriting 'Preludium of the Kyrie the organ loud and diminishing to *p*. before the Kyrie' (i.e. the entry of the voices).
[2] The evidence of the sketch-books suggests that it was probably the fugue in the 'Gloria'. See p. 222 footnote.
[3] Schindler, op. cit., p. 322.

given out that Beethoven would appear in his small office, which holds six or eight people, at 4 o'clock and invited guests so generously that . . . some fifty brilliant people overflowed into the street and waited for him, in vain.'[1]

Almost all the letters of this year are concerned with the trial or with Karl's settling at Blöchlinger's Institute. Apart from these are letters to the Archduke Rudolf, congratulating him on his appointment (see p. 95), excusing himself from giving lessons and, in one case, referring to his own study of early music in the Archduke's library, presumably in connection with the Mass. The following is dated 29 July, from Mödling

I was in Vienna to collect from Y.I.H.'s library what I needed . . . the older composers do us double service, since there is generally real artistic [as opposed to merely technical] value in their works (among them, of course, only Händel and Sebastian Bach of the Germans possessed genius). But in the world of art, as in the whole of creation, freedom and progress are the main objectives. And although moderns are not quite so far advanced in solidity as our ancestors, yet the refinement of our manners has enlarged many of our conceptions as well.

It was during this summer that the young music-publisher Moritz Schlesinger endeared himself to Beethoven by sending him some roast veal by special carrier from Vienna to Mödling, from which Beethoven returned at the end of October.

The first months of 1820 were again taken up with the lawsuit almost to the exclusion of any other interest, for it was the period of Beethoven's heavy counter-attack on his sister-in-law. He was living, according to a conversation-book of March this year, 'opposite the Auersperg Palace, in the same house where the coffee-house is on the Josephstadt Glacis' (it is difficult to avoid the impression that Beethoven's confusing descriptions and directions somehow reflect his deep resentment at having to concern himself with the mechanics of everyday existence). He stayed there until May, when he went as usual to Mödling, but to a different lodging from last year's, which he had been asked to leave because of the noise that he made. Most of this year's correspondence is with publishers, and a letter to Adolf Martin Schlesinger written in April mentions a new project. 'I shall be willing to hand over to you new sonatas—but only at 40 ducats a piece, a sort of undertaking to consist of three sonatas for 120 ducats.'[2]

[1] Letter to Goethe, 14 September, quoted in Leitzmann *Beethovens Persönlichkeit* (1914) Bd. II, p. 243.
[2] The ducat (=4½ gulden) was worth roughly 9 shillings (1961).

Moritz Schlesinger's present of roast veal was in fact to pay the most handsome dividend that such a humble gift can ever have earned —the three piano sonatas op. 109, 110, and 111. The sketches for op. 109, which was finished this September, are to be found among those for the Benedictus, the Credo, and the Agnus Dei of the Missa Solemnis. Among them also are sketches for nos. 7–11 of the Bagatelles op. 119, commissioned as Part III of Starke's *Wiener Pianoforteschule*. Meanwhile his Viennese publisher Steiner was asking for the repayment of an old loan, and negotiations for the publication of the Missa Solemnis (which should have been ready for the consecration of the Archduke at Olmütz on 20 March of this year,) were carried on with Simrock's of Bonn. The conversation-books for the early months of this year, when Beethoven was seeing a lot of the Lobkowitz's tutor Peters and the journalist Bernard, contain some of the few traces of slightly risqué conversations that Schindler for some reason did not think necessary to excise; also a great deal about procuring Beethoven his favourite fish-foods (including oysters and smoked salmon) and Hungarian wines. His unfortunate taste for heavily adulterated wines was not only disastrous to many of his guests (see p. 60) but also further contributed to ruin his own already weak bowels, and there are repeated references to attacks of diarrhoea, which his friends always attributed to these wines, to his excessive water-drinking or to the food that he often left standing for so long that it was indigestible, if not inedible.[1]

An unusual visitor this year was a music-loving Turk, who gave Beethoven the then unusual, if not wholly accurate information that Turkish and Greek music 'have much in common with the Jewish ecclesiastical chant'. But in Beethoven's own eyes no event in the year could compare with the information, dated 20 April, that

The Appellate Court has seen fit to ordain that, with the complete exclusion of the mother Johanna van Beethoven from the eventual guardianship over the minor Karl van Beethoven, whereby the appointment of a co-guardian in the person of Leopold Nussböck, brought about only by virtue of the law

---

[1] See Appendix A. An entry in Schindler's handwriting in the conversation-notebooks of August–September this year is revealing:

'You are said to have recently had a terrible access of rage during the night, is it true ?'
'In the "Cum Sancto Spiritu"'.
'But don't lock yourself in at night. No stranger will get into your room, and the housekeeper must come in sometimes.'
'In that case you can't complain if all your meals are badly cooked, or over-cooked, and inedible: and you mustn't thunder.'
(hear! hear!)

applicable to her, is automatically cancelled, the appellant Herr Ludwig van Beethoven and the Prince Lobkowitzian Councillor Karl Peters, proposed by him, are to be appointed joint guardians of the said minor, Karl van Beethoven.

Legally, at least, Karl was now his and the Queen of the Night was finally dispossessed of her child. The piano sonata op. 109 was perhaps written in the mood of thankfulness and optimism that this deliverance (as Beethoven felt it to be) inspired.

CHAPTER 5

1821–1822

Despite Beethoven's suggestions in his negotiations with Simrock, the Missa Solemnis was far from being finished by the end of 1820. There had been a misunderstanding about the fee, Simrock understanding Beethoven's price of 100 louis d'or as the equivalent of 100 friedrichs d'or.[1] He explained this to Beethoven in a letter of 23 September, which was not answered; and when in November Brentano, Beethoven's agent, confirmed that Simrock was to have the Mass—of which he had meanwhile despaired—Simrock found it difficult to put his hands on the necessary sum, and wrote to Beethoven suggesting the payment of an 'equivalent' sum in florins. At the end of November 1820 Beethoven accepted this offer, although he pointed out that he would be losing at least 100 florins in doing so.

During the first months of 1821, when Beethoven was still living in the Landstrasse suburb, he was seriously ill, first with what the *Allgemeine Musikalische Zeitung* called 'rheumatic fever' and later, when he moved to summer quarters at Unterdöbling, with jaundice. In September his doctor sent him to Baden to take a cure, but he told Brentano in a letter from Vienna in November that 'it soon became cold at Baden and I was overtaken by an attack of diarrhoea so violent that I could not continue the course of treatment and had to flee here'. This mismanaged, and no doubt half neglected, case of jaundice almost certainly accounts for the deterioration in the condition of Beethoven's liver, which played an important part in his final illness.[2] Work on the Mass continued, but was interrupted 'since I have been compelled to write a considerable number of potboilers, as I must unfortunately call them' (letter to Brentano). This presumably refers to the Eleven Bagatelles, op. 119. Sketches for op. 110 appear interspersed among those for the Agnus Dei of the Mass and for the last piano sonata op. 111, which seems to have been completed only three

[1] The French louis d'or was worth roughly 20 shillings, the friedrich d'or (Prussian) 16 shillings.
[2] See Appendix A.

weeks after op. 110. Schlesinger published op. 109 during this year (1821) and Beethoven's letters of this autumn include several concerned with proof-reading.

The Missa Solemnis was sufficiently near completion in the early months of 1822 for Beethoven to send 'a score and parts' to the Archduke, who returned them, so that publication should not be delayed. On 19 May Beethoven promised his agent Brentano that Simrock, who was becoming impatient, would receive the score by the end of June. Meanwhile, however, he had been in correspondence over op. 111 with his other publisher, Schlesinger, who seems to have put out a feeler about the Missa Solemnis. A letter to Schlesinger on 9 April contains the following passage 'as to the Mass I have already agreed to let you have the work itself, together with the pianoforte arrangement, for an honorarium of 650 Reichsthaler[1] in Prussian currency'. It seems that Beethoven, disappointed by the prospect of losing money on his contract with Simrock, now had the idea of putting up the Missa Solemnis to the highest bidder. Peters of Leipzig no doubt got wind of this, and approached him in May of this year. At the beginning of June Beethoven answered 'The greatest work that I have composed so far is a grand Mass with choruses, four obbligato voices and a large orchestra. Several publishers have made me offers for it. I have been offered 100 full weight louis d'or. . . . .' In the same letter he regretted the 'duplicity' of his Viennese publisher, Steiner, who had—we may think reasonably—said nothing to him about Peters' interest in Beethoven's music, though the two men had met at the Leipzig Fair. He also assured Peters that 'in no event will Schlesinger ever get anything more from me; he has played me a Jewish trick, but apart from that he is not among those who might have received the Mass'.

The 'trick' was probably the innocent enquiry whether Beethoven had forgotten to send the finale of op. 111, since there seemed to be only two movements. The quarrel was in any case only temporary; but it is psychologically interesting to observe how free Beethoven is with his accusation of 'Jewish' trickery just at the time when he himself might well have been accused of double-dealing with his publishers.

He spent the summer of 1822 first at Oberdöbling, then at Baden, and the negotiations over the publication of the Mass must have taken up a great deal of his time. At the end of June he had agreed to deliver the score to Peters by the end of the following month, and by

[1] Approximately £97 (1961).

September the agreed fee had been sent; but on 22 November he still had not delivered the score to Peters and was forced to give an explanation.

'This is the state of affairs with regard to the Mass', he wrote, 'already I have finished one completely, but another is not yet complete.' This was the second time that Beethoven had made this excuse, for he had finally extricated himself from his obligation to Simrock by offering him *a* Mass instead of *the* Mass. Furthermore during August of the same year (1822) he wrote to the Viennese publishers Artaria, offering them the Mass for 1,000 florins, but asking them to keep the offer secret. So that by the end of 1822 four publishers had been offered the Mass, two of whom, Schlesinger and Artaria, still hoped to receive it eventually. The fact that he already owed 1,000[1] florins to Artaria but did not wish his repayments on this debt to be deducted from his possible fee, shows that he was in low water financially. In the following January we even find him borrowing money to pay a tailor's bill. This would easily be explained by his frequent changes of lodging, his never-ending doctor's and chemist's bills, the chaos of his domestic affairs and the fact that he now had Karl living with him when he was not at Blöchlinger's. But whatever the reason, factual and objective or psychological and subjective, Beethoven was entering a period of his life when he was literally obsessed by money and figures. This was clearly observed by Schindler, who wrote of Beethoven's very last works:

Reflection is accorded an extensive domain, indeed it almost wholly dominates the artist who previously had always created freely, beyond these limits [of introspection]. On the other hand arithmetic had so strikingly taken possession of the master that the room which was opened to artistic reflection was taken up by mercantile speculation. For a third interest there was hardly anything left, if newspaper-reading and politics be left out of account. . . . This strange turning-point in his essential self became fully manifest during the course of the year 1824, but there had been many premonitions during the two previous years, even in his artistic productions (see the second movement of the sonata op. 111).[2]

This obsession (not unconnected, according to Freudian psychology, with Beethoven's well attested concern with his intestinal functions) seems in a sense to have taken the place of his hostility to Karl's

---

[1] Approximately £100 (1961).
[2] This reference is obscure, unless Schindler seriously regarded the variations of op. 111 as in some sense the result of arithmetical calculations—a complaint often made against music of any complexity.

mother, as soon as she was rendered helpless and Karl himself had turned against her, as he did at this time. She was ill and in financial difficulties (half her pension had to be surrendered for Karl's upkeep) and it seems likely that her illness was connected with the birth of a second illegitimate child. Karl's remarks about his mother in the conversation-books at this period are heartless enough to content even the jealous Beethoven, whose aggressive instincts, as we shall soon see, were now deflected on to his other sister-in-law, Therese, wife of Johann.

Throughout the summer of 1822 there was a very marked rapprochement between Beethoven and his remaining brother, with the initiative on Beethoven's side. The postscript to a letter written from Oberdöbling in May, suggesting setting up house together, is strongly emotional in character and suggests a recent flaring-up of the old quarrel

Peace, let us have peace.[1] God grant that the most natural bond, the bond between brothers, may not again be broken in an unnatural way. In any case my life will certainly not last very much longer. I repeat that I have nothing against your wife, although her behaviour to me on a few occasions has greatly shocked me. In any case owing to my indisposition, which has now lasted for three and a half months, I am very sensitive and irritable, I might even say extremely so. . . .

Another letter to Johann, written on the last day of July, is not simply affectionate, but even skittish 'Now all good wishes, most excellent little brother! Read the Gospel every day. Take to heart the epistles of Peter and Paul. Travel to Rome and kiss the Pope's slipper.'[2] Johann's name occurs repeatedly in the conversation-books at this time, and even his wife is allowed to give advice on domestic matters. She treats her difficult brother-in-law with a good deal of formality ('Wollen der Herr Bruder jetzt Kaffee oder noch warten?') which suggests that Beethoven's momentarily dormant mistrust of her was perhaps mutual. And the inevitable storm began to rumble in the distance when Johann persuaded Beethoven, on his return from Baden, to move into a house next door to one owned by his wife's

---

[1] See *Letters*, II, p. 946. Was Beethoven perhaps at this time reworking the Agnus Dei of the Missa Solemnis—that 'prayer for internal and external peace', as he called it, that has such a personal character?

[2] This may possibly be an echo of an amusing story told by Grillparzer in his autobiography, and relating to his journey to Rome in 1819. It was probably handed round in the circle to which Grillparzer belonged, and this contained many acquaintances of Beethoven's. See Franz Grillparzer, *Sämtliche Werke* (Leipzig, 1902) Band 12: 'Selbstbiographie' and 'Erinnerungen au Beethoven' (1844–5).

brother. The lodgings, which were in the unpromisingly named Kothgasse,[1] proved disastrous and Beethoven was not long in declaring his dissatisfaction.

Before returning to Vienna from Baden, however, Beethoven was visited by one of the most intelligent and articulate of all the musicians who reported their impressions of him during these last years. This was Friedrich Rochlitz, first editor of the Leipzig *Allgemeine Musikalische Zeitung*. On his first visit Beethoven was amiable enough but, he discovered, had heard almost nothing of what he had said. The second occasion was at a restaurant (possibly the 'Blumenstöckl' in the Ballgasse) where Rochlitz was taken by Schubert. He found Beethoven sitting among his friends, conducting what amounted to a monologue.

Those around him contributed little, merely laughing or nodding their approval. He talked about life and, after his own fashion, about politics. He spoke of England and the English, of whom he had an incomparably high opinion, which in part sounded rather fantastic. Then he told stories of all kinds about the two occupations of Vienna by the French; for them he had no very kind words. His delivery was absolutely natural and free of any kind of restraint, and whatever he said was spiced with highly original, naïve judgements and humourous fancies. He impressed me as a man with a rich, aggressive intellect and a boundless, indefatigable power of imagination. He might have been a gifted adolescent who had been cast on a desert island and had there meditated on any experience or learning that he might have accumulated, until these fragments of experience and knowledge had become a view of life and his imagination had become convictions—both of which he now produced with complete ease and confidence. After his meal he got up and came over to me. 'Na, gehts gut im alten Wien?' ('Well, how do you like it in our old Vienna?') he said in a friendly way. . . .

The third meeting between Rochlitz and Beethoven was at Baden

He arrived looking quite neat and clean, even elegant. Yet this did not deter him from going for a walk—and it was a hot day—in the Helenental. This meant taking the main road, used by the Emperor and his family among many others, who crowd along what is usually a narrow footpath. Undismayed by this, Beethoven took off his fine black frock-coat, slung it on a stick over his shoulder and wandered along in his shirt-sleeves. . . . His talk and his actions were one long chain of eccentricities, some of them most peculiar. Yet they all radiated a truly childlike amiability, carelessness and confidence in all who approached him. Even his barking tirades, such as those against his Viennese contemporaries, were only explosions of his fanciful imagination and his momentary excitement. They were uttered without any haughtiness, without

[1] Mud Street.

any feeling of bitterness or resentment, simply blustered out lightly and good humouredly. . . . He often showed . . . that to the very person who had grievously injured him, or whom he had just most violently denounced, he would be willing to give his last thaler, should that person need it.[1]

The Viennese public provided Beethoven with a fresh source of complaint this year (1822) by the enthusiasm with which they received Rossini, who now visited the city for the first time. His operas were already popular,[2] but his presence raised this popularity to the point of a craze. Beethoven already knew and admired the *Barber*, and he was such an admirer of Italian singing that he told the Viennese singer Karoline Unger that he would write an opera for Barbaja's company, which was then in Vienna. He received Rossini, who said later that he found it impossible to communicate owing to the fact that he had no German and Beethoven (contrary to Cipriani Potter's account) very little Italian, even if he had not been almost stone deaf. Beethoven was put out by Rossini's popularity ('a pretty talent and pretty melodies by the bushel') and facility ('his music suits the frivolous and sensuous spirit of the age, and his productivity is so great that he needs only as many weeks to write an opera as the Germans need years'). He could afford to be generous, however, secure in the knowledge that—as he put it—'they can't rob me of my place in musical history'.

His own association with the theatre was revived for a short time this year. In September he provided music for the ceremony of the opening of the Josephstadt Theatre. This consisted of an arrangement of what he had written for Kotzebue's *Ruins of Athens*, for a similar occasion at Budapest in 1812, and an entirely new overture—*Zur Weihe des Hauses* ('For the consecration of the house'). The other event was the revival on 3 November, 1822 of *Fidelio*, a benefit performance for the seventeen-year-old singer Wilhelmine Schröder (later Madame Schröder-Devrient). Both she and Schindler left accounts of the dress-rehearsal which, after much consideration, Beethoven decided to conduct himself with the help of Michael Umlauf, the musical director of the theatre. Although differing slightly in details, both accounts show that this must have been a terrible experience for Beethoven, whose deafness soon destroyed all rapport with the orchestra. Wilhelmine Schröder describes him 'with

---

[1] Letters of 28 June and 9 July, to Härtel, published in Rochlitz *Für Freunde der Tonkunst*, IV, (1832).
[2] The first performance in Vienna of an opera by Rossini was on 26 November, 1816— *L'Inganno Felice*.

a bewildered face and unearthly, inspired eyes, waving his baton back and forth with violent gestures. . . . If he thought it should be *piano*, he crouched down almost under the conductor's desk, and if he wanted *forte* he jumped up with the strangest gestures, uttering the most uncanny sounds.'

Let Schindler continue—

already uneasy in his seat, he turned now to the right, now to the left, scrutinizing the faces around him to learn the cause of the breakdown. Everywhere was a heavy silence. Then he summoned me . . . and handed me his notebook. . . . Hastily I wrote 'Please do not continue; more at home.' At once he sprang into the parterre and with an 'Out, quick!' started running to his lodgings. Once there he threw himself on the sofa, covered his face with his hands and remained thus until we sat down to eat. During the meal not a word passed his lips . . . and afterwards he begged me not to leave him until it was time to return to the theatre.[1]

Next day he went with Schindler to Dr. Smetana, who had some reputation as an aurist; but as on every other occasion, he lost heart and discontinued the suggested treatment since it brought him no immediate and noticeable relief.

[1] Schindler op. cit., p. 335.

CHAPTER 6

1823

To the second half of 1822 we can trace the seeds of all the works which were to occupy Beethoven for the remaining four years of his life as a composer. In several cases these works had been planned and partly written. For example when Beethoven wrote to Ferdinand Ries, in July, and asked him 'have you any idea what fee the Harmony Society would offer me for a grand symphony ', he had been working intermittently at least since 1817 on the work which was eventually to be the Ninth Symphony. In the same way his letter to Antonio Diabelli, written in November ('the fee for the variations would be 40 ducats[1] at most') refers to the same work that he offered to Simrock as early as February 1820—'grand variations on a well known German waltz, which, however, I cannot yet promise you'. These so-called 'Diabelli Variations' had been begun early in 1819, at the same time as the Missa Solemnis, and they were finished in March–April 1823, probably immediately after the final touches were put to the Mass (October–December 1822). What was entirely new was the commission for 'one, two, or three new quartets' which the Russian prince Nicholas Galitsin addressed to the composer in November and was accepted by him on 25 January 1823.

A month earlier Beethoven wrote to Ries accepting the Philharmonic Society's offer of £50 for a 'm.s. symphony'—'even though the Englishmen's honorarium cannot match that of other nations' and he goes on 'for myself I would willingly write gratis for the first artists in Europe, if I were not still the poor Beethoven. If I were in London, what would I not write for the Philharmonic Society? for Beethoven can compose, thank God, though he can do nothing else in this world.'[2] Although work on the Ninth Symphony continued all through 1823, a great deal of Beethoven's time was taken up with the details of his new plan for publishing the Missa Solemnis. This consisted of selling manuscript copies by subscription to all the sovereigns of Europe. It is not known how many of these invitations

[1] Approximately £20 (1961).
[2] See *Letters*, II, p. 978.

to subscribe to the Mass were in fact sent out, but Beethoven took great trouble in discovering the correct forms of address and the most promising avenues of approach in each case. Apart from the many German courts approaches were made to Paris, St. Petersburg, Copenhagen and Stockholm, but not London, because George IV had never acknowledged the dedication of *The Battle of Vittoria*. The Viennese court was not approached, but the Grand Duke of Tuscany (a Habsburg dependant of Vienna) was among the ten monarchs who answered Beethoven's invitation favourably. Private subscribers included Galitsin and Prince Radziwill, the governor of the Prussian province of Posen, who had already received the dedication of 25 *Schottische Lieder*, op. 108, the previous year and was to receive that of the *Namensfeier* overture (an earlier work issued as op. 115 in 1825).

Among the private individuals whom Beethoven tried to interest in the Missa Solemnis were Goethe and Cherubini, the one in his capacity as Minister of the Grand Duchy of Weimar and the other as Director of the Paris Conservatoire. His letters to both show a touching humility, and by an unhappy chance neither of them was answered. To Goethe he wrote

The admiration, love and esteem which I have cherished since my youth for the one and only immortal Goethe have persisted. Such feelings are not easily expressed in words, particularly by such an uncouth fellow as I am, whose one aim has been to master the art of music. But I feel constantly prompted by a strange desire to say all this to you, seeing that I live in your writings.

Goethe, who had noted in his diary but not acknowledged the receipt of Beethoven's setting of his *Meeresstille und glückliche Fahrt* the year before, was seriously ill during the month of February 1823, when he received Beethoven's letters. His convalescence during the summer was dominated by his senile infatuation (he was seventy-three) with Ulrike von Levetzov.

To Cherubini, who apparently never received the letter, Beethoven wrote that he was 'enraptured whenever I hear a new work of yours and feel as great an interest in it as in my own works—in brief, I honour and love you'. Then, after making his request about the Mass, he breaks into schoolboy French 'vous resteres toujours celui de mes contemporains, que j'estime le plus si vous me voulez faire une extrème plaisir c'etait si m'ecrireres quelques lignes, ce qui me soulagera bien. L'art unie tout le monde, how much more then true artists, et peut êtres vous me dignes aussi, de me mettre, to count me too among that number'.

Meanwhile Beethoven's family affairs were mounting to a new climax. He was still living in the unsavoury Kothgasse lodgings found him by his brother Johann, whose concern with Beethoven's financial affairs was clearly irritating the composer. He wrote to Ries in February 'My brother here, who can afford to keep a carriage and pair, has nevertheless been trying to make money out of me as well.' The conversation-books of April and May show Karl making fun of the dyed hair and the ludicrous musical pretensions of his uncle Johann.

Your brother says he would give half of what he possesses to be able to detect a mistake in an orchestral performance. Now he wants to learn the piano—just imagine, with his fingers!
He maintained he could detect a mistake in my playing, so I sat down and, just to take him in, played correctly, though he said he heard a mistake.

Schindler reports that Johann wanted to learn to conduct. However, if Karl curried favour with the more formidable of his uncles by making fun of the other, he was by no means always in Beethoven's good books himself. On one occasion he evidently made the cardinal mistake of becoming involved in one of the quarrels between Beethoven and his servants. The occasion was, as usual, in the highest degree trivial, Beethoven's wrath and resentment unbounded. Karl writes

I don't know what you're angry about. I don't remember laughing but I must admit that I found her [the servant] in tears complaining that you torture her and that she would rather leave than be so mistreated in her old age. If you told her to do the washing, she was only doing what she should—though she admits that she may have misunderstood you. When I told you what I thought, it never occurred to me that you would take me up wrong, if I said what I believed to be true . . . I can't eat anything until I have stopped crying . . . food eaten in such misery would be poison to me.

And in the way that such quarrels always develop, when the real cause lies far deeper than the apparent one, the wretched Karl is forced to go over the whole pathetic story again from the beginning. Beethoven had obviously agreed to forget the incident but had then returned to to the attack. Karl writes

I wanted earlier to write down for you the reason for my behaving as I did, but you wouldn't let me, and I was content that the matter would be dropped as you had promised. I now see, though, that you are so annoyed with me that you won't even look in my direction, so I must give my reasons. As I said before, I thought that I could speak my mind, and while the old woman was in the room I said nothing to lead her to suppose that I took her side. You misunderstood entirely what I wrote. I never said that the old woman was in the right, but simply wrote down *her own words*, meaning to add nothing. However, when you asked me to give my opinion, I gave it, feeling certain that you would not forbid my speaking freely. If I had known that you would be offended by my speaking freely, all I could have done was to say 'You are right'. As I thought I could speak openly, I told you the truth—that if, as she says, you yourself told her to do the washing at once, she was right to do it. But I shall be careful in the future of saying even that, as I see that it offends you.

The whole scene is painfully clear—the ill, stone-deaf man and the old servant, who is terrified of him and cannot really understand what he says; and the seventeen-year-old boy, trying to mediate with reason and good humour and meeting with the formidable displeasure of the uncle, who cannot help still regarding him as a child and resenting any display of independent judgement.

During this summer the uneasy truce between Beethoven and his brother Johann's wife was rudely shattered. Johann was ill, and his wife and her daughter—whom Beethoven had charmingly nicknamed 'Fatlump' and 'Little Bastard'—were apparently neglecting him. Therese was suspected of having a lover in the house and Beethoven, was talking, as usual, of police measures. Therese, however, who no doubt had clear memories of her brother-in-law's attempt to prevent her marriage in the first place, was more than a match for him now. In the conversation-book Schindler writes—'the nurse said the mistress was standing in the hall with the poker and waiting for you, intending to receive you with it. I was terrified by this atrocious behaviour and did not know what to do, except to keep you away by the excuse that your brother wanted to sleep.' Therese had clearly got the measure of the kind of arguments that Beethoven himself used, and would therefore be likely to understand, in such a situation. One cannot help having a sneaking sympathy for her robust vulgarian common sense in her own defence, though such scenes as these form an improbable and almost macabre background to the Ninth Symphony, which was coming to birth during these months.

Had Beethoven a sudden new access of physical, as well as psychic, energy at this time? In a playful letter to Ries—in which he once again complains of his servitude to the Archduke—he writes skittishly 'Give my best greeting to your wife until I arrive in London. Take care. You think that I am old, but I am a youthful old man.' Were this warning to Ries, to be ready to protect his young and pretty wife from a potential rival, and his violent hostility to his sister-in-law and her daughter simply obverse and reverse of a recrudescence of sexual vitality? If so, it was a flame that no doubt contributed to the furnace of the Ninth Symphony, and the word 'sublimation' was perhaps never more justly used.

That Beethoven's thoughts were carried back to an early love at this time we can see from the conversation-books. Count Gallenberg, who was in charge of the musical archives of the Kärntnerthor Theatre and was now in touch with Beethoven about the score of *Fidelio*, had married in 1803 the Countess Giulietta Guicciardi, a pupil of Beethoven's with whom he had certainly been in love. Now, twenty years later, Beethoven becomes reminiscent to Schindler, for some reason breaking into his halting French 'j'etais bien aimé d'elle, et plus que jamais son époux'; and to what incident, before or after her marriage, can he be referring when he writes 'et elle cherchait moi pleurant, mais je la méprisois'? Had Giulietta Guicciardi been prepared to marry Beethoven in 1803 and been refused by him? or had she sought him out after her marriage and tried to revive their previous relationship? It is impossible to say, but Beethoven's reflection on the whole affair is unambiguous, as he returns from sentimental reminiscence to common sense (and his native German): 'if I had been ready to expend my vital energy on a life of that sort, what would have remained for all that is noble and higher?'

From May until the middle of August this year Beethoven was the guest of a certain Baron von Pronay at Hetzendorf. Pronay was a *Kammerherr* or Gentleman in Waiting at court, and in the conversation-books we find Karl warning Beethoven not to indulge in his anti-royal diatribes while he is Pronay's guest. Pronay was also a great gardener and we can follow Beethoven round the garden, being shown the flowers and enquiring their names. However, Pronay's excessively respectful manner and his incessant bows when he encountered Beethoven proved finally beyond endurance. He had made only one stipulation when he offered Beethoven rooms in his villa—that there should be as little noise as possible in the one that was over his own bedroom. In order to invent an excuse for leaving, or being asked to leave, Beethoven deliberately made as much noise as possible, as late as possible, in this room and then took himself off to his favourite Baden, where he arrived on 13 August. His letters at this time are concerned largely with proofs (of the Diabelli Variations, the sonata op. 111 and the Missa Solemnis) or enquiries about the progress of the subscription list for the Mass. The landlord of the ill-fated Kothgasse lodgings was behaving badly and Beethoven was, as usual, in search of police help in the matter. His eyes gave him serious trouble from April onwards and soon after his arrival in Baden he wrote to the Archduke complaining of a cold, catarrh, eye-trouble and the usual stomach upsets 'due to my *faithful servants*!'

An entry of Schindler's in one of the conversation-books for April this year at least partly relieves Beethoven's servants of responsibility for his bad health: 'don't drink this wine, it is grossly adulterated . . . my gums are covered with blisters', and Beethoven seems to have been regularly eating food that had been cooked hours beforehand and left standing, because his hours of eating depended on his work and the caprice of the moment. Some of his friends thought that he ate far too much fish—his favourite food, with eggs and macaroni.[1]

His health, however, improved at Baden and it is significant that, with this improvement, went a marked decrease in his deafness so that he could hear J.R. Schultz, a young Englishman who visited him at the end of this September, without using an ear-trumpet. On 5 October Beethoven received the visit of the composer Weber and his pupil Julius Benedict. Weber had come to Vienna to conduct the first performance of *Euryanthe*, and although he and Beethoven had at one time had no very high opinion of each other's music, Beethoven had revised his opinion of *Der Freischütz* and Weber had been enthusiastic about *Fidelio*, which he had produced this year in Dresden. Now his reception was warm indeed[2]. 'You're the devil of a fellow! a good fellow!' said Beethoven and then, Weber continues, 'this rough, repellent man actually paid court to me, served me at table as if I had been his lady'.

When Beethoven was given to understand that *Euryanthe* suffered from a bad libretto, he was sympathetic: 'Always the same story; the Germans cannot write a good libretto.' He himself was full of opera plans at this time, and received two visits from the poet Grillparzer during 1823, one at Hetzendorf[3] and the other after he returned to

[1] In an undated letter of this year he tells the Archduke that he is taking a whole bottle of purgative medicine every twenty-four hours. For Schindler's reminiscences about Beethoven's tastes in food and drink see S. pp. 541–2.
[2] Though we need surely not go as far as the Sterbas, op. cit., p. 222, and read a homosexual element into Beethoven's behaviour on this occasion, unless the word 'homosexual' is to be used to cover any relationship between members of the same sex in which warm friendliness and admiration are given natural physical expression. Beethoven was merely uninhibited. The account of this meeting is in Max Maria von Weber, *Carl Maria von Weber*, II, p. 509.
[3] The two bachelors—Beethoven was fifty-three, Grillparzer thirty-two—obviously discussed marriage. One of Grillparzer's entries perhaps summed up the conflict that troubled them both 'Die Geister unter den Weibern haben keine Leiber und die Leiber keine Geister'. ('Wits lack beauty and beauties lack wit'.)

Vienna from Baden towards the end of October, when he had lodgings in the Landstrasse suburb, on the corner of the Bockgasse and Ungargasse. Two other visitors this year deserve mention. The first is Louis Schlösser, whose account of his visit will be discussed in another chapter, and the second is Franz Liszt, at this time a boy of eleven and a pupil of Beethoven's friend Carl Czerny. The boy's visit with his father to Beethoven is recorded in the conversation-books; but the story of Beethoven submitting a theme to the boy for public improvisation and kissing him on the forehead at the end of his performance is apocryphal. Several entries in the conversation-books show the writer (probably Schindler) trying to persuade Beethoven to attend the boy's concert on 13 April; but it seems that in the end Beethoven sent his nephew instead.[1]

---

[1] Schindler gives different accounts in the 2nd and 3rd editions of his biography. See S. p. 525.

CHAPTER 7

1824

The year 1824 opened with an act of grace on Beethoven's part, and one that nothing in the previous nine years would have led us to expect. On 8 January he wrote to Karl's mother, that 'Queen of the Night' whose iniquities had obsessed him for so long, a friendly, almost solicitous letter. He had heard that she was ill and in financial difficulties—

Our many occupations made it quite impossible for Karl and me to send you our best wishes on New Year's Day. But I know that without this explanation you are fully assured of both my own and Karl's wishes for your welfare. As for your need of money, I would gladly have helped you out with a sum. But unfortunately I have too many expenses and debts . . . so that I cannot prove to you at once and on the spot my readiness to help you. Meanwhile I assure you now in writing that henceforth and for ever you may draw Karl's half of your pension. . . .

and the letter ends

Both Karl and I wish you all possible happiness
Your L. van Beethoven, who is
most willing to help you.

'Karl and I' makes it quite clear that in Beethoven's mind his sister-in-law had finally forfeited all claims to association with her own son. He will be generous to her as long as those terms are observed; and by renouncing on Karl's behalf the share in the pension, Beethoven asserts finally his complete control over the boy. Letters to Josef Karl Bernard written this same month, asking him to make inquiries from Johanna's doctor about her real circumstances, make it clear that there was no fundamental change in his attitude. A man named Hofbauer was supposed to be paying her what amounted to alimony. 'Since Hofbauer, I understand, believes that he is the father of her child, he is probably right. And as she has become such a strumpet, I consider that after all I should make Karl realize the guilt of her wicked behaviour. . .' It is the old story over again, only now Beethoven feels secure and can afford to be a little generous. He eventually sent her 11 gulden,[1] asking for a written receipt.

In February the Ninth Symphony was finished, and Beethoven emerged for a moment from the maelstrom in which he had lived while he was working on the piano sonata op. 106, the Missa Solemnis, and the symphony, the years of the lawsuit and his wrestling with what he once called 'the demons of darkness'. A contemporary account quoted by Thayer speaks of him 'no longer grudging himself occasional recreation' and 'being seen again strolling through the streets of Vienna, gazing into the shop-windows through eye-glasses which dangled at the end of a black ribbon, greeting friends and acquaintances as they passed'.[2] The conversation-books report much discussion of Grillparzer's libretto *Melusine* early this year,[3] and there was the recurrent embarrassment of the oratorio *Der Sieg des Kreuzes* by his friend Bernard. He had undertaken to compose this for the Viennese Gesellschaft der Musikfreunde, but he was not alone in finding Peters' dramatic handling of the story of Constantine and the battle of the Milvian Bridge wholly uninspiring. Instead, he began work in the spring on the first of the quartets commissioned at the end of 1823 by Galitsin, the quartet which eventually emerged as op. 127. But before that there was the question of the grand concert of his works.

Beethoven was naturally anxious to hear performances of the Missa Solemnis and the Ninth Symphony as soon as possible. But believing that the Viennese taste was wholly corrupted by Rossini and not wishing to risk a fiasco, he put out feelers in Berlin. When his friends heard of this they decided to take action and a number of them, headed by Prince Carl Lichnowsky, drew up a long document requesting for Vienna the right to be the first city to hear Beethoven's latest works. The terms of this document were extremely flattering to Beethoven who, once he had got over the malicious rumour that he had himself prompted its preparation, allowed himself to be persuaded.[4] This, however, proved only half the battle, and the real difficulties arose when Beethoven was asked to decide on the theatre in which the concert was to be given. He wanted Michael Umlauf to conduct and

---

[1] Approximately 22 shillings (1961).
[2] *Life of Beethoven*, ed. Forbes, (1964) pp. 886–7.
[3] See Chapter 12, p. 101.
[4] It is interesting to note that of the thirty signatories only one, the Abbé Stadler, was a professional musician. The rest were aristocrats, civil servants, publishers, or journalists. This is perhaps a more damaging reflection on the position accorded to musicians in Metternich's Vienna than on the musicians themselves.

Schuppanzigh to lead the orchestra, and this was not possible to arrange at the Theater an der Wien. At the alternative theatre, the Kärntnerthor, there were other difficulties, and the project seemed to have reached a stalemate. Beethoven saw through a ruse prepared to extract a decision from him, cancelled the concert and dismissed Moritz Lichnowsky, Schindler, and Schuppanzigh from his favour. This did not last long, however, and all through March and April we can follow the negotiations in extracts from the conversation-books, where Lichnowsky is concerned with keeping expenses down yet having the requisite forces of players and singers, Schindler with the prices of admission. Although the Landständischer Saal and the Redoutensaal both came into consideration and as late as 21 April it was publicly announced that the concert would be given in the Theater an der Wien, Beethoven finally decided for the Kärntnerthor Theatre. On 24 April Schindler wrote to the director Duport specifying Umlauf and Schuppanzigh as conductor and leader, orchestra and chorus to be augmented by amateurs from the Gesellschaft der Musikfreunde; the soloists were Henriette Sontag (soprano), Karoline Unger (contralto) Anton Haitzinger (tenor) and Seipelt (bass). Even when the date was fixed for 7 May the programme still remained to be settled. The original plan of giving first performances of both the Missa Solemnis and the Ninth Symphony would have made this one of the longest as well as most remarkable concerts in the history of music. Realizing that the whole Mass could not be performed, Beethoven decided to omit first the Gloria and then the Sanctus. A certain amount of sophistry was required to obviate the ecclesiastical objection to liturgical texts being sung in a theatre, but permission was finally obtained for the performance of what appeared on the programme as 'Three Grand Hymns' but were in fact the Kyrie, Credo, and Agnus Dei of the Mass. These were preceded by the overture *Die Weihe des Hauses* op. 124 and followed by the Ninth Symphony. A suggestion that Beethoven should conduct 'with Umlauf' was reported by Schindler

You could surely conduct the overture by yourself.
It would put too severe a strain on your ears, and for that reason I should not advise you to conduct the whole concert.

Was Beethoven really considering this, and could he have forgotten so soon his humiliating experience at the dress-rehearsal of *Fidelio* only eighteen months earlier?

When the concert at last took place its success exceeded the expectations of even Beethoven's greatest friends. Beethoven was oblivious of the ovation and had to be prompted to acknowledge it. Schindler reports in the conversation-books

> on one occasion the second movement of the symphony was completely interrupted by applause' [this was prompted by the dramatic entry of the timpani, apparently] and 'there was a demand for a repeat'
> 'the wind instruments gave a good account of themselves'
> 'when the parterre broke out into applause for the fifth time, the Police Commissioner shouted "Silence!" '

Beethoven was delighted with his women soloists, whom he had known since 1822, although they complained that his music was terribly difficult to sing, which meant very different from Rossini's, in which they both excelled. We find him giving them lunch on 24 March— chicken, 'meat from the restaurant' and *Guglhupf* (a kind of sponge-cake)—and less happily, one of the wines which he himself particularly liked but were in fact grossly adulterated—Sontag is on record as having vomited fifteen times the following night. At the performance the bass, Seipelt, had no top F sharp and only a few voices of the chorus attempted the top B flat entries in the Credo; but Beethoven himself was happy, until he discovered that even the wretched 420 florins[1] that remained after paying the chief expenses of the concert could not be be regarded as profit, and that there were still further expenses to be taken into consideration. Someone, probably his brother Johann who was jealous of Schindler's position with Beethoven, suggested that the concert's meagre financial success was Schindler's fault—in short, that he had defrauded Beethoven. There was a dreadful meal at a restaurant in the Prater, at which Beethoven charged Schindler with this in the presence of Umlauf and Schuppanzigh, who defended him but eventually retired with Schindler to finish their meal elsewhere. Schindler was soon exonerated, but the antagonism and irritation caused by his tactlessness and the banality of his conversation prompted a strange letter

> I do not accuse you of having done anything wicked in connection with the concert, but stupidity and arbitrary behaviour have ruined many an under-taking. Moreover I feel a kind of fear that some day a great misfortune may befall me owing to you. Stopped up sluices often overflow suddenly, and that day in the Prater I was convinced that in many ways you had done me great harm. In any case I would much rather try to repay with frequent small gifts the services that you do me, than have you at my table. For I confess your presence irritates me in many ways. If you see me looking not very cheerful,

[1] Approximately £42—(florin = gulden).

you say 'nasty day again, isn't it?' .... I will certainly invite you occasionally, but it is impossible to have you beside me permanently, as this would upset my whole existence

and this charmingly frank letter concludes with one of those self-congratulatory remarks that are so much harder to forgive Beethoven than any of his exhibitions of temper or jealousy. 'I must declare that the purity of my character does not permit me to reward your kindness to me with nothing but friendship, although I am of course willing to be of service to you in any matter connected with your welfare.'

A second concert, to which Beethoven had been opposed, brought in even less money than the first. The programme on this occasion included the overture op. 124 and the Ninth Symphony but only the 'Kyrie' of the Mass. To these was added a trio 'Tremate, empi' composed by Beethoven more than twenty years earlier, and . . . 'Di tanti palpiti' from Rossini's *Tancredi*! Beethoven did not assist his own financial situation by this year paying for three sets of lodgings simultaneously throughout the whole summer. He retained his town rooms in the Landstrasse suburb when he moved on 1 May to Penzing, where he took a room for the whole summer. But after only three weeks he left Penzing (on the pretext that people on a small footbridge near the house stared at him while he was shaving) and betook himself once again to Baden, where he remained off and on until November. Little wonder, therefore, in the face of such unnecessary expenditure, that he was desperately concerned with the profits that he could hope to make from the publication of the Missa Solemnis and the Ninth Symphony.

On 25 February of this year (1824) he had offered Schlesinger the Mass for 1,000 florins and the symphony for 600,[1] though with the stipulation that it should not be published until 1825. On 10 March he made exactly the same offer to Schott of Mainz and to Probst of Leipzig. Twelve months earlier he had told Ries that the Philharmonic Society could keep the symphony for eighteen months before he would publish it; hence the proviso to Schlesinger, which was not, however, made to Schott or Probst.[2] Beethoven must presumably have understood the Society's 'exclusive right' to the symphony for eighteen months to apply only to England, since he himself planned

[1] i.e. £100 and £60 respectively.
[2] Beethoven's ambivalent attitude to the whole question of publishing these two works, is reflected in the strange phraseology of his letter to Schott dated 20 May, 'I have the honour to inform you that I am more or less willing to let you have my grand Mass and the new symphony.'

the first performance in Vienna in May 1824, a month after he had sent the score of the symphony to London, where the first English performance took place in March 1825.

In a second letter to Probst, written from Baden in August this year, he says that the Mass is 'really disposed of already' but he repeats his offer of the symphony, with a rather clumsy threat

You must make up your mind with all speed, for I have already received a portion of the fee for this symphony. At the same time I could give this man other works for the money he has already paid me. Although God has specially blessed me, enabling me to help whenever I can, and although I am never at a loss for publishers, yet you are well aware that I like simple honesty in business dealings. Since I could give him other works, I should have no further trouble there, and I could let you have the symphony, although it could not be engraved and published until July of next year . . . . Meanwhile do not abuse my confidence or speak of this offer of mine in conversations with other people. My fee is 1,000 gulden. . . . .

It is not difficult to follow the course of Beethoven's thoughts as he wrote this letter, and it is easy to understand them in his situation. But he might have spared Messrs. Probst the reference to his simple honesty. If his behaviour over the publication of these works was not downright dishonest, it was certainly an example of sharp practice, if poor Beethoven's muddled financial dealings can ever be called 'sharp'.

One visitor to Beethoven at Baden this September seems to have caught him in a quite unusually expansive mood. This was Johann Andreas Stumpff, a harp-maker of German extraction but settled in London. Beethoven accepted his invitation to dinner and entertained Stumpff himself, played his Broadwood piano, gave him a print of one of the portraits of himself and promised to stay with him when he went to London. Stumpff's account shows Beethoven railing against everything and everybody in Vienna and filled with the highest regard for everything English—'England stands high in culture. In London everybody knows something and knows it well; but the typical Viennese talks of nothing but food and drink, and sings and pounds away at completely trivial or home-made music.' He talked of sending Karl to London to complete his education[1] and the evening ended with much drinking of toasts, praising of Handel and deploring of 'Rossini and Co.' Beethoven was plainly relaxed after the good food and drink and in

[1] Karl had studied English at Blöchlinger's, as one of the conversation-books shows him reciting 'To be or not to be' on the occasion of Frau Blöchlinger's birthday; and he helped Beethoven with his English correspondence.

sympathetic company. 'Today I am my real self and what I ought to be', Stumpff records him as saying, 'all unbuttoned.'[1]

Stumpff's visit was towards the end of September, and Beethoven's carefree mood was rudely interrupted a week or so later by the momentary disappearance of Karl. He had just celebrated his eighteenth birthday, and it was not very surprising or tragic that there was one night on which Beethoven discovered that he had not been home to their Vienna lodging. When he did appear the next day, Beethoven was beside himself with relief and justified his anxiety by speaking of 'these wretched institutions . . anxiety about a young fellow who is growing up . . . and in addition there is that poisonous breath coming from dragons'. In any case Beethoven disapproved of one of Karl's friends, a young man called Niemetz whom he had met at Blöchlinger's. In what was obviously a stormy interview with Karl, recorded in the conversation-book marked autumn 1824, Beethoven describes Niemetz as 'completely lacking in decency and manners' and 'rough and common . . . no friend for you'. Karl defends his friend with sense and spirit, never showing anything but respect for his uncle but maintaining his own point of view. He was in fact developing ideas of his own not only in the matter of his friends; and there had been serious altercations with his uncle when he expressed the wish to join the army. During the winter of 1824–5 he was still, unwillingly, pursuing his philological studies at the university, and no doubt amusing himself in the bad company (Beethoven's 'breath of dragons' expresses clearly a fear of his contracting a venereal infection) to which he was, perhaps, introduced by his friend Niemetz. We know that the quarrels continued during the winter, because Beethoven's first landlady when he returned that autumn to Vienna (a Frau Kletschka in the Johannesgasse) was so disturbed by 'the quarrels with nephew and housekeeper and the pounding of the piano' that she asked him to leave, whereupon he moved for a time to the Krugerstrasse.

As evidence of Beethoven's health at this time Thayer quotes a letter of 18 November in which Beethoven excuses himself from giving the Archduke a lesson on the grounds of 'a chill'. This may well have been true, but these excuses were very frequent in their correspondence and we cannot attach more importance to them as objective evidence of Beethoven's actual health than did the Archduke himself. Yet we can be fairly certain that for most of the time during these last years Beethoven felt so ill that the wonder is that he led so normal a life, let alone composed.

[1] Account copied from Stumpff's manuscript by Thayer, op. cit., p. 919, footnote 51.

CHAPTER 8

1825

The month of January 1825 saw what might have been the end of Beethoven's financial worries, if only he had been able to cure himself of the indecision and multiplicity of aim that were the result of his physical condition. Beethoven's poverty, in as much as it was real and not imaginary, was entirely the result of his inability to manage his own affairs and his unwillingness to entrust them to anyone else; and these traits were almost certainly caused by the deterioration in his health. Whenever he did make up his mind to take others' advice, as in the case of his brother Johann and in a lesser degree at various times of Schindler, Karl or (as we shall shortly see) Holz, his impatience and suspiciousness always brought the arrangement to grief; for if he did not see an immediate improvement in his situation, Beethoven at once concluded that his adviser was a knave and dishonest or a fool and useless. He adopted very much the same attitude to doctors, and his health (including his hearing) fluctuated in exactly the same way, no doubt often for the same reasons, as his financial stability. It is certainly mistaken to lay the blame for his poverty on his contemporaries and for his ill-health on his doctors. The truth lies rather in a passage of a letter exchanged during the March of this year (1825) between two publishers, J. A. Streicher of Vienna and C. F. Peters of Leipzig—'what am I to say about Beethoven's behaviour to you, and how can I endeavour to excuse it? I can only do this by letting you have his own opinion of himself, as he once expressed it at my house—"everything I do apart from music is badly done and stupid".' His double dealings with publishers can be explained partly by his obsession with the idea of saving money for his nephew and partly by the shortness of ready money in a household where domestic chaos reigned and the householder was inclined to let himself in for paying for three lodgings simultaneously for three months of the year. If to this we add Beethoven's sheer muddleheadedness with figures (to which the conversation-books bear repeated witness) we may well be surprised that he did not become involved in real financial disaster.

In January 1825, however, the long and complicated manœuvres

over the publication of the Missa Solemnis and the Ninth Symphony
were concluded when the composer wrote 'I, the undersigned, declare
by virtue of my signature that Bernhard Schotts Söhne at Mainz are
the sole rightful publishers of my grand solemn Mass and also of my
grand symphony in D minor. In addition I accept these editions as
the only rightful and correct ones.' Furthermore, a week before Beethoven concluded this arrangement, he had written to Charles Neate
accepting a new offer from the Philharmonic Society, and a most
satisfactory one. He was to receive 300 guineas for conducting at least
one of his works at each of the Society's London concerts during the
coming season; and it was added that he could expect to make a
further sum of at least £500 by giving a concert of his own, and £100
by the sale of his quartets. None of these was finished, though op. 127
was largely written. Beethoven's request for a further 100 guineas
for travelling expenses was refused, it is true; but this was certainly
not the sole reason for his vague procrastinations, which found
expression in a letter to Neate in answer to his reminder that London
was impatient for Beethoven's arrival, 'je ne pourrai guère venir à
Londres durant le printemps mais qui sait quel accident m'y conduit
peut-être en automne'. His acceptance of Neate's offer two months
earlier is already half forgotten, and he is attributing to 'who knows
what accident' the visit to London which had been firmly planned as
long ago as 1817. Yet his family were urging him—Karl reminding
him of the financial gain, Johann of the possible benefit to his health,
while the violinist Schuppanzigh became impatient with the indecision
(typical of Beethoven's mental condition at this time)[1] of which he had
already had ample experience over the concert in the previous spring.
'I wish he would pick up enough courage to make the trip; he would
not regret it'.

It was indeed courage that failed Beethoven, the courage needed
by an ill, stone-deaf man to travel to a country whose language he did
not know and to appear in public in a role which recent experience
had proved he could no longer fill. Why, we may ask, did Beethoven
ever accept the London invitation to conduct, after the *Fidelio*
experience? It is significant, perhaps, that Schindler, who had witnessed
the full humiliation of that occasion and its effect on Beethoven, is not
found among those who pressed him to make the journey to London.

Meanwhile the first of the Galitsin quartets—op. 127 in E flat
major—was completed, and after much preliminary trouble but
insufficient preliminary rehearsal, was given its first performance

[1] See Appendix A.

on 6 March. Before this Beethoven sent a humorous document to the players—

Best ones! Each of you is herewith given his part and is bound by oath, and indeed pledged on his honour, to do his best, to distinguish himself and to vie with his neighbour in excellence. Each participant is to sign this sheet.

and their names followed—Schuppanzigh,[1] Weiss, Linke ('the grand master's accursed violoncello')—Holz ('the last[2] but only in signing').

The performance was, at best, a *succès d'estime* and the fault was attributed to Schuppanzigh, who showed a clear grasp of the work's problems when he said 'it would not be true to say that any isolated passages are too difficult for me technically; it is the ensemble that is difficult.' However that may be, Beethoven was angry and disappointed, and determined on another performance of the quartet led by Joseph Böhm, who had been giving quartet concerts in Vienna during Schuppanzigh's absence. Under Böhm the quartet, which had three performances before the end of March, was a great success and during April it was given by Mayseder's quartet at several concerts in private houses. Two months later Beethoven, dictating a letter to Karl, told him to tell Galitsin

that the quartet was admittedly a failure the first time, because it was performed by Schuppanzigh, who owing to his stoutness now requires more time than he did formerly to master a work quickly; and add that many other circumstances contributed to its failure and that I warned him that it would be a failure. For although Schuppanzigh and two others draw pensions from persons of princely rank, yet the quartet is no longer the same as it was when all the players were constantly together On the other hand the quartet has been splendidly performed six times by other artists, and received with the greatest applause. On one evening it was played twice in succession and again after supper. . . .

[1] Schuppanzigh had given Beethoven violin lessons as long ago as 1794, when he used to play at Prince Carl Lichnowsky's quartet evenings, where Weiss was viola. From 1808 till 1815 these two formed, with Mayseder (violin) and Linke, the Razumovsky Quartet. After Razumovsky's Viennese palace was burned down on the night of 31 December 1814, the quartet was disbanded and Schuppanzigh toured Germany, Poland, and Russia, only returning to Vienna in 1824. His large bulk earned him the position of a butt in Beethoven's circle, where he was called 'Falstaff'. Karl Holz, a well-trained amateur, seems to have met Beethoven for the first time in the spring of 1825 when, besides playing in Schuppanzigh's quartet, he conducted in the Redoutensaal a performance of the Fourth Symphony. His account of his relations with Beethoven is to be found in L. Nohl, *Beethoven, Liszt und Wagner*.
[2] See *Letters*, III, p. 1182.

Beethoven was by now hard at work on the A minor quartet (op. 132), when he was overtaken by an illness more serious than his colds, catarrhs, diarrhoea and digestive troubles.[1] Schindler wrote in the conversation-books in mid-April, when the trouble started, 'Dear master, think of the future. What will be the result of your working at night? without that this would never have happened.' The entries by the doctor whom Beethoven summoned, Braunhofer, seem to bear out Schindler's opinion:

no wine, no coffee, no spices of any kind. I'll arrange matters with the cook . . . you must stick to the diet, you won't starve on it . . . you must do some work during the daytime so that you can sleep at night. If you want to recover completely and live a long life, you must live according to nature. You are very liable to inflammatory attacks and have narrowly escaped a severe inflammation of the bowels—the predisposition is still in your body . . . I can promise you that if you drink any spirits, you will be lying weak and exhausted on your back in a few hours.

On 7 May he went to Baden and four days later sent his doctor a humorous report of his condition, asking to be allowed to drink white wine again 'as this mephitic beer is simply revolting'. That Beethoven had received a serious shock is suggested first by the words of the canon which he sent to Braunhofer ('Doctor, shut the door on death—Notes, help us in our need'), and then by the entry in a conversation-book of May–June 'Hymn of thanksgiving to God from an invalid on his convalescence. Feeling of new strength and reawakened feeling'— where we find the idea of the third movement of op. 132, which dates from these weeks.

During the summer and autumn months at Baden Beethoven was even more than usually worried about his nephew, who had at his own request left the university and entered the Polytechnic Institute at Easter. The vice-director of the Institute, a Dr. Reisser, had been appointed co-guardian with Beethoven, so that Karl was well supervised; and he was supposed to spend his Sundays with his uncle at Baden. The first letters to Karl from Baden are pathetic

I am getting thinner and thinner and feel ailing rather than well, and I have no doctor, not a single sympathetic soul at hand. If you can manage to come on Sundays, please do. But I don't want to interfere with your plans in any way, if only I were certain that your Sundays away from me were well spent. Indeed I must learn to give up everything . . . oh! where have I not been wounded, nay more, cut to the heart?![2]

[1] See Appendix A.
[2] *Letters*, III, pp. 1199.

This form of self-pity, and the thinly disguised emotional blackmail which it involves, often do more to alienate the young than any amount of abuse or hard treatment from their elders; and if Karl was not very regular in his visits to Baden this summer, we can hardly blame him. Soon, however, Beethoven was taking a much firmer line, for he had heard that Karl was seeing his mother again. He threatens to give Karl the choice between his mother or his uncle ('if the bond is to be broken, so be it. But you will be detested by all impartial people who hear of this ingratitude') and ten days later he wishes to be rid of all his family

God is my witness, I dream only of getting completely away from you and from this wretched brother and that horrible family which has been thrust on me. God grant my wishes, for I can no longer trust you
Unfortunately your father
or, better still, not your father.[1]

Beethoven seems to have had an unusually dreadful couple of servants to look after him this summer, and they appear throughout his letters as 'the old witch' or 'the old beast', and 'the wench' or 'Satan'. He was therefore doubly annoyed when he discovered that Karl was borrowing money from them. Beethoven retorted by loud complaints and by making him account for every sum he received, though he also entrusted him with various household shoppings. In fact the same alternation between extravagant affection and extravagant displeasure marked his relationship with his nephew now, as it had always done. Only at eighteen Karl was beginning to find this emotional tie irksome, and such admonitions as to 'choose the best stuff for his new trousers, but to be careful to save his clothes by wearing old things at home', simply ludicrous. In a hot July Beethoven fussed over Karl's health and in September we see him entering into an unattractive arrangement with his new friend Karl Holz, whom he set to spy on the boy. In the conversation-books Holz writes—'I have lured him into a beer-house to see whether he drinks a lot; but that does not seem to be so. Now I will get him to play billiards, and shall see at once whether he has been playing a lot.' There follows a clear hint of Beethoven's overriding anxiety, his nephew's sexual morals, 'what harm can come to him if he goes through the city from the Alservorstadt?' and a pathetic suggestion of bribing Karl into more cultivated tastes, 'I also told him that his uncle would be more inclined to give

[1] *Letters*, III, pp. 1216.

him money if he heard some classical works at the Burgtheater once
or twice a month'.

When the time for Beethoven's move back to Vienna from Baden
came in October, Karl was expected to make himself useful and did
not always satisfy his uncle, who upbraided him for his gross selfishness
and followed this with the usual self-pitying, self-righteous sentiments,
'Well go on, then, persist in your behaviour, but you will regret it.
This does not mean that perhaps I may die all the sooner, though that
may be what you want. But as long as I live, I shall cut myself off
from you completely—without forsaking you, of course, or failing to
support you. . . .' A week later the quarrel ended in the usual emotional
outburst prompted apparently by Karl's utter misery—

Not a word more. Only come to my arms, you won't hear a single hard word.
For God's sake do not abandon yourself to misery. You will be welcomed
here as affectionately as ever. We will lovingly discuss what has to be considered and what must be done for the future. On my word of honour you
shall hear no reproaches, since in any case they would no longer do any good.
All that you may expect from me is the most loving care and help—only
come, come to the faithful heart of
                        your father
                        Beethoven

Come home as soon as you receive this note.

    Si vous ne viendres pas, vous me tueres surement. . . .
    For God's sake do come home again today. If not, who knows what danger
may confront you? Hurry, hurry.[1]

Had Karl already thrown out hints of suicide? It seems probable.

By the beginning of September Karl Holz had become Beethoven's
inseparable companion and completely ousted Schindler, who had
never fully recovered his place in Beethoven's good graces after the
concert of May 1824. It is unfortunate, therefore, that our chief
source for Holz's relationship with Beethoven at this time is Schindler
himself, who was naturally jealous and inclined to show Holz in a
bad light. We know that he was a cultured amateur musician, well
read, a good talker, handsome and amusing (which could not be said of
Schindler). Beethoven himself admitted in a letter to Karl that Holz
was a heavy drinker, and Schindler may not be wrong when he says
that under Holz's influence Beethoven drank more heavily than usual
at this time. Schindler also credits him with radical political ideas,
and this may have endeared him to Beethoven, who was always ready

---

[1] *Letters*, III, pp. 1258.

F

to abuse the Austrian royal family and court. Certainly Holz was a dashing and amusing companion compared with Schindler, and Beethoven's affection for him blossoms into a number of the verbal jokes that always accompanied his good humour. 'Holz' in German means wood, and there are repeated references in Beethoven's letters to 'our best mahogany', 'chip', 'wood of Christ', 'splinter from the Cross of Christ', etc. During the months that he was seeing most of Beethoven, Holz married and this gave rise to innumerable references and jokes on the part of Beethoven, whose account of the dream in which he saw Holz's parents begetting him is perhaps an indication of the deep impression that the young man had made on him.[1]

Beethoven's visitors during this summer (1825) included young Ludwig Rellstab who was anxious to provide him with a libretto and suggested as possible subjects Attila, Antigone, Orestes, and the sixth-century Byzantine general Belisarius but without arousing the composer's interest.[2] The German-Danish composer Friedrich Kuhlau was present at a supper-party with Holz, Tobias Haslinger the publisher and a number of others in Beethoven's Baden lodgings. Whether under Holz's influence or not, a great deal was drunk at this party and Kuhlau did not remember how he got home, or to bed. Beethoven himself seems to have been in excellent spirits and wrote a canon for his visitor on the B–A–C–H theme, which was much in his mind at this time as the subject for a possible overture. The feebly punning text— 'kühl, nicht lau' ('cool, not tepid')—suggests that it was composed fairly late in the evening. Moritz Schlesinger was also in Vienna this summer, lured by Beethoven's offer of 'two new grand violin quartets', presumably the A minor op. 132, completed this August, and the B flat major (op. 130), which was not in fact completed until November. He flattered Beethoven by telling him that Cherubini had said to his Conservatoire pupils in Paris that 'the greatest musical minds that ever lived, or ever will live, are Beethoven and Mozart' and he urged him to go to England, promising him a profit of at least £1,000. At dinner at Schlesinger's toasts were drunk to Goethe and Cherubini, the two of his contemporaries whom Beethoven most admired and both of whom, rather bitterly, owed him a letter at this time.

During the month of September the A minor quartet was rehearsed and then performed at the inn 'Zum Wilden Mann', where Schlesinger

---

[1] Letter of summer, 1826, probably to Holz. 'Last night I dreamed that your parents were begetting you, and I saw in my dream how much sweat it cost them to bring to light such an amazing piece of work. . . .'

[2] Rellstab, *Aus meinen Leben* (Berlin, 1861), II, pp. 224 ff.

was lodging. On that occasion the audience included an English
visitor, Sir George Smart, who left a detailed account:[1]

There was a numerous assembly of professors to hear Beethoven's second new
manuscript quartette, bought by Mr. Schlesinger. This quartette is three-
quarters of an hour long. They played it twice. The four performers were
Schuppanzigh, Holz, Weiss, and Lincke. It is most chromatic and there is a
slow movement entitled 'Praise for the recovery of an invalid' . . . Beethoven
directed the performers and took off his coat, the room being warm and
crowded. A staccato passage not being expressed to the satisfaction of his eye
(for alas! he could not hear) he seized Holz's violin and played the passage a
quarter of a tone flat. I looked over the score during the performance.

Smart, in listing those present on this occasion, mentions Beethoven's
nephew Karl 'who is like Count St. Antonio'.[2] Two days later he
heard another performance of the quartet in the same room, after
Schuppanzigh, Lincke and Czerny had played the trios opp. 70 and 97
(Smart mistakenly says 79). Schlesinger gave a dinner party after the
concert, attended by Smart, Beethoven and his nephew, the members
of the quartet, Czerny and a flautist called Sedláček; and Beethoven
himself extemporized 'for about twenty minutes in a most extraordinary manner, sometimes very fortissimo [sic] but full of genius'
on the theme

(cf. no. 2 of the Elf Neue Bagatellen op. 119)

When he arose at the conclusion of his playing, he appeared greatly
agitated. No one could be more agreeable than he was—plenty of jokes. He
was in the highest of spirits. We all wrote to him in turn, but he can hear a
little if you halloo quite close to his left ear. . . .

From the conversation-book of 16, 19, and 24 September, dates
when Smart visited Beethoven at Baden, it is clear that there was much
discussion of Beethoven's long projected English tour. On the final
visit Smart tells us that he overheard Beethoven (Schindler would no
doubt have said under Holz's influence) say, 'We'll try how much the

[1] To be found in H. Bertram Cox and C. L. E. Cox, *Leaves from the Journal of Sir George
Smart* (1907), pp. 104–15.
[2] 'A Sicilian who later became Duke of Cannizzaro: he married the daughter of Governor
Johnstone of Penascola.' *Journal of Mrs. Arbuthnot*, edited by Duke of Wellington, I, 374.
He played the flute.

Englishman can drink'; and having passed this test satisfactorily, Smart made his farewells. He gave Beethoven his diamond pin in remembrance of the gratification of his visit, and received in return a canon on 'Ars longa, vita brevis'. It is interesting to note, in view of Beethoven's complaints of his neglect by the Viennese, that during these autumn months in Vienna there were performances of the 'Archduke' and E flat trios, the Mass in C, the Choral Fantasia and the septet, quite apart from the quartet performances already mentioned and a number of others.

Beethoven returned to Vienna from Baden in October and moved on the 15th into lodgings in the Schwarzspanierhaus, so called because of its original connection with a community of Spanish Benedictines. This move, which was to be his last, had the happy result of bringing him together with an old Bonn friend, Stephan von Breuning, a *Hofkriegsrat* (Councillor in the War Department) with whom Beethoven had quarrelled over the guardianship of his nephew. Meeting now in the street, they discovered that they were to be neighbours, and Beethoven enlisted Frau von Breuning's help with his household affairs. According to her daughter, Frau von Breuning found Beethoven—who had apparently showed her rather marked attention at one time—embarrassing owing to his 'animated gestures, his loud voice and his indifference towards others' which 'surprised people in the street . . . who stopped and took him for a madman'. She also observed to her husband that 'Beethoven's habit of expectorating in the room, his neglected clothing and his extravagant behaviour were not particularly attractive!' To which Stephan von Breuning retorted 'and yet he has had a great deal of success, especially with women'.[1]

The days of those successes, however, were long past in 1826, the last complete year of the composer's life, which we must now examine

[1] See Gerhard von Breuning, *Aus dem Schwarzspanierhaus* (1874).

CHAPTER 9

1826

In January 1826 Beethoven was suffering from the usual trouble with his bowels and also with his eyesight. A letter to his doctor shows that at the end of February he was better, but still not well; and he speaks of his complaint as 'rheumatism or gout'.[1] Meanwhile his B flat major quartet op. 130 was given its first performance by the Schuppanzigh Quartet on 21 March, when the concert also included a performance of the 'Archduke' trio, with Anton Halm as the pianist. The second (scherzo) and fourth (danza alla tedesca) movements were encored and the Cavatina was an immediate favourite; but, as the players themselves had foreseen, the final fugue presented great difficulties to both performers and listeners. The publisher Matthias Artaria, who had purchased the rights in the work, persuaded Beethoven to write a new finale and offered to publish the Grosse Fuge as a separate work, to be paid for also separately. Beethoven asked Anton Halm to make a four-handed piano arrangement of the fugue, but was not content with his version and made one himself, published as op. 134. A music-loving amateur, Ignaz Dembscher, who wished to arrange for a second performance of the new quartet at his house, was refused permission by Beethoven on the grounds that he had not subscribed to Schuppanzigh's original concert. When Holz conveyed this message, Dembscher asked whether there were no way of mollifying Beethoven, to which Holz replied that the first step would be to send Schuppanzigh the 50 florins[2] subscription. 'Must I really?' ('muss es sein?') said Dembscher, and his unwillingness so amused Beethoven when Holz told him the story that he at once wrote a comic canon on the incident, with the words (answering Dembscher's question) 'It must be, it must be so. Out with your purse.'[3] Meanwhile the C sharp

---

[1] See Appendix A.
[2] Approximately £5 (1961).
[3] This is Holz's version—and that favoured by Thayer—of the origin of the 'question and answer' which formed the finale of the quartet op. 135, which Beethoven was to write this autumn. Schindler connects it with Beethoven's unwillingness to hand out the housekeeping money. All that is certain is that the composer used some humble, even trivial occasion and that the 'cosmic' interpretation of the question and answer is at most an allegory. Schindler op. cit., pp. 500–7.

minor quartet op. 131 was being written; the theme of the opening
fugue occurs in the conversation-books of December 1825, the theme
of the variations before the end of January. But although the quartet
was finished during the spring or early summer of 1826, there is no
account of Beethoven ever having heard it performed. The conversation-books show that he was full of plans for the future—a tenth
symphony, a Requiem, and an oratorio or a concerto. According to
Holz Beethoven was at this time very taken by Handel's *Saul* and
also interested in ancient Hebrew music. Theatres in both Berlin and
Vienna expressed their interest in his project of writing an opera,
although Grillparzer's *Die schöne Melusine* was not favoured in Berlin,
owing to its similarity to the *Undine* of de la Motte Fouqué and
E. T. A. Hoffmann.

A tantalizing reference to Schubert occurs in the conversation-
books at this time. Holz has seen him reading a Handel score; he was
at all Schuppanzigh's quartet-concerts; 'he has a great gift for songs';
and 'he spoke very mystically, always'. 'Mystical' was not a term of
praise in Beethoven's circle, whether applied to the new Romantic
movement in the arts or to the intense, emotional religion preached
in Vienna at this time by the 'Ligorianer' or Redemptorists. It is
difficult to imagine how Schubert can have laid himself open to this
charge, but a possible explanation may be found in Braun von Braunthal's account of Schubert's eulogy of Beethoven in this same year
(1826). According to this witness—who described Beethoven entering
a restaurant this year 'like someone walking in their sleep'—Schubert's
words were as follows—

He (Beethoven) can do everything, but we cannot yet understand all that he
does, and a lot of water will flow under the Danube bridges before this man's
creations are generally understood . . . Mozart's relationship to Beethoven is
like Schiller's to Shakespeare; Schiller is already understood, but Shakespeare
by no means. . . . No one understands Beethoven unless he has a high share of
intelligence and even more of feeling and has been very unhappy in love or in
some other way.[1]

If Schubert's words are accurately reported, we have here one of the
fundamental tenets of the Romantics: that unhappiness, because it
forces a man to look into himself, is a key to the understanding of great
art, and to be rated on a par with strong intelligence and an ability to
feel deeply. Such a belief might well, in the fundamentally eighteenth-

[1] This account appeared in *Süddeutsche Zeitung* in 1840 and is not wholly trustworthy,
however tantalizing. See O. E. Deutsch, *Schubert—memoirs by his friends* (1958), pp. 249–50.
Schubert had already paid an abortive visit to Beethoven in 1822. See Schindler, p. 522.

century atmosphere of Beethoven's circle, have been written down as *mystisch*.

A visitor who, if his memories are to be trusted, was singularly well received by Beethoven this spring was Friedrich Wieck, whose seven-year-old daughter Clara was already a prodigious little pianist and was later to marry Robert Schumann. Wieck was something of an expert on deafness and on hearing-aids, as well as a professional musician, and therefore doubly welcome to Beethoven who 'improvised for more than an hour, with his hearing-aid on the sounding-board'. Their conversation, as reported by Wieck,[1] is a good indication of the range of Beethoven's interests at this time. 'Music at Leipzig—Rochlitz—the Gewandhaus, his housekeeper and his perpetual moves; his walks; Hietzing and Schönbrunn; his brother and various "Viennese fools"; the aristocracy, democracy; the French Revolution; Napoleon.' Then back to music—'Mara, Catalani, Malibran, Fodor and the singers of genius, Lablache and Rubini; the perfection of Italian opera—always better than German owing to the language and the better singing; Wieck's ideas about piano-playing and teaching; the Archduke Rudolf.' Wieck reports that Beethoven asked a lot of questions and understood very quickly, before his guest had finished writing the answer. There was always a certain rough kindness in his manner and he had characteristic 'deeply expressive' movements of the eyes, and often took his head or his hair in his hands. He expressed himself rather crudely, but gave the impression of being a noble, sympathetic, and sensitive character, friendly and enthusiastic in his attitude but politically a pessimist.

Wieck says that he visited Beethoven at Hietzing, but either his memory played him false or Beethoven was out of Vienna for a short visit. His usual move to the country was postponed, perhaps because he was waiting for money from Prince Galitsin, and he could not decide where to go, though he thought of Ischl. Very early in 1826 the conversation-books show a recrudescence of his anxiety about Karl, who complains that he is overworked but wants to go to a carnival ball. Beethoven apparently considered accompanying him—he already embarrassed the poor boy by often appearing at noon at the Institute, like an anxious mother fetching a small child—and had to be dissuaded by Holz, who offered to go in his stead. To the fear of 'bad company' was now added, probably with reason, the suspicion that Karl was gambling. He had to account for every penny that he received from

[1] Details communicated in a letter, reprinted from *Dresdener Nachrichten*, in *Signale* no. 57, December 1873.

Beethoven and no doubt wanted money for pleasures whose nature he could not confess to his puritanical uncle. In any case, he came home less and less, explaining his absences to his uncle Johann (who communicated the explanation to Beethoven) by 'his fear of the frequent quarrels and reproaches for his past behaviour, also the frequent rows with servants'. One entry of Holz's suggests that there was an occasion on which physical violence was used between the two; but this, though it deeply shocks Thayer, was not in itself very significant in a family so given to fisticuffs as the Beethovens.

It was probably a variety of motives that prompted Karl towards the end of July to form the plan of committing suicide. He was worried about his approaching examinations and about his debts; he had been reduced to despair by the alternating extremes in his uncle's attitude towards him; and he was no doubt spurred on by a long banked-up resentment, to which his affection for his mother contributed further. Moreover suicide was then, as it is now, far more commonly attempted in Vienna than in countries where the sheer instinctive physical hold on life is stronger or the moral fibre tougher. It was not for nothing that Schiller in the *Xenien Almanack* of 1797 referred to the Viennese as *Phäaker*—'Phaeacians',[1] a sobriquet eagerly seized on by their hostile critics (including Beethoven) and, with a certain self-complacency in their failings that recalls the Irish, by the Viennese themselves. A histrionically staged suicide attempt, in a romantic ruined castle, by a student just before his examinations, worried by some debts and a difficult family background—this, if not an everyday occurrence, would certainly have excited much less comment in Vienna than in any other European capital. Thayer describes Karl as 'a bungler with firearms'; but did Karl ever really intend to kill himself? or only to take a spectacular revenge on the uncle who tortured him? He made the attempt at the Rauhenstein ruins near Baden, on Sunday 30 July, and was found wounded but conscious and carried to his mother's lodgings. Beethoven was informed, and tried to send a doctor of his own, who would hush up the affair. However, the boy's mother had already found a doctor, and Holz himself reported the matter to the police, who removed Karl to the general hospital on 7 August. Nothing could be clearer evidence of Karl's real mentality than his threat 'to tear the bandages from his wound if another word were spoken to him about his uncle'. To the magistrate who eventually investigated the case Karl said that he tried to shoot himself

[1] Homer describes Odysseus's visit to the island of Scheria, where the Phaeacians lived a carefree existence, entirely dedicated to pleasure. See *Odyssey*, Book VI.

'because my uncle tormented me too much' and 'I grew worse because my uncle wanted me to be better'. Beethoven's implication in the case became common knowledge, and those who saw him immediately after the incident reported that he suddenly looked like a man of seventy. According to Austrian law Karl, as one who had attempted suicide, was entrusted while in hospital to a priest who visited him regularly, and whose business it was to discover the motives behind the attempt and to convert the patient to a Christian attitude to his situation. Karl was entrusted to one of the proverbially strict Redemptorists. 'These Liguorians are like leeches' observed Holz. He was in hospital from 7 August to 25 September, and during the later weeks it was decided that he should be allowed to enter the army, as he had long wished to do. Stephan von Breuning, as a member of the War Council, was able to put Beethoven into touch with a Baron von Stutterheim, who gave Karl a cadetship in his regiment, then stationed at Iglau, where he was to report a week after his discharge from hospital.

Beethoven, though originally opposed to the army as a career for Karl, was overjoyed at this solution, and in his gratitude dedicated his C sharp minor quartet to Stutterheim; but he was in despair at the thought that Karl might see his mother in the interval between his discharge from hospital and his joining his regiment. He even confided his anxiety to the magistrate and obtained permission to have Karl with him, although Stephan von Breuning frankly disapproved of the idea. His second letter to the magistrate contained a plea for police supervision—'A warning from you would be most effective, and it would do no harm for him to know that he will be watched unseen while he is with me.' However, three days after leaving hospital Karl accompanied his two uncles to the country. Johann had invited Beethoven to his estate at Gneixendorf earlier in the summer, and received an unequivocal reply 'I will not come. Your brother?????!!!! Ludwig.' Now he accepted a second invitation and took Karl with him, ostensibly for a week but in fact for a much longer period, as Karl did not eventually join his regiment until 2 January 1827. Beethoven's objection to visiting his brother had been largely an objection to his sister-in-law with whom, it will be remembered, he had had the most recent of many violent quarrels in the summer of 1823. A year after, however, Johann wrote in Beethoven's conversation-book, 'My wife has surrendered her marriage-contract and entered into an obligation which permits me to turn her out without notice at the first new acquaintance that she makes.' Karl further mollified Beethoven by saying, 'you will scarcely see the woman. She is treated as a housekeeper, looks after the house, and works.' And so the ill-assorted family party settled down to what was hardly more than an armed truce in the autumn countryside on this high, rather bare plateau overlooking the valley of the Danube, treeless but covered with fields and vines. Beethoven, who was working on his F major quartet op. 135 and the new finale of op. 130 (to replace the Grosse Fuge), ate with his brother and sister-in-law but spent his time working in his room or walking the countryside, where his strange appearance and behaviour were remembered many years later. His sister-in-law had detailed the son of one of her husband's vine-dressers, a lad called Michael Krenn, to act as his personal servant, and Beethoven took one of his sudden, intense likings to the boy—giving him money, getting him out of trouble when he failed to do an errand for his mistress, making him report the conversation at meals and finally expressing a desire to take him back to Vienna. With Karl, on the other hand, it is clear from the conversation-books that the old nagging started again, the suspicions and the demand for unquestioning devotion

I beg of you once more not to torment me as you are doing; you might regret it, for I can stand much but too much I cannot endure. You treated your brother the same way today with no reason. You must remember that other people are human too.

Will you let me go out a little today? I need recreation. I will come back later.

I only want to go to my room.

I am not going out, I only want to be alone for a little.

Will you let me go to my room?

It is a relief to know that he also played four-handed piano pieces—mostly Lannoy's[1] Marches—with his uncle.

At the end of November Johann, obviously nervous of a scene with his brother, wrote him a note in which he said very strongly that Karl ought to leave Gneixendorf and join his regiment. It seems clear that Beethoven was unwilling to let him go, having fallen again under the old spell of his nephew; and Karl himself was anxious to stay at least until his hair had grown long enough to hide the scar on his face. Beethoven was already suffering from the beginnings of dropsy, for Johann mentions swollen feet and the fact that 'his belly became larger and larger, and he wore a bandage over it for a long time'. How advanced his illness was when he finally left Gneixendorf with Karl,

---

[1] Baron Eduard von Lannoy, one of the directors of the concerts given by the Gesellschaft der Musikfreunde. In 1824 he conducted a concert in which Beethoven's 'Opferlied' was performed, in its third version.

probably on 1 December, it is impossible to know. Transport was
difficult and after several hours in a rough cart the two had to spend
an unseasonably cold night in a primitive unheated inn, Beethoven
still in summer clothes. During the night he was seized with fever and
what was plainly pleurisy ('dry hacking cough accompanied by violent
thirst and cutting pains in the side'). His reaction, which was that of a
child rather than a man of fifty-six whose health had been bad for
years, was to drink large draughts of ice-cold water; so that when he
arrived in Vienna he was in a dangerous condition. No doctor could
at first be found, but finally a Dr. Wawruch was obtained by Karl.
In the account published later[1] he wrote, 'I found Beethoven afflicted
with serious symptoms of inflammation of the lungs. His face glowed,
he spat blood, his breathing threatened to choke him and a painful
stitch in his side made lying on his back painful.' A week later, however, the pneumonia and pleurisy had yielded to treatment and the
patient could leave his bed, walk about his rooms and read or write.
But almost immediately he was laid low with a very severe attack of
jaundice, whose onset Wawruch attributed to 'a violent rage, a great
grief because of long continued ingratitude and undeserved humiliation. . . . Trembling and shivering he bent double owing to the pains
which raged in his liver and intestines, and his feet, hitherto moderately
swollen, became enormous. From this time on dropsy developed, and
there was an increase of jaundice.'[2] The reference to the 'violent
rage' and 'ingratitude' seem to point to a final climactic scene with
Karl, but there is no further evidence of this. The dropsy was tapped
for the first time on 20 December, and again on 8 January, 2 February, and 27 February. The conversation-books contain references to
Beethoven's drinking water surreptitiously during the night, to an
enema and to all the usual humiliations of the sickroom. On the other
hand he was overjoyed when he received, on 14 December, the
bound volumes of Handel that Johann Andreas Stumpff had promised
him; and the young Gerhard von Breuning in his memoirs[3] remembers
him turning the handsome leather-bound volumes over and over, like
a child with a new toy. Gerhard was a boy of thirteen at the time, and
was given the freedom of Beethoven's sickroom in a way that would
be considered strange today. He delighted the sick man by his chatter,
his interest in everything and his lively solicitude (we even find him

[1] 'Aerztlicher Rückblick auf L. van Beethovens Letzte Lebenstage', published in *Wiener Zeitschrift*, 30 April 1842, and reproduced in L. Nohl, *Beethoven nach den Schilderungen seiner Zeitgenossen* (1877), pp. 247 ff.
[2] See Appendix A.
[3] *Aus dem Schwarzspanierhaus*, 1874.

dealing with the bed bugs), and significantly earned the nicknames of *Hosenknopf* (trouser-button)—once used with reference to Karl—and 'Ariel'. The conversation-books show that, right until the day of his departure on 2 January 1827, Karl continued to be the unwilling object of his uncle's solicitude and suspicions. On that day he disappears from the scene for the last time, though he wrote a number of letters to his 'dear father' giving news of himself and inquiring for news of Beethoven's health. When the end came, he was still at Iglau and the slow transport of the day made it impossible for him to attend Beethoven's funeral. His subsequent career showed that Beethoven's early hopes of his gifts and subsequent fears of his depravity were equally unfounded. Karl was in fact an ordinary young man, who made a good husband and father and on leaving the army had a quiet and respectable career as a minor civil servant. His tragedy was that, when still a child, he was asked to be the vessel into which an ageing and ill genius discharged all the pent-up tenderness and possessiveness that had never found its normal outlet in the relationship first of husband and then of father.

CHAPTER 10

1827

The year 1827 opened badly. Karl went to his regiment on 2 January, and it was clear that Beethoven would have to undergo a second tapping for dropsy in the near future. Schindler had resumed his old place as factotum, replacing Holz after the first few days of Beethoven's return to Vienna, but complaining of Karl, Johann (who arrived on 10 December) and Holz intriguing against him. Dr. Wawruch soon shared the fate of all Beethoven's doctors, and Schindler warmly seconded Beethoven's wish to consult the Dr. Malfatti with whom Beethoven had quarrelled many years before. Malfatti at first refused, on the grounds of professional ethics, but eventually consented. When he came, he took the patient off all the medicines prescribed by Wawruch and substituted drafts of iced punch, cold fomentations and a kind of primitive sauna bath. Beethoven was delighted with the punch and he very soon exceeded the original prescription of one glass a day, with the result that he not only intoxicated himself but started the diarrhoea to which he was always prone. The bath, whose effect was equally disastrous, is referred to in the conversation-books of 27–8 January:

The dry hayseed bath is supposed to make you sweat, and Malfatti says that this must be tried now, since the internal medicine is not having the desired effect.
It is nothing but hayseed in two piles placed on warm jugs.

According to Gerhard von Breuning, Beethoven's body 'which had been emptied of water by the scarcely completed tapping [the third, on 2 February] attracted the moisture developed by the bath, like a block of salt; it swelled visibly in the apparatus and in a few days it was necessary to reinsert the tube into the still unhealed puncture'.

An entry in the conversation-books during the first days of February reveals that the real source of Beethoven's trouble was now identified, 'The condition of the liver is the key to the whole illness.' His visitors included the publishers Haslinger and Streicher as well as Bernard and the singer Nanette Schechner, who brought with her the tenor Luigi

Cramolini. There is some doubt of Cramolini's accuracy, but he tells in his memoirs of singing *Adelaide* and an aria from *Fidelio* in the sickroom, accompanied by Schindler. At first he was overcome by the pathos of the scene and could not master his voice, until Beethoven encouraged him with the words 'I cannot hear anything alas! I only want to *see* you sing.'[1]

In writing to thank Stumpff for the Handel scores, Beethoven mentioned his acute financial embarrassment and raised the question of a possible benefit concert to be given by the Philharmonic Society. This was on 8 February, and he repeated the suggestion in letters to Smart and Moscheles two weeks later. The suggestion was put before a directors' meeting held on 28 February, when it was unanimously decided to send Beethoven a gift of £100. Beethoven did not, however, receive Moscheles' letter, dated 1 March and telling him of the Society's intention, until more than a fortnight later, and in the interval he had written two further letters to England. According to Wawruch, Beethoven abandoned all hope of recovery after the fourth tapping (27 February), and it was in a state bordering on despair that he wrote to Smart on 6 March and to Moscheles on 14 March:

Truly my lot is a very hard one! however, I am resigned and will accept whatever Fate may bring; and I only continue to pray that God in His divine wisdom may so order events that as long as I have to endure this living death I may be protected from want. This [assurance] would give me sufficient strength to bear my lot, however hard and terrible it may prove to be, with a feeling of submission to the will of the Almighty.

He received the money on 15 March, and Schindler reported to Moscheles his pathetic relief and delight. Pasqualati, Streicher, Breuning, and Malfatti sent him presents of food or wine and, at his special request, Schott dispatched a small consignment of Rüdesheimer Berg which, however, did not arrive until Beethoven was already dying.

During the month of February Schindler showed Beethoven a collection of sixty songs by Schubert, and these so delighted him that he wanted to see Schubert's instrumental compositions. The songs that Schindler mentions as especially pleasing Beethoven were 'Der Taucher', 'Bürgschaft', 'Die junge Nonne', 'Elysium', and some Ossian settings. He spoke to several of his visitors of Schubert 'possessing the divine spark' and when a few days before his death the visit of

[1] Cramolini's 'Reminiscences' were published in the *Frankfurter Zeitung* of 29 September 1907.

Hüttenbrenner and Schubert was announced by Schindler, 'Let Schubert come first', he said. Another old friend who visited him was Hummel, who appeared on 8 March, and again on the 13th, the 20th, and the 23rd, accompanied by his pupil Ferdinand Hiller.¹ On the 20th, at Beethoven's special request, Hummel brought his wife, whom Beethoven had known and very much admired before her marriage. On the 20th his condition was noticeably worse (Wawruch says that the doctors gave up hope on 16 March) and he whispered to Hummel 'I shall no doubt soon be going above.' On the 23rd he was unable to speak and lay with the sweat standing out on his forehead. When Frau Hummel wiped his face with her handkerchief, says Hiller, Beethoven gave her a look of ineffable gratitude. On the same day he signed, with difficulty, the will drafted by Breuning, making Karl his sole heir. It was on this day too—according to Gerhard von Breuning, after the doctors' visit—that Beethoven 'in his favourite sarcastic-humorous manner' quoted the Latin tag 'plaudite amici, comoedia finita est' (applaud friends, the play is over).²

The last conscious act in Beethoven's life took place the next day, when he received the final anointing and communion of the Catholic rite. The account of this we owe to his brother Johann, to Schindler, to Wawruch, and to Hüttenbrenner. Johann tells us that 'a few days after 16 March' he urged his brother to make his peace with God, and that Beethoven agreed 'with the greatest readiness'. Dr. Wawruch, confirmed by Schindler, says that he 'wrote with the greatest delicacy the words of admonition on a sheet of paper, which Beethoven read with unexampled composure, slowly and thoughtfully, his countenance like that of one transfigured. Cordially and solemnly he held out his hand to me and said "Send for the priest".' Schindler's³ account says that Beethoven accepted Wawruch's suggestion 'quietly and firmly' with the words 'I wish it'. Hüttenbrenner, writing over thirty years later, attributed the suggestion to a certain Johann Baptist Jenger and —supreme irony—to Johann's wife Therese, who also told him that after receiving the Last Sacraments Beethoven said to the priest 'I thank you, reverend sir. Your have brought me comfort!' On the evening of the same day, 24 March, he became unconscious and the death-agony began. Incredible as it may seem to us, the young Gerhard von Breuning was still allowed to come and go in the sick-room, and the impression this final spectacle made on the thirteen-

---

¹ Hiller's account is to be found in his *Aus dem Tonleben unserer Zeit* (1871), pp. 169 ff.
² A common closing line in the old Latin comedy.
³ Op. cit., p. 476.

year-old boy was naturally profound. 'The strong man lay completely unconscious, in the process of dissolution, breathing so stertorously that the rattle could be heard at a distance. His powerful frame and his unweakened lungs fought with approaching death like giants. The spectacle was fearful.'

It is not known for certain who was with Beethoven when he died. The only account is Anselm Hüttenbrenner's, written, like Gerhard von Breuning's, many years later. Both agree that at 3 o'clock on 26 March—nearly forty-eight hours, that is to say, after Beethoven had finally lost consciousness—there were in the room besides themselves Stephan von Breuning and the portrait-painter Joseph Teltscher, who had begun to make a drawing of the dying man and was dismissed by Breuning. Gerhard von Breuning says that Johann van Beethoven was there and the housekeeper. Hüttenbrenner adds Schindler and 'Frau van Beethoven', Johann's wife. When Breuning and Schindler went to choose a place for Beethoven's grave, Hüttenbrenner says that he was left alone in the room with Frau van Beethoven and the dying man. It seems possible that Gerhard von Breuning and Hüttenbrenner may have confused Johann's wife with Beethoven's housekeeper, the 'Sali' whom Frau von Breuning had found for him. Whichever of the two it was, she played no part in the final scene, which is best told in Hüttenbrenner's own words:[1]

After Beethoven had lain unconscious, the death-rattle in his throat, from 3 o'clock in the afternoon till after 5 there came a flash of lightning, accompanied by a violent clap of thunder, and garishly illuminating the death-chamber. Snow was lying on the ground at the time. After this unexpected natural phenomenon Beethoven opened his eyes, lifted his right hand and looked upwards for several seconds, with his fist clenched and a very serious, threatening expression as if he were trying to say 'Hostile powers, I defy you! Away with you! God is with me!' . . . When he dropped his raised hand to the bed, his eyes half closed. My right hand was under his head, my left resting on his breast. Not another breath, not a heartbeat more!'

The autopsy, performed the next day, though unsatisfactory and inconclusive by modern standards, revealed a liver 'shrunk to half its proper size, leathery in consistency and greenish-blue in colour, covered with bean-sized nodules on its tuberculated surface as well as in its substance, and with all its vessels very much narrowed and bloodless. The spleen was more than double its proper size.' The fact that the report of the autopsy disappeared was at one time used to reinforce

[1] Hüttenbrenner's account is to be found in a letter dated 20 August 1860 to A. W. Thayer, quoted in Leitzmann op. cit., vol. 2, pp. 412 ff.

the suspicion that death was due to syphilis. This, however, is no longer medically acceptable.[1]

The funeral at the parish church in the Alserstrasse was three days later, on 29 March at 3 in the afternoon, and attended by an enormous crowd. The Italian singers from Barbaja's company took part and the music included two of Beethoven's trombone *equali*, with Latin texts fitted to them, and the funeral march from the piano sonata op. 26 played by a brass band. Eight of Vienna's leading musicians were pall-bearers—Eybler, Hummel, Kreutzer, Seyfried, Gänsbacher, Gyrowetz, Weigl, and Würfel—and among the torchbearers were such friends as Bernard, Böhm, Czerny, Haslinger, Holz, Linke, Schubert, Streicher, Schuppanzigh and Steiner, as well as Grillparzer, who had written the funeral oration. This was spoken by the actor Anschütz. The body was buried at the Währing cemetery, but removed in 1888 to the Central Cemetery.

[1] See Appendix A.

CHAPTER 11

Social and political attitudes

Beethoven was twenty-two, and the main lines of his character were therefore firmly set, when he settled in Vienna in 1792. His initially flattering experiences as a lion of Viennese aristocratic society, and his subsequent resentment of the changes brought about in that society by the years of war and foreign occupation, may have modified his childish impressions but certainly never effaced them. These impressions were gained in the Rhineland town of Bonn, where he was born and brought up, and to understand their nature we must look for a moment at the circumstances of his early life there.[1]

The Electoral Principality of Cologne, in which the town of Bonn stood, was a prince-bishopric and one of the first of the small German states to feel the influence of the German *Aufklärung*, or movement of 'Enlightenment', that wind of change that began to blow a whole generation before the French Revolution and had, indeed, by 1789 already begun to thaw the huge ice-floes of irrational legal, social, religious, and political tradition which had accumulated from feudal days. The Enlightenment was before all else a movement of reason-ableness. It was by reason that its prophets sought to break down the feudal system of privilege, and reason inspired the philanthropic ideals and the social conscientiousness that gave the movement its emotional power. Although springing from middle-class intellectual origins, the Enlightenment was patronized by rulers with either a genuine social conscience (like the Austrian Emperor Joseph II, who died in 1790) or intellectual pretensions, like Frederick the Great of Prussia and Catherine II of Russia, who took a dilettante interest in the intellectual side of the movement but for the most part steered clear of its practical implications, social or political.

There were not a few cases in Europe of an 'enlightened' minister, like Pombal in Portugal, leading an unwilling or indifferent (but generally unintelligent) royal master by the nose along the path to reforms that were long overdue. Bonn saw an example of such a

[1] For a full discussion of Beethoven's early years in Bonn see L. Schiedermair's admirable *Der junge Beethoven* (1925 and 1939).

minister during the first decade of Beethoven's life (1770–80) in Belderbusch, under whose influence the Electoral Prince Maximilian Friedrich initiated a national theatre in Bonn, in order 'to elevate the dramatic art into a school of manners for the German people'. In 1784 both he and his minister died, and the Principality passed to the Habsburg Archduke Maximilian Franz. He fortunately shared the ideas of his eldest brother Joseph II who, in this very decade (1780–90) was reorganizing the Austrian crown-lands and much of the empire according to the principles of the Enlightenement, curbing feudal and ecclesiastical privilege and laying the foundations of the first fully centralized welfare state in Europe.

The new Elector professed, and practised, the highest principles— 'to rule a country and a people is an office, a form of state service', he announced—and under his benevolent and far-sighted government Bonn's cultural development continued without interruption. Friends and patrons of Beethoven's early years were intimately concerned in this cultural flowering: Franz Gerhard Wegeler, for instance, forwarded the study of anatomy and gynaecology and Bartholomäus Ludwig Fischenich, a friend of Schiller's, promoted the study of law. The clergy were not alienated at Bonn, as they were in most countries, where the Enlightenment became identified with anti-clericalism. When the Scientific Academy at Bonn was raised to the status of a university (1786) a Minorite friar, Elias van der Schüren, lectured on Kant's philosophy and another, Philipp Hedderich, came out as a champion of the nationalist, anti-Roman movement in church affairs, while the Carmelite Anton Dereser earned himself a comparison to Luther by his bold pleas for ecclesiastical reform. The Bonn bookshops in the seventies and eighties sold the latest editions of Plato, Plutarch, Rousseau, and Montesquieu as well as the modern German authors Herder, Schiller, and Goethe.

This, then, was the young Beethoven's first experience of public life and of the 'state'; and it was no doubt the contrast between these predominantly happy impressions and the political and social conditions in Vienna after the second French occupation (1809) that explains the violent political jeremiads of Beethoven's last years. His early experience of an 'enlightened' political régime in Bonn proved an effective and lifelong immunization against the extremer doctrines of the French revolutionaries, which as a general rule found least sympathy in those countries where the Enlightenment had been most effective. Not, of course, that Beethoven never as a young man came into galling contact with the formalities and privileges, the poverty and the injustice which marked eighteenth-century society even at its best. But it was only in Vienna that he was to encounter the spirit of caste in its crudest form,[1] and it came to him as a surprise after his own experiences in Bonn, where he had been accepted as a friend and an equal in families like the Breunings and Wegelers, who were themselves leading members of the community, and had seen another composer, Haydn, accorded the highest honours on his visit to Bonn in 1790.

If Beethoven remained, as he did to the end of his life, a man of the eighteenth century, both in his emotional reactions and in his opinions, this was because he only became fully aware of the social and political evils of the *ancien régime* when his character and opinions were already formed. In Vienna the presence of the Imperial court and a strong and numerous cosmopolitan aristocracy fostered an atmosphere of luxury and display on the one hand, and a servile mentality on the other, both of which were on the wane in Bonn before Beethoven was born. Nevertheless, as a young man in Vienna Beethoven was happy to find not only his patrons, but his friends among members of the aristocracy who appreciated his gifts. His political obsessions—they can hardly be called opinions—date from twenty years later, when the French wars and occupations had reduced the despairing government to bankruptcy and to a policy of nervous reaction that saw a French sympathizer or 'Jacobin' in every Liberal, while the power and wealth of his aristocratic patrons had been greatly diminished. Beethoven was no egalitarian. He had no objection to kings, until he thought that he had been robbed of his savings by Franz I and heard that Franz suspected genius of any kind and wanted only *brauchbare Menschen* (useful citizens) for his subjects.[2] He had still less objection to aristocrats as such, rather counting himself as one of their number by virtue of his artistic

---

[1] A characteristic instance of this is to be found in an anecdote in one of the conversation-books for 1823. A certain Niederstaetter was engaged as tutor to the children of the Countess Wrbna, one of the most admired beauties at the Congress of Vienna and married to a man who enjoyed the special confidence of the Emperor. The children were lazy and insolent, and Niederstaetter on one occasion tweaked the nose of one of them. The child complained at once to its mother, and she appealed immediately to the count, who became abusive and even used physical violence when rebuking the tutor. 'How dare you, a mere outsider, lay hands on someone of noble blood?' he asked. Niederstaetter was dismissed and, when he wished to make an official complaint of the violent treatment that he had received, he was advised to let the matter drop, since no one would take any action against the Wrbnas.

[2] This is confirmed by Beethoven's attitude to Louis XVIII—not a king generally popular with Democrats—who in 1824 had responded to a request for a subscription to the Missa Solemnis by sending the composer a gold medal. Writing to the editor of the *Wiener Zeitung*, asking for this information to be inserted in the press, Beethoven says—

You doubtless realize that to circulate news of this kind is well worth while, both for my
continued on page 89

gifts; his attitude changed only when they claimed privileges on the grounds of birth alone, when they humiliated him or neglected to patronize the arts. In all of this he was a typical man of the Enlightenment rather than of the French Revolution; an admirer of a benevolent despotism like that of Joseph II rather than a republican; an enemy of feudal privilege and a believer in *la carrière ouverte aux talents* rather than a democrat in any but the vaguest sense of the word. Although he detested tyranny, he had never really experienced it himself, because he never encountered in Bonn, and was protected by his noble patrons from becoming acquainted in Vienna with that fear which, according to Montesquieu, is the hallmark of tyranny. Beethoven's inspiration remained to the end of his life the eighteenth-century ideals of human dignity, morality, and tolerance. Of real democracy, as the nineteenth century came to know it, he had no knowledge; nor does anything in his character lead us to suppose that he would have felt sympathetic towards it. His ideal was rather what he knew (or imagined) of the English constitution, and in this admiration he again resembles such eighteenth-century liberals as Voltaire, Montesquieu, and Pombal.

'You in England have heads on your shoulders', he said to Cipriani Potter, while nothing was too bad for the Viennese. At first he wrote of them with the tolerant, amused contempt still today common among Germans. After the first Austrian defeats by the French, in 1794, he had written, 'People say that a revolution may break out here, but I think that as long as the Austrian still has his dark beer and his sausage he won't revolt.'

During the last ten years of Beethoven's life his political antagonisms were far more violent. He calls the Viennese 'worthless from the Emperor downwards' and characterizes them with a typically clumsy pun 'Oesterreicher, Eselreicher' (Austrians, Ass-trians). If this increasing intolerance was partly explained by the suspiciousness caused by his deteriorating health and increasing deafness, we should not forget the real deterioration of standards characteristic of a post-war age. Beethoven was not the first middle-aged bachelor, ill, deaf, and suspicious, to have been exploited by his servants; nor need we imagine that even in these years of acute poverty Vienna produced the monsters of dishonesty, inefficiency, and immorality depicted in Beethoven's letters and conversation-books. In fact his relations with

---

honour and the king's. It is clear that His Majesty did not want just to fob me off by paying for his [subscription] copy. This action shows, to my mind, that he is a generous King and a man of refined feeling.

the innumerable people—mostly women, but in a few cases men—
whom he engaged to run his household do no credit to his love of
humanity, and often reveal a quite unregenerate *ancien régime* conception of the relationship between master and servant. According to
him servants were all, without exception, rogues and 'cattle', who
must be schooled by fear since they understood no other motive. He
was free with verbal abuse, though very close with the housekeeping
money, and not above resorting to physical violence, even with the
women. Most damaging of all, perhaps, in modern eyes, was his
attempt to initiate a system of spying among his household staff.
Between 1816 and 1818 when he was desperately trying to form a
stable household in order to make a home for his nephew, he turned
for help to Frau Nanette Streicher, an old friend who proved most
generous with advice and help. In January 1818 he wrote to her—

Please instruct and train the kitchenmaid who is now taking up her duties, so
that she may side with you and me against N. (the housekeeper). As a reward
for doing so, I will make her an occasional present; but the other need not
know anything about this.

When Beethoven spoke or wrote at this time of 'the utter moral
rottenness of the Austrian state' or exclaimed that 'all other misfortunes in this city can be ascribed to the immorality of servants', he
can hardly have realized the demoralizing effect of his own actions.
In the late summer of 1819 this dislike and distrust of servants led to
hysterical outbursts in his letters, 'Oh! may the whole miserable rabble
of humanity be cursed and damned!' 'Cursed, damned, execrable,
abominable rabble of Vienna'. Since the invention of the telephone
outbursts such as these are not normally committed to writing, and
for this reason biographers today may sometimes wonder how much
they really know of their subject's more undignified lapses.

There can be little wonder that Beethoven, with his strong feeling
of personal superiority, bitterly resented the relegation of the lawsuit
over his nephew Karl from the nobles' to the commoners' court. He
does not, he says, belong to the 'plebeian mass', and the conversation-
books make his meaning quite clear 'The ordinary citizen must be
separated from superior people, and I have fallen among them [i.e.
the former].'[1] He showed no immediate anxiety to contradict the
rumour, which was circulating, that he was a natural son of Friedrich
Wilhelm II; and we have seen his lively interest in such honours as the

---

[1] See Schindler op. cit., p. 307. I find disingenuous the attempt to confine Beethoven's anti-
egalitarian sentiments to Vienna only. Nothing is commoner than egalitarian theory combined with a strong practical sense of personal privilege.

medal sent him by Louis XVIII and the membership of the Swedish Academy of Sciences, which he tried to announce in the Viennese press. This very human concern with recognition, and even with royal favour, may strike us as pathetic in a man of Beethoven's stature. If it cannot be ranked, as some writers have tried to rank it, as outright snobbery, it certainly shows a keen and conscious desire to mark himself off from the common run of humanity; and this is not the instinct of a democrat.

Another strangely illiberal trait, as it seems to us, in Beethoven's character was his readiness to call in the police, not only in cases of real or imaginary grievances against his servants, but in order to get his own way with members of his family. The régime of Franz I and Metternich, was a combination of paternalism and repression characteristic of all 'benevolent despotisms'; and not only the police, but even royalty, was often invoked in the most trivial cases. Thus Johanna van Beethoven and Beethoven himself appealed to Archduke Ludwig in the matter of Karl's being sent out of the country, and Karl's mother eventually appealed to the Emperor himself. Members of the royal family used to appear masked at balls in the Redoutensaal and mix freely with the dancers; and readers of the poet Grillparzer's autobiography will have been astonished by the cases in which the most trivial points of official discipline or promotion were referred to the very highest authorities. The police, to which Beethoven appealed on equally trivial occasions, was not of course the Secret Police whose chief concern was with possible political subversion; but it was nevertheless the organ of authority, which settled disputes by main force. Beethoven had no hesitation in using his position, as a protégé of the Archduke Rudolf and a well-known public character whom the police would instinctively support against those in a humbler position, to enforce his wishes. A letter written from Hetzendorf in May 1823 makes unpleasant reading:

Many compliments to the Director of Police and to Herr von Ungermann [a Commissioner of Police whom Beethoven had already contacted in connection with Karl's mother]—The six gulden will follow, but they should not be given to (the landlord) until he has taken down the placard and delivered the receipt for the house-rent to the worshipful police and has also undertaken to behave in future like a civilized person.

NB. The worshipful police are most politely requested to settle the matter today with the landlord as quickly as possible, seeing that a much more important affair will demand their attention immediately afterwards.

This 'much more important affair' was that of Therese, his sister-in-law, whom Beethoven wished his brother Johann to divorce. It is difficult to know whether Beethoven made himself more odious or ridiculous by this calling in of 'authority' to impose his wishes in matters which were not really his concern.

The instinctive appeal to force in any emergency was no doubt part of Beethoven's very primitive emotional nature, whose spontaneous reactions he seems never to have questioned and certainly never learned to control. Such immediate, unthinking emotional reactions also explain Beethoven's generous sympathy with what presented itself to his imagination as noble, though he might not have investigated it closely. The enthusiasm for Napoleon, which he had imbibed at the house of the French ambassador in Vienna, Bernadotte, during the last years of the eighteenth century, provides a good example of this. Napoleon at this time appeared to Beethoven as a hero in the antique mould, a character out of the Plutarch whom he had been reading, and a politician who would realize Plato's ideal of the philosopher-king. The English intellectuals who shared this delusion had much more excuse, since they never had the French contacts that Beethoven enjoyed at Bernadotte's. He was to learn by bitter experience that the First Consul's character and ambitions promised anything rather than an era of sweetness and light, but it simply did not occur to him to compare the ideal which he had formed with the facts. This inability to believe, or even to understand, that human beings or situations were different from what he imagined them was probably the cause of most of Beethoven's personal unhappiness. The realization of the truth was often the more agonizing for being long delayed. It was not until the summer of 1825, as we have seen, that he could bring himself to face the truth that his nephew Karl was neither exceptionally good nor exceptionally bad, but simply a rather ordinary, young man. Moreover the realization hardly helped him, for the letter in which he writes, 'if only you had some depth of character, you would always act quite differently', was followed within a month by the pathetic *cri de coeur* 'come soon! come soon! come soon!'

His disillusionment with Napoleon, though absolute for a time, seems never to have included the realization that it was Napoleon, rather than the Emperor Franz, whom he should have blamed for 'robbing' him of his money. In 1820 he observed approvingly in one of the conversation-books that 'Napoleon everywhere destroyed the feudal system and protected right and law', and he seems to have accepted without protest the description of Napoleon by Josef Karl Bernard, editor of the *Wiener Zeitung*, as 'a good fellow who wanted to blockade England in order to destroy her' and a 'Maecenas'.

The mood of disillusion with all political movements and with government in general, common in countries exhausted by war and subject to a petty rather than a violent tyranny, makes itself frequently felt in the conversation-books.[1] In 1820 there is an entry, probably in Bernard's handwriting—'Before the French Revolution there was great freedom of thought and political action. The revolution made both the government and the nobility suspicious of the common people, and this has led by degrees to the present policy of repression.' Three years later another entry, in an unidentified hand, runs—'All over Germany things are exactly as they were before the so-called democratic disturbances—the most that has been achieved is that the real revolutionaries have been marked down and removed. The real scholar and independent thinker was no more persecuted in Germany then than now.' Both of these entries suggest a clear distinction between the writer, who identifies himself with liberal policies, and the 'common people', between the revolutionary hotheads and the scholar or thinker. Beethoven and his friends were still living in the world of Joseph II, where reason, humanity, and tolerance were the ideals; and they rejected egalitarian democracy as unequivocally as they rejected the paternalistic Austrian police-state organized by Metternich, his secretary Gentz, and his censorship chief Sedlnitzky. This régime is more mocked than condemned in the conversation-books. We find Joseph Blöchlinger, for instance, Karl's headmaster, observing in 1820 with a humour that we can already recognize as Viennese—'The Congress [at Laibach] is working on a law that will lay down how high birds may fly and how fast hares may run.' Another of Beethoven's journalist friends, August Friedrich Kanne, who became editor of the *Allgemeine Musikalische Zeitung* in 1824, observed wryly that one reason for Europe's disastrous financial situation lay in the fact that 'Germany has to support thirty-eight courts and something like a million princes and princesses'. On the other hand the revolt of some 8,000 starving peasants on the Palffy estates in Hungary prompts a just, factual comment rather than a spontaneous reaction of warm sympathy or indignation, 'the fault lies in the landowners' oppressive

---

[1] According to Schindler (p. 345) Beethoven particularly resented the Emperor's patriarchal habit of holding 'public audiences' every Wednesday in the winter months. From 200 to 300 people from all over the Empire were admitted to hand over their requests or complaints; but any hint of 'democratic' opinions formed an absolute bar to admission. Schindler (p. 337) sums up Beethoven's general attitude to politics as entirely dominated by the ideal of personal freedom. 'Absolute personal freedom of every kind, even if accompanied by misery and lamentation, and limited only by the laws of morality—this was the norm of life in the eyes of this exceptional character.' This he would hardly have claimed for his servants.

treatment—in many cases worse than serfdom'. This is the voice of reason rather than of moral indignation or true compassion.[1]

A further indication of Beethoven's social and political attitudes can be found in his relationship to his pupil, the Archduke Rudolf, eighteen years his junior, youngest brother of the Emperor and a nephew of the Prince-Elector of Bonn, Maximilian Franz. They met, probably through the Lobkowitzes, some ten years after Beethoven arrived in Vienna, when he was in his early thirties and the Archduke a boy in his early teens. Piano lessons began in 1803 or 1804, and these were followed by composition lessons which lasted until the year before the composer's death. Rudolf, whom family pressure rather than personal inclination destined for the priesthood, was exceptionally intelligent though delicate in health, genuinely gifted for music and well aware of his difficult master's great qualities. He not only assured Beethoven an annual pension from 1809 until his death, but helped him unostentatiously whenever he could, instructed his own household to dispense with the usual formalities of protocol which so irritated Beethoven, and protected him from the police interference which his public outbursts against the government and the royal family would have unfailingly brought upon him otherwise. In return he expected Beethoven to give him composition lessons when he was in Vienna and was probably not surprised, though he may well have felt himself honoured, to receive the dedication of a large number of Beethoven's greatest compositions, including the trio opus 97, the piano sonatas opus 106 and 111, and the Missa Solemnis.

Beethoven's response, as we can trace it in letters that are spread over more than twenty years, was complex and variable. He seems to have felt genuine affection and gratitude, but to have grudged the time needed to give lessons and the sensation of being in any way indebted. The manner of the letters is always respectful, and the present-day reader has some difficulty in distinguishing between what were the normal forms of address used to royalty in Beethoven's day and what often appears to be unnecessary fulsomeness. He could occasionally write, as in 1819, 'I never was a courtier, am not one now and shall never be able to be one', but there seems to be more than a little of the courtier about a letter written in September 1817:

[1] Beethoven's philanthropy or public spirit certainly did not extend to a reasonable acceptance of his obligations as a tax-payer. According to Schindler—'he had 21 gulden [according to Emily Anderson's reckoning about 2 guineas] to pay every year in *Klassensteuer* [a form of tax intermediate between poll-tax and income tax proper] and these 21 gulden must have provided material for quite 21,000 jokes and allusions during the year'.

I hear that Your Imperial Highness is looking wonderfuly well; and though it is quite possible to draw therefrom wrong conclusions about excellent health, yet I hear people talking about the improvement in Y.I.H.'s condition, and in this I certainly do take the most lively interest. I hope, too, that when Y.I.H. returns to the town I shall be able to assist you in the sacrifices you make to the Muses. Surely God will hear my prayer and will once more liberate me from so many calamities, seeing that since my childhood I have served Him trustfully and have performed good actions whenever I could. Hence on Him alone do I place my reliance, and hope that in all my manifold miseries the Almighty will not let me utterly perish.

If the first part of the letter suggests ill-concealed boredom (Beethoven was, as so often, excusing himself on the grounds of ill-health from giving the Archduke a lesson), the conventionally pious language and stock, rather childish sentiments of the second half suggest something painfully close to hypocrisy.[1] In his defence it should be said, first, that Beethoven was never a master of words and therefore easily fell into commonplace phraseology: and secondly that a man of his mercurial moods and uncritical character easily comes to feel sincerely the emotions that he has begun to express in the first place from a sense of duty or propriety.

There is an even stronger passage of the same kind in a letter written in June 1819, where Beethoven congratulates the Archduke on his election as Archbishop of Olmütz and speaks of his plans for the Missa Solemnis:

The day on which a Mass composed by me will be performed during the ceremonies solemnized for Your Imperial Highness will be the most glorious day of my life; and God will enlighten me so that my poor talents may contribute to the glorification of that solemn day. . . . I beg you to forgive me for writing and I implore Our Lord to let His Blessings flow down in rich measure on the head of Y.I.H. Y.I.H.'s new profession, which so fully embraces the love of humanity, is certainly one of the finest: and in it Y.I.H. both as a human and as a spiritual leader will always provide the finest example.

Once again both the style and the sentiments seem suspect to us. They suggest not so much an independent-minded artist as a rather toadyish old family servant. It is impossible to connect such expressions and attitudes with Beethoven, unless we realize that apart from his music Beethoven always preserved much of the naïve feeling and conventionality of thought and expression of the semi-educated.

[1] Beethoven could be merciless towards such conventionally pious language in others, as when Moscheles wrote 'FINIS—with God's help' at the end of a score and Beethoven scrawled 'Man, help thyself' across the page.

CHAPTER 12

General culture

There has been a great variety of opinion about the character and
extent of Beethoven's general, non-musical education. On the
one hand he has been represented, largely on the evidence of his
ill-written and often ill-spelt letters and inelegant personal habits, as
little better than an illiterate boor. On the other hand it has been
possible to quote his early admiration for Schiller, his lifelong enthusiasm for Goethe, his references to Plato, Homer, Plutarch, and Kant
and the fact that he was accepted in aristocratic circles not only as
a musician but as a friend, in order to argue that he possessed a degree
of culture by no means common among musicians in any age, and
almost unknown in his own.

The son of a lay-clerk in the Prince Elector's chapel at Bonn in the
last quarter of the eighteenth century could not expect anything more
than a rudimentary education. In Beethoven's case there were two
special circumstances that made his conventional schooling even
sketchier than it might otherwise have been—his unusual musical
gifts, which were naturally cultivated at the expense of his general
education, and the fact that he was the eldest member of his family
for which, with a drunkard father, he very soon became virtually
responsible. Beethoven met the cultured world in the Wegeler and
von Breuning families, but his reading was done comparatively late
and in his spare time, so that in his maturity he showed all the
characteristics of a self-educated man. Albert Leitzmann expresses
very well the advantages and the drawbacks of such an education.[1]

Beethoven was the last of the hermit autodidacts of genius, whose patchy
culture and insufficient education made a real liberation of the spirit impossible
. . . wild forest-plants of disturbing beauty and overwhelming power. This
kind of human existence will never return. Goethe's phrase describing
Beethoven as 'an untamed personality' referred to the creative impulse, the
idealism, the extreme emotional violence, the childlike innocence in worldly
matters and the grotesque manners of genius—all coming from a single
source.

[1] Albert Leitzmann, *Beethovens Persönliche Aufzeichnungen* (1914) p. 3.

The disadvantages of the self-educated man are partly practical. It seems to us incredible that Beethoven never learned simple multiplication, and although his financial anxieties were generally rooted in deep psychological traits of character rather than in objective fact, this helplessness with figures must have exposed him to every kind of petty dishonesty, while the knowledge of this no doubt increased in him the suspiciousness common to all deaf people. In his dealings with publishers, and to a much greater extent with servants, he must often have had the sensation of a man entering a dark room filled with unknown people whose language he could not understand.

Less obvious, but wider in their effect on his mentality, are the general handicaps of the self-educated man. In the first place he is likely to move in a small world. He can form only the vaguest, if any, ideas of the past or of human beings, systems, societies and ideas other than those with which he has come into personal contact, until he supplies this knowledge himself; and the sources to which he goes will often be decided by chance circumstance. When he reads, he must make his own standards which will be largely instinctive, and he will be liable to intense surprises, disappointments and volte-faces in his mental life, such as are for the most part spared to those whose wits have been sharpened and their faculties of judgement, comparison and selection trained, however simply, according to a deliberate educational system.

Beethoven's conscious attitude to literary culture was compounded of genuine humility and a very characteristic pride. In 1809 he wrote to his publishers Breitkopf and Härtel, asking them to send him translations of Homer, Euripides, and Ossian and works by Wieland, Schiller, and Goethe.

Without claiming to possess real erudition, I have tried ever since childhood to understand the thoughts of the best and wisest men of all ages. Shame on the artist who does not think it a fault not to take things at least so far.

Beethoven was in his fortieth year when he wrote this letter. We know that he had had a great enthusiasm for Schiller during his teens at Bonn, and that the first plan to set the *Ode to Joy* dates from those years. Schiller was a Rhinelander like himself and has been described[1] as 'a Frenchman who wrote in German because he happened to be born in Swabia'. Schiller's rhetoric and pathos, the often naïve contrast between virtue and vice in his dramas and a certain plebeian coarseness and vigour in his writing all have obvious parallels in the music of Beethoven's early and middle periods. In 1823 Beethoven's lega

[1] Albert Einstein, *Greatness in Music*, p. 74.

adviser, Dr. Bach, suggested that *Fiesco* would make a good opera book, but there were plainly difficulties at which the composer hinted when he said to Czerny, 'Schiller's poems are extremely difficult for music. The composer must be able to rise far above the poet. Who can do that in Schiller's case? Goethe is much easier in this respect.'[1] What did Beethoven mean? No man, least of all Beethoven, should be held pedantically to chance expressions of literary preferences made at different times in his life. But the fact remains that Beethoven did on one occasion say that Homer was his favourite among the poets and that he preferred Schiller to Goethe ('Goethe is more of an egoist') and on another, as late as 1824, that 'he preferred to set Homer, Klopstock, Schiller to music', without mentioning Goethe. On the other hand in his letter to Goethe of February, 1823 he speaks of himself as 'still ever living, as I have lived since my youth, in your immortal and ever youthful works' and referred to his projected setting of lyrics by Goethe including 'Rastlose Liebe'. It is true that Beethoven in this letter was asking Goethe a favour—to obtain a subscription to the Missa Solemnis from the Grand Duke of Weimar—and that four years earlier there is an entry in Beethoven's hand in one of the conversation-books, 'Goethe ought to stop writing—he'll be like the old singers'— [who go on singing after their voices have gone, presumably]. But there can be no doubt of Beethoven's original admiration, and he was perhaps only slightly exaggerating when he said to Rochlitz in 1822

I would have gone to death, yes, ten times to death, for Goethe. Then when I was at the height of my enthusiasm, I thought out my 'Egmont' music. Goethe is really alive, and wants us all to live with him. It is for that reason that he can be set. Nobody is so easily set as he—but I don't like composing songs.

Egmont lay twelve years behind him in 1822, and in fact 'Rastlose Liebe' never got beyond the sketch-stage; but right to the end of his life Beethoven was hoping to make a musical setting of *Faust*—'the highest that there is both for me and for art' (see p. 11). Goethe, he told Rochlitz, had killed his early taste for Klopstock, about whose works he makes a confession very typical of the self-educated man—

I carried Klopstock about with me for years, on walks. . . . True, I didn't always understand him. He skips about so, and always begins so far away, above or below—always *maestoso*! D flat major, isn't that so? He's great nevertheless and uplifts the soul. When I couldn't understand him, I sort of guessed at his meaning.[2]

[1] To Karl Czerny, 1809.
[2] Letter to Härtel, reprinted in Rochlitz, *Für Freunde der Tonkunst*, IV (1832).

It was the scholar in Klopstock, just as it was the sophisticated man-of-the-world in Goethe, that puzzled or alienated Beethoven. Whatever happened exactly when Goethe and Beethoven met at Teplitz in 1812, and however much the story of their different reactions on meeting the court became embellished or twisted in the telling, a whole world separated the two men. Goethe was gently bred, never in need of money, naturally at home in elegant society as well as in a variety of intellectual fields, refined, reflective, and sophisticated. On the other hand Beethoven was humbly born, barely educated in any field but music, forced into a subordinate position by lack of money, coarse and clumsy in manner, spontaneous as a child in his emotions and boundlessly naïve. If there was a touchingly humble note in Beethoven's admiration for Goethe, this was sometimes modified by an unmistakable note of resentment; while Goethe, though he could not fail to be aware of Beethoven's greatness as an artist, politely deplored the primitiveness of the man. 'I have never met an artist more concentrated, more vigorous or more deeply sincere in feeling . . unfortunately as a man he is completely lacking in self-control.'[1]

Beethoven's commonplace book, in which he copied out favourite passages from his reading, contains an astonishingly large number of lines from Homer. These are mostly simple episodes or images which show that Beethoven felt, as we should expect him to feel, the fascination of an art which seems to confer magic on the mere description of the most trivial or everyday details of life. In Homer it is, as Walter Pater[2] puts it, as though 'there had been no effort in it: that here was but the almost mechanical transcript of a time, naturally, intrinsically poetic, a time in which one could hardly have spoken at all without ideal effect, or the sailors pulled down their boat without making a picture "in the great style", against a sky charged with marvels'. That Beethoven was looking for the same quality in Ossian we can be sure; and if he occasionally imagined that he found it, this was not owing to his lack of education, since it was a commonplace of literary criticism to compare Ossian to Homer, however ludicrous it may seem today. How much of Shakespeare Beethoven knew is not known, but certainly *Macbeth*, *The Tempest*, and perhaps something of *Henry IV* and *Henry V* since he nicknamed his large violinist friend, Ignaz Schuppanzigh, 'Falstaff'.

If the disadvantages under which the self-educated man suffers are

[1] Letter of Goethe to Karl Friedrich Zelter, dated 2 September 1812, quoted in Leitzmann, op. cit., I, p. 148.
[2] Walter Pater, *Marius the Epicurean*, 1885, p. 74.

clear enough, what are the advantages? His palate is not spoiled by indoctrination, and he is hardly aware of what the accepted good taste of his day expects him to admire; or if he becomes aware, it is at an age when he no longer feels any urgent need to conform. In Beethoven's case we may very much doubt whether a formal education would have had any beneficial effect on his music, though it might well have destroyed the simplicity of the man and the spontaneity of his emotional responses, which is one of the greatest attributes of his music. It is possible that it would have made him happier, in the sense of being better able to understand and so to live with others, to see things from their point of view as well as his own, and to control his feelings. But then the world might have simply gained a reasonably good citizen (and Franz I another *brauchbarer Mensch*) while music would have exchanged a unique artist of the highest rank for yet another 'excellent composer'. It seems certain that the greatness of Beethoven's music is inextricably bound up with his violent, undisciplined nature and the suffering that it brought him.

Like many German composers he was unable to discover a satisfactory libretto for the opera which his friends were urging him to write in succession to *Fidelio* (itself a good instance of Beethoven's imagination investing commonplace literary material with real sublimity). It is a strange fact that among what may be called the cronies of Beethoven's last years—the names which recur in the conversation-books, that is to say—there is a high proportion of literary figures, not poets but journalists of the better sort. We have already met August Friedrich Kanne and Josef Karl Bernard, and to these must be added Johann Schickh, editor of the *Wiener Zeitschrift für Kunst, Literatur, Theater und Mode*. Not unnaturally Beethoven received countless suggestions for a new opera from these men. Bernard himself was, as we have seen, the author of the text of an oratorio, *Der Sieg des Kreuzes*, which Beethoven undertook to compose but understandably failed to write. Among the suggestions that were at least considered by Beethoven perhaps the most astonishing are Metastasio's *Ruggiero, ossia l'Eroica Gratitudine* and Voltaire's tragedies (brother Johann's suggestion) and the most tantalizing Byron's *Corsair*. In 1819 Beethoven apparently bought a copy of *Der Vampyr*[1] (which Marschner and Lindpaintner were to use in 1828) and the following year Bernard told him that *The Corsair* was 'particularly suitable for an opera', adding (no doubt in order to whet the composer's appetite) that 'Byron

---

[1] A story by J. W. Polidori, first published in 1819 and believed at the time to be the work of Byron.

gets two guineas a line in London'. Beethoven's own taste seems to
have returned most often to *Wanda, Königin der Sarmaten* by the
eccentric romantic playwright Zacharias Werner, whom we shall
meet in a later chapter in a very different role. *Wanda* was a tragedy
based on Slavonic history and mythology, and Beethoven considered
seriously another tragedy of very much the same complexion, *Drahomira*, by another and much greater writer than Werner, Franz Grillparzer, the only Austrian tragedian of the nineteenth century still
remembered today.

Grillparzer was a lawyer's son and some twenty years younger than
Beethoven. His autobiography, to which allusion has already been
made, provides an excellent picture of how the French wars and
occupations affected a Viennese family growing up in the first decade
of the nineteenth century; and how between 1815 and 1848 the strict
literary censorship, instituted by Metternich and administered by
Count Sedlnitzky, discouraged any imaginative writing that was not,
directly or indirectly, propaganda for the Habsburg dynasty or the
government, slowly wearing down the poet's spirit by a succession of
pin-prick attacks, by silent disapproval, and finally by simple neglect.[1]
Grillparzer's mother was an ardent musician, and as a boy the poet
met Beethoven casually on several occasions. In 1823, when Beethoven was inquiring on all sides for possible librettos, he was put in
touch with Grillparzer either by Count Moritz Lichnowsky or by
Count Dietrichstein, director of the court theatres. Grillparzer, whose
musical taste was for Mozart rather than Beethoven, thought at first
of his early *Drahomira* but changed his mind, because he did not want
to give the composer 'the opportunity of moving still closer to the
extreme limits of music which lay nearby, already threatening like
precipices, by introducing him to a story already half diabolical in
character'. Instead he chose the story of Melusine—a fairy-play
with ballets, choruses, and some passages of melodrama, not unlike
Dvořák's *Rusalka*—and sent this to Beethoven. Anything less suited to
Beethoven at any time, and particularly during the last years of his

---

[1] Any reader of the autobiography will be struck by the close resemblance between political
censorship of the arts in all ages. When Grillparzer earned official, and court, disapproval for
his poem on the Colosseum 'Die Ruinen des Campo Vaccino'—the disapproval that in fact
blocked his career as a civil servant for at least ten years—he was given three grounds of
complaint—(1) that no Christian should have written such a poem (a confrontation of
ancient and modern Rome), (2) that a Royal and Imperial employee should have been more
discreet, (3) that he had been travelling to Italy in the Royal and Imperial suite. The last
charge was not even true, while the other two reveal a narrowness and nervousness of mind
that would be hard to credit, if totalitarian censorships of the present day did not furnish
examples of exactly the same kind.

life, it would be difficult to imagine, and the work was never composed. Beethoven was embarrassed, but clearly anxious not to hurt the poet's feelings; and he even on one occasion informed Grillparzer 'your opera is ready', when he can at most have meant that it was composed in his mind. The two men agreed in conversation on the mortification of living under an inept, tyrannical government and yet being unable to drag themselves away from the fascination of Vienna.

Another of Beethoven's would-be collaborators at this time, Christoph Kuffner, observed in the conversation-books that 'although words are subject to the censorship, the sounds that represent [?] and give force to words are not'. Grillparzer, on the other hand, had the impression that Beethoven envied poetry its scope, because he considered it wider than that of music; but he shrewdly observed that 'Beethoven had by this time become accustomed to allowing his imagination such unbounded freedom of scope that no libretto in the world could have contained within the necessary limits the outpourings of that imagination'.[1]

Rather unexpectedly Grillparzer comments on the freedom of speech in Beethoven's circle of friends—'who were not afraid of grossness, cynicism, or insults'. The conversation-books, no doubt prudishly edited by Schindler in this as in other respects, still occasionally give glimpses of a society whose moral tone was certainly nearer that of Beethoven's sister-in-law Johanna, with her two illegitimate children, than to the often puritanical standards adopted, at least in formal conversation and in writing, by Beethoven himself. During 1820, for instance, when the Lobkowitz tutor Peters was a frequent visitor, there are number of jokes about a certain Frau Janitschik, a common acquaintance of the circle.

She says I can't sleep with her, the bed's too small.
You're supposed to have slept with her too (to Beethoven).
Peters says that his overcoat was taken off his back at Frau Janitschik's, just as Joseph's was by Potiphar's wife.

Beethoven's sense of humour, a good indication of the real character of any man, was very much his own. He was fond of puns and verbal jokes of all kinds, especially those connected with his friends' names, and he repeated such jokes with merciless frequency. We have seen

[1] See Franz Grillparzer, *Sämtliche Werke*, Band 12, 'Erinnerungen an Beethoven' published (1844–5) to correct the impression given by Rellstab. To Weber Beethoven said that in his opinion the best librettos were those of Cherubini's 'Les Deux Journées' and Spontini's 'La Vestale'—the first a *comédie larmoyante* recalling Greuze's pictures, the second a neo-classical tragedy à la Canova.

him amusing himself with Holz's name, and the comic canons which he frequently composed during the last decade of his life are often based on such quips, e.g. 'Sankt Petrus war ein Fels' (Peters), 'Kühl nicht lau' (Kuhlau), 'Schwenke dich' (Schwenck), 'Hoffmann, sei kein Hofmann' (Hoffmann), and the many devoted to Tobias Haslinger, member of Steiner's publishing firm in the Paternostergasse, who was the recipient of countless good-humouredly punning letters, and the subject of a comic biography which appeared[1] in Schotts' magazine *Caecilia*. This is a painfully laboured, donnish production, full of learned musical allusions and poor puns.

Fux's *nota cambiata* which has now appeared, is discussed with Albrechtsberger, the appoggiaturas are meticulously analysed, the art of creating musical skeletons is dealt with exhaustively, and so forth. Tobias then envelops himself like a caterpillar, undergoes another evolution. . . . His scarcely grown wings now enable him to fly to the little Paternostergasse. . . . Having passed through the school of appoggiaturas (*Wechselnoten*) all that he retains is bills of exchange (*Wechsel*) . . . he finally becomes a member of several home-made learned (Beethoven writes *geleert*—literally 'emptied'—instead of the correct *gelehrt*) societies, etc. . . .

Beethoven's verbal humour was plainly of the kind that friends tolerate, and even come to enjoy, not because it is in fact amusing but because they associate it with the good humour and the happy moods of a man they love and admire.

Beethoven's reading included a considerable amount that was not purely literary or imaginative. The conversation-books are starred with notes of new books that he wishes to obtain, though probably the majority of these were forgotten. The subjects include cookery, botany, ornithology, carriage-building, history, travel, and medicine. He is said to have read Kant's *Allgemeine Naturgeschichte und Theorie des Himmels* and *Metaphysische Anfangsgründe der Naturwissenschaft* and Schelling's *System des transzendentalen Idealismus*. But it would probably be truer to say that he had read 'in' these books and assimilated just what he could digest in his art. It is surely not credible that a man who could not master—or at least did not master—the principle of simple multiplication, can have understood the marshalling of philosophical arguments, or attached anything more than a sense of vague emotional grandeur and elation to the abstract terms in which those arguments are conducted. We know that in the world-histories that Beethoven read, or dipped into, it was not the isolated events or

[1] Beethoven protested against the publication (see *Letters*, III, p. 1232) but did not deny the authorship.

the detailed logical sequence of cause and effect that concerned him, so much as the 'grand design'. In the same way we may safely suppose that Beethoven's famous quotation (or in fact misquotation) of Kant— 'the moral law in us and the starry sky above us'—sums up the inspiration that he received from philosophy. In any case, it appears in the conversation-books in connection with the Director of the Observatory, a certain Littrow, rather than in any philosophical context. Kant, like Schiller, formed part of Beethoven's Bonn background, and was a symbol of moral aspiration rather than an intellectual master. The fact that in the world of conceptual thinking and the manipulation of numbers, or 'figuring', Beethoven was naturally clumsy and poorly trained does not, of course, detract one iota from his greatness either as a composer or as a human being. On the contrary, the contrast only enhances his achievement.

If we had no positive reason to doubt Beethoven's strictly intellectual interest in philosophy (or indeed anything else), there would still remain the strong negative evidence of the notebooks in which he copied favourite passages or confided his most intimate thoughts and hopes. The character of these is anything but philosophical. It is in fact almost always moral or religious, personal in application and emotional in tone. Although Beethoven's religious beliefs are not always easy to discover, there can be no mistaking the character of his religious attitudes and emotions; and it is to this side of his character that we must now turn.

CHAPTER 13

Religious attitudes and beliefs

Beethoven remained to the very end of his life, as we have seen, a man of the eighteenth-century Enlightenment, both in his emotional and intellectual attitudes and in his literary tastes. The same is true of his religion; but the problem in this case is more complex, since the attitude of the Enlightenment to religious belief and practice was not uniform. Christianity, both Catholic and Protestant, was at a low ebb in the middle of the eighteenth century, and the Enlightenment in many cases arose as a protest against Christian indifference, the worldliness of established churches and the widespread neglect of the social, humanitarian side of Christ's teaching. For this reason the Enlightenment was generally most anti-clerical where the Church had most power and religion was identified with the State, while it took on an almost Christian colouring where religion was weak or had remained solely as a spiritual force. The enormous medieval legacy of power enjoyed by the Church in Catholic countries, and the clergy's resentment of any interference with the *status quo*, brought the Enlightenment into direct conflict with Catholicism almost everywhere; but the exact nature of the conflict, and the means taken to resolve it, differed widely between countries. It is therefore difficult to speak of a single 'enlightened' attitude even to the Church, still more towards religion in general.

Beethoven, brought up in Bonn and moving to Vienna in his early thirties, experienced two very different religious atmospheres. In the 1780s, while he was growing from a boy to a man, Bonn was a stronghold of the new ideas under its 'enlightened' Electoral Prince Max Franz, who was by virtue of his office a high church dignitary. As we have seen earlier, members of the Catholic clergy were active in the new university, and the Church at least in Bonn itself— in neighbouring Cologne the situation was different—never showed a declared hostility towards the movement. As Schiedermair well describes it—

The attitude of the church in the Electoral Principality, of the Elector himself and of the Bonn theologians never forced sympathizers with the new ideas into rebellion; nor on their side did such sympathizers feel obliged to break completely with the Church.

Elsewhere he speaks of

a Catholicism based on firm foundations in both the upper and lower ranks of society, and among the higher classes a movement towards a religious Enlightenment, an acceptance and development of many modern ideas . . . yet something irreconcilably opposed to a purely intellectual religion (*reine Vernunftreligion*).[1]

Beethoven must, of course, have encountered in his youth plenty of examples of 'unenlightened' religion, the remains of medieval superstition, ecclesiastical privilege, and mere formalism. But these were not the dominant impressions left by his years in Bonn; and if he arrived in Vienna a thorough-going and enthusiastic liberal, with little interest in institutional religion of any kind and an instinctive distrust of the clergy, the natural springs of religious feeling in him were unspoiled, and it was not long before the tragedy of his deafness forced him to turn inward and to explore, from a religious point of view, the significance of what seemed at first unmitigated disaster. Those who will reasonably trace Beethoven's intolerance of all authority, and his hostility to father-figures of all kinds (from the Emperor Franz to Father Fröhlich at Mödling), to his early experiences of a drunk and bullying father will see an instinctive correction of the psychological balance in the prominence in his most intimate religious effusions of the idea of God as an all-powerful, all-loving Father.

The history of the Enlightenment in Austria was markedly different from that in Bonn. The 'enlightened' Joseph II had a mere ten years (1780–90) in which to carry through what he felt to be the most pressing reforms, and he set to work with all the feverish haste and fanatical thoroughness of a man who has been frustrated for fifteen years—the period of his co-regency with his mother Maria Theresa—and only becomes his own master at the age of forty. The extraordinarily detailed ecclesiastical legislation of these years, which earned him the contemptuous name of 'my brother-in-law the sacristan' from Louis XVI, covered every field in which the Church was concerned, from purely liturgical matters to the abolition of the contemplative orders and the state control of seminaries, and changed the face of Austrian Catholicism in a decade. Joseph himself seems to have been a

---

[1] Schiedermair, *Der junge Beethoven*, pp. 326 sqq.

sincerely believing and practising Catholic, but the effect of his reforms (and more particularly the course of training which he instituted in the Austrian state seminaries) was to produce a dry Erastian form of religion, strongly influenced by nationalism and administered by a clergy which could reasonably be described as a branch of the civil service. This 'Josephine' Catholicism appealed to a number of the educated classes and was passively accepted, with varying degrees of distaste and infidelity, by the remainder.[1] On the uneducated, that is to say the vast majority, it had as little hold as the Church of England exercised in this country at the same period. In Austria as in England extreme economic distress, caused respectively by the Industrial Revolution and the Napoleonic Wars, gave rise to widespread political and emotional unrest. This was rendered most acute in the case of Austria by the French occupations of 1805 and 1809, and it provided the soil in which a spontaneous, popular religious movement sprang up within the Church itself. John Wesley's movement, originating within the Church of England but eventually forced outside it, was viewed with a mixture of contempt and distaste by educated people, who considered that its emotionalism was suited only to the lower orders and a few eccentrics. The corresponding movement in Austria, which sprang up after 1810 and is frequently referred to in Beethoven's conversation-books, met with very similar disapproval or contempt.

The guiding spirit in that movement was the ninth of twelve children born to a Moravian butcher named Dvořák, who translated his family-name to Hofbauer. This young man started life as a baker's assistant and had been a formally professed hermit in Italy (1771–2) and his native country (1776–9) before he began to study for the priesthood in Vienna (1780–3). The chief formative influence in his early years in Vienna was the ex-Jesuit Father Diesbach, one of the strongest opponents of the Josephine ecclesiastical reforms, and it was Joseph's insistence on training the Austrian clergy in state seminaries that sent Hofbauer to Rome, where he was ordained (1785) and joined the recently formed order of the Redemptorists. From 1787 to 1808 Hofbauer—who had taken the names Clemens Maria —administered a highly successful Redemptorist mission in Warsaw, but he was ejected in 1808 by the express orders of Napoleon, who suspected the Redemptorists' influence and resented their independence

---

[1] Again Franz Grillparzer's autobiography gives an admirable picture of a sensitive, intelligent man's contemptuous attitude to the religious Establishment of these years. It is significant that religion plays almost no part in the memoirs of the conventionally patriotic and conservative Caroline Pichler.

of local ecclesiastical authority and direct responsibility to the Pope only. Returning to Vienna, Hofbauer led a retired life at first as convent chaplain, though he was on excellent terms with Archbishop Hohenwart and with the Papal Nuncio, Severoli. During the French siege of Vienna in 1809, Hofbauer worked in military hospitals, and in the years following his influence as assistant priest at the Italian church in Vienna, the Minoritenkirche, gradually spread. His sermons, his work in the confessional and the selflessness of his personal life won him an enormous following among the poor and uneducated, untouched by Josephine Erastianism and spiritually neglected yet able to recognize at once the purely spiritual quality of Hofbauer's teaching and example. The same qualities also appealed to the circle of romantic neo-Catholics which gathered in Vienna after 1808 round Friedrich Schlegel and his wife Dorothea (a Mendelssohn by birth), both converts. At various times this circle included the political thinker Adam Müller; the poets Clemens Brentano, Eichendorff, and the brothers Matthäus and Heinrich von Collin (author of the 'Coriolanus' to which Beethoven wrote occasional music); the painter and educationist Klinkowström and the painter Philipp Veit, Dorothea Schlegel's son by her first marriage. During the Congress of 1814–15 Hofbauer worked in close collaboration with the Papal delegate Cardinal Consalvi and with Archbishop Hohenwart, to counter the plans of the so-called 'Febronianists', led by the German Prince-Primate Dalberg, for the nationalization of the Church in Germany. At the same time Hofbauer did much for Catholic education, especially at the university, where he became a kind of unofficial chaplain.[1] Under his influence, too, there appeared a number of specifically Catholic journals—*Friedensblätter* (1814–15), *Die Oelzweige* (1819–21) and Schlegel's *Concordia* (1820–3). Hofbauer's work was under uninterrupted police supervision, and in February 1819 he was only saved from banishment by the direct intervention of the Archbishop with the Emperor Franz.

Of much less spiritual importance, but considerably more in the public eye than Hofbauer, was Zacharias Werner, already mentioned as the author of a tragedy that Beethoven considered for an opera. Werner was a Prussian who had spent a number of years as a civil servant in Warsaw, where he was an active Freemason and violently opposed to Hofbauer's work at the Redemptorists' mission. He had

---

[1] It is also worth noting that when Karl, Beethoven's nephew, was in hospital after his attempted suicide, the priest who was in charge of his case was a Redemptorist. Hospital work would hardly have appealed to the 'high and dry' clergy of the Josephine Establishment.

written a number of successful plays and moved in intellectual circles in Berlin. Werner's mystical identification of sexual love, religion, and art disgusted Goethe (though it may have inspired some of the ideas in his novel *Die Wahlverwandtschaften*), but his strongly erotic temperament won him immediate success with women disciples on his first visit to Vienna (1807) and later in Madame de Staël's circle at Coppet. In 1810 at the age of forty-two his turbulent and contradictory temperament, which recalls Liszt's in many ways, brought him to the verge of a nervous breakdown during a visit to Rome, where he finally became a Catholic. Four years later he was ordained priest and went to Vienna, where he fell immediately under Hofbauer's spell. His sermons caused a furore during the Congress by their grossly histrionic style and imagery, and are frequently referred to in contemporary memoirs, in Beethoven's conversation-books and in the police records, where it was noted disapprovingly that 'even Jews and their wives attend Father Werner's sermons'. Dorothea Schlegel commented unfavourably on his 'lowered eyelids, deep bows, huge tobacco pouch, and common Berlin dialect', while another witness writes that 'Werner rages like a madman, uses the expressions of a cabby, and is delighted to have somewhere [i.e. the pulpit] where he is not contradicted'.

Both Werner and Hofbauer understood that the weakness of Josephine Catholicism lay in its aridity. Hofbauer observed that 'the Reformation was spread and maintained not by heretics and philosophers, but by men who really demanded a *religion for the heart*'. The type of simple, popular devotion spread by Hofbauer and the Redemptorists had much in common with Wesley's Methodism—a strong insistence on penance, a deeply emotional relationship to the person of Christ, a lively fear of Hell and hope of Heaven, and in general a language and style of piety well suited to the uneducated but calculated to repel the ordinary educated man.

In the conversation-books Zacharias Werner is mentioned more often than Hofbauer. In 1819 Beethoven makes a note of his *Spiritual Exercises for three days* and a visitor speaks approvingly of Werner's sermon against 'the Minister'—probably Metternich, since he mentioned 'the whore' (Metternich's affair with the Duchesse de Sagan was being freely commented on). In the next year the Lobkowitz tutor, Peters, writes that 'Pepi Lobkowitz' (his charge, Prince Joseph) 'saw Bernard at Werner's sermon today'. Bernard, who had an official position as editor of the *Wiener Zeitung*, was at Hofbauer's funeral in the spring, and this prompted the following remarks from Karl's headmaster, Blöchlinger, who felt strongly about the religious situation, 'Times are troubled. Religion, too, is concerned and the so-called Liguorians are beginning the old Gnosticism again, while the world approves, because no one knows what else to do.'[1]

He describes Hofbauer himself as 'the head of the new clerical party, so called Ligorianer. He was a wretched fanatic and dogmatizer', while Bernard equates 'pietists, fanatics, Ligorianer and mystics'. Blöchlinger then goes on to attack Adam Müller and Friedrich Schlegel. 'All these converts are converts for self-interest, not by conviction—especially Schlegel'. Even the normally charitable Caroline Pichler surmised that Dorothea Schlegel's 'ultramontanism' or 'Liguorianism' is to be explained as 'a reaction from her earlier escapades'. These had been chronicled in novelistic form, but many thought in execrable taste, by Schlegel (who was her second husband) in his *Lucinde*. Not even Blöchlinger, however, accuses Hofbauer of self-interest. Most of those who came into personal contact with him —as Blöchlinger certainly did not—seem to have agreed with Zacharias Werner, who said that he had known 'only three strong characters: Napoleon, Goethe, and Pater Hofbauer'. Hofbauer was beatified in 1888 and finally canonized, as St. Clement Maria Hofbauer, in 1909.

One of Karl's masters, Joseph Köferle, observed in the conversation-books that 'the Klinkowström Institute would be good for Karl, but the Ligorianer are in control there and the tone is therefore bigoted— more hypocrisy than real piety'. And he adds—'it would be sad if the old darkness were to return'. Beethoven's voice is never heard on these subjects directly, but it is interesting to see that he seems twice to have bought *Die Oelzweige*, perhaps from curiosity. On several occasions he makes an oblique jocular reference to 'the expiations we go in for here', and there may be a similar echo of disapproval in his flippant jokes based on the Passion, a devotion which loomed large in Redemptorist piety. Thus he calls Holz 'lignum Christi' (a reference to the Good Friday liturgy), observes that a servant who is unwilling to carry wood should remember that even our Redeemer had to drag his cross

---

[1] The Redemptorists were often called Ligorianer, or Liguorianer, after their founder Alfonso Maria Liguori. Gnosticism (which appears oddly misprinted in the latest (Forbes) edition of Thayer as 'agnosticism') is the generic term used to describe the medley of magical, mystical, and apocalyptic beliefs which in the second century threatened to engulf the Christian church, especially in Asia Minor. Blöchlinger is probably referring to such popular devotions as the Nine First Fridays, scapular of Our Lady of Mt. Carmel, miraculous medals, etc., which Hofbauer introduced to Vienna from Italy. The whole subject is admirably dealt with in Rudolf Till *Hofbauer und sein Kreis*, 1951.

to Golgotha, and writes to Haslinger 'as for my most gracious master, surely he can but follow the example of Christ, i.e. suffer'.

Beethoven certainly had no sympathy with the popular forms of Counter-Reformation or baroque piety, with its southern, histrionic colouring and rhetoric, often saccharine sentimentality of expression, and exclusively emotional appeal. That Hofbauer and the Redemptorists were blacklisted by the government might have told with him in their favour; but the fact that they were protected by Archbishop Hohenwart —who complained in 1817 of their Erastian opponents that 'their sermons would not have offended Socrates, Plato, or Hippocrates'[1]— and thanks to him by the Emperor Franz himself, could not have endeared them to him. We have seen Zacharias Werner boldly attacking the all-powerful Metternich's private morals in a sermon; and it is perhaps significant that the frequent references to Divine Providence in Metternich's memoirs—acting, it need hardly be said, without exception in Metternich's own interests—are classically Josephine in their vague, undenominational character. Josephine Catholicism, like 'High Church principles' in England at the same time, was in fact the hallmark of the conservative patriot, and often more a profession of faith in the existing social and political order than a religion.[2] If we extend the parallel and think of Hofbauer as Wesley, or one of the Evangelical leaders, we shall have a fair idea of the religious alignments in Vienna, and their social and political corollaries, in Beethoven's last years.

We certainly should not expect Beethoven to share the religious beliefs and attitudes of either Hofbauer or Metternich. But can we therefore accept the common conclusion that he had no positive relationship to the Catholicism in which he was brought up? Schindler opined that he was a 'deist',[3] a vague philosophical rather than religious attitude that is plainly contradicted by the note of intensely personal religious fervour in Beethoven's intimate jottings and prayers, and by the deep commitment of the Missa Solemnis. We are not helped in our inquiry by Beethoven's declared principle (reported by Schindler) that 'religion and thorough-bass are settled matters concerning which there should be no disputing'. This observation suggests that Beethoven, like most people whose concern with religion is practical and real rather

---

[1] See C. Wolfsgruber *Hohenwart* (1912), p. 275.
[2] It is interesting to note in this connection that the conservative courtier Baron von Pronay, in whose villa Beethoven spent part of the summer of 1823, observes that 'the Liguorians are a bad sign of the times in Austria'.
[3] Schindler op. cit, p. 505.

than simply theoretical, found it a difficult and unprofitable subject of discussion. We are given a much clearer indication of his religious beliefs and feelings by the contents of his library, his commonplace book and his diary. Very little evidence is to be found even here of his attitude, positive or negative, towards Catholicism; but there is one exception, and although it is not of primary importance in determining Beethoven's general attitude to religion, it must be mentioned before we pass on to these more general considerations.

Among the books that Beethoven left at his death were three by Johann Michael Sailer—*Kleine Bibel für Kranke und Sterbende* ('Small Bible for the Sick and Dying'), *Christians Vermächtnis an seine lieben Söhne* ('Christian's Legacy to his Dear Sons') and *Goldkörner der Weisheit und Tugend* ('Golden Seeds of Wisdom and Virtue'), all three directly Christian, devotional works. The author was the son of a Bavarian shoemaker who ended his life as Bishop of Regensburg, and occupied a unique position in the German Catholic revival. Educated by the Jesuits at Ingolstadt, he taught first at Dillingen and then from 1799–1821 in the university at Landshut. In 1821 he was sent to Regensburg as vicar-general to the ageing bishop, whom he succeeded in 1829, dying himself three years later. He was early in trouble with the ecclesiastical authorities owing to the close connections that he cultivated with non-Catholics, including Matthias Claudius and Lavater. These contacts, and the fact that he was chosen by the 'enlightened' Bavarian minister Montgelas as professor of moral and pastoral theology at Landshut, made him suspect to the Jesuits; and they account for the delation of his first book to Rome and the rejection of his name for the bishopric of Augsburg. Sailer's career, in fact, recalls in many ways that of Fénelon, a similarity that did not pass unnoticed in his lifetime. The accusations that carried weight against him in Rome make strange reading today. They came under three headings of (1) 'quietistic mysticism', prompted by his insistence on a 'truly interior religion of personal conviction', (2) 'leniency to Protestants', (3) 'ideas of reunion between Christians' in view of the spread of irreligion. In the conversation-books both Bernard and Kanne voice what we may take to be Sailer's sentiments when they say that, 'the church too (like the state) needs a constitution . . . councils must be summoned again, in which the whole body of bishops from all over Christendom consider questions of doctrine in the right relationship to the religious needs of each country, according to its cultural development'.

If Sailer was anything but a Josephine Catholic, he also remained poles apart from the other extreme of Hofbauer's devotionalism. Although he had little feeling for Roman centralisation or devotion to the papacy, he rejected what he called 'scholastic', i.e. rationalistic religion as wholeheartedly as he did 'mechanical' religion with its 'dangerous superstition'. In opposition to both of these he proclaimed a 'spiritual', i.e. a 'real' or 'active' religion, to be achieved 'not only by individual thought, but before all else by an individual experiencing of traditional and revealed truth'. This personal, subjective approach to religious truth, various forms of which have in the past been condemned by the Church under the name of Fideism, formed the second and more fruitful branch of the Catholic Enlightenment. It has been summed up well by Karl Eschweiler—

A man conscious of his human dignity can only accept as real and true that part of the traditional body of belief that he has made his own, either by the work of his own personal intelligence or by the sincerest, most interior feeling.[1]

When we come to the discussion of the Missa Solemnis we shall return to this definition.

Sailer was the first Catholic theologian to grasp the religious significance of the romantic movement, and his own theory of the organic development of the Church, which foreshadows John Henry Newman's, had much in common with the romantic theory of poetry. The importance that he attached to art, as an expression of the divine in human terms, can be seen in the following passage from his *Bund der Religion und der Kunst*,[2] ('The Union of Religion and Art'), the very title of which is revealing.

If we consider the one, true, eternal religion according to its inner life in a man, we find that it is nothing more than the life of a childlike temper in the one, true God; the life of faith in God as eternal truth; the life of love for God as eternal beauty; the life of trust in God as the one immutable ground of existence. Only this religion, where it exists, is interior by nature and character, spirit and life, invisible. And yet religion, as the interior life of man, has an irresistible impulse to reveal itself, to make itself visible, audible, sensible and to form for itself a body that can be seen, heard, felt, and enjoyed. It is one and the same artistic impulse that sees in the night sky Nature's own great cathedral and conceives and produces St. Peter's in Rome, St. Paul's in London, the Stephanskirche in Vienna and the Frauenkirche in Munich. . . .

[1] Quoted in A. Schmitz, *Das romantische Beethovensbild* (1927) p. 85.
[2] Quoted in Moriz Brühl, 'Johann Michael Sailer—systematische Anthologie und Lebensbild,' pp. 69–70. Taken from 'Neue Beiträge zur Bildung des Geistlichen', also mentioned by Beethoven himself in the conversation-books (Nohl, 100).

This impulse is never content with the expression of the inner life of religion in ever new forms of celestial music and sacred eloquence . . . does not rest until the deepest feelings have been brought to their full culmination, until human voices and the deep notes of the strings, the organ and innumerable other instruments have been combined in marvellous harmony with the music of the spheres and become one celestial music, and the great hallelujah of the heavenly choirs is echoed in the human chorus below.

The sentiments, and even the high-flown style, are just such as Beethoven admired (since he copied such passages into his common-place book) and imitated in his own more modest jottings. And we possess further, even more convincing proof of how highly he rated Sailer in the fact that he possessed three of his books. When in April 1819 he was in despair at the apparent impossibility of removing Karl from his mother's influence, it was to Sailer at Landshut that he wished to entrust him. (See p. 26.) The suggestion came from Councillor Matthias von Tuscher, one of the boy's co-guardians, who in answering the magistrates' objection to sending Karl out of the country, mentioned Sailer's 'reverence for the talents of the composer Beethoven' which would ensure Karl's receiving 'the strictest over-sight and care' at Landshut. We know that Beethoven's old friend Antonie Brentano, who was to receive the dedication of the Diabelli Variations begun about this time, wrote to Sailer on 22 February 1819 a letter in which she described Beethoven as 'even greater as a human being than as an artist'. The plan only failed because Karl's mother pleaded successfully against sending him out of the country.

In a very different class from Sailer, but not perhaps without bearing on Beethoven's religious attitudes, was the author of a book which the police in fact confiscated after his death—Ignaz Aurelius Fessler's *Ansichten von Religion und Kirchentum* (Views on Religion and Church Membership) (1805). Fessler was a Capuchin friar from Silesia, favoured by Joseph II for his 'enlightened' views and promoted by him to a professorship at the university of Lemberg (Lwow) in what was then Austrian Galicia. Three years later we find him, now a Protestant, as a member of Fichte's circle in Berlin, where he remained until 1810. In that year he went to Russia to teach philosophy at the St. Petersburg Theological Seminary. After playing an important part in the Pietistic interconfessional movement in Russia, he died thirty years later as general superintendent of the Lutheran community in St. Petersburg. This religious *Wandervogel*, whom his baptismal names seemed to have predestined to a life of religious contrasts, expresses large views such as may well have found an echo

in Beethoven. The religious man, says Fessler, does not cut himself
off from church membership—

because he wants eternal religion to become general, each man following his
own path and developing his religion individually; because he knows that this
is only possible in the half-light (*Helldunkel*) of Church membership, and that
in its meaningful forms Church observance is still of benefit to him and that
his irreligious brothers still feel the need of it—and finally because his participation may bring institutional religion itself into better ways and arouse it to
a stronger life. For all these reasons he will support his church loyally,
honestly, and gratefully, honouring and revering it and supporting it by
bearing his share of responsibility.[1]

Was something of this kind in Beethoven's mind when he imagined
himself ending his days as a church musician? or at the very end of his
life, when he planned still another setting of the Mass and of the
eucharistic hymn *Tantum ergo*—strange choices if he had really ceased
to attach any meaning to Catholic teaching and devotion,[2] particularly
when he was urged on all sides to make the large sum of money that
he so urgently needed by writing an opera. Was it in a state of mind
half-way between Sailer's and Fessler's that, at the very end, he himself
received the Church's last sacraments? It is impossible to know, but
this seems nearer the truth than any picture of Beethoven as a rationalist philosopher, a sentimental humanitarian or a modern humanist.

If Beethoven's beliefs are hard to discover, the prayers or *cris de
cœur*—there is no other word for them—which occur repeatedly
in his diary or notebooks make it clear that his religious feelings
were strong. Most noticeable is the feeling of dependence, of humility
before a power inconceivably greater than himself and yet somehow
intimately concerned with the smallest details of his life and personality. This is the root of any religion, just as the opposite sense of
pride and self-sufficiency is the contradiction of the religious spirit.
As a young man Beethoven was indeed both proud and self-sufficient,
and it was only the experience of his deafness that broke this pride,
slowly and painfully turning the heaven-storming, largely extrovert
composer of the early and middle period works into the self-commun-
ing and contemplative visionary of the last ten years. Beethoven first

[1] Fessler 'Ansichten von Religion und Kirchentum' (Berlin, 1805) III, Brief XXI, pp. 430 ff.
[2] An entry in one of the 1820 conversation-books shows that he was not hostile to the
practice of confession—
My feelings about confession may be judged from the fact that I myself took Karl to
confession to the Abbot of St. Michael's, who said that it was no good Karl going to
confession as long as he was still obliged to see his mother.

faced the certainty of his deafness as early as 1798. Its full implications
were dawning on him in 1800, when he wrote a confidential letter to
Wegeler, and made their full impact in the Heiligenstadt Testament of
1802. This intensely human document contains an unmistakable note
of self-pity, but is chiefly remarkable for its clear-sightedness, 'Forced
to become a philosopher in my 28th year—oh! it is not easy, and for
the artist far harder than for anyone else', and 'Patience they say is
what I must now choose for my guide, and I have done so.' But it was
resignation, a much sterner quality, that Beethoven was eventually
called upon to show, when all cures proved useless; and resignation
came harder to him than perhaps to any artist who has suffered a
comparable affliction. Ten years after the Heiligenstadt Testament
there are two entries in his diary which show something of the
struggle—

Resignation, resignation deep and sincere to your fate! only this can give
you the [self-]sacrifice—for your obligation. . . .
    Endurance and resignation—resignation! it is by this that we can be
gainers even in deepest misery and make ourselves worthy of God's forgiveness![1]

How Beethoven had developed since 1800, when he thought of
resignation as a kind of stoical, negative virtue and deplored its necessity in his letter to Wegeler!

I have often cursed my existence; Plutarch taught me resignation. I shall, if
possible, defy fate, though there will be hours in my life when I shall be the
most miserable of God's creatures. Resignation! what a wretched resort, yet
it is the only one left to me!

In the dozen years separating these quotations Beethoven moved from
a position of militant stoicism, which is a philosophy of pride and self-
sufficiency, to an acceptance which, whatever his everyday life may
have been, bears in his music the unmistakable character of joy, that
unearthly joy such as is only achieved through suffering. We shall
discover more about its nature, perhaps, when we come to the Missa
Solemnis and the last quartets. For the moment we must return to the
non-musical evidence of Beethoven's religious feelings and beliefs.
    All the contemporary accounts by friends and visitors emphasize
Beethoven's intense love of the countryside round Vienna, where he
spent sometimes as long as four months of the year. It was here that a
great deal of his composition was done, and his notebooks show how
closely he related the experiences of solitude, serenity, and union with

[1] Leitzmann op. cit., p. 10

nature to the awareness of a transcendental, personal God. No nature lover has ever been less of a pantheist—'Almighty One in the woods! I am blissfully happy in the woods; every tree speaks through Thee, O God! what splendour! in such woodlands as these! on the heights is peace to serve Him.'[1]

Unskilled with words, Beethoven here makes the trees 'speak through God' when he presumably means that God speaks to him through every tree. This is what he in fact says on another occasion: 'It is as though every tree in the countryside said "Holy, holy!" Ecstasy in the woods! who can express it all?'[2]

It is not surprising that one of the books from which he copied most into his commonplace book was Christopher Christian Sturm's *Betrachtungen über die Werke Gottes im Reiche der Natur und der Vorsehung*—('Considerations of God's works in the realm of nature and providence'). The author was a Protestant minister, who died in 1786, and the work has a very characteristic eighteenth-century flavour In 1818 Beethoven copied two significant passages from Sturm—

Nature is a glorious school for the heart! Well, I will be her pupil and bring an eager heart to her instruction. Here I shall learn wisdom, the only wisdom that is free from disillusionment; here I shall learn to know God and enjoy a foretaste of heaven in that knowledge. Among such occupations my earthly days will flow peacefully by, until I am taken up into that world where I shall be no longer a student, but a knower of wisdom.
    I will humbly submit to all life's chances and changes, and put my sole trust in Thy immutable goodness, O God!

Many other entries in the commonplace book show that an important element in Beethoven's religion was his awareness of this immutability and ineffability of God, his sense of the inconceivable difference between creator and creature which is suggested so strikingly in the contrast between the humblest supplication and the greatest imaginable majesty in the Missa Solemnis. He found verbal expression for this in a number of oriental texts which appeared in translation during his lifetime. After Goethe's imitation of Persian and Arabic amatory poetry in the *West-östlicher Divan*, the Schlegel brothers had turned their attention to Indian religious literature. Beethoven probably copied the following passage from one of their popularizing works—

---

[1] Scrawled on a sheet of music paper once in the possession of Joseph Joachim, probably dating from September 1812. Leitzmann op. cit., p. 25.
[2] July 1814.

I

O God, Thou art the true, the eternally blessed and immutable light of all time and space. A thousand laws, and more than a thousand, bear witness to Thy wisdom, and yet Thy acts are always free and redound to Thy glory. . . . To Thee be all praise and adoration! Thou alone art the truly Blessed One (*Bhagavan*), Thou art the essence of all laws, the image of all wisdom.

Beethoven's favourite quotation of this kind, and one which he kept always on his desk, was not (as was long believed to be the case) an original oriental one but a quotation from Schiller's *Die Sendung Moses* ('Moses' Mission') a philosophical *conte* in an Egyptian setting.[1] 'I am that which is. I am all that is, that was and that will be. No mortal man has raised my veil. He is solely from himself, and all things owe their being to Him alone.' It is open to any reader to call such a passage (as Renan called the Old Testament) 'vague oriental eructations'; but Beethoven, lacking all personal and literary sophistication, clearly found in these words an adumbration of the mystery that he felt to exist at the root of all existence, human or in a wider sense cosmic. It was a mystery which, by its nature, could never be fully comprehended but of which he was conscious of being in some sense a priest, as we can see from his letter to the Archduke Rudolf in 1823, 'There is no loftier mission than to come nearer than other men to the Divinity, and to disseminate the divine rays among mankind.' Of Beethoven's own attitude to that central mystery of creation we shall have more to say when speaking of the 'Sanctus' of the Missa Solemnis.

What then is our final conclusion about the nature of Beethoven's religion? The nature of his religious feelings is clear, the evidence of the commonplace book and diaries confirming the far more important evidence provided by his music. The humility and sense of personal relationship found in both writings and music suggest belief in an omnipotent, personal God; transcendent yet approachable (nature outpourings) and a father in whom all men are brothers (diary and Ninth Symphony) yet infinitely removed from humanity, mysterious and never wholly comprehensible or knowable (Oriental quotations, the 'Sanctus' of the Missa Solemnis, and the 'Heiliger Dankgesang' in op. 132). For institutional religion he seems to have had little use, or even for any specifically Christian doctrine, although he certainly acknowledged the obligations of the Christian moral code. To Haydn's pious simplicity he had seemed 'an atheist'; and whatever the truth, or circumstances, of the story that on one occasion 'he narrowly escaped

---

[1] A similar quotation can be found in Karl Leonhard Reinhold's 'Die Hebräischen Mysterien oder die älteste religiöse Freimauerey', lectures given at the Viennese lodge 'Zur wahren Eintracht' and published at Leipzig in 1788.

excommunication for having said that Jesus was only a poor human being and a Jew', there is no evidence at any time of his life to suggest that he believed in the divinity of Christ.[1] The original prompting of the Missa Solemnis may well have been largely musical and circumstantial: he was interested in the music of the past, especially Handel, and wanted to write a large choral work for which the Archduke Rudolf's appointment to the see of Olmütz provided an obvious occasion. Coming, however, to the text of the Mass in a very different frame of mind from that in which he wrote his first setting in 1807, matured now by suffering and forced by his deafness to turn his mind inwards, he found unexpected new meaning in the central Christian doctrines of the Incarnation and the Redemption, less in the specifically sacramental doctrine of the Eucharist. Such wresting of personal conviction from traditional Church doctrine was certainly in the spirit of Sailer's Catholicism; and although Beethoven was plainly not a practising Catholic during his lifetime, his acceptance of the last sacraments on his death-bed confirms the impression that he had not consciously separated himself from Church membership. To call him, as Schmitz does, a '*katholischer Aufklärer*, rationalistic in most points but fideistically inclined in the Masses'[2] is true in fact but misleading in its emphasis. It would perhaps be truer to say that he was a deeply religious man who was brought up formally as a Catholic Christian and never formally renounced his Church membership, but only came at the end of his life, through misfortune and illness, to understand the close connection between the religious sentiments and often unformulated convictions of a lifetime and the fundamental teachings of the Church, to which he had been for the most part indifferent or hostile.

[1] Friedrich Kerst, *Beethoven—the man and the artist, as revealed in his own words* (1964). p. 102.
[2] A. Schmitz, *Das romantische Beethovenbild*, pp. 100–1.

Part Two

CHAPTER 14

Introduction

We have found Beethoven's character and moral ideas, his culture and his religion all deeply founded in eighteenth-century origins and determined by eighteenth-century ideals and principles; and it will therefore be no surprise to discover that certainly until well past middle life he was at bottom a man of the eighteenth century in the field where alone he excelled—the field in which he stood head and shoulders above his contemporaries, absolutely confident and unique, that of music. In every other field of activity, not only the practical organization of his life, but even in the expression of his feelings in speech or writing, we have seen Beethoven afflicted by a helplessness or an indecision that prompted Schindler, in a rare moment of poetry, to compare him to 'a boy fallen to the earth from some ideal world' or 'a ball thrown from one hand to the other—all his life the prey of conflicting advice'. In everything concerning music, on the other hand, he knew his own mind instinctively, never asked advice and worked his way indefatigably to the end which he had had in view from the beginning. If we see him lumbering clumsily, like a sea-lion, on the dry land of everyday existence, as soon as he can plunge into music, which was his natural element, he moves with a power and a certainty of aim that revealed, from the very start of his career, the natural master.

Beethoven was not, however, one of those artists like Mozart and Mendelssohn (or in our own day Ravel and Britten) who seem to be born already possessing an instinctive knowledge of musical craftsmanship. Whereas their works are from the very beginning marked with a natural grace and elegance which never leaves them even if the 'inspiration' of their music falls below its normal level, Beethoven's music was always less remarkable for grace and elegance than for its power, for the directness, economy, and forcefulness of its utterance and the purity and truthfulness of its emotional character. Moreover there is about Beethoven's music a sense of achievement, of obstacles surmounted and difficulties squarely faced and doggedly eliminated, that gives it what has always been felt to be a moral quality. Beethoven was in fact often obliged, as his sketch-books show, to revise, re-shape, file, or extend his original ideas over a period of months or even years; and so the final product was indeed an achievement in quite a different sense from that in which we use the word of, say, Mendelssohn's octet or Mozart's wind quintet K.452. If there is indeed a strong air of moral bracingness about Beethoven's music, it comes in the first place from the very conditions in which that music was born, conditions which represent a victorious struggle over recalcitrant material. Without strength of character Beethoven's music would hardly have been written, or would have been written quite differently, so that there is something moral in its very essence. The additional fact that his character was not only strong but also profoundly and positively ethical, merely added, as it were, a further dimension to the moral character of his music.[1]

The fact that Beethoven did not enjoy the same instinctive ease as many far lesser composers have enjoyed in his handling of the material of music was an important factor in determining the nature of his development as an artist. Combined with the deafness which attacked him before he was thirty and was all but total less than twenty years later, it partly explains the unique nature of the music that he composed during the last ten years of his life. As a pupil during his early years in Vienna he had found Haydn too easy-going and sought out the most distinguished theorist and contrapuntist of the day, Johann Georg Albrechtsberger, showing that it was facility in the exercise of pure craftsmanship that he still lacked and wished to acquire. He was more thorough in his contrapuntal exercises than in his study of fugue, a form whose close restrictions he found irksome as a young man when freedom and expressiveness seemed contradicted by strict discipline. It was only towards the end of his life that he learned that it was precisely the combination of a strict formal discipline with the widest free-ranging fantasy that gives their character to the greatest musical creations, a discovery almost certainly due in the first place to his study of Handel. Even so, formal perfection was never with Beethoven an end in itself, only a means. In this he differed from the lesser composers of his own day and earlier generations, but in fact followed, only more consciously and articulately, the great men of the preceding generation. We cannot, it is true, imagine either Haydn or Mozart saying, as Beethoven said, 'yes, what is to touch the heart must come

---

[1] Arnold Schmitz (*Das romantische Beethovenbild*) even goes so far as to say that 'art for Beethoven was a matter of morality (*eine moralische Angelegenheit*) . . . of purely aesthetic values he had no very great understanding', pp. 75–6.

from above; otherwise it is merely notes, body without spirit', or marking a movement 'from the heart—may it penetrate to the heart'; but in both their cases this was the unspoken, perhaps unconscious prompting of their greatest works and it was only in their lesser, occasional music that they were content with the exercise of craftsmanship alone. It is because Beethoven, and after him the whole nineteenth century, was unwilling or unable to compose without this strong personal prompting that composers' outputs became so small compared with those of the eighteenth century. It was a return to the eighteenth-century conception of the composer as craftsman that brought back the huge proliferation of opus-numbers in the case of Saint-Saëns and Reger, and more recently Milhaud and Villa-Lobos.

As a young man in Bonn Beethoven had been initiated by Neefe into the 'language of the emotions' (*Affektenlehre*). We know that he valued C. P. E. Bach's treatise on *The True Art of Clavier-playing* and can be certain that he played the same composer's sonatas in which that 'language' finds expression.[1] That Beethoven felt himself, even at the end of his life, in some sense still an inhabitant of that more innocent, unsophisticated world is suggested by his answer to a question that Schindler put to him in 1823—why did he not append poetic programmes to his piano sonatas, for example op. 10, no. 3, and the two sonatas of op. 14, both dating from the 1790s? Beethoven, apparently, far from rebuking Schindler for a foolish irrelevance, merely replied that 'those days were more poetical and such hints were therefore unnecessary. Everyone at that time recognized in the Largo of op. 10, no. 3 the pictured soul-state of a melancholy being . . without requiring a key in the shape of a superscription; and everybody saw then in the two sonatas of op. 14 the picture of a contest between two principles or a dialogue between two persons, because it was obvious.' Many men in their fifties have felt that the world was more poetical when they were young; but although Beethoven himself (or, as he believed, the times) might have changed, he does not suggest that his own attitude to his music has undergone any revolutionary alteration. Without offending Beethoven's own principles, therefore, it would be legitimate to look for some such portraiture or emotional dialogue in the last piano sonatas, where the composer's language and terms of reference have changed rather than his aesthetic.

[1] On 26 July 1809, Beethoven wrote to Breitkopf and Härtel asking for scores of Haydn, Mozart, Johann Sebastian Bach, Emmanuel Bach, and so forth—'I have only a few samples of Emmanuel Bach's compositions for the clavier: and yet some of them should certainly be in the possession of every true artist, not only for the sake of real enjoyment but also for the purpose of study'.

It is clear from many of his remarks that Beethoven never considered himself a revolutionary in either the language or the aesthetics of music. We know that he classed the rules of thorough-bass with religion, as being both matters on which discussion was out of place; and he wrote to his pupil the Archduke Rudolf, 'the old masters are most useful to us. But freedom and progress are, in the world of art as in the whole of creation, our object; and if we moderns are not quite so advanced as our ancestors in solidity (*Festigkeit*) yet the refinement of our manners has enlarged our scope in many ways (*manches erweitert*).' (29 July 1819)

That the freedom and progress in which he believed did not involve jettisoning the past is made very clear by the fact that Beethoven turned with renewed interest during the last decade of his life not only to such academic devices as canon and fugue, but even to the polyphonic masters of the sixteenth century (especially Palestrina) and to what seemed in 1820 a musical archaeologist's interest, namely the modes. Beethoven in fact expressed in a nutshell his attitude to innovation in music when he observed that 'what is new and original appears of its own accord (*gebiert sich selbst*) without one thinking about it'. This is the attitude of the truly original creator, whose concern is primarily with creation, not with originality, which he can afford to take for granted.

Beethoven's own musical tastes were, as we know, conservative. He rated Handel most highly of all composers,[1] having heard his music first at Baron van Swieten's at least as early as 1794, when he may also have heard some of Bach's choral music (he was famous as a young man at Bonn for his performance of the '48'). Thanks to van Swieten, Handel's music continued to be performed in Vienna. Caroline Pichler in her *Memoirs* tells us that she and her daughter sang in performances of *Alexander's Feast*, *Samson*, *Acis* and *Messiah* during the years 1813–14 in Vienna; and Beethoven was much impressed by reading the score of *Saul* during the last years of his life. In 1824 we find Beethoven writing to Nägeli, the Swiss publisher, asking to be sent 'Sebastian Bach's five-part Mass'—an edition of the B minor Mass advertised in 1818 but not appearing in fact until 1833, after Beethoven's death.[2] Beethoven spoke of Palestrina with great admira-

[1] To Stumpff (1823): 'Handel is the greatest composer who ever lived' (M.S. communicated to Thayer pp. 919–20). Handel died in 1759. We may form an idea of Beethoven's conservative taste by comparing the situation with that of a composer who in 1960 rated Brahms most highly of all his predecessors.
[2] His quotation from the 'Crucifixus' in a letter of 1810 makes it clear that Beethoven only knew the B minor Mass by hearsay at that date.

tion, but added that 'it would be absurd to imitate him without possessing his spirit and his religious ideas'.[1] When Beethoven was working on the Missa Solemnis we know that he consulted the library of the Archduke Rudolf and that he got Peters, the Lobkowitz's tutor, to scour the Lobkowitz Palace library for treatises on old music. Among these he found Glareanus (presumably the *Dodekachordon* of 1547) and Zarlino's *Istitutioni armoniche* (1558), from which he may have learned that 'the Lydian mode is most suited to tragedies and songs that can move the soul and draw it out of itself', with obvious results in the Missa Solemnis and the A minor string quartet op. 132.

Among contemporary composers Beethoven rated Cherubini the highest, a judgement that witnesses to his eighteenth-century criteria and the primary value that he attached to impeccable academic craftsmanship. It was originally as a dramatic writer that Cherubini had impressed him, and he had certainly heard *Les Deux Journées* (known in Germany as 'Der Wasserträger' and in England as 'The Watercarrier') and *Faniska*, which were given in Vienna during Cherubini's visit in 1805–6. But the work of which Beethoven spoke with the greatest admiration at a later date was the first (C minor) Requiem, written in 1817. This he unaccountably preferred to Mozart's and proposed to take as a model for his own setting of the Mass for the Dead, which was among the many works planned during his last years. It is easy to recognize the reasonable man of the eighteenth century, and to understand his admiration for Cherubini, if Holz's memory served him well when he reported Beethoven as saying, 'A Requiem should be a melancholy remembering of the dead; the Last Judgement may be given a miss (*mit dem Weltgericht müsse man nichts zulieb machen*) . . . a tranquil music, no need for the last trump; remembering the dead does not demand a great racket (*Getöse*).'[2] We can, I think, be fairly sure that Beethoven would have substantially shared Cherubini's view of Berlioz's music.

Of Haydn Beethoven seems to have admired, as we should expect, particularly the *Creation*, and of Mozart *The Magic Flute*. But whatever he may have felt about their music as a younger man, in the last ten years of his life he barely mentions Haydn and he complains of *Don Giovanni* that 'our sacred art ought never to permit itself to be degraded to the position of being a foil for so scandalous a subject', without saying a word of the symphonies, concertos, chamber music,

---

[1] To Karl Gottfried Freudenberg (1824), recounted in his *Erinnerungen eines alten Organisten* (1870), pp. 39 ff.
[2] To Holz; cp. L. Nohl, *Beethoven, Liszt und Wagner*, p. 112.

or any other opera except the *Magic Flute*. There is no doubt that during these last years Handel eclipsed all other masters in Beethoven's eyes.

With the music of his younger contemporaries he had, on the whole, little sympathy. In the last months of his life, it is true, he was deeply impressed by the volume of Schubert songs shown to him by Schindler, and he came to admire Weber's *Freischütz*, though he distrusted the accentuation of colour as an element in music, because he felt that this was alien to his profoundly human ideal. It was no doubt the exploitation of harmonic colour for its own sake that he was alluding to when he observed that 'Spohr's music is so rich in dissonances; pleasure in his music is marred by his chromatic melody'. He summed up Spontini accurately when he observed that 'he understands theatrical effect and martial noises admirably' and described his *Olimpia* as 'much ado about nothing'[1]. Meyerbeer had still shorter shrift on every occasion when he came into contact with Beethoven— as the nervous bass-drummer in a performance of the *Battle of Vittoria*, on the occasion of his *Die beiden Kalifen* being performed in Vienna in 1814, and finally when his *Emma von Leicester* was given there in 1820. As we have seen, Beethoven and his circle of friends had little use for what they called the 'mystic', i.e. romantic approach to music; but they had less still for the purely sensational. 'I cannot deny', wrote Beethoven in 1808 to Heinrich von Collin about the magic ballet *Alcina*, 'that on the whole I am prejudiced against this sort of thing, because it has a soporific effect on both reason and feeling.'

Just as we possess in what remains of the conversation-books a unique key to Beethoven's everyday life, so in the sketch-books we possess a unique form of insight into Beethoven's processes as a composer. Our knowledge of these sketch-books is due almost entirely to one man, Gustav Nottebohm (1817–82), who made a close study of all the available manuscripts and published his findings in isolated journals during the 1860s before collecting them in a single volume, *Beethoveniana—Aufsätze und Mittheilungen*, in 1872. Fifteen years later, in 1887, when the author himself was dead, Mandyczewski collected all Nottebohm's remaining essays on Beethoven and published them as *Zweite Beethoveniana*. As in the case of the conversation-books, Beethoven's handwriting, his abbreviations and the signs meant only for his personal eye make the task of deciphering extremely difficult; but how rewarding the information obtained from these sketches can be to the student of Beethoven's music we shall see when we come to

[1] 1824 to Karl Gottfried Freudenberg.

examine each work of these last ten years in detail. It is also interesting to observe that the character of Beethoven's autographs changed at exactly the same time as we shall find his music beginning to take on the characteristic colour and consistency that we associate with this last, third period of his creative development—namely with the piano sonata op. 101 and the cello sonatas op. 102. According to Schünemann[1]

Beethoven's script becomes progressively more delicate. The cello sonatas op. 102 show more careful forming and joining of notes and, in general, lighter pressure on the paper. The stems of the notes are smoothly, almost lovingly drawn, and even the spurs and dots of quavers lose their firm, thick, broad up-down and cross-strokes.

In the piano sonata op. 111 this process of refinement has been carried much further. In the final theme and variations everything is widely spaced, and there are only one or two bars to a line.

One can recognize the light penmanship, the fine strokes of the demisemiquavers and the minute heads of the notes, which are sometimes no more than hinted at. The notes suggest the sonority itself, which seems to have passed beyond what is earthly or corporeal . . . as though the composer's thoughts and visions belonged to another world. The very look of the notes seems to have become the expression of a higher, eternal harmony.

The sketch-books amply confirm Beethoven's words to Karl von Bursy in 1816, when he told him—'no, I do not work uninterruptedly at any one thing. I always work on several at the same time, taking up now one, now the other'. The conjunctions shown in the sketch-books are often informative, throwing light on both the works concerned, as we shall see. As to his method of working, we have his own description. It may be remembered that in 1822 Beethoven received the visit of a certain Louis Schlösser, violinist in the court orchestra at Darmstadt. He must clearly have found the young man (Schlösser was only twenty-two) sympathetic, as he answered in some detail the question as to how he in fact composed. The following is taken from Schlösser's account,[2] written some fifty years later yet probably in the main accurate, so far as we can judge—

I can remember for years a theme that has once occurred to me. I alter a lot, reject and experiment until I am satisfied; and then begins in my head the

[1] Georg Schünenmann, *Musiker-Handschriften* (1936), pp. 74–5.
[2] 'Persönliche Erinnerungen an Beethoven', published in *Hallelujah*, VI (1885) nos. 20 and 21.

development (*Verarbeitung*) in breadth, concentration, height, and depth. Since I know what I want, the basic idea never deserts me; it rises and grows, I hear and see the picture in its complete extent, as in a mould, and there only remains the task of writing it down. . . . Ideas come I know not whence, uncalled for, indirectly or directly. I could seize them in my hands—out of doors, in the woods, on walks, in the middle of the night, in the early morning, suggested by moods such as the poet translates into words and I into sounds.

Braun von Braunthal[1] was taken by Schubert to an inn where Beethoven was sitting: 'From time to time he took a second and larger notebook from his pocket and wrote in it, with his eyes half shut, "What is he writing?" I asked . . . "He is composing", answered Schubert. "But he is writing words, not notes." "That is the way he works. He uses words to describe the course of his ideas . . . and at most intersperses them with a few notes."'

The actor Anschütz (who was to speak Grillparzer's funeral oration over Beethoven's grave) tells of finding him in the country 'lying in a meadow . . . his head supported by his left hand. His eyes were fixed on a sheet of music, on which he drew with his right hand heavy, mystical characters, drumming with his fingers in the intervals.' At Gneixendorf, too, during the last months of his life, we hear of Beethoven not only roaming the countryside in the throes of creation (and frightening the cattle) but sitting at his table, conducting with his arms and beating time with his feet, much to the amusement of the cook who was making his bed.

This description of the process of musical creation accompanying, and as it were permeating, every hour of the day and much of the night, of course provides the corrective to the picture that we otherwise possess of Beethoven's life. Here we have the lens, as it were, without which we see his whole existence out of perspective. The world of sounds was the real world to Beethoven, far more real than the world in which bills had to be paid, servants engaged and overseen, publishers bullied or cajoled, and small-minded and uncomprehending people somehow persuaded to live up to Beethoven's exalted idea of their functions. His rages and hates were the rages and hates of frustration, of resentment at the unreal world of everyday needs impinging on his creative activities, and at human beings who seemed to conspire to ignore or misunderstand the purity and nobility of his intentions. Because the ideal world of musical creation, in which those intentions were indeed wholly pure and noble, was so much more real to him

---

[1] He published in 1840 his 'Recollections', described by O. E. Deutsch in *Schubert—a Documentary biography* (1946), as 'rather dubious'.

than that of everyday, he was often unaware that his behaviour suggested the exact reverse of what he wished to express; that his bursts of affection could be as untimely and misleading as his rages, and his indignation with what seemed to him absolutely evil wholly misplaced, a naïve irrelevancy. There were no half-way measures in Beethoven's human relationships, and there are no half lights, no sophistication, no unspoken reservations in his music. It would hardly be an exaggeration to say that it was in musical terms that Beethoven saw life (as when he described Klopstock's poetry as always 'maestoso D flat major') rather than vice versa. Mozart's Queen of the Night was probably quite as real a figure to him as his sister-in-law Johanna, and it would no more have occurred to him to make allowances for one than for the other. How in fact Beethoven maintained against all the odds of illness and personal anxieties his inner, creative life at the intensity and for the long periods needed to create the great works of his last ten years will never cease to be a marvel.

CHAPTER 15

The Violoncello Sonatas.
Op. 102 nos. 1 and 2

When the Viennese palace of the Russian Ambassador, Razumovsky, burnt to the ground on the last night of 1814, there was plainly no prospect of Razumovsky continuing the opulent kind of life that had impressed the Viennese for the last decade. Among other changes the string quartet associated with the Russian embassy since 1808 was disbanded, and this freed the cellist Linke, who was soon engaged as 'chamber virtuoso' by the Countess Marie Erdödy, at whose summer residence in Jedlersee he spent the months of July and August 1815. As a member of the Razumovsky Quartet Linke was a personal friend of Beethoven's as well as being intimately acquainted with his music, which had formed a staple part of the quartet's repertory. Since Beethoven was also on very friendly terms with the Erdödy family, it is not surprising that during his own summer stay at Baden during 1815, he should have been a visitor at Jedlersee; or that finding Linke there, he should have set about writing him two cello sonatas. An undated letter to Countess Erdödy, certainly belonging to this period, runs—'Let the violoncello apply himself; starting on the left (*linke*) bank of the Danube he is to play until everyone has crossed from the right bank. In this way the population will soon be increased.'

What population? It is hard to say, but the whole letter is full of such puns, that may have appalled his friends yet always indicated a state of happiness, or at least contentment. Of the two sonatas, which were eventually published in 1817 by Simrock as op. 102, the first was written 'towards the end of July', the second 'at the beginning of August'. Both show a combination of characteristics which do not appear in any earlier works of Beethoven's with anything like the same consistency or concentration. In fact these two sonatas are the earliest examples of what we come to recognize as a new style, the style of the Third Period. Beethoven's earlier music contains plenty of isolated examples of each of the traits which together form this Third Period style—the overriding interest in counterpoint and especially in canon and fugue; the use of trills and other ornamental figures for not strictly ornamental purposes; the use of syncopation, and particularly anticipation, for expressive purposes; instrumental recitative carried to a new point of expressive intensity; the contrasting or combination of extremes of pitch; bold harmonic progressions by means of 'side-slipping' rather than conventional modulation; variation-form invested with a wholly new significance; and the emergence of what can per-haps best be described as a new transfigured 'play' element comparable in quality, though not in actual character, to that which we find in Mozart's last works, such as the finales of the string quintet in G minor K.516 and the piano concerto in B flat major K.595. The fact that every major work composed by Beethoven from these two cello sonatas of op. 102 to the end of his life is characterized in different degrees by different combinations of these features is the justification for Lenz's distinguishing a definite Third Period style.

The first of these two sonatas, which is in C major—A minor, opens with an Andante introduction of twenty-six bars, based entirely on the cello's unaccompanied opening phrase

and the piano's response, which already contains an imitation of the cello in the left hand

Throughout there is a strong emphasis on the interval of the third, either in the keyboard part alone or in the movement between the two instruments. The mood is withdrawn and meditative, yet warm with benignity and very close to that of the first movement of the piano

K

sonata in A major op. 101. Here, as there, the listener has the sensation of overhearing an interior monologue, or a dialogue between
two parts of the composer's personality complete with questions and
hesitations (bars 5 and 10). When in bar 16 the music modulates to the
dominant, the piano prepares the cello's return to Example 1. with a
dominant pedal trill, which is later taken over by the cello, and this
short introduction ends with a cadence ushered in by a phrase in which
each note is ornamented with a trill and leads to a harped and held
chord of the dominant seventh. The language in its broad outlines is
simplicity itself, as so often with Beethoven; the originality lies entirely
in the lay-out—the close-lying harmony between the two instruments,
their conjunct motion and the frequency of points of imitation that
may easily escape the casual listener but give this whole introduction
its unified consistence.

The Allegro vivace (A minor) which constitutes the body of the
first movement, and forms with its dotted rhythms a strong contrast
to the smooth motion of the introduction, is comparatively conventional in character. The development section is unusually short
(only twenty-two bars against the forty-eight bars of the exposition
and recapitulation) but contains an incident very characteristic of
Beethoven's last period. After the two instruments have exchanged
an antiphonal dialogue for some nine bars, passing through G minor
and D minor, they reach an abrupt A minor cadence. This is followed
immediately by four and a half bars in which the cello sustains B flat
while the piano executes a succession of pianissimo chords in the key of
E flat major, moving to B flat, and so back to the D minor and the A
minor in which the recapitulation begins

Ex. 3

Passages such as this, where a semitone sideslip seems to shift the whole
plane of Beethoven's thought to an entirely different world for a few
seconds, are increasingly common in his later works. (The chordal
progression clearly anticipates bars 53 ff. in the final movement of the

last string quartet op. 135). They seem like moments of distraction or
dissociation, such as are familiar to everyone, accepted and used by the
composer for the contrasting emphasis that they give the return to that
mental thread which they interrupt.

The second movement returns to the C major of the sonata's
introduction, and at first to the close harmony between the two
instruments. Six bars of this adagio are in effect florid instrumental
recitative, passing from C major through a series of diminished
harmonies, elaborated in the piano part, to the dominant G. The cello
then rises from its deepest register to a protracted cadence marked
'teneramente'; and this in its turn introduces a return to the opening
bars of the first movement's Introduction, varied and ornamented
with the trills and repeated notes, as well as the canonic imitations,
which are so prominent a feature of these late works.

This Introduction, here greatly curtailed and amounting to no
more than a seven-bar reminiscence, leads without a break into the
next movement. This final Allegro vivace opens with the two instruments echoing each other in a phrase which develops a striking similarity to a passage from Davy's 'The Bay of Biscay':

Ex. 4a   Op. 102, No. 1

Ex. 4b

all that_ day there she._ lay in_ the_ Bay._ of _ Bis-cay - o

This cell-phrase (A) does not play a large part in the exposition or
recapitulation, but dominates the short development section and
reappears at the beginning of the enormous coda (66 bars in a movement of 233). There are many precedents for this type of phrase-
dislocation, but perhaps the most striking is the final Scherzo of
Beethoven's piano sonata op. 14 no. 2 (written between 1795 and
1799), while several features in the rest of the exposition recall the
final Presto of another piano sonata dating from much the same time,
op. 10, no. 2:

Ex. 5a
Op. 10 No. 2
Presto

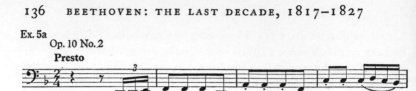

Ex. 5b
Op. 102 No. 1
allegro vivace

The exposition concludes conventionally in the dominant, and there is a bar's rest before the exposition opens with the cello's mysterious low E flat, which soon becomes a fifth and re-introduces the echo-game with which the movement opened (cp. Ex. 3).

Ex. 6

This is repeated twice, first in C major and then, by that leap to the flattened sixth of the scale which always has a strong significance for Beethoven, in A flat major. We now hear the 'Bay of Biscay' theme in canon, at the fifth between the pianist's two hands (Ex. 7), and then at the octave between cellist and piano left hand (with minor third), while the right hand adds a countersubject (with major third).

Ex. 7

A long chain of suspensions, first in the cello and then in the piano part, accompanied by the cell phrase (A) in contrary motion, comes to a momentary rest on the Neapolitan D flat major sixth, and then moves through a prolonged conventional cadence to C major and to the recapitulation. When this comes to a regular conclusion in C major, Beethoven opens his coda by making a show of repeating the development section, initiating the same round of fifths, only this time moving from A flat, to F, to D flat. The cellist holds his D flat fifth for fifteen bars while the pianist executes what amounts to a short cadenza, based largely on the material of the development section. This ends with the predictable Neapolitan shift from D flat to C major, which the remaining thirty-seven bars of the coda never even hint at abandoning. The two instruments imitate or accompany each other in triplets, scales, and trills, finally coming together in the last thirteen bars in unison statements of the theme cell (A) whose dislocations have prompted the greater part of the movement.

This whole sonata is a blend of old and new elements, or perhaps rather an alternation between passages whose general physiognomy is familiar from the composer's earlier works and others in which the elements may be familiar but their combination and accentuation is new. Thus the main body of the first movement and the exposition and recapitulation of the finale can be paralleled, as we have seen, in earlier works. On the other hand it would be difficult to find a precedent for the Andante introduction to the first movement or the Adagio and return of the Introduction that precede the finale. These look forward to the world of the late string quartets[1] and it is there—perhaps in the Lento assai of op. 135, based on the same theme of four descending and ascending notes—that we must look for a parallel. In the finale it is the proportions of the movement and the close contrapuntal writing in the development section that are new, while the moment of distraction or dissociation in the first movement (see Ex. 3) anticipates the harmonic leap or slip that introduces the development section in the last movement.

The second sonata of op. 102 is strongly contrasted with the first. The opening Allegro con brio D major first movement begins with a direct hit very much in the manner of earlier D major works, such as the piano sonata op. 10, no. 3 and the trio op. 70, no. 1 (another work dedicated to Countess Marie von Erdödy). The piano's leap of an octave,

Ex. 8

immediately (as it were) trumped by a tenth, is counter-balanced by the wide span of the cello's sensational entry from the low D (f) diminishing to the high tenor A and at once descending an octave to p dolce and a cadential phrase whose extraordinary nobility it is difficult to analyse

---

[1] The parallel with op. 135 has already been suggested for a passage in the first movement, see p. 134. It is perhaps worth noting that the poco sostenuto introduction in the trio op. 70, no. 2, also dedicated to Countess Marie von Erdödy, makes use of a similar opening figure to that in op. 102, no. 2, but soon develops a more playful mood.

Ex. 9

Although the first group of subjects ends conventionally in A major at the sixteenth bar, Beethoven slyly inserts another eight bars, in which he returns to the piano's opening theme (Ex. 8) which he gives for the first time to the cello, before embarking on the second subject. This consists of two themes, the first hardly more than a broken chord pattern but combined with a harped chord with which Beethoven makes great play later in the movement, and the second a four-square full-blown melody, which provides little material for development. There is only one very small eccentricity in this whole exposition, in bars 47–8, where Beethoven wrenches the movement away from the B minor to which it has already once modulated and is plainly modulating again, into the D major that ends the section. He does this by one of the harmonic side-slips that we shall meet increasingly in the works of this last period.

Ex. 10

In the development which follows, the opening phrase of the sonata
is first set twice against a chromatic kaleidoscope provided by the piano,
and then skilfully combined with the first of the second subject group,
whose harp-like ornament is countered by a series of mordents in the
piano part

Ex. 11

The recapitulation is introduced by a canonic statement in G major of
the opening phrase and a rush of scales in contrary motion. At the
end of the recapitulation the same phrase introduces the coda, which
opens with a strain of the second subject melody, but soon dissolves into
a sequence of sempre pianissimo chords passing from G major to F

sharp minor, D major, C major, F minor, E flat major and so, by the familiar Neapolitan progression, back to the D major scales in contrary motion which bring the movement to an end.

The second movement, marked 'Adagio con molto sentimento d'affetto' forms the greatest possible contrast. It starts with a simple, hymn-like eight-bar theme in the cello, accompanied by low-lying piano harmonies. This theme moves within a narrow span, hardly extending beyond the compass of a fifth, and is marked by Beethoven 'mezza voce'. The key is D minor, modulating to the minor of the dominant at the eighth bar. The following eight bars, which carry the music back from A to D minor, open with a phrase (which the composer marks 'espressivo') as extrovert, even operatic in character as the opening of the movement was inward-looking.

Ex. 12

The piano is answered by the cello, and the two instruments come together in unison in the fourth bar, which introduces the return of the hymn-like, chordal theme of the opening. These eight bars are then repeated, with the cellist and pianist reversing their roles. The remote resemblance to the D minor Andante in the piano sonata op. 28, where there is a rather similar contrast of the hymn-like and the operatic, diatonic and diminished harmonies, is continued in the D major middle section. Here again there is a continual exchange of material

between the two instruments. The main theme, which Beethoven
marks 'dolce', appears always with the same countersubject

Ex. 13

The twenty-six bars of this section are occupied to a great extent with
protracted and ornamented cadential passages, and the last of these
leads the movement back to the opening theme. This time the hymn-
melody is given to the piano and punctuated by dotted demisemiquavers
in the cello. Once again the roles are reversed in the complementary
A minor strain, where the cello has the melody, while the piano
combines the dotted demisemiquavers with an ostinato rhythmic
figure in the left hand. The long coda begins with a twelve-bar
pianissimo episode in B flat major, and seems to introduce new
material, until we realize that Beethoven is in fact re-viewing cadential phrases from the D major middle section in the light, as it were, of
the hymn-like main theme of the movement. At the twelfth bar he
reaches the dominant of D, characteristically descends a semitone to
the tonality of C sharp minor and slowly rises to a pause on the
dominant seventh of D.

The Allegro fugato, which follows without a break, is the earliest
of the many strictly contrapuntal movements to be found in the works
of Beethoven's last period. These form the indispensable counterbalance to the lyrical, song-like movements with which they are often

paired—as in opp. 101 and 106. In each of these cases an inward-turning, lyrical movement, psychologically searching but still (as the composer's express markings show) *con molto sentimento d'affetto*, is followed by an intensely dramatic display of that kind of musical skill which comes nearest to forensic intelligence and even forensic eloquence. Although even here there are episodes that the composer marks 'dolce', the main body of these strictly contrapuntal movements is rugged, blunt, and marked by a bewildering number of heavy sforzando markings, the majority of them on the conventionally weak beats of the bar. These produce a violently dislocated rhythmic effect as well as something approaching that produced, in a verbal argument, by paradox. There are no fugal devices that Beethoven uses with greater relish and effect than inversion and the treatment of the subject by reversal of accents, both of which suggest an obvious parallel with verbal contradiction; but this revelation of a basic unity in apparently contradictory statements is a specifically musical activity that has no exact parallel in the other arts. It is here that music shows, para-doxically, its superiority in precision to words. The precision is not in the conceptual field and therefore resembles that of poetry rather than of prose; but poetry itself can offer no parallel to the neat and immedi-ately perceptible identity between, for instance, the two following statements—in fact the fugal subject of this movement and its inver-sion

Ex. 14 (a) **Allegro fugato**

Beethoven invested the whole repertory of contrapuntal ingenuities with an overtly dramatic character that was entirely new. That he was quite deliberate in doing this is shown by his often quoted remark that anyone could write a fugue and that he himself had written many as a young man but that 'now something different is needed'.

The new episode that Beethoven introduces after the long fermata at bar 138 is based on a familiar contrapuntal subject, a version of which appears as the subject of the G minor fugue in Book I of the '48'

Ex. 15

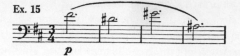

Here it serves Beethoven for only a short time (some thirty bars) and then disappears in a welter of trills and stretto passages, involving much use of scales in contrary motion or in sixths. These last two pages illustrate Beethoven's confident ignoring of merely sensuous beauty, or perhaps rather his confidence in being able to allow such claims an entirely secondary place when the drama, as well as the argument, of a movement demand it. That this is ungrateful music to the performer is of no importance to the composer, though how any musician could write, like the cellist Robert Haven Schauffler, of its 'lack of poetic relief' is a mystery.[1]

[1] R. H. Schauffler, *Beethoven*, 1946, p. 356. [This is] 'the first of the nine fugues which form such a gloriously characteristic feature of the third period. Thirty years study of this rough-hewn movement, as violoncellist and critic, has never altered the writer's conviction that its brutality, inflexibility and lack of poetic relief make the first fugue of the nine the worst of them'.

CHAPTER 16

The Pianoforte Music.
Opp. 101, 106, 109, 110, 111, 119, 120 and 126

It was as a pianist that Beethoven had originally made his name in Vienna, and although his deafness and his many other musical interests prevented him playing in public during the last years of his life, between 1816 and 1822 he still turned to the instrument as a means of expressing some of his most intimate thoughts and some of his boldest conceptions. It was not until the spring of 1823, when he finished the Diabelli Variations, that he finally abandoned the piano, and it was probably a year or so later that he said to Karl Holz that the pianoforte 'is and always will be an unsatisfactory instrument'.[1] He had already (July 1823) expressed in a letter to Ferdinand Ries his dissatisfaction with pure virtuosity—'the *allegro di bravura* . . . that only encourages mechanical playing to an undue extent'. There was no hint of sour grapes in this judgement, since according to Czerny Beethoven 'excelled all his contemporaries in the fire and brilliance of his playing, his manipulation of hair-raising leaps and thunderous scale passages'.[2] Goethe, it is true, preferred Hummel's playing to Beethoven's; but Goethe was no musician and was in any case quite out of sympathy with Beethoven's orchestral approach to the instrument.

Napoleon treated the world as Hummel treats his piano . . . for he was in harmony with every moment and every circumstance, just as to Hummel it is a matter of indifference whether he plays an Adagio or an Allegro.

Beethoven's friends, on the other hand, considered Hummel a mere virtuoso (*Passagenmacher*) who could not make the piano 'sing' as Beethoven did. In fact Hummel was the representative of an older school of piano-playing which went back to Mozart, whose pupil he

[1] See L. Nohl, *Beethoven, Liszt und Wagner*, p. 112.
[2] See N., I, pp. 356 ff. 'Clavierspiel', based on Czerny.

was; and this was the reason for Goethe's preferring him to Beethoven, who represented the new, forceful, orchestral style which Goethe no doubt found insufferably aggressive and lacking in emotional balance.[1] Not that Beethoven's piano-music appealed exclusively to the *Klavier-tiger* type of performer even then, for it contains moments of tenderness and tranquillity quite as unforgettable as the great displays of dynamic forcefulness and intellectual power. Goethe and the members of the older generation of connoisseurs, on the other hand, may have found the speaking intimacy and emotional intensity of Beethoven's lyrical music as distasteful, even embarrassing, as his dynamism. They were certainly equally novel. It is in his last piano works that Beethoven most clearly anticipates the aesthetic of the nineteenth century; for even when he continues to use traditional forms, he uses them in so personal a manner and in such unusual combinations that the effect is entirely new.

The last five piano sonatas fall into two rough groups, as Schindler was already suggesting when he observed that the 'tempo must be observed strictly in the so-called bravura style sonatas', opp. 106 and 111. This suggests that in opp. 101, 109, and 110 Beethoven himself was freer in his style of playing. Not only the character of these works but Beethoven's own marks of expression confirm this.

Opus 101. Sonata in A major

The first of the group, the sonata in A major op. 101, is also the first work that belongs quite unequivocally to Beethoven's 'third period'.[2] It combines, that is to say, great freedom of design and intimacy of feeling, which may find expression in forms that are irregular or fragmentary, with strict canonic and fugal episodes in the dramatic style with which Beethoven always now invested his contrapuntal music. Other features that we shall observe as common in this third period style—syncopations, anticipations, individual use of the trill and extremes of pitch contrasted or combined—are also to be found most markedly in this sonata.

The work was finished, as we know from the composer's autograph, in November 1816, and seems to have been composed chiefly during the summer months of that year, which he spent at Baden. It was a particularly bad time for Beethoven, who was deeply disturbed

[1] Caroline Pichler's remark about Weber's piano-playing being 'like that of Mozart and Beethoven—whom I often heard—rather than Liszt or Thalberg', probably refers to Beethoven's 'notably calm manner, dignified behaviour and upright, motionless seat at the instrument' (Czerny).

[2] On the prophetic character of the two cello sonatas op. 102 see p. 133.

emotionally by the new responsibility for his nephew and by his fears and guilty feelings about the boy's mother. The sonata in A major seems like an oasis in this wilderness, the escape into an ideal world from cares that only find, perhaps, an occasional echo in the finale's fugato. There could be no stronger contrast than that between this sonata and op. 106, begun the next year.

We first hear of the A major sonata in a letter of 19 July in which the composer offers Härtel of Leipzig 'a new sonata for pianoforte solo', an offer which he repeated on 1 October to Robert Birchall in London. In November, however, when the sonata was finished he wrote to the Vienna publisher Steiner, 'as for a new sonata for piano- forte solo, well! as soon as sixty fully armed men [i.e. gold ducats][1] present themselves, it can be produced immediately'. There followed the concern with the title. Beethoven had learned (possibly from the young Schindler, who was a member in 1816) of a society that wished to purify the German language and social manners of French influence and to return to German ways (*deutsches Wesen*); and with character- istic enthusiasm he decided to substitute the German *Hammerklavier* (or *Hämmerklavier*, as he first said) for the Italian word 'pianoforte' on all his future works, starting with the new sonata.[2]

In the last movement of the sonata, at bars 223–7, Beethoven made use for the first time of the instrument's low E. He draws attention to this in a letter to Tobias Haslinger, characteristic in its humour.

Most Excellent A(djutan)t
Second S(coundrel) of the Empire
The guilty and the innocent are commanded to see to the proof-reading with all speed and to return the proofs to me.
In the last movement, in the passage where low E appears in the four chords, I should like the letters to be added, thus

$$
\begin{array}{ccccc}
E & E & E & E & E \\
A & F\sharp & G\sharp & A & B \\
E & E & E & E & E \\
\end{array}
$$

[1] Approximately £27 (1961).
[2] When he writes to Tobias Haslinger (January 1817) 'Hämmerklavier is certainly German and in any case it was also a German invention', he was of course mistaken and wronging Cristofori. But we may think ourselves fortunate that Beethoven did not adopt any other of the proposed neologisms, which included *Tonwerkerei* (music), *Zussammenklangwerk* (sym- phony), *Tonstreitwerkversammlung* or *Tonkampf* (concert). The attempt was not a new one and has been made since. Theodor Hierneis (*The Monarch Dines*, p. 93) was in despair at having to learn *echt deutsch* culinary terms when he went to Potsdam in 1890 from the royal kitchens in Munich, and Hitler did his best to 'purify' the language of alien elements. In our own time Percy Grainger made a similar attempt to oust Italianisms with his 'louden lots' (crescendo molto) and so forth.

Furthermore, the words which have been added in certain places must be noted and inserted—The innocent and the guilty, the rude and the courteous second S(coundre)l of the Empire etc. etc. etc. cannot be promoted.

'The words which have been added' are presumably marks of expression, which are particularly frequent in the first and last movements. The markings of each movement were not given in German only (as in op. 90) but in German and Italian (as in op. 81 a). Hans von Bülow[1] found that the two languages throw light on each other; but although his is an opinion not indeed lightly to be rejected, it is difficult to see what light the conventional Italian 'allegretto ma non troppo' of the first movement throws on the much more explicit 'etwas lebhaft und mit der innigsten Empfindung' ('rather lively and with the profoundest sensibility') or how the 'allegro' of the finale in any way illuminates 'Geschwind, doch nicht zu sehr, und mit Entschlossenheit' ('Fast, but not too fast, and with decision'). In the other two movements the German is an accurate translation of the Italian and adds little or nothing to it—'Vivace alla marcia' ('Lebhaft, Marschmässig') and 'Adagio ma non troppo, con affetto' ('Langsam und sehnsuchtsvoll')— though the German 'Sehnsucht' (yearning) is a more specific emotion than the generic 'affetto'.

The sonata opens with such suddenness and so little preliminary manœuvring that we feel, as on other occasions in Beethoven's later works, that we are interrupting music already in progress. It is as though a door were suddenly opened and we overheard a conversation that was not meant for our ears, a conversation in this case of unearthly tenderness and warmth. The comparison is borne home more strongly when we discover how much of the movement is shaped like a dialogue, with one phrase answering another (bars 16–25) or a single voice repeating something with a slightly different inflexion (bars 1–2 and 5–6). The web of this dialogue is so finely woven that although the movement is in a very compressed 'sonata' pattern, it is virtually impossible to label precisely a second subject. There seems equally good reason to begin this at bar 9 or 12 or 16; and this ambiguity is only a further proof of the movement's closely unified character. Rhythmically the gentle 6/8 flow is only interrupted by the syncopations that introduce and form the pedal accompaniment to the development section, and even these are hardly more than the slight holding of a breath in anticipation.

---

[1] *Beethoven's Werke für Pianoforte Solo in kritischer und instructiver Ausgabe.* Quotations are from the revised and improved fourth edition, 1878.

Ex. 1

It is only after almost fifty bars that Beethoven suddenly indulges in a series of heavy sforzandos off the beat, quite out of character with the rest of the movement, and two bars of energetic right-hand chords against staccato octaves in the left, such as were to become great favourites with Brahms (bars 50–1).

The return to tempo primo is marked 'molto espressivo' and the antiphonal dialogue carries us without any preparation into the recapitulation, which is itself so masked (as Lenz calls it) that the short movement (102 bars) is over almost before the listener is conscious of its shape.

This combination of great expressiveness with absolute simplicity, which becomes increasingly important in Beethoven's latest works, presents the performer with a problem whose solution is nothing less than the index of his artistic personality. Such movements mercilessly reveal any element of insincerity or pose, any dryness or shallowness in an artist. In fact this whole movement is full of such pitfalls for the performer who is in any way, either from the inexperience of youth or the hardheartedness of age, other than mature. One figure in particular, which seems to belong more naturally to the strings than to the keyboard, presents great difficulty; it carries much of the movement's emotional weight and is repeated in many different forms but always with the same phrasing

Ex. 2

To find the exact tone and touch for that, tender without sentimentality and caressing without sensuality, questioning yet not expecting an answer and breathing acceptance rather than resignation, is not the task for any ordinary artist. It should be said, perhaps, in their favour, that ordinary artists generally avoid this sonata, no doubt by instinct.

The second movement forms the strongest possible contrast in tempo, rhythm and general character: a lively march in F major, marked by dotted rhythms throughout, after the floating 6/8 A major of the first movement. The change from A major to F major—the tonality of the flattened sixth of the scale—was a favourite with Beethoven and always marks a dramatic change of mood. The second half of the march brings a certain amount of imitative counterpoint, in three parts and widely spaced on the keyboard, awkward for the player and not even ideally to be performed without giving that impression of a difficulty mastered, a feat of mind and hand, which gives Beethoven's contrapuntal writing its essentially dramatic character. It is characteristic of him that he immediately follows a tough, bare stretto by a playful passage in which the hands are crossed and the extreme ranges of the instrument humorously contrasted.

Ex. 3

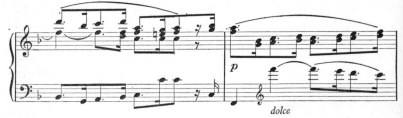

The whole march is full of such contrasts, especially of pitch and volume, whereas the first movement contains not a single fortissimo marking and few above *mf.*

The trio which follows is in B flat major and flows as smoothly as the march moved jerkily. In the sketches for this movement, which is strictly canonic, Beethoven at first notated no dotted notes at all, nothing but evenly moving quavers and crotchets after the first two bars, though it may be guessed that this represents merely the working of the canon, and that a more varied rhythmic scheme was always in his mind.[1] The character of the trio is difficult to define. By nature it is a *jeu d'esprit,* a moment of repose alike from the tenderness of the first movement and the bluff good humour of the march; but it is more than that, for Beethoven imprints his personality on everything that he writes.[2] Here, for example, we notice his refusal to plane away the angularities involved in strictly canonic writing, his deliberate relishing of false relations in the stretto, his improbable marking 'dolce' against two successive entries and his insistence on a dramatic crescendo, first in the stretto and then in the return to what turns out to be a transition to the repeat of the March. The sketch-books show that Beethoven originally meant the first half of the March to end in A major, and not to be repeated; and the final sketch for the second part is also followed by a cryptic reference to the key of A major.

As it is, the March ends in F major, and the Adagio which follows starts unambiguously on the dominant seventh of A. Only twenty bars long, this forms an introduction to the final Allegro into which it passes without a break.[3] This was a scheme that Beethoven had

[1] See Nottebohm, *Zweite Beethoveniana,* p. 342. It should, however, be said that changes in *rhythm* between the first ideas in the sketch-books and the final versions are the commonest of all.

[2] The D major fugue for string quintet op. 137, written the following year (1817) but published posthumously is perhaps the nearest thing to an academic exercise among his works.

[3] The notebooks suggest an entirely different gait (Nottebohm I, p. 343).

3tes Stuck poco Allegretto

already used on several occasions—in op. 27, no. 1, in op. 53 (where the Molto adagio is actually marked 'Introduzione') and in op. 81a. None of these movements, however, starts with the immediate eloquence of this Adagio's first eight-bar phrase, where the listener is reminded of a note that Beethoven made in one of Archduke Rudolf's books: 'Good singing was my guide; I tried to write as flowingly as possible and trusted in my ability to justify myself before the judgement-seat of sound reason and pure taste'. After a cadence in C major, a single idea is developed in imitation between the two hands

Ex. 4
Op. 101

and the final cadence is reached by a succession of diminished sevenths which von Bülow compares to those at the end of J. S. Bach's Chromatic Fantasy. Certainly Beethoven is here improvising (*fantasieren*), as a short cadenza based on the E major arpeggio leads the music back to the opening four bars of the first movement—marked 'dolce' and 'tutto il cembalo ma piano', i.e. without using the soft pedal. But instead of continuing he pauses after the last of the four bars, repeats the final phrase and then carries it up by ever faster sequences to a top E. From there a presto scale and a series of rising trills introduces us to the finale.

Ex. 5   Op. 101

This apparently tentative, rhapsodic approach to the finale, which is almost the rule in Beethoven's last works,[1] often conceals close thematic relationships behind what seems to be improvisation. In the present instance we can follow the working of Beethoven's imagination, as he halts on the phrase with the falling major third and repeats it ponderingly, as though examining its potentialities. Then, having found the needed transformation, he rises like a hawk hovering over its prey before pouncing down on the finale. This is founded on a novel assertion of the descending major third from the first movement, contradicted angrily in the development section where it becomes a minor third, whose questioning character is answered in the fugato.

The recalling of the opening movement makes the character of the finale seem, by contrast, almost brutally, or at least bluntly, decided and Beethoven, it will be remembered, marks it 'with decision'. The imitations between the two hands which appear at once in the first eight bars give the contrapuntal nature of the music. Inversion, in which the two hands exchange parts, and canonic imitation appear almost unceasingly throughout the first group of themes, even if it is only in what appears to be accompaniment to another of Beethoven's marvellously simple espressivo melodies.[2]

Ex. 6   Op. 101

---

[1] We find it in the piano sonatas opp. 106 and 110, the Diabelli Variations and the string quartets opp. 131 and 132: and of course the most remarkable instance of all is the Ninth Symphony.

[2] Hans von Bülow, op. cit., suggests that this theme should be played 'with that warmth which can be learned from violinists of the Belgian or French, but unfortunately not of the German school'. This no doubt refers to such players as Charles Bériot, César Thomson, Eugène Ysaye, Henri Vieuxtemps and M. P. Marsick, the teacher of Kreisler, Thibaud, Enesco, and Carl Flesch.

The character of the exposition, including the second group of subjects which opens with a phrase of great simplicity, is energetic and extrovert, demanding a youthful and brilliant style of playing. The fugal development section in the minor is something of a puzzle. Tovey's likening of Beethoven's fugal finales to the trial-scenes in a novel or play is not relevant in this case, if only because the conflicts and tensions here resolved belong solely to this movement and not to the sonata as a whole, whose unity is not so much psychological, i.e. that of a drama, as vegetable, i.e. similar to the bond that unites the acorn and the oak. We do not find here, as in the final fugues of op. 106 or the Diabelli Variations, what Tovey calls the drawing-in of all the threads of the story. It is much more as though the secret dialogue of the first movement, which was brushed aside by the March but returned in a different guise for a moment in the trio and seemed to have reached some tranquil conclusion in the Adagio, had in the finale turned into a debate conducted with great brilliance and excitement, and with all the characteristics of a speaker (or rather four speakers) who wish not only to be heard but to convince. The style of the music, with its frequent staccato passages and strong upbeat rhythms, the organic thirds and sixths which thicken the texture, and the dramatic insistence on extremes of pitch and even of conventional dissonance is not so much the contradiction as the complement of the suave, floating euphony of the first movement.

Ex. 7

Op. 101

When the fugue ends and the recapitulation starts it seems as though the display of violence might become monotonous. Beethoven evidently felt this instinctively and so provided a variant to the inverted counterpoint of the exposition. This variant is equally contrapuntal in character but marked 'dolce poco espressivo' (to be understood presumably as 'un poco espressivo' rather than in the negative sense of 'poco'), and a touch of brilliance is added by the expansion and ornamental furbishing up of the semiquaver passage that leads to example 6. There is a charming touch of humour in the pianissimo repetition of the last bars immediately before the coda, where Beethoven foreshadows, for just the half-dozen bars (305–11) that it takes to establish, that mood of blissful innocence that Mahler was to exploit in whole movements[1]

Ex. 8

The coda threatens the listener with what seems to be going to be a repetition of the whole fugal development; and it is as though Beethoven had seen the look of despair on his audience's face and taken pity on them, when he bursts into the ornamented inversions, the scales in thirds and the crossed hands, the pianissimo drum roll in the

[1] Cp. 'Verlorene Müh', 'Wer hat dies Liedlein erdacht' and 'Rheinlegendchen' from the Knabenwunderhorn songs, and the Ländler of the first symphony.

deep bass the ritardando that seems to be fading in the distance, until a salvo of A major chords brings the movement to an end.

Good humour, deep and tender reflection, the acceptance and transfiguration of suffering, and the high spirits of creative achievement —the sheer joy of exercising a faculty that is art and craft, an intellectual activity, an emotional release and a unique means of communication with oneself and one's fellow men—this is all to be found in this sonata, which is the most physically euphoric of all the last five. Here certainly there is not a trace of anything that could be possibly called literary or metaphysical or speculative, or indeed anything but unadulteratedly musical. In this connection it is perhaps significant that the sonata was dedicated to an amateur pianist whose playing of his works Beethoven particularly admired. The Baroness Dorothea Ertmann was the daughter of a businessman of Offenbach-am-Main, named Graumann, and married in 1798 an Austrian officer, with whom she moved to Vienna. She was a favourite pupil of Beethoven's and in 1817 was rated 'die erste Klaviervirtuosin in Wien'.[1] Beethoven's relations to her are well suggested in the letter which accompanied an engraved copy of op. 101.

My dear and beloved Dorothea Cecilia!
    You must often have misjudged me, for I must have seemed unpleasant to you. A good deal should be put down to my circumstances, particularly in former times when my Muse was less appreciated than now. You know the explanation given by the unbidden apostles who made shift with means very different from the Holy Gospel.[2] Well, I did not want to be reckoned among their number. Please accept now what was often intended for you and what may be to you a proof of my devotion both to your artistic aspirations and to your person. . . .

Reichardt, who heard Baroness Ertmann play Beethoven's music in 1808–9, said

I have never seen such power and inmost tenderness combined, even in the greatest virtuosi; from the tip of each finger her soul poured forth and from her hands, both equally skilful and sure, what power and authority were brought to bear over the whole instrument! Everything that is great and beautiful in art was turned into song with ease and expression.[3]

Years later (1831) Mendelssohn visited her and her husband, by then a general, in Milan and was charmed by both of them.

[1] Schindler op. cit., p. 321.
[2] Emily Anderson (*Beethoven's Letters*, vol. II, p. 671 footnote), relates this to Acts chap. 8, vv. 9–24.
[3] Reichardt, *Vertraute Briefe auf einer Reise nach Wien*, (1810), p. 296–8.

Opus 106 in B flat major

The next of the piano sonatas, op. 106 (which shared with op. 101 the title of 'für das Hammerklavier' but alone of the two has retained it today), was written in very different circumstances. In a letter to Ries Beethoven says 'the sonata was composed in distressful conditions, for it is hard to write almost for the sake of bread alone, and to this pass I have come'. Indeed the work was begun not very long after Beethoven had written (21 August 1817) to his old friend Zmeskall, 'As for me, I often despair and should like to die. For I can see no end to all my infirmities. God have mercy on me, I consider myself as good as lost. . . . If the present state of affairs does not cease, next year I shall be not in London but probably in my grave.'

London was where he was planning to be, for he was just contracting to write a symphony for the Philharmonic Society. True, the sketchbooks show that during the autumn of 1817 and the spring of 1818 he was working on the first two movements of the Ninth Symphony as well as the new piano sonata; but it was the sonata that chiefly occupied him during these months, when all four movements were begun, in the order in which they eventually appeared. During the composition of the first movement, the second and then the third were sketched; and during the composition of the second and third, the final introduction and fugue were begun.[1] It also appears from the sketches, and from a later letter to the Archduke Rudolf, that the first movement of the sonata was in some way connected with a work designed to celebrate his patron's name-day. In the letter (June 1819) Beethoven speaks of 'despondency and so many sad circumstances, and my health so bad at the time all made me so discouraged . . .' The 'sad circumstances' were, of course, those connected with his nephew Karl and the quarrel with the boy's mother. During the last months of 1817 and the first half of 1818 (roughly the period when the first two movements of op. 106 were conceived and finished) this quarrel was in a state of uneasy truce. But from May 1818, when Beethoven took Karl to Mödling and the boy was expelled from the local school, until the following spring, when the last two movements of the sonata were finished, the case flared up again and Beethoven's position deteriorated steeply, ending with his humiliating dismissal from the Landrechte court in December 1818 and his resignation from the guardianship at the end of March 1819. The conversation-books from March and April 1819 reveal him in a state of despair.

[1] Nottebohm, II, pp. 123 ff.

It might perhaps be said that the lawsuit over the guardianship of Beethoven's nephew bears the same relation to the sonata op. 106, as the trial of Guido Franceschini for the murder of his wife, Pompilia, and her parents in 1698 bears to Robert Browning's poem of *The Ring and the Book*. In each case a sordid and, objectively considered, trivial case prompted a great artist to review the whole human predicament and to embody his findings in a monumental work whose proportions, novelty of conception and language, and profound thought and feeling entirely dwarf the original facts, which acted simply as a precipitant. Beethoven saw his struggle with his sister-in-law for the guardianship of her son in terms of absolute right and wrong; and the scale which that struggle assumed in his mind was hardly less than that of Milton's *Paradise Lost*. This may seem a pathetic delusion when it prompts the outbursts that we find in Beethoven's letters or conversation-books. In music, whose *proxima causa* is always subjective and may often seem trivial and disproportionate, all that has objective value is the work of art precipitated.

Beethoven himself was convinced of the unique character of his op. 106. 'There you have a sonata that will give pianists something to do,' he said, 'a work that will be played in fifty years' time.' Yet the sketch-books show[1] that the origins of some of the sonata's most striking and apparently 'inevitable' features were almost as humble as the circumstances that precipitated the work. In the first movement the leap of an octave and the interval of the third (or tenth) were predominant features from the beginning; but both here, and even more strikingly in the scherzo, the traits which give the music its character—defiant rhythm in the one case and humorous asymmetry in the other—are almost totally absent. We can observe here how little of Beethoven's 'third period' originality lay in the first *Einfall*, or inspiration, and how much in the subsequent working-over, or elaboration. The first sketch for the scherzo, for instance, is conventionally eighteenth century in cut, even down to the half close

Ex. 9

[1] Nottebohm, I, pp. 123–36.

There is also clear evidence that Beethoven had in mind an entirely different Presto movement after the canonic trio, and the sketch-books contain what seems more like an ancestor of the scherzo in Tchaikovsky's Fourth Symphony

Ex. 10
Presto

The subject of the final fugue, as we shall see later, went through innumerable metamorphoses before reaching its final form.

The question of tempo presents an immediate difficulty in the opening Allegro.[1] There is no ambiguity about this movement's character, and Schindler was clearly right in classing it, with op. 111, among the 'so-called bravura-style' sonatas of Beethoven's last years— works in which 'the tempo must be strictly observed'. But what tempo? Czerny, who played the work to Beethoven, gave the metronome marking ♩=138, which was considered for something like a century impossibly fast, just as Moscheles's correction to ♩=138 is certainly impossibly slow. On the grounds that Beethoven himself revised his original metronome markings for the first movement of the Ninth Symphony from ♩=126 to ♩=88, Hans von Bülow adopted ♩=112 (also pleading the difference between Beethoven's lighter pianos and those of the present day), Tovey ♩=80–92 and Weingartner ♩=80. Rather more than forty years ago, however, Artur Schnabel decided to take Beethoven at his word and to play the

[1] See Appendix 2 for a fuller discussion of this whole problem.

first movement of op. 106 at the tempo so long considered impossible. If he did not wholly convince listeners by his own performance, in which the fullness of the fast chordal passages and the wealth of detail in inner parts were not ideally clear, he restored a principle which has been triumphantly vindicated by a later generation of virtuosi, with larger hands and greater technical facility. We can, in fact, say that although the development of the heavier modern instrument may have made op. 106 even more difficult to perform than it was in Beethoven's own day, there is still no reason for adopting any slower tempo than $\downharpoonleft = 138$.

It is the richness of *intention*, quite as much as the purely physical *extension* of the hands, that presents the difficulty in this first movement; and it was no doubt in order to miss none of this detail, and to avoid the impression of hurry or scamping, that earlier generations of pianists insisted on the slower tempo. Both the first and second groups of themes are so full of interest and character, the contrapuntal imitations lie so close together and the chromatic alterations seem to crowd so thickly on each other, that it is not enough for the player to possess an exceptional technical mastery of the instrument. He needs a clear intellectual grasp of the musical events that come to life in what can easily be a bewilderingly kaleidoscopic variety under his hands; and even then the final interpretation of the movement has hardly begun. For having first understood what he is playing and then mastered its physical problems, he must go on to grasp the whole musical significance of the grand design and to render plausible to the listener the extra- ordinary alternation of defiance and tenderness, the violent contrasts of pitch and dynamics. The interval of the third is literally omni- present, not only in each of the many themes, but in every apparently unimportant detail of 'accompaniment' (if such a word may be used in speaking of music in which everything is organic), and transition. Often, as in the opening theme or the first of the second group, in G major, it is either unadorned or only slightly altered chromatically; but on other occasions it is half concealed, though only to gain in richness and profusion of meaning by the intermingling of major and minor intervals.

Ex. 11

The declamatory rising minor third with which the exposition ends provides an obvious link with the first movement of the Ninth Symphony (bars 23–4); and Tovey even finds an echo (or pre-echo) of the Agnus Dei of the Missa Solemnis in the 'distant thunder' of the deep bass drumrolls in the coda.[1]

The harshnesses and shrillnesses of this and the last movement of op. 106, though very real, should not (as Tovey says) dominate the player's imagination, any more than they should be 'bowdlerized' away. They impressed the earlier, romantic generation of pianists by their 'otherness', their defiance of what was still musical convention. Seen in the longer perspective of today they lose nothing of their power (which is a different thing from violence) because they are without exception organic and logical, far more frequent in the dense contrapuntal web of the finale but already appearing in milder form in this first movement.

Ex. 12

Op. 106

If the third (tenth) is omnipresent throughout this movement, the bare octave is hardly less prominent, whether in leaps (bars 121–3) in mysterious transition (bars 32–3, 38–9, 188–91, etc.) or in the heaven-storming double-octaves that usher in the coda. Yet against this fundamentally austere harmonic character must be set the many chromatic variations within the material itself (bars 5–16, 19–25), the richly modulating character of, for instance, bars 69–90 and, supremely, the G flat major 'cantabile e legato' in the recapitulation. It is interesting, too, in view of Beethovens' own scepticism,[2] to find the diminished

---

[1] A more striking parallel with the Mass is to be found in the B flat major scale *sempre piano e dolce* earlier in the coda (bars 373–4). This anticipates an exactly similar passage at the end of the Credo (bars 457 ff.).

[2] 'My dear boy', he said to K. F. Hirsch during the winter of 1816–17, 'the surprising effects attributed by many simply to the composer's natural genius may often be quite easily obtained by the correct use and solution of this chord'. Frimmel, *Beethoven Studien* II, pp. 55–69. In connection with Beethoven's dynamic markings in this movement it is well to bear in mind Tovey's sage observation that they should be understood as 'degrees of excitement rather than degrees of force'.

sevenths at the very climax of the development section (bars 194–7).
Verdi, it may be remembered, was to express a similar theoretical
scepticism belied by a similar continuation to employ them in practice.

The tempo of the Scherzo (assai vivace♩=80) is Beethoven's own.
We have already seen that the original version of the opening theme
(see Ex. 9) was built up in conventional two-bar sequences, which
Beethoven changed into one-bar sequences. At the same time the
sketch-books show him concerned with accentuating the upbeat, even
in ways that seem oddly old-fashioned (cp. the opening of the piano
sonata in B flat major op. 22)

Ex. 13

meilleur

Once again Beethoven is concerned with the interval of the third,
rising and falling; and it would hardly be an exaggeration to say that
the whole Scherzo is concerned with this single interval pursued
through a rhythmic maze further complicated by strong dynamic
contrasts and frequent accentuation of weak beats in the 3/4 bar, as
at bars 6–7

Ex. 14

This rhythmic quirk not only recurs throughout the scherzo but
resounds within the very vitals of the trio's canon, where it presents
the performer with the problem of producing what von Bülow
admirably describes as a *quasi pizzicato*. The mysterious character
of the trio derives from the extreme simplicity of the material (broken
B flat minor/D flat major triads) combined with the extreme closeness
(one beat only) of the canonic interval. Beethoven has enhanced the
strangeness of the effect by laying out much of the music four or five
octaves apart, with no comfortable 'filling' between. This is a layout
common in the works of his last years, but no more a miscalculation or

due to his deafness than Bach's delight in high trumpet parts, Brahms's preference for closely written passages in the lower register of the piano or the occasional flouting of traditional musical grammar and syntax by Berlioz or Mussorgsky.

The presto separating the trio from the return of the scherzo was a second thought and ends with a characteristic joke—the pursuit of thirds across five octaves of the keyboard, from top to bottom, followed by a *prestissimo* scale of F major retracing the journey from bottom to top, and a strange tremolo, marked *pp* in the sketch-books (a) but eventually given a rhythm which suggests a thematic concealment (b)

Ex. 15

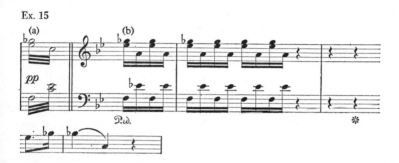

The suggestion that the scherzo and trio should here be repeated (oddly sponsored by von Bülow) is admirably answered by Tovey:[1]

> The great doubly rotating scherzos [of the Seventh and Ninth Symphonies, for instance] seize us in a whirlwind which nothing can stop; the present scherzo trips us up in dialogue by quips and in dance movements by booby-traps. But we are not invited to go through booby-traps twice.

In the coda, which follows the repeat of the scherzo, Beethoven indulges in what amounts to a semantic joke, though it cannot satis-factorily be rendered in words. The movement is in B flat and seems to have come to a satisfactory close in that key, when Beethoven appears deliberately to contradict himself by quietly asserting B natural. The game goes on until B flat eventually wins and the listener is left saying to himself 'so it was not the B flat that was really A sharp, but the B natural that was really C flat—in other words the perfectly respectable flattened supertonic' (Tovey). A wispy reminiscence of the scherzo's opening capers across the stage for a moment, makes three short bows and disappears in the wings, rather like the Moorish boy in *Der Rosenkavalier*.

[1] See *A Companion to Beethoven's Piano Sonatas* (1931).

Before going on to consider the Adagio sostenuto which forms the heart of op. 106, we must return for a moment to the sonata's history. When Beethoven returned the corrected proofs to Ries in March 1819 he said:

Should the sonata not be suitable for London, I could send another one; or you could also omit the Largo and begin straight away with the Fugue, which is the last movement; or you could use the first movement and then the Adagio, and then for the third movement the Scherzo—and omit entirely no. 4 with the Largo and Allegro risoluto. Or you could take just the first movement and the Scherzo and let them form the whole sonata.

Mussorgsky himself was, in fact, hardly more accommodating about the order in which the scenes of his *Boris Godunov* were to be given. Moreover to this must be added a letter to the Archduke Rudolf, written from Mödling in early June 1819, in which Beethoven says, 'To the two pieces in my handwriting composed for Y.I.H.'s name-day[1] I have added two more, the second of which is a grand Fugato, really amounting to a grand sonata, which will soon be published. . . .'

It is of course theoretically possible that Beethoven wrote the first two movements of op. 106 together, as the key and subject-matter suggest, and then wrote separately the great Fugue and the Largo introduction, and separately again the Adagio; and that their organic connection was no closer in his mind than the organic connection between any one of them and the music of the Missa Solemnis or the Ninth Symphony, both of which he was either planning or actually writing at this time. Whatever the truth of the matter, Beethoven's apparent indifference as to how much of the sonata was published in London and in what order, appears to have been neither sardonic nor cynical; and it remains inexplicable, particularly when we remember how adamant he could be about other, comparatively trivial details in the publication of his works. It may well be that the equally unexpected gesture by which he added, in another letter to Ries, what is now the first bar of the Adagio, is closely connected with one of the permutations of the sonata that he had countenanced for London. In one of these the Adagio was to follow the first movement whose fortissimo close makes some transition to the Adagio even more necessary than the pianissimo close of the Scherzo. In either case the F sharp minor threnody of the Adagio needed, he must have felt, some 'distancing'—a step or pedestal, as it has been called, setting it above either the heroic extroversion of the first movement or the boisterous witticisms of the scherzo.

[1] Presumably the first two movements of op. 106. See above p. 38.

Perhaps no single movement, even of Beethoven's, has prompted so much literature as this Adagio. Lenz[1] began it, by speaking of 'une immense lamentation, assise sur les ruines de tous les bonheurs'. Liszt's performance was compared to that of 'an eyewitness of secrets of a world beyond the grave,'[2] while in our own day J. W. N. Sullivan speaks of the movement as 'the deliberate expression, by a man who knows no reserves, of a cold and immeasurable woe . . . as inimical to human existence as the icy heart of some remote mountain lake.'[3] Hans von Bülow's footnote in his edition warns the aspiring pianist off the movement as off holy ground, 'Almost no other movement of the master's demands such pious and awe-ful devotion to do justice to its dolorous nobility. This is no longer a question of "playing the piano": let anyone who cannot "speak" on the keyboard with his whole soul content himself with reading this music.'

Without echoing the tone of such effusive appreciation, we may still count this Adagio among the greatest—and perhaps indeed the greatest—of all Beethoven's slow movements. The key of F sharp minor following on B flat major is a variation of that shift to the key of the flattened sixth (F$\sharp$ = G$\flat$) so common in the composer's last works. But there is nothing in the whole of music like the whispered shift, resembling a momentary shaft of light, from the dominant (C sharp)— a transition suggested by the movement of the hands on the keyboard —to the remote Neapolitan world of G major

Ex. 16

---

[1] Detailed considerations of the sonata in Willehlm von Lenz, *Beethoven—eine Kunststudie* (1855–60), V, pp. 30–52.
[2] In the *Sankt Peterburgsky Vestnik dlya muzyki i teatra* (1858), no. 36.
[3] J. W. N. Sullivan, *Beethoven—his spiritual development*, p. 207.

This passage alone seems to demand that all talk of immense lamentations, ruined happiness and cold, immeasurable woe should be seriously qualified. We do not need to indulge the supremely profitless game of finding 'meanings' for such music to feel that, if the opening thirteen bars of this movement are indeed an expression of grief—or, rather, are grief made audible—these two bars are in some sense the voice of a consolation so absolute that, even if they never reappeared (as they do almost at once) and had no echo in the rest of the movement (as they in fact have) it would still be impossible to consider the Adagio a movement of anything approaching unqualified lamentation, let alone despair.[1]

So far the keyboard writing of the movement has been of hymn-like simplicity, and Beethoven has specified the hushed, silvery tone of 'una corda mezza voce'. Now, however, the pace quickens a little, the whole strength of the instrument is brought into play ('tutte le corde') and the writing becomes more complex. Over gently staccato chords in the left hand (almost operatic in their cushioning accompaniment) and a syncopated middle voice, there develops a long and ornate cantilena *con grand' espressione*, whose chromatic anfractuosities, trills, and suspensions recall the great slow movements of the Baroque and look directly forward to the highly ornamented cantabile style that Chopin was to develop under the influence of Italian opera (bars 30–34).

Ex. 17

[1] Paul Bekker, *Beethoven*, Eng. translation, p. 134, 'we feel the religious atmosphere of the second Mass about us: the mood of consolation, of reliance on supernatural promises, as it exists in the "Benedictus".'

This rises slowly crescendo to a piano espressivo of closely imitative writing between the three voices over a pedal A, which is already preparing the way for the second group of themes in D major.

Now, as the tenor part maintains an uninterrupted murmuring movement, we hear (or at least I hear) the same ineffably consoling voice[1] as in example 16—only now it sounds in the deep bass of the instrument (bars 45–7) and is only taken up later in imitation by the treble. Once again a long mounting crescendo ends in a pianissimo, while Beethoven's marking 'una corda' prompts von Bülow's observation that the passage must sound 'as though from another world' (bars 57–8)

Ex. 18

[1] How differently this can strike another listener may be seen from a passage in Fritz Cassirer's *Beethoven und die Gestalt* (1925) p. 137, which provides a good example of the more modern type of rhapsody prompted by this movement. 'The suffering of all creation figured in the suffering of the third! a real suffering, without direction or rhythm, now major, now minor, now almost squeezed out of existence, wandering through the house without any fixed resting-place—yet always a third, suffering as a third.' This personification of an interval and the conception of that personification suffering, like the ancient Jewish scapegoat, on behalf of the whole community, recalls nothing so much as the medieval interpretation of Scripture by parable and analogy.

That this passage was connected in Beethoven's mind with the earlier bars quoted in example 16 is suggested by the fact that in both he resorts to the upper octave in the middle of the bar, in search for still greater expressiveness.

This revelation is followed in bars 59–60, by what the listener feels to be some inner cataclysm—whether of awe or self-abasement it is impossible to say—which shakes the composer to the very core of his being and causes him to shrink into himself, until in the last six bars of the exposition, a pianissimo chordal hymn, monumental in its diatonic solidity, witnesses to the restoring of his inner balance.

That the short development section of the movement opens (in the left hand bar 69 and the right hand bar 73) with the rising minor third that Beethoven added, apparently as an afterthought, to the beginning of the movement, suggests that its significance was already implicit and that Beethoven was only anxious to make it explicit to the listener. Like the scherzo, this development section (which is only some twenty bars long) consists entirely of a long sequence of major and minor thirds, often in false relationship and stressed by sforzandos on the weak beats of the bar.

Ex. 19

The alternating of 'una corda' and 'tutte le corde' gives the impression of an antiphonal dialogue which dies away on a dominant pedal, whose initial pianissimo is diminished almost to silence as the recapitulation is ushered in from the deep bass. The ornamentation or variation of the opening theme in demisemiquavers, playing round the interval of the octave but seldom touching it (sevenths and ninths), gives it a character of effort or strain enhanced by the heavy chords in the left hand. The

hymn-like passage at the end of the second group (now in F♯ major
and ornamented with suspensions) takes on a more ecstatic character[1]
and a note of finality which makes the sudden move from the tonic F
sharp major to the B minor, which opens the coda, the more
unexpected.

The coda's opening bars ('*pp* una corda'), which sound at first
spare to the point of bareness, are in fact richly and exclusively thematic
and organic.

Ex. 20

A simply factual chronicle of what happens in these bars (154–7) will
perhaps give an idea of the density or 'specific gravity' of the movement.
Two bars of the main theme, over its counterpoint, in B minor break
off at the beginning of the second bar. This is completed by the bass
in a move down the second inversion of the G major triad and the
two bars are inverted in double counterpoint in that key, the second
bar being filled by an echo in an inner part that leads to a close in the
next bar. The first theme of the second group (in G major) is built
sequentially over a long crescendo into a climax of extreme intensity
where a single note is repeated in the right hand with the *Bebung*
effect of the old clavichord, against stormy broken chords in the left
hand (bar 165). Then, after a pause like the orator's *aposiopesis*,
the final restatement of the movement's opening theme, foreshortened
yet still containing the crucial shift to G major (example 16), ends with
four bars in which the 'suffering third' at last finds rest and fulfilment,
(as Cassirer might say), in its most amplified and expanded form—the

[1] Hans von Bülow speaks of 'ein enthusiastischerer Charakter'.

major tenth, suggesting (if we are to adopt such language) a triumphant acceptance of the suffering that has gone before.

The sketch-books[1] do not contain very rich material for the Adagio, but for the Largo, which follows immediately and introduces the finale, there is a very clearly defined tonal scheme

Ex. 21

Orgelpunkt

Beethoven adheres closely to this in the final version, although the points of rest are sometimes different from those shown in the scheme. Most revealing and significant is the fact that the system of descending thirds shown above is very close to that in bars 80–7 of the Adagio, surely evidence of kinship quite as final as that required to prove a common paternity in human beings. The elaboration of this scheme in the Largo is intensely characteristic of Beethoven in this last period of his creative life. In the first place we have the recitative form, apparently improvisatory, yet tied, as shown above, to a very firm harmonic skeleton. Then there are the atmospheric use of the extremes of the keyboard, the mysterious harping of a single note over five octaves, the tonic-cum-dominant pedal and the fragmentary rhythms. Against these evidences of a novel freedom in the handling of every element—melody, harmony, rhythm, and colour—stand the passages of regular, severely rhythmic imitative counterpoint, the B major scales in contrary motion and the G sharp minor Allegro, which could be taken from a two-part invention though still marked by Beethoven's unmistakable personality in the accentuation alone. When he has closed the circle of keys from A to A—through F sharp minor, D major, B minor, G major, E minor, C major, A minor, F major, D minor back to A major—the fortissimo prestissimo excitement of

[1] See Nottebohm, I, pp. 123–36.

the restatement suddenly dims; and when the A alone is left sounding
pianissimo in both hands, Beethoven suddenly shifts his bass by the
interval which had special significance for him and passes straight to an
F major which is the dominant of the finale's B flat major.

Beethoven called this last movement a three-part fugue with occasional freedoms ('fuga a tre voci con alcune licenze'). In the sketch-
books Nottebohm found a great number of fugal subjects, three of
which show characteristics of the theme finally chosen (always the
leap of the tenth, the impetuously descending scale passages in a and b,
the all-important trill in c, where however the accentuation is different).

Ex. 22
(a)

What in fact is this mammoth finale? In proportions and complexity
it has no parallel among Beethoven's works, except the Grosse Fuge
which he was to conceive seven or eight years later as the finale of the
B flat major quartet op. 130. But although Beethoven was finally
persuaded to write a different, more light-hearted finale for op. 130,
no one has ever suggested substituting another finale for op. 106.

If, as von Bülow says, the Adagio of op. 106 is no longer a question
of 'playing the piano', the final fugue on the other hand is just that; or
rather a transcendental keyboard technique must be taken for granted
in anyone who is going to confront the further, purely interpretative
problems of the movement. In fact, the fugue raises in acutest form
the question of virtuosity and its justification, not as an end in itself
but as a means to an end. To appreciate fully the character and stature
of this finale it is necessary not only to understand the structure of the
fugue and the ingenuities of the contrapuntal writing, but also to have

some perception of the superhuman task that Beethoven here sets his performer. The technical difficulty of the music is part of its character, an element as integral as the intellectual power behind the whole conception and the emotional energy displayed in its carrying out. A four-handed arrangement for two pianos would unquestionably promote clarity and balance, accuracy of accentuation and correct chording; but the element of individual effort and mastery—the experience of a single man confronting and overcoming what appear overwhelming obstacles—would be lost, and with it something far more important to Beethoven's idea than formal elegance or mere correctness. If we read Czerny's description of Beethoven's own piano-playing, we cannot avoid the conclusion that the finale of op. 106 was conceived in terms of precisely this kind of playing 'distinguished by immense power and character, unimaginable bravura and agility . . . a legato then considered by all other players impracticable on the fortepiano . . . a style wholly dependent on his ever changing moods'.

It is impossible, I think, to deny that there is in this finale, as in the Grosse Fuge, an element of excessiveness or what Coleridge called 'nimiety', an instinct to push every component part of the music à outrance, not just to its logical conclusion but beyond. This instinct, which is more frequently found among German than any other artists and may well contain strongly aggressive elements, was to be indulged on an immense scale by Wagner.[1] But Beethoven, too, must have known that in the finale of op. 106 he was in a sense doing violence to his listener. It may even be that there is a connection between the blind rages against human meanness and ignobility, such as we find in his letters and conversation-books at the time when this movement was being written, and the violence that marks many incidents of the fugue. Already in the theme itself the strongly accented trill on the weak second beat has this character of aggression, repeated in the energetic octave leap of the countersubject, while the all pervading rhythm of ♪ ♩ ♩ | is as pugnacious as a well aimed and delivered blow of the fist. When Beethoven returns to the subject after the first episode and treats it by reversal of accents (bars 42–8) this pugnacity is increased rather than diminished, while the overlapping of the three-note figure between the two hands in the following episode (51–5) leads to a new order of asperities, this time in the harmonic sphere. Even the G♭ major independent episode (bars 85–93), although a kind of interlude, very quickly loses its playful character and passes through an angry cadenza (bars 94–5) into one of the areas of maximum violence where

[1] And after him, in their different ways, by Richard Strauss, Reger, and Schoenberg.

the theme is first treated by augmentation (bars 97–110) and then
a stretto by augmentation and inversion introduces the most revolutionary sonorous combinations that European music was to know until
the days of Schoenberg.

Ex. 23

This is the first great climax in the finale, and it is followed by a
repetition, this time in A flat instead of G flat, of the scherzando
episode, which in its turn introduces an entirely new element—a
'melancholy cantilena' (von Bülow) in B (C flat) minor which rises
over the cancrizans version of the original subject, heard in the left
hand (bars 153–161).

Ex. 24

The three appearances of the cancrizans, even if not consciously recognized as such by the ordinary listener, possess a mysterious character owing to the reversion of the upbeat (letter A in example 24). The episode arising from the cancrizans (bars 180–92) still bears this hallmark, of course, but becomes increasingly virtuosic in character. This virtuosity is enhanced by the passage beginning at bar 184, where the scales in contrary motion take on a brilliant, almost 'martellato' character. The well prepared cadence with which this section ends contains one of Beethoven's most effective surprises—the unexpected appearance of the fugal subject in the left hand while the right hand is still engaged with the cadence; and the short episode that follows (201–7) introduces the semiquavers of the theme in the middle part ingeniously shared between the two hands and even, on isolated occasions and by octave transposition, between the two upper parts.

Beethoven has now reached an unambiguous G major and proceeds to examine the possibilities of his fugal subject in its inverted form—statement in the upper followed by answer in the middle voice and then, after a short episode, a stormy E flat entry in the bass (bar 229). The increasing closeness of the accents in the following episode plainly announces a climax which is not long in coming (bars 243–5).

Ex. 25

This clean and unambiguous break, very characteristic of Beethoven's dramatic conception of the fugue, provides not only a breathing-space for performer and listener, but a point of vantage from which to survey the whole enormous territory of the finale before attacking what is in fact the last third of the movement. Beethoven now introduces an entirely new subject, tranquil and smoothly flowing and as different as possible from that of the fugue. This D major 'una corda, sempre dolce e cantabile' provides an ideal contrast with the B flat or E flat thunderings and lightnings that have gone before—'and after the storm a still, small voice'

Ex. 26

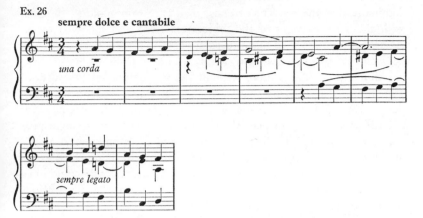

sempre dolce e cantabile

una corda

sempre legato

The voice is unmistakably trinitarian, for the three-part fugal texture continues and even reaches an unostentatious stretto before Beethoven introduces once again the original fugal subject and combines it with the newcomer. The stretto between the theme and its own inversion leads into the formal peroration, which begins in bar 317, with a dominant pedal in the key of the tonic, and is concerned chiefly at first with the countersubject. The last stretto is followed by the appearanace of the theme simultaneously with its inversion, and it makes one final re-entry, in the very highest register of the instrument, before a totally unprepared and unexpected cadence which introduces the coda proper (bar 367).

This opens with a gesture in mockery of the subject's ascending major tenth, in the form of a falling minor tenth.

Ex. 27

p cresc.

A long trill on the sub-dominant in the deep bass is followed by a mysterious, yet perfectly logical double tonic-dominant pedal (B flat —F) which recalls a similar passage in the introductory Largo. The hum of double trills finally subsides on to a pianissimo chord of the dominant, and the movement ends, thematically organic to the last, with the scale passages of the subject extended and followed by an electrifying sequence of tenth-leaps crowned with the trills that have pervaded the whole movement. Liszt, who played the whole finale at 'an almost incredible tempo, without the loss of the smallest detail'[1] played the final trills in octaves, a practice sanctioned by his more puristically inclined quondam son-in-law, Hans von Bülow, who himself was the first to play all the last five sonatas in a single programme, at Vienna in 1881. His boldness in so doing amazed Hanslick. Only Clara Schumann and Brahms had up till then played single examples of these last five sonatas in Vienna, and 'nobody could have come for pleasure . . . a music-history lecture in examples, illustrations without text'.

The sonata op. 106 was sold to the Vienna publisher Artaria for 100 ducats and published on 1 October 1819. A fortnight earlier Artaria inserted in the *Wiener Zeitung* an advertisement as follows:

We shall now put aside all the usual eulogies, which would in any case be superfluous for the admirers of Beethoven's great artistic talent, and in so doing also meet the composer's wishes. We note only in a few lines that this work, which excels all this master's other creations by its rich and grand fantasy, artistic perfection, and sustained style, will mark a new period in Beethoven's piano works.

The sonata was dedicated to the Archduke Rudolf and the title page was suitably imposing

Grosse Sonate für das Hammerklavier Seiner Kais.[erlichen] König[lichen] Hoheit und Eminenz, dem Durchlauchtigsten Hochwürdigsten Herrn Herrn Erzherzog Rudolph von Oesterreich Cardinal und Erzbischoff von Olmütz etc. etc. etc. in tiefster Ehrfurcht gewidmet von Ludwig van Beethoven Op. 106.

Opus 109 in E major

Between the composition of op. 106 and the next of the piano sonatas (op. 109) Beethoven had started to work on the Missa Solemnis. In fact the Adagio of op. 106 suggests that his mind was already moving in the world from which the Mass was to emerge. It was during 1819, when the last two movements of op. 106 were completed and the Mass begun, that Schindler spoke of Beethoven as being, as at no other time, 'rapt away from the world' (*erdenentrückt*).[2] The second

[1] *St. Peterburgskiy Vestnik dlya muzyki i teatra* (1858), no. 36.
[2] See Schindler, op. cit., p. 321.

of the Missa Solemnis sketch-books contains the beginnings of a 'sonata in E minor'. Sketches for the second and third movements of what eventually became the sonata in E major op. 109 are to be found among notes on the 'Benedictus' and advanced sketches of the 'Credo'. Almost certainly related to op. 109 is a sketch in C sharp minor headed 'next sonata—adagio molto sentimento moltissimo espressivo', though this was never used. Beethoven wrote to his publisher, A.M. Schlesinger, on 20 September 1820 that 'the first of the sonatas [op. 109] is quite ready save for correcting the copy, and I am working uninterruptedly at the other two [opp. 110 and 111].' The opening theme of op. 109 is noted in a conversation-book of 1–14 April.

Beethoven had his first attack of jaundice during the summer of 1820, which he spent (May to September) in Mödling; but it was in April that the court gave him full charge of his nephew Karl, and his sister-in-law's protest against this was finally rejected in July. The sunny and relaxed mood of the E major sonata seems to reflect Beethoven's satisfaction and relief after more than four years of often despairing worries over the one human being on whom he had now centred all his affections and all his hopes for the future. The music is overwhelmingly lyrical in character and free in construction, and demands more variation in tempo, even within the movements, than op. 106. Lenz[1] saw the whole work as 'a single movement in several phases (*Bewegungen*)—one and the same idea stated in the recitative, teasingly alluded to in the Vivace, drained of its lifeblood in the Prestissimo and achieving beatitude in the variations'. This is an exaggeration but the exaggeration of a truth, although it seems belied at the tenth bar of the initial 'Vivace, ma non troppo'. Here the simple flowing opening melody, in which broken chords are so disposed between the two hands that both are truly melody-bearers, is unexpectedly interrupted by a richly expressive 'adagio espressivo', chromatic in harmony (the expected modulation to the dominant B major is repeatedly postponed), free and rhapsodic in rhythm, widely spread over the keyboard and generously provided by Beethoven with dynamic and expressive markings. The approach to B major (for the 'adagio expressivo' in fact represents the second group of themes in this sonata movement) is through the dominant minor ninth of C sharp and then, by two of the harmonic side-slips that are characteristic of Beethoven's latest style, through D sharp major to B.

---

[1] *Beethoven—eine Kunststudie* V, pp. 54–67.

Ex. 28

The highly ornamented writing of the whole section is in the greatest possible contrast to the extreme simplicity of the opening theme, which completely dominates the very short (thirty bars) development. At the recapitulation this theme appears with the suspensions and anticipations which form almost as remarkable a hallmark of this sonata as the interval of the third formed in op. 106. If the harmonic side-slips (Ex. 28 marked x), which are most frequent in the keyboard works, are partly manual in origin (see Ex. 16 for a parallel instance in the Adagio of op. 106) these suspensions and anticipations suggest rather the reserving of psychic energy, the savouring of contrast and tension

before its solution and possibly an emphasis on the syntax of music—
its intellectual structure—at the expense of its purely sensuous
pleasingness.

The coda of this short movement is once again based on the first
theme and includes a dozen bars of absolutely simple, hymn-like
cantabile chords that provide a severe test of the player's quality.

Ex. 29

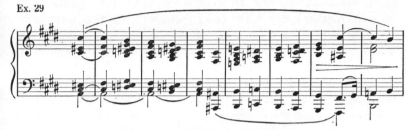

The tender sentiment of a Mendelssohn and the unction of a Liszt
are equally out of place here, where only the 'pure in heart' can tread
without stumbling.

The Prestissimo movement which follows has all the tightly-packed
meaning and concentration of contrapuntal thought typical of Beethoven's scherzos in his latest phase. The blunt, spare opening has a
strongly thematic bass line, which is to furnish material for a two-part
anon in the development section (bars 70–82).

Ex. 30

ben marcato

The restless, uneasy movement of inner voices in the first group of
themes becomes even more marked in the second, where the B minor
tonality is disturbed by much sequential chromatic writing and a
mysterious pianissimo passage of Neapolitan harmony (dominant of C
natural in B minor). Very characteristic also is the foreshortening by
which the end of the exposition is telescoped into the opening of the
development section (bars 65–6). By a similar device of compression the
recapitulation is ushered in by a chord of the dominant of the dominant
(F sharp major preparing the return to E minor) and bar 112 is both
the last bar of one period and the first of the next. The restlessness and
very fast tempo of this movement seem both abolished in the short coda,
a bare succession of chords in strict time and without any strongly
characterized expression.

In the theme and six variations, which form the sonata's last movement, expressiveness is of the first importance. Beethoven even returns
to a bilingual marking, such as he used in op. 101, in order to ensure
that the theme should be given the right character—'gesangvoll mit
innigster Empfindung', translated as 'andante molto cantabile ed
espressivo'. This hymn-like melody (3/4 E major) falls into two regular
eight-bar halves. The first half is characterized by a particularly elegant
contrary motion between the outer parts, which almost meet at the
first beat of the fourth bar and again on the first beat of the seventh.
The modulation to the dominant at the end of the first half of the
melody is through the chord of the German sixth—harmony that was
to appear again in Schubert (C major symphony) and Schumann
(*Dichterliebe*) and to play an important role in Wagner's *Tristan*, in the
music of Liszt and the Russians. Here, in a register of the instrument
and a lay-out that suggest soft trombones rather than strings, the effect
is not sensuous but spiritual, not a caress but a movement of with-
drawal of the soul within itself.[1] (A)

Ex. 31

The second half of the melody brings, in place of the contrary motion
in the first half, a movement in thirds between the alto and bass parts,
a modulation to G sharp minor in the fourth bar and a strong emphasis
on a chord of the ninth before the simple 'mezza voce' cadence.

It is a remarkable fact that all six variations are in the same key as
the theme (E major) yet each treats a different element or aspect. In
the first half of the first variation ('molto espressivo' 3/4) Beethoven
introduces a new melody, a kind of solemn mazurka, harmonically
simple (barely a reference to the German-sixth cadence of the original)
but marked by a threefold rising appoggiatura, in each case an octave
leap on the dominant. Given the marking 'molto espressivo' we can
be certain that Beethoven here intends an arpeggiato similar to that
effect, which he has already used twice in the theme itself (bars 13 and

[1] Cp. bars 59–60 in the Adagio of op. 106.

14).[1] In the second half of the variation, which follows closely the harmonic pattern of the theme's second half, these appoggiaturas are even more frequent and varied, including sixths as well as octaves. A certain similarity in style, though not in lay-out to Chopin's mazurkas has often been remarked.

Ex. 32

The second variation ('leggieramente' 3/4) is most unusual in form. The first eight bars follow the theme very closely in broken chords (semiquavers), but with explicitly Neapolitan harmony representing the German sixth before the close on the dominant. The eight bars that follow are divided into two groups of four. In each the falling major third, with which the theme opens is the subject of the variation —the first ('teneramente') in warmly sung quavers, and the second in dancing semiquavers, but both over a dominant pedal. Exactly the same pattern is followed in the second half of the variation. First the second half of the theme is set out in broken chords; and when this is completed, first the singing and then the dancing variation appear. Now, however, the harmony is different. The singing variation opens with a piano but insistent D natural, which the ear may understand as B minor until it establishes itself as the dominant minor ninth of F sharp (minor), through which the music returns to G sharp minor (half close in the second half of the theme)

Ex. 33

[musical notation]

---

[1] See Nottebohm, I, pp. 460–2.

and so, through the 'dancing' variation to E major. This whole double variation, which contains such variety of harmonic character, texture, and layout, is in strong contrast to all the other five variations, which are marked by exceptional unity of style and material.

The third variation ('allegro vivace' 2/4) moves brusquely out of the espressivo world into that of a two-part invention in double (invertible) counterpoint, with sforzato accentuation and occasional anticipations that provide the spice of the unexpected. A much freer polyphony marks the fourth variation (9/8) where Beethoven is at pains (even to the point of maltreating the Italian language)[1] to establish the gently flowing tempo. The extraordinary power of plastic or visual suggestion—something very rare in Beethoven's music—inherent in the passing of a single semiquaver figure from part to part, up and down, above or beneath the fragment of melody recalled to von Bülow Goethe's description of angelic activity in the first monologue in *Faust*

Wie Himmelskräfte auf und nieder steigen
Und sich die gold'nen Eimer reichen.[2]
(Like angelic powers that rise and sink and pass from hand to hand the golden vessels.)

Harmonically the scheme of this variation is simpler than that of the theme. In the first part is it not until the seventh beat of the seventh bar that Beethoven abandons the tonic E major and modulates through the German sixth to the dominant. After the repeat he moves, as in the second variation (see p. 181) to the unexpected D natural which, as before, again proves to be a dominant minor ninth of F sharp, and this initiates a wonderful dialogue, as it were, between two manuals, gradually swelling—with the manifest effort suggested by sforzato accents on the weak beats of the bar—into a return of the original 'plastic' theme and an apparently aimless, yet in fact strictly thematic, wandering of gentle semiquaver scale figures in contrary motion.

Ex. 34

---

[1] 'un poco meno andante cioè un poco più adagio come il tema'—moving slightly less, that is to say a little slower than (the 'come' mistranslates his German 'als') the theme.
[2] Part 1 Act 1 lines 96–7.

This world of angelic activity and contemplation gives way in the fifth variation ('allegro ma non troppo') to a bluff, blunt march-like fugue in three parts with the falling major third of the theme as its subject, heard already in the first bar in its inverted (rising) form in the bass. The German-sixth harmony of the theme is faithfully reproduced at the explosive cadence immediately before the appearance of the countersubject and answer (Ex. 35). The fugue's second part is taken up

Ex. 35

with an inversion of the inverted form of the original subject—a falling (minor) sixth in place of a rising (major) third. This comes in bars 23–4 to a violent clash of anticipations enhanced by the extremities of pitch. The eight bars that follow this ('forte') and introduce a new countersubject in the bass, are then repeated exactly 'piano' to form a transition to the final variation, where Beethoven explored territory entirely new not only to the instrument but to the musical imagination.

The most immediately salient technical feature of this final variation is that it is based all but entirely (thirty-three out of thirty-five bars) on a dominant pedal. This is heard first of all in the soprano and tenor parts, while the alto has the original theme and the bass provides the harmony. As the pedal moves from part to part, it changes both rhythm and tempo (from crotchets and quavers to quaver triplets and then to semiquavers and demisemiquavers), until finally it becomes a trill that lasts twenty-three bars. The trill has started in effect—in slow motion, that is to say—in the sixth bar of the variation. It is when both the inner parts, at an interval of two octaves, are trilling and the soprano and bass have quaver triplets three octaves apart that we move into a wholly new world of sound

Ex. 36

It would be tempting to speak of impressionistic effects, of sonorities used for their own sakes, if the passage were not so soberly thematic and organic, so logical despite its novel sound; and there are stranger variations of this sonority to come. After the cadenza-like broken chords in bars 17–24, the dominant trill moves from the deep bass to the alto part. Above this, high among the leger lines, the theme is heard in a fragmentary form—isolated quavers plucked, off the beat, by the player's little finger—while the left hand executes a series of descending demisemiquaver scale passages

Ex. 37

The effect of this passage is hardly any longer pianistic; it seems to look forward rather to the imitation of gamelan sonorities that we find in the piano music of Debussy's middle period. This is particularly noticeable in the last four bars of the variation (Ex. 38), where the dominant pedal constituted by the trill is expanded in the left hand, three octaves lower, by what is in effect a tonic trill which also incorporates the notes of the dominant seventh chord which are also heard descending slowly, like isolated harp notes, from the extreme heights.

This transfiguration of the theme in an atmosphere so rarified that not many pianists can breathe it, the absence of all ballast in the shape

Ex. 38

of a solid middle register and the impression of a music that hovers at a great height above the world of everyday experience to which it is connected by only the most tenuous links, has no parallel in any earlier work of Beethoven's, not even in op. 106. We shall find it again in op. 111, in the Missa Solemnis, though in a different form, and most of all in the last string quartets. Whether or no Beethoven himself associated the crystalline, ethereal character of these last pages of op. 109 with something of the same other-worldliness as that of the Missa Solemnis (which he was composing at the same time), the hymn-like character of the original theme is unmistakable when it finally returns in its original form, bringing an extraordinary reminder to the listener of the distance that he has travelled during the space of these comparatively short six variations.

The sonata in E major was dedicated to Maximiliane Brentano, the daughter of Franz Brentano—a Frankfurt merchant who also acted as Beethoven's agent with the publisher Simrock—and his Viennese wife, who was born Antonia von Birkenstock. She was a girl of nineteen when Beethoven sent her the following letter, dated 6 December 1821:

A dedication!!!! well, this is not one of those dedications that are used and abused by thousands of people. It is the spirit which unites the noble and finer people of this earth and which time can never destroy. It is this spirit which now speaks to you and which calls you to mind and makes me see you still as a child, and likewise your beloved parents—your most excellent and gifted mother, your father imbued with so many truly good and noble qualities and ever mindful of the welfare of his children. . . . The memory of a noble family can never fade in my heart. May you sometimes think of me with a feeling of kindness. My most heartfelt wishes. May heaven bless your life and the lives of all of you for ever.

Opus 110 *in A flat major*

The last two piano sonatas, op. 110 in A flat major and op. 111 in C minor, seem to have been written concurrently during 1821. They are mostly referred to by Beethoven as a pair and the autograph dates are only a month apart—op. 110 being apparently finished on 25 December 1821[1] and op. 111 on 13 January 1822. The sketches for both works are scattered among those for the Agnus Dei of the Misssa Solemnis.[2] There is, however, a very marked difference in character between the two.

The sonata in A flat op. 110 is the most frequently played of Beethoven's five last piano sonatas, and even appears as a test piece in competitions among young players. Schindler was the first to utter a warning.

The study of Beethoven's music should not be begun seriously until the student has reached an advanced state of general as well as purely musical culture, without which it will have an exhausting (*ermattend*) effect on those who have little sensibility to musical poetry. This music sprang in the first place from a profound personality and is only fully intelligible and useful to profound personalities.

Although the works of Beethoven's early and middle years are technically within the grasp of many young artists and have become so much part of the language of music that they are 'understood' by all musically educated people, many of them still demand a quality of musical perception and depth of emotional experience that no child can possess (and many of the technically most brilliant and most sophisticated young artists are still emotionally children). The works of Beethoven's last years, including all five of the last piano sonatas, should be regarded, like the great operatic roles, as something that no physical, or even intellectual gifts, however exceptional, justify a young artist in attempting. A pianist of seventeen who attempts op. 110 should be regarded as no less presumptuous than a singer of twenty-five who attempts Brünnhilde. It was in connection with this sonata that Hermann Wetzel wrote, 'In late Beethoven one must weigh every note until one has realized its motivic significance. . . . Not a single note is superfluous, and there is no passage . . . that can be treated as you please, no trivial ornament' (*belangloser Floskel*).[3] Tovey is uttering the same warning when he calls the development section of the first movement of op. 110 'the *locus classicus* for those Greek simplicities of Beethoven's later style where the player can do nothing but leave the text to speak for itself'—notoriously the most difficult of all feats for any artist, and more particularly a young one.

[1] According to Kinsky *Das Werk Beethovens. Thematisch-bibliographisches Verzeichnis seiner sämtlichen vollendeten Kompositionen*, p. 314, the last movement was revised early in 1822.
[2] See Nottebohm, II, pp. 464–7.
[3] See Herman Wetzel, *Beethovens Sonate op. 110—eine Erläuterung ihres Baues*, in Frimmel, *Beethoven Handbuch*, 1909.

The exact tone of the sonata's opening movement is even more difficult than usual to define. Beethoven's marking is 'moderato cantabile molto espressivo', and he qualifies the opening bars 'con amabilità' adding in brackets the German 'sanft'. 'Amabilità' suggests the same idea as the 'piacevole' that Beethoven uses for the fourth variation in op. 109. Fuller Maitland[1] suggests that this means 'to be played in a placid and graceful way, without passion'. Like op. 109 this sonata belongs to the lyrical and intimate rather than the so-called 'bravura' category (opp. 106 and 111), demanding considerable freedom in the treatment of tempo. Czerny's ♩=76 seems too fast to von Bülow, who is persuaded that this opening has 'an adagio character' and suggests ♩=69.

The chordal introduction and the extraordinarily vocal first theme which completes it vanish, as it were, into a cloud of fine spray at bar 12, where espressivo melody is replaced by the lightest arpeggio demisemiquavers. These are spread over the whole keyboard and are only supported by harmonies in the deep bass, until their ethereal, ornamental character gradually gives place to a recognizably thematic shape and the second group of themes is introduced 'molto legato'. Here the rhythm of the descending octaves clearly recalls the opening of the recapitulation in the first movement of op. 109. But Beethoven's written-out appoggiaturas (bars 22–3), demand an expressive treatment and the increase in weight of tone that later editors suggested by tenuto markings. They herald a characteristic crisis of intensity, in which the two hands move further and further apart, opposed not only in direction but in character, and end separated by over four and a half octaves of empty

Ex. 39

[1] In *Grove*, vol. vi, p. 723.

keyboard. Here the extremes of pitch are used for purely expressive purposes, whereas in op. 109 Beethoven's intention was rather to create a
remote, ethereal atmosphere; and it is striking how differently he uses
the keyboard on each occasion, with the maximum of elaboration in
op. 109 and the maximum of simplicity here.

The heavily phrased melodic bass in the second of this group of themes
and, once again, the contrary motion of the two hands lead to another,
though less emphatic sforzato climax and the exposition ends with a codetta
containing a repeated but tranquil assertion of the key of the dominant.

The development section is introduced by a single solemn step—a
descent in open octaves from E flat through D flat to C. All sixteen
bars of this short section are concerned with the opening two bars of
the movement, held up in different lights against a recurrent semiquaver
pattern in the left hand. The key-scheme is simple (F minor, D flat
major, B flat minor to A flat major at the recapitulation) and the music
progresses (as Tovey's observation quoted earlier suggests) with the
simplicity and apparent inevitability, the dignity and lack of self-
consciousness, that do indeed recall the great art of the remote past.[1]
At the recapitulation Beethoven, by a stroke of genius, combines the
singing melody of the opening four bars with the restless 'spray-figure'
in feather-light demisemiquavers in the left hand. Then reversing the
roles, he gives the melody to the left hand in the singing tenor-register
of the instrument beneath a high tremolando pedal in the right—the
first of the many alterations or embellishments in this recapitulation.
The main theme of the first group, appearing now in D flat major,
modulates through the minor to the key of F flat (the apparently
remote E major of the text) and this necessitates one of those passages
of harmonic 'sleight of hand' in bar 77 where, by what seems a purely
manual shift, Beethoven returns to the tonic (A flat) for the second
group of themes. Written as below and not in the more convenient E
major used by Beethoven, the passage is clearer theoretically, although
the ear persists in feeling that it has been the victim of some kind of
confidence trick or practical joke

Ex. 40

In the coda (bar 110) we have another example of the *aposiopesis* or sudden breaking-off of an idea (in this case the mounting demisemiquavers that threaten to reach the upper limit of Beethoven's London Broadwood) and the taking up of the sonata's opening lyrical idea in half a dozen quiet bars which reiterate the movement's lyrical essence.

At the root of the scherzo which follows there probably lie two memories. The first we can trace directly to a letter that Beethoven wrote to the publisher Simrock on 18 March 1820. This contains the following passage,

As I know that businessmen like to save postal expenses, I am adding here two Austrian folk-songs to refund you for your expenditure. You may do what you like with them. I wrote the accompaniments—I am inclined to think that a hunt for folk-songs is better than the man-hunts of the heroes who are so highly extolled—

Ex. 41

(Our cat has had kittens—Three and six, nine—One of them has a mark on its head (?)—that'll be mine).[1]

This seems almost certainly to lie at the root of the first four (*piano*) bars of the scherzo, which Beethoven answers with a C major shout. A rather more sophisticated humour shows itself in the next six bars, where the accents of the right and left hands are deliberately contradictory. But any hint of sophistication disappears again in the movement's third idea

[1] 'Riegerl' seems to be a dialect word for a kind of cap.

Ex. 42

Ich bin lü-der-lich, du bist lü-der-lich

This, as its rhythm alone suggests, seems to be the memory of another folksong, quoted by A. B. Marx[1] as 'Ich bin lüderlich, du bist lüderlich' ('I am a draggle-tail, you are a draggle-tail'). Von Bülow is careful to warn the player against 'the trivialization of this popular idea', and gives the impression that, if it were possible, he would have preferred Beethoven not to indulge his naïve sense of humour in this way. This is, in fact, the last appearance in the piano works (if not altogether) of what might be called that Dutch vein of humour which reminds us that the composer's forbears may well have been among the peasants whose gross amusements we know from the pictures of the Breughels.

The humour of the trio is much more sophisticated, taking up the 'misplaced' and contrasted accents that characterized bars 9–14 of the scherzo, making much play with anticipations emphasized by two-octave leaps and with periphrases or *Umspielungen*, by which a note is more often suggested by its neighbours than directly stated. The general effect is spiky and deliberately awkward, humorous perhaps but in a far more intellectual, even self-conscious way than the scherzo. This trio, in fact, belongs with the canonic trios of opp. 101 and 106. After the return of the scherzo the movement ends with a coda of fifteen bars, five of which are silent. These silent bars are in fact those which would naturally carry a strong accent, so that the whole coda makes a syncopated effect on the listener.

In the third movement of op. 110 we have one of the most original and personal constructions in all Beethoven's works. It is a double movement, in the sense of combining Adagio and finale, and also by reason of the repetitions that it contains. Although the movement opens in the key of B flat minor (whose key signature Beethoven uses), this lasts only one bar, and the recitative which follows is first of all in A flat minor and then (a modulation that echoes the first movement) in F flat, before reaching the A flat minor cadence that introduces the 'Arioso dolente'.

The first twenty-eight bars of the movement consist of a 'scena ed aria' in a manner that suggests the opera of the late eighteenth century —orchestral strings (bars 1–3), vocal recitative with harpsichord

[1] A. B. Marx, *Ludwig van Beethoven—Leben und Schaffen*, 5th ed., (1901) Part ii, p. 416.

support (bar 4). Three chords on the strings ('andante crescendo'), modulating from A flat minor to F flat, lead to a dominant chord above which the right hand executes a crescendo and diminuendo on a single note. This is the singer's 'messa di voce', so much admired by the connoisseurs of the castrati's art, represented by an imitation of the archaic clavichord device of the *Bebung* and it leads to a final cadence 'dimin. smorzando' (or 'colla voce', as it might have been) in A flat minor. The Arioso dolente which follows, translated by Beethoven 'Klagender Gesang' (Song of Lamentation) is exquisitely vocal in general character but unmistakably instrumental in the rhythmic articulation of the first three bars. No voice could give their full value to the anticipations which give the melody its heartrending character, any more than it could compass the wide span that is part of Beethoven's design.

Ex. 43

The accompaniment of repeated chords, though conceived for the lighter instrument of Beethoven's day and more difficult to manipulate successfully on today's fuller-toned pianoforte, emphasizes the forlorn character of the melody, which is further enhanced by its frequent isolation (bars 15–16) from the accompaniment.

The arioso comes to a full, formal close, with a postlude that seems to be conclusive. The twenty-eight bars of the movement have been packed with experience, mostly painful in character, but so shaped and mastered that any further comment seems impossible. The fugue that follows, growing with hardly a pause out of the arioso is, as it were, the answer to the lament of the arioso, an answer as unexpected as it is convincing. For whereas in the Adagio of op. 106 a single voice brings consolation to a multiple, polyphonic distress, here the single voice of lament is answered by a triple, or rather a triune, reassurance. Like that earlier voice, this is still and small, at least when first heard. Beethoven further qualifies his Allegro, ma non troppo with 'sempre piano' and legato phrasing is of the utmost importance. Bülow quotes in connection with this fugue Beethoven's remark to Karl Holz—'To write a fugue is no great art, I wrote dozens when I was a student. But the imagination (*Phantasie*) also insists on its rights, and nowadays the traditional form must be penetrated by another, genuinely poetical element.'

It is noticeable at once to the hearer that the rising fourths of the

fugal subject answer, counter, or act as a corrective to the drooping
line of the arioso,[1] whose broken, hesitant rhythms are in the same
way braced by the even, confident march of the dotted crotchets and
the smooth, untroubled flow of the countersubject's quavers. Yet
although there can be no questioning the poetic element in this fugue,
it is almost immaculately traditional in form; and Beethoven's
observation about the imagination insisting on its rights would apply
more obviously to the highly dramatic fugue of op. 106 with its
irregularities ('alcune licenze', as he himself called them). It is only
at the forty-first of the eighty-five bars that we reach the first long
crescendo marked by Beethoven, a passage where the uppermost voice
prolongs the subject by rising sequences. The fortissimo entry of the
second half of the subject in the deep bass, striding upwards in another
short crescendo, comes to an end on the high D flat in the left hand
voice at bar 81; and although the final appearance of the theme in
the tonic (bass octaves, starting in bar 101) is introduced by a short
crescendo and marked forte, there is absolutely no other fortissimo marking until the final chord of the dominant. From here the
music suddenly loses its abundant vitality. The dominant seventh of A
flat wanders disconsolately up and down the keyboard and in a single
gesture becomes G minor, as the repeated accompaniment chords
announce the return of the arioso. The tonality is a semitone lower
than before and Beethoven adds to the original 'dolente' the marking
'perdendo le forze' or 'ermattet' (exhausted). This mood of something
approaching despair is reflected in the broken rhythms and fragmentary
phrasing which destroy all the former linear beauty of the melody,
while emphasizing its emotive quality. These 'sanglots entrecoupés'
(Bülow) vividly suggest a human voice under the stress of extreme
emotional distress and physical exhaustion[2] and the final cadence is
marked, unlike that in the first version of the arioso, 'una corda,
foreseeing the 'quasi niente' of a century later. The singer's grief has
sung itself out and we expect the same formal ending as before. But
instead of ascending to the unadorned octave we hear, to our surprise,
the major third repeated with increasing confidence until at the tenth
stroke the whole dynamic range from pp to $f\!f$ has been covered. Each
of these chords is off the beat and their effect is therefore of breathless
anticipation, though of what the listener cannot tell; perhaps the
merely physical excitement of a final allegro, a deliberate search for

---

[1] They also reproduce the skeleton shape of the first movement's opening theme.
[2] Compare the C flat major episode marked 'beklemmt' in the Cavatina of the string quartet
op. 130, and bars 120 ff. in the fourth variation of the finale of op. 111.

oblivion in physical activity? Nothing could be less expected than what in fact emerges, with firm steps if slightly hesitant gait, from the deep shadows—the inversion of the fugue, stated pianissimo 'sempre una corda' in the least dramatic register of the keyboard (the fugue subject when it first appeared was in the singing tenor register of the instrument). It is—if such fancies are permissible—as though the grief-stricken soul, that had refused the answer, the reminder, or the admonishment of the original fugue and fallen into an even more absolutely despairing questioning, was now to be offered an answer which, although substantially the same, approaches the problem from a different angle. However we regard it, we can hardly avoid the impression that Beethoven's reply to the human grief and distress of the two arioso stanzas is the contemplation of a harmonious world whose laws are absolute and objective, neither subject to human passion nor concerned with anything beyond themselves. Mozart gave the same answer in the finales of the G minor quintet K.516 and the B flat major piano concerto K.595. How far either composer identified this world of absolute values with that of religious belief and feeling (as Bach seems to have done) it is impossible—and in the last resort irrelevant—to know. Beethoven's deep philosophical optimism, which bound him closely to the eighteenth century, makes this identification more probable, I think, in his case than in that of his predecessor, the naturally more melancholy and sceptical Mozart.[1]

The first sixteen bars of the new fugue are all limpidity and innocence and demand the greatest simplicity and tranquillity in performance. At bar 152, however, Beethoven embarks on a stretto (by augmentation in the right hand and by diminution in the left) which not only disturbs the surface and troubles the transparency of the music but alters the rhythm, as well as the tempo, of the theme. This complexity begins to weaken first the flow, and then even the basic rhythmic character of the music, when the anticipations weaken the sense of the bar-line between bars 156–62;

Ex. 44

[1] In discussing the role of the fugue in op. 110 we should not forget that in the sketch-books the fugue-subject appears before the sketches for the scherzo and the Adagio, though this is not conclusive evidence of where Beethoven originally meant it to appear in the sonata.

In the first three bars of the stretto by double diminution (168–70) the listener unfamiliar with the work wholly loses his bearings, until Beethoven orientates him by introducing for the last time the inverted fugue subject, unmistakable in its rhythm and character although with all its intervals augmented. Finally, as the pace of the music quickens, the original fugal subject reappears, first in octaves in the bass, then in the middle voice and, as the fugal peroration moves into the coda, in the topmost voice, where full chords are supported by rolling broken chord figures in the left hand. The coda, in which this keyboard layout continues, is based on precisely those bars of the fugal subject that led (bars 67–70) to the climax which forms the central point of the first fugue. The passionate impetus of these sequences sweeps onwards and upwards to the topmost C (c''') of his instrument, while the intensely rhythmic broken chords in the bass, four octaves and more below, recall not so much the distant drum-rolls of the coda in the first movement of op. 106 as the relentless beating of waves hundreds of feet beneath the eagle mounting to the sun, whose blaze envelops the huge swoop and soar of the A flat major arpeggio in the last five bars.

The passionate, heroic nature of the coda is the last of the many surprises in this final movement of op. 110. We do not instinctively feel it to be out of place, contradicting either the distress of the arioso or the luminous verities of the fugue; and it may be that, on the emotional level, Beethoven was expressing in this unique movement the same idea as that expressed by Goethe's angels.[1]

> Wer immer strebend sich bemüht,
> Den können wir erlösen.
> (The tireless struggler in life's toils,
> It is he that we can redeem.)

Opus 111 in C minor

Although Beethoven's original intention was to dedicate both opp. 110 and 111 to Antonia Brentano, the mother of Maximiliane to

[1] *Faust*, Part 2, Act 2, Scene 6.

whom op. 109 was dedicated, in fact op. 110 appeared without a dedication. The C minor sonata op. 111, on the other hand, which was finished in January 1822 and published by Schlesinger before April 1823, was dedicated eventually to the Archduke Rudolf. ('Y.I.H. seemed to find pleasure in the C minor sonata', Beethoven wrote in July of the same year, 'and I therefore feel that it would not be presumptuous if I were to surprise you with its dedication.') As we have seen, the sketches for this sonata are among those for op. 110 and both jostle sketches for the Agnus Dei of the Missa Solemnis. The first theme of the first movement of op. 111 appears among the op. 110 sketches with '3tes Stück presto' pencilled against it.[1]

We know that the question of op. 111 not having a third movement was a sore one with Beethoven. Schindler's story that Beethoven omitted a third movement saying that 'he had no time and must work on the Ninth Symphony' infuriated all romantically-minded commentators including Bülow, whose nobly indignant footnote refers to Schindler as *jener Strohkopf*, ('that addle-pate'). The nineteenth century believed in the divine right of artists and preferred a mystical to a factual explanation of all aesthetic phenomena. It is indeed difficult to imagine any movement that could have followed the theme and variations of op. 111, and there was the precedent of op. 109 ending with a movement in this form. Beethoven himself, on the other hand, made no mystical claims for his music; and he might well have given Schindler this very practical answer in perfectly good faith and not, as Bülow believes, in witheringly sardonic scorn for the incomprehension that could ask such an abysmally irrelevant question. What annoyed Beethoven, far more than Schlesinger's suggestion that a movement had been omitted from the parcel containing the sonata, were the endless misprints which he found in the Paris edition and in the Leidesdorf copy of this which appeared in Vienna.[2] When Diabelli produced another edition, Beethoven kept a close watch over the proofs.

Among Beethoven's thirty-two piano sonatas only three, besides this last of the series, open with a slow introduction. These are op. 13

---

[1] Paul Mies, op. cit., p. 149, finds evidence of the theme going back as far as 1801–2 in the sketch-books.

[2] Beethoven's letter to Diabelli on this subject contains an example of the anti-Semitic language into which Beethoven sometimes fell when riled ('the two beach-pedlars and rag-and-bone Jews called Schlesinger'). In this matter he was very much a man of the age and the place in which he lived. Like the rest of Vienna, he was ready to consort with the *haute juiverie* in the salons of the Itzig sisters (the Baronesses von Eskeles and von Arnstein) but was quick to attribute any fault in a Jew to his 'race'.

written in 1798-9 and opp. 78 and 81a, written in 1809-10. There is a strong similarity between op. 13 and op. 111, not only in tonality[1]—both are in C minor—but also in the character of the opening, marked 'grave' in the earlier work and 'maestoso' in the later. In both of these slow introductions Beethoven 'hurls defiance' (as the old commentators used to say) at the world or its creator. The harmony of both is concerned in the first place with the diminished seventh, introduced immediately in op. 111 and after a more discreet tonic passage in op. 13; and after that with a rigorously controlled sequence of chromatic modulations leading in each case with a cadenza-like gesture into the main body of the movement. It is significant that in op. 13 Beethoven engages in a manifest dialogue, with fortissimo chords in the bass answered by an eloquently pleading phrase in the treble, while in op. 111 we have a monologue. Whereas the young man exteriorized the struggle in himself, dramatizing his 'opponent' as a force outside himself, one whom it was possible to defy or placate, middle age brought the knowledge that this opponent was his own dark shadow, a rejected aspect of his own self still sharing with him a common identity. If this first movement is in fact an expression of heroic resistance, Beethoven has long outgrown the days (if they ever really existed) when he played at being Prometheus and defying the Almighty. The opening five bars of op. 111 are a cry of agony rather than a shout of defiance, and they are followed by a wonderful five bars in which Beethoven seems to be looking with tender amazement at his own human wretchedness, turning it in his hands as though to discover its meaning.

Ex. 45

---

[1] Cp. similarities of the same kind between op. 106 and op. 22.

The chromatically rising bass (G flat to D natural), narrowing the intervals in the left hand against the widening intervals in the right creates a feeling of agonized pressure, which is only released when the bass line drops to the lower octave and the détente begins. The sensation of constriction is all the more acute because the whole passage is pianissimo. This is an interior, mental agony which has nothing to do with loud noises—in fact the crescendo only comes when the relief of the cadence is in sight. Having found that meaning at the cadence in bars 10–11, he ponders on it in the cantabile phrase (12–13) and its repetition, and then plunges into the grim struggle, with the confidence of one who already knows its conclusion—wholly unlike the young man who plunged into the 'molto allegro e con brio' of op. 13. This movement, too, is marked 'allegro con brio ed appassionato' and it has a number of virtuoso traits—the semiquaver passages in octaves, the dizzy climbs and descents over the whole range of the keyboard—but these are always subordinate to musical, expressive considerations. The nature of the material, on the other hand, was almost certainly determined by Beethoven's interest at this time in counterpoint. The first dramatic, questioning phrase (A) is perhaps an operatic memory, since it is found note for note in Act 2 of Sacchini's *Dardanus* Ex. 46 (1), which was given at Bonn in the season of 1782–3, when it may have been heard by Beethoven as a boy. The triplet *Schleifer*, or slide upwards, which accentuates its dramatic character, is not in the sketch-books.

Ex. 46
(1)

cf Op. III

(2)

The building up of bar 3 in Ex. 46, in six bars of semiquavers crescendo after the deliberately hesitant 'ritenente' of bar 23, does not conceal the fact that this theme suggested itself to Beethoven primarily as a cell that combined contrapuntal workability with the harmonic interest of the 'diabolical' interval of the diminished fourth. There are four quasi-fugal entries of this subject (complete with countersubject) after its original statement and before the appearance of the second group of themes. This is heralded by two bars in which Beethoven leaps from top to bottom of the keyboard—a gesture suggesting an extreme tension which finds its relief in the first theme of the second group, a short, sunny and intensely expressive six bars of recitative-like music, before virtuosity takes over again and the bass introduces the second of the second group of themes (B), itself a close variation of the first theme (A).

Ex. 47   B.

At the opening of the development section, B is first presented with the *Schleifer* characteristic of A and is then combined with A in augmentation. This is surely the origin of the fugato in Liszt's piano sonata, where contrapuntal and manual vituosity are in exactly opposite proportion to what we find here. The development section, as in all these last sonatas of Beethoven's, is extremely short—a mere 20 bars in a movement of 158—but the recapitulation shows a number of interesting variations from the original. Thus in bar 98 a new D flat major passage (i.e. Neapolitan harmony) carries the second fugal entry into F minor, thus preparing the way for the appearance of the second subject in the conventionally correct key of C major. This is extended

and developed, first in an eloquent passage in F minor, which seems
for a moment, like an echo from op. 57 (bars 124–5) and then in a
chain of rapidly rising sequences introducing B. The coda falls
through *sforzando* chords off the beat to an austerely triumphant close
in which the diminished seventh of the introduction is released into a
C whose major character is emphasized by the broken tenths in the
left hand.

Ex. 48

That single diminished seventh, which already has a pedal containing
the tonic beneath it, like a foregone conclusion, is the only reference
in the coda to the agonized cry of the introduction. In op. 13, on the
other hand, four bars of the Grave return as part of the coda, in
whose twenty bars there are no fewer than eight chords of the diminished seventh either sforzato or on a naturally strong beat. There the
battle is by no means played out, whereas in op. 111 Beethoven, we
may feel, has come to honourable terms with his opponent, who is
half a friend and in any case wholly himself.

In both sonatas the first movement is followed by a theme and
variations. In op. 13 the Adagio cantabile is an extrovert hymn and the
variations are decorative. In op. 111 the simplicity and static quality of
the Arietta, where each half consists of four bars grouped round a
dominant pedal and four bars climax and cadence, suggests a spirit
completely at rest, at peace with itself, not so much resigned to suffering
as willingly accepting and transfiguring it into something that is
indistinguishable from joy. The stages by which Beethoven reached

this final form of the Arietta can be seen in the sketch-books. Once again the difference between the original conception[1] and the definitive version are chiefly rhythmical. The following shows how humble were the origins of this sublime melody—

Ex. 49

Beethoven marks the Arietta 'adagio molto semplice e cantabile' and the two ideas, as Bülow points out, are in fact complementary. 'Cantabile' suggests the melody's expressive character and 'semplice' warns against any hint of passion or rhetoric. In fact the movement must, even at its opening, be bathed in a quiet glow whose source is only gradually revealed as the listener is taken through the successive initiations represented by each variation. The harmonic scheme remains almost primitively simple—the tonic C major, its corresponding A minor and the dominant G major—for the first two variations. Here the music flows at first smoothly and then with a regular, gently dotted rhythm; and there are no forte, let alone sforzato, markings.

In the third variation the mood changes suddenly and with it the metre. The Arietta itself and the first variation are written in 9/16, that is to say each bar contains three groups of three semiquavers, explicit or implicit. In variation 2 Beethoven changes to 6/16 i.e. three groups of two semiquavers in each bar; and now in variation 3 to 12/32, i.e. three groups of four demisemiquavers to a bar. Forte and sforzato markings appear again and the performer has to guard against the piling up of unwanted accents, which destroy the original shape of the theme and also the continuity of tempo (Beethoven marks 'l'istesso

[1] See Nottebohm, II, pp. 469–70.

tempo') with that of the foregoing variation. If the mood of this variation is violent, it is a violent joy, a stamping dance of triumph, only modified in the second half by the dialogue between forte left hand and cantabile right.

Ex. 50

The multiplication of units has been exhausted for the moment (there are few pages in classical piano literature that present to the eye so many notes, so many black lines and so many ties) and we return in variation 4 to the 9/16 and the hushed mood of the Arietta. Over a tonic-dominant pedal in the left hand—strictly rhythmical demisemiquaver triplets—the harmonies of the Arietta are heard on the weak beats of the bar (second, fifth, and eighth) enriched in several instances by chromatic alterations. Instead of the repeat Beethoven writes a variation within a variation: a pianissimo episode with the two hands of the pianist moving in thirds and sixths, high in the treble range of the instrument and executing delicate demisemiquaver figures over a supporting staccato which follows the harmonic skeleton of the Arietta. Bülow speaks of this passage as a 'dance of the sylphs', but the association of 'sylph' seems to me wholly misleading. If this is in some sense a dance, then it is the morning stars, the motes of the sunbeam, or the Lucretian atoms that are dancing, in any case creatures belonging to an order of creation infinitely removed from that of the nineteenth-century theatre, to which sylphs (whatever their original habitat) belong irrevocably by association. After the second half of the Arietta has been varied in the same way, the pianist finds himself with both hands above the leger lines in the treble clef and within the same octave. The atmosphere is rarified at this height above the *terra firma* of the keyboard, but peaceful, and Beethoven is unwilling to descend. Instead he prolongs the ecstasy, to which he gives a momentary touch of blurredness by the repeated cluster of fourths.

Ex. 51

Then, descending at last, he embarks on a long cadence, still in an undimmed C major, exploring long, wave-like figures in the bass to counter the high oscillations of the treble that have occupied the ear for so long. This comes to rest on a trill which seems to herald the end of the variation, a D which the ear takes to be the supertonic of C but which becomes, in an exquisite diminuendo change of perspective, the leading note of E flat. It is on the dominant seventh chord of E flat that this floating, fluttering cadenza-like passage comes to rest, in a long triple trill, through which the root B♭ sounds rhythmically in the left hand like a quiet bell (Ex. 52). Again the ear expects a cadence, but again the music moves away—a series of single-note trills moving slowly, crescendo, up to the very topmost octave of the keyboard, where once again there is a halt on D countered in the deep bass by a B♭.

Ex. 52

The two hands move still further apart from each other in a quotation from the Arietta, which gains an extraordinary poignancy (and one that needs no underlining from the player) by the extreme contrast of pitch. The broken melody that follows, 'espressivo' over repeated chords, recalls the arioso of op. 110 and through its gradual descent we finally approach the fifth and last variation.

Here the theme returns in its simple contours but accompanied by the demisemiquaver figures and triplets which have been developed during the fourth variation—repeated chords in the right hand below the melody and widely spaced, rolling and harmonically shifting broken chords in the left. But Beethoven's longing for the air of the heights is still not satisfied, and the last time we hear the melody of the Arietta (or rather its first half) it is surrounded by a long (eleven-bar) dominant trill and delicate demisemiquaver triplets providing the harmony—an ethereal, floating effect that hardly ceases when the whole complex of sound is transferred to a lower pitch, and returns undimmed in the crystalline scales in sixths that lead to the ultimate cadence.

Opus 120. Diabelli Variations

What Schindler or Schlesinger or anyone else expected to follow this movement is indeed hard to imagine. It was after finishing op. 111 that Beethoven remarked that the pianoforte 'is and always will be an unsatisfactory instrument'[1]; but since early 1819 he had been working on another work for the instrument which was not finished until more than a year after op. 111. This was a set of variations commissioned by the music-publisher Anton Diabelli, who had recently left the firm of Steiner and set up on his own with a certain Peter Cappi. Diabelli was a musician in his own right, teaching the piano and the guitar and composing popular piano pieces, songs, easy church music and a number of unpretentious stage-works. The aim of his commission was to produce a volume representing contemporary Austrian composers, and it was accepted (Beethoven is said to have refused at first) by fifty-one composers in all, including Schubert, Liszt, and Beethoven's pupil, the Archduke Rudolf, who displayed his craftsmanship rather than his sense of humour by writing a fugue on Diabelli's little waltz. The first reference in the letters to these variations is in February 1820, when Beethoven wrote to Simrock of 'grand variations on a German waltz'. In April 1823, immediately after the work was completed, he offered it to Pacini in Paris, to Ries

[1] L. Nohl, Beethoven, Liszt and Wagner, p. 112.

in London (with a dedication to his wife), and a month later to Lissner in St. Petersburg. In fact, however, he received proofs from Diabelli in June and the work appeared in Vienna that month, with a dedication to Antonia Brentano. No wonder that Beethoven felt obliged to give Ries some explanation, and this he did in a letter dated 5 September:

You say that I ought to look around for someone to attend to my affairs. Well, that is the very thing that I did in the matter of the variations—I mean my friends and Schindler looked after them for me, but alas! how badly. The variations were to appear first of all in Vienna after they had been published in London. But everything went wrong. The dedication to Brentano was only to apply to Germany. I was under a great obligation to her and could publish no other work at the time. In any case only the Viennese publisher Diabelli got these variations from me. But everything went through Schindler's hands. I have never met a more wretched fellow on God's earth, an arch-scoundrel whom I have sent packing. . . .

Schindler, as Thayer says, was a convenient whipping-boy for the confusion and consequent embarrassment that accompanied Beethoven's excursions into practical affairs.

The variations, of which Beethoven planned at first six or seven and later twenty-five, rose finally to the number of thirty-three. He was ready to laugh at the theme's 'cobbler's patch' (*Schusterfleck*—colloquial German name for the *rosalia*, or identical repetition of a phrase a step higher in the scale) but Diabelli's waltz revealed an unexpected number of characteristics necessary in a variation theme—a strong if primitive harmonic structure, salient rhythmic traits and a melodic nullity that was itself a kind of virtue. Beethoven's variations are an epitome or microcosm of his musical world. The variety of treatment is almost without parallel, so that the work represents a book of advanced studies in Beethoven's manner of expression and his use of the keyboard, as well as a monumental work of art in its own right. A few statistics will show that this diversity was founded in a quite extraordinary unity, and that this apparently unpretentious set of pieces does indeed deserve to be called monumental.

Diabelli's waltz, C major 3/4, has thirty-two bars, and nine of Beethoven's thirty-three variations preserve all these three characteristics (two more are in C major 3/4 and have, by elision, thirty-one bars). No fewer than twenty-eight variations retain the C major tonality, while four are in C minor, and the fugue is in the relative major (E flat); there is thus no instance of a distant remove from the original key. The 3/4 metre of the original is preserved in seventeen variations, becomes 3/8 in three, 6/4 in one and 9/8 in one. Only eleven variations desert triple time (ten in 4/4 and one in 2/4). The actual structure of the original is preserved almost as strictly— fifteen variations have the same number of bars as Diabelli's waltz (thirty-two), seven have plain multiples of this number (four have sixteen bars, two have forty-eight and one has sixty-four) and the two variations (counting the finale, without the coda, as one of these) that have twenty-four bars are still manifestly regular. Only one variation, beside the four with thirty-one bars compressed by elision, has the odd number of thirteen, and there is one each with twelve and eighteen bars.

These figures suggest that the wide range of variety and interest in the Diabelli Variations is not achieved, as might be supposed, by any cavalier treatment of the theme. Beethoven seems, on the other hand, to pride himself on the immense wealth that can be extracted, by a balanced mixture of craftsmanship and imagination, from so apparently unpromising a matrix. Although it is possible, and certainly convenient in performance, to make at least one, and possibly two, breaks in the variations, the attempt to force the work into some semblance of a four-movement sonata is a mistake.[1] The first break, after the Presto variation no. 10, does not conclude a first movement in the technical sense; and if we try to regard variations 11–23 as forming a scherzo, we come up against variations 14 and 20, which can belong to no scherzo and are too widely separated to form anything approaching a trio section. The section formed by variations 24–8 inclusive has no unity of character, since it starts with the Fughetta but continues with virtuoso variations; and even the final group starting with no. 29 is really only united by the C minor tonality of the first three variations, which passes through the E flat major of the fugue into the C major of the final Tempo di minuetto.

Where Beethoven himself intended a close affinity between two consecutive variations, he made this clear, either by the similarity of figuration (nos. 16 and 17, 26 and 27) or by relating the tempo of a variation to that of its predecessor. If we accept that this tempo-relationship always implies a further, deeper bond, we must make the following groupings—numbers 2, 3, and 4; 6 and 7; 11 and 12; as well as 16–17 and 26–7, as already noted. The links become much rarer after the early variations, and this is what we should expect in view of the fragmentary nature of the later sketches.[2] Many of these

---

[1] It is with the Bagatelles rather than the sonatas that the Diabelli Variations belong—pithy, witty, penetrating, fugitively touching or noble but always self-contained miniatures, such as the next generation was to elaborate. Such *mutatis mutandis* are Schubert's *Moments musicaux*, Chopin's Preludes and Schumann's *Carnaval, Davidsbündlertänze, Kreisleriana*, etc.

[2] See Nottebohm, II, pp. 568–72.

are on loose single sheets of paper. From the end of 1822 comes a group of sketches for seven variations, clearly numbers 1–7. Among these we can recognize the embryos of variations 3, 4, and 7 in those that the composer has marked 1, 2, and 6. The Alla Marcia which came to form the first of the set (and has for obvious reasons been called the *Meistersinger* variation) was apparently an afterthought, whose aggressive break with the theme's waltz-rhythm probably accounts for the unprepared listener's early abandonment of the thread which in fact so closely links each variation to the original.

It is interesting to see how Beethoven remains true to the distinguishing marks of Diabelli's tune without ever repeating himself. The strong upbeat of the opening, for instance, is found in all but three of the variations (22, 23, and 29) but in every imaginable form—from a single note (8, 20, and 32), a sforzando trill (6, 16, and 21), a two-quaver or triplet figure (3, 4, 5, 7, 9, 10, 11, 12, 15, 17, 18, 19, 26, 27, 30), a chord or chords (1, 2, 13, 14, 28, 33) to the elaborate ornamental septuplet of 31.

In the same way Beethoven's handling of the modulation to the subdominant in bars 8–10 of the first half, and 7–8 of the second half, of the theme is amazingly versatile. He cannot always wait to develop the latent possibilities of this change in direction, and even in no. 2 the dominant of F major appears as early as bar 5 in the second part, prompting Beethoven to a series of highly coloured 'altered' chords containing the melody in the inner parts. In no. 3 the innocent, carefree counterpoint is suddenly interrupted in the same place (bar 5 in the second half) by a patch of dark colour in which the bass murmurs almost without rhythm the phrase that has been passed in clear contrapuntal dialogue from part to part

Ex. 53

The simpler and more limpid the character of the variation the more notable is Beethoven's use of this dark patch as a contrast.[1] It is most marked in no. 12 (nine bars before the end, again rhythmless), no. 15 (bars 8–12) and in no. 18, where in both halves it prompts passages that look forward to the 'romantic' composers of the next generation —Brahms[2] in the mysterious unison quavers of bars 8–16 and Schumann in the breaking up of a 3/4 bar into two groups of three quavers in the last nine bars. It is this modulation in the original that prompts the distant modulations in the minor variations nos. 9, 29, and 30, where Beethoven substitutes the flattened supertonic for the dominant of the theme. In the second half of no. 9 the return to the tonic is an amusing duel between the strong accents on the first beat of the bar in the chromatically rising bass and the insistent counter-accents in the right hand, and this metrical struggle is reflected in the deliberate harmonic misunderstandings between the two hands.

Ex. 54

Neither the Fughetta (no. 24) nor the Fugue (no. 32) adheres closely to Diabelli's harmonic scheme, which is also mocked rather than followed in no. 22. This 'allegro molto alla "Notte e giorno faticar" di Mozart', as Beethoven entitles it,[3] is a musicians' joke, and a very

---

[1] In the highly excited Allegro of no. 16, on the other hand, the reverse contrast is found—an unexpected patch of *pp* D flat major (bars 4–5 of the second part), static in the surrounding tumult.

[2] There is another noticeable pre-echo of Brahms's keyboard manner in no. 8—the close-lying figure in the left hand and the chains of thirds with octave in the right.

[3] Dr. Hans Hollander suggests that this was Beethoven's humorous reaction to Diabelli's persistent pressure to finish the variations.

good one, though to call it as Bülow does 'a sparkling epigram on the
history of the opera from Mozart to Meyerbeer' is characteristically
extravagant. The second half of the variation starts in the remote key
of A flat, by the familiar semitonal 'screwing-up' of the dominant
close to the first part, which left us in G major (cf. op. 106 scherzo,
bars 161 sqq.). This A flat is in its turn turned by an implicit enharmonic pun into E major (A flat = G sharp), and then by progressive
flattening of note after note the tonic C major is reached in two bars

Ex 55

Contrapuntal imitation plays a large part in at least twenty of the
thirty-three variations, and many of them (nos. 4, 6, 12, 14, 19, 20, 23,
and 30) consist wholly or in part of canons. Here again the variety is
prodigious. What seem at a first hearing exercises in finger virtuosity
prove without exception to be thematically derived and organic—
as in no. 23, where the semiquavers in contrary motion in the left hand,
prove to be cancrizans of the right. In no. 14, on the other hand,
the slow, heavy canonic entries with which the second half opens pile
up like blocks of Cyclopean masonry (Bülow speaks of 'high-priestly
solemnity' and advises the player to think of the 'mighty vaults of a
Gothic cathedral'). In no. 20 this solemnity and massiveness take on
the character of a procession entirely in a single unit—two dotted
minims to the bar in 6/4 time. Contrary to all superficial impressions
Beethoven clings almost more closely to Diabelli's original in this
variation than anywhere else. The metamorphosis may be strange, but
it is quite real—

Ex. 56
a (1)

(2)

b (1)

(2)

In a (2) Beethoven delights in converting the conventional *Schuster-fleck* or *rosalias* into the most recondite and elided progressions; and in b (2) he fastens on the F sharp appoggiatura of the theme (b 1) and gives it overwhelming thematic importance in the shape of an accented diminished fourth, ascending in canonic imitation from the deep bass. This Shakespearean combination of, as it were, verbal humour and profound meaning[1] is one of the outstanding traits of Beethoven's last period.

[1] Cp. Goethe's shrewd observation, 'Whenever Lichtenberg makes a joke you will find some problem hidden.'

At the opposite extreme come the purely playful canons of nos. 6 and 9 and no. 4, which opens 'piano dolce' but contains two seven-bar crescendos that gather an enormous momentum. By itself stands no. 30, not one of the two variations in which Beethoven dispenses with the upbeat of the original but one in which this upbeat takes on such importance that its original character is forgotten. This is one of the five minor mode variations, and the closeness of the canonic entries (at two beats distance) combined with Beethoven's strong Neapolitan inclinations (D flat major in C minor) give the whole piece a richly chromatic character. That Beethoven intended this chromatic colouring to be intensely expressive is shown by his generous markings of *legato*, *cantabile* and *espressivo*. In the opening of the second half Bülow even sees, perhaps not too unreasonably, 'the original seed from which all Schumann's romantic harmony was to develop'

Ex. 57

If this passage looks forward to Schumann, it is for a moment difficult to tell whether the delicate ornamentation of no. 31 ('largo, molto espressivo' 9/8) looks backward to the slow movements of the Baroque, or forward to Chopin's harmonically subtle fioriture. But except in bar 2 of the second half, the ornamentation itself and its organic character look backward to the late eighteenth century rather, though the free, rhapsodic handling of bar-lines is as personal to Beethoven as is the intense, concentrated quality of the lyricism. Moreover this variation passes without a break into the fugue of no. 32, where Beethoven is far more under the spell of his master Handel than in the fugal movements of the last piano sonatas.

This is neither a virtuoso movement, like the finale of op. 106, nor a lyrical drama, like the finale of op. 110. There has already been a miniature 'fughetta' in no. 24, a wonderfully limpid yet warm interlude between the fireworks of no. 23 and the transfigured peasant dance of no. 25, with a stretto (bars 6–10 of the second part) whose unaggressive expressive quality prepares the listener for the last tenor and soprano entries of the subject, which Beethoven himself marks, as it were, with a star. The fugue in no. 32 is entirely different from this in character—a double fugue with one subject reproducing the repeated notes of Diabelli's right-hand accompaniment and the other inverting his rising, into falling sequences.

Ex. 58

Beethoven makes use of both subjects inverted and even finds room for tender episodes before the short stretto, ending on a fermata, that introduces the big epilogue. Here the tempo is slightly faster, quaver figures appear for the first time and the main subject is given a new rhythmic shape, with its strong opening upbeat transferred to the downbeat and the phrasing telescoped accordingly. This finally mounts to a climactic chord of the dominant minor ninth over a tonic pedal, widely spread and returning to rest without its bass. Then come six bars of transition, made by an enharmonic process such as we have observed in no. 22 (cf. Ex. 55).

Ex. 59

Poco adagio

This leads into the final variation, no. 33, 'Tempo di minuetto moderato'—but not to be dragged, adds Beethoven—marked 'grazioso e dolce'. In this variation, which Bülow compares to Schumann's 'farewell to the listener' movements, Beethoven transfigures the eighteenth-century dance-form used by Haydn and Mozart, very much as he has transfigured the J. S. Bach adagio movement in no. 31 and the Handelian fugue in no. 32.[1] The writing in this last variation is

---

[1] Was it this that Hanslick had in mind when he wrote that, until Bülow played all Beethoven's last piano works in Vienna in 1881, only Clara Schumann and Brahms had played isolated sonatas 'and nobody could have gone to hear them for pleasure. . . .[It was] a *music-history lecture in examples, illustrations without text*'?

transparently clear and almost tenderly euphonious, the mood relaxed
and serene. As in the finales of opp. 109 and 111 Beethoven seems
drawn instinctively to the upper registers of the instrument; and as
in the finale of Mozart's last piano concerto K.595, the imperceptive
might fail to understand that the simplicity is not the trivial simplicity of
a child's game, but that of a spiritual genius who has apprehended the
ultimate peace and joy that lie behind and beyond life's struggles and
agonies, a genuinely childlike simplicity achieved after a lifetime of
battles and suffering. Already in both halves of the variation itself
the music has taken on the qualities of a kind of celestial ballet, with
rising leaps of tenths and a cascading fall of semiquaver chords. In the
coda, which is as long as the variation itself, these passages return
again, like a gentle firework display illuminating the whole sky in
whose clear upper air all these events take place. For a moment we
return to something very like the last variation in op. 111—a whispered, crystalline figure sounding like a bell and developing into an
exquisite design of broken tenths, such as Chopin was to use twenty
years later in his 'Berceuse'

Ex. 60

A fourfold reference to the subdominant modulation in Diabelli's theme, a cascade of quietly descending figures in imitation and the work ends on a diminuendo, which reaches a pianissimo C major triad followed only two beats later by an explosive sforzando.

Bagatelles opp. 119 and 126

Of the two sets of Bagatelles published by Beethoven in 1823 (op. 119) and 1825 (op. 126) the former set contains, despite Schindler's assurance to the contrary, at least four pieces that almost certainly date from much earlier. These bagatelles, or trifles, resemble in form and character the Moment Musical, the Albumblatt, the Prelude or the genre-piece to which later generations of composers attached considerable importance. To Beethoven they were, like his songs, nothing more than occasional pieces. The publication of these two sets during the last years of his life does not argue any change in his attitude, only the need for ready money. The Bagatelles were in fact pot-boilers; but, as we should expect, Beethoven's pot-boilers are often quite as interesting as other composers' most ambitious and carefully considered works. Hardly one is entirely without interest.

The first piece in op. 119 (Allegretto 3/4 G minor) resembles so closely the scherzo of the violin sonata op. 96, written in 1812, that some relationship must exist. Despite the date in the manuscript '1822, November', the music still belongs to the eighteenth century, and its simple elegance, light staccato, transparent harmony (only warming to a rather thicker texture in the E flat major trio section) recall the works that Mozart wrote for Paris. The second piece (Andante con moto 2/4 C major) may well date back still further, as it bears a distinct resemblance to the coda of the Andante in the C minor trio (op. 1, no. 3) of 1795.[1]

The third of the op. 119 Bagatelles (à l'Allemande' 3/8 D major) dates back to a sketch of 1804 and has no connection with the 'alla tedesca' movement of the B flat major quartet op. 130. The fourth ('Andante cantabile' 4/4 A major) has no known history, but its transparent charm and 'grazioso' marking suggest an early date. The fifth ('Risoluto' C minor 6/8) is an aggressive dance movement, but marked with a strange, faintly exotic quality[2] that marks Pedrillo's serenade ('In Mohrenland gefangen war') in Act II, Scene 3 of *Die*

---

[1] There is a slight but interesting similarity between the theme and that of Beethoven's last public improvisation (see ch. 8, p. 71).

[2] Although the Neapolitan harmony which characterizes Mozart's serenade is only heard in one bar of the Bagatelle, the rhythmic similarity is plain.

Entführung aus dem Serail. The date of the original is before 1804.[1]

With no. 6 we enter a different world. Nottebohm (*Zweite Beethoveniana*, pp. 146–7) argues that no. 6 was written in 1820–1, on the evidence of the first known sketch, which is on the reverse of a page bearing sketches for the Credo of the Missa Solemnis. This is not in itself conclusive; but there are traits in this Allegretto G major 2/4 that suggest a late date. The combination of canonic writing and recitative style in the Andante 3/4 introduction is one of them; and another is the changing of the rhythm as the theme is heard in diminution in bars 31–5 of the Allegretto. Almost conclusive is the coda, which recalls the Allegro vivace of the cello sonata op. 102, no. 1 (see p. 135).

Ex. 61

The last five (nos. 7–11) of the Bagatelles op. 119 were originally Beethoven's contribution to Part III of Friedrich Starke's *Wiener Pianoforte Schule*, which appeared in 1821. Unlike the publisher Peters, who returned the Bagatelles to Beethoven with the remark that he should consider it beneath him to spend his time on trifles such as anyone could write, Starke observed, 'the connoisseur will soon realize that not only is the individual genius of the famous master brilliantly displayed in each piece, but that what Beethoven with characteristic modesty calls 'trifles' (*Kleinigkeiten*) are in fact full of instruction (*lehrreich*) for the performer and demand the most complete penetration into the spirit of the composition'.

No. 7 (3/4 C major) and no. 8 ('Moderato cantabile' 3/4 C major), both belong to the world of the Diabelli Variations. In no. 7 two ideas

[1] Nottebohm, II, pp. 146–7.

are contrasted—a pedal trill which moves from one part to another, and a scherzando figure moving upwards in the right hand and downwards in the left, and then vice versa. The tranquillity that marks most of the twenty-seven bars is rudely shattered in the last five, where the theme is heard in diminution over a pedal trill in the deep bass

Ex. 62

There is a momentary hark-back to the finale of op. 106 in bar 5 of the example (compare bar 197 of the fugue in op. 106). No. 8 is a close relation of the Fughetta, variation 24, in the Diabelli Variations, as is shown by the last six bars

Ex. 63

No. 9 ('Vivace moderato' A minor 3/4) is a waltz, such as Beethoven might have improvised, on an A minor broken triad with a
Neapolitan cadence. No. 10 ('Allegramente' A major 2/4) starts
clearly in E major, and only reaches the tonic in the fifth of its twelve
bars. Thirds and sixths in the right hand and a syncopated tonic and
dominant ding-dong in the left; the formula could hardly be simpler,
but no other composer would have lit on just this lay-out. No 11
('Andante ma non troppo' B flat major 4/4) is a hymn-like piece of
great simplicity, and shares with variation 11 of the Diabelli Variations
the unique marking 'innocentemente e cantabile' ('innocente' in op.
120) There are at least two unmistakable Beethoven finger-prints
both melodic—(a) from *Fidelio*[1] and (b) the Ninth Symphony

Ex. 64 (a)

Ex. 64 (b)

The importance which Beethoven himself attached to the Six
Bagatelles of op. 126 is clearly shown by the studies which exist in the
sketchbooks.[2] There seems no doubt that all of these pieces, even if in
some cases based on earlier ideas, were composed entirely during the
period immediately before their publication. The first, 'Andante con
moto' (G major 3/4) is an eight-bar song-like melody, which Beethoven immediately varies in a purely ornamental way. After four bars
of what starts as a second strain, in the dominant, Beethoven's attention is suddenly caught by a single phrase, and instead of continuing
the melody he embarks on variations of this phrase

[1] But compare also the final cadence of Schubert's song 'Geheimes', whose rhythm appears in
the development section of the first movement of the B flat major quartet op. 130, see p. 373.
See Nottebohm, *Zweite Beethoveniana*, pp. 193 ff.

Ex. 65

When the D major cadence is reached, a cadenza supervenes, after which the original theme appears in the bass, but only for four bars. The right hand then takes up the same four bars a third higher; and after a G major cadence, eight bars of delicately imitative writing form a coda. This whole second half of the piece, after the coda, is richer harmonically and more eloquently flowing than the opening; and it is difficult to avoid the impression that the composer did indeed change his mind at the 2/4 'l'istesso tempo' (ex. 65), not only about the course of the music at that moment but about the whole nature of the piece.

No. 2 Allegro (G minor 2/4) originally started an octave lower and the typical keyboard figuration—what can have persuaded Hans von Bülow that the piece was 'obviously conceived for string quartet'?— was entrusted to the left hand alone, an octave lower. The cantabile middle section is suddenly halted at a C minor cadence by a series of stormy interjections culminating in a characteristic exploitation of keyboard extremes

Ex. 66

After a repeat of the middle section the piece ends quietly.

No. 3 Andante (E flat major 3/8) is a serene, hymn-like piece. Indeed the first twenty-four bars, up to the cadenza, might easily have been conceived for a quartet of wind instruments. After the sweeping, harp-like cadenza and two bars recitative the theme returns cantabile in the left hand beneath a long trill in the right. The melody is on the weak beats of the bar, and then passes to the right hand, which executes elegant demisemiquaver variations in Beethoven's earlier manner. The four bars postlude are based on what, in the sketch-books, seem to have been designed as a prelude to the piece.

No. 4 Presto (B minor 4/4) has the rhythm of the bourrée and contrapuntal passages alternate with simple homophony and even unisons. The B major trio is constructed on a single rhythmic figure repeating over an open-fifth drone in the left hand. Both sections repeat, making this by far the longest of the Bagatelles in either set. No. 5 Quasi allegretto (G major 6/8) is described by von Bülow as an idyll, and its flowing quaver figures, one hand answering the other, have a pastoral charm which in the middle section seems to anticipate that of the rural scenes in Liszt's *Années de pélérinage*.

Ex. 67

The sixth and last of these Bagatelles, Presto (E flat major 4/4) followed by 'Andante amabile' 3/8, bears a superficial resemblance to no. 3. Here the prelude has survived, and takes the form of six bars of very fast scale passages ending with a dramatic flourish, as though setting the stage for an operatic aria. The melody which follows, though, is entirely instrumental in character and the semiquaver triplets are a reminder that these pieces were written within a few years of Chopin's early works and the glittering, salon piano music of Weber, Mendelssohn, and Hummel.

Ex. 68   Andante amabile e con moto

Very different from this last, and weakest, of the Bagatelles of op. 126 is the 'Rondo a capriccio' found among Beethoven's papers and given the opus no. 129 by his publisher. Von Bülow regarded this as an authentic 'parergon of the last creative period' and flays Lenz for referring to the work as '449 bars from the composer's earliest period, and quite without interest'—a judgement, says von Bülow, 'worthy of that Kalmuk Ulybyshev'.[1] The discovery of the autograph in 1945 prompted an article by Erich Hartmann (*Musical Quarterly*, April, 1946) which showed that the work was written probably between 1795 and 1798. The title was originally 'Alla ingharese, quasi un Capriccio' ('ingharese' being a confusion between 'ongarese' and 'zingarese'). The words 'Die Wut über den verlornen Groschen ausgetobt in einer Kaprize' are not in Beethoven's handwriting.

[1] Alexander Dimitrevich Ulybyshev (1794–1858) author of a *Nouvelle Biographie de Mozart* (Moscow, 1844) in which he depreciated Beethoven. When attacked on this score, he published *Beethoven, ses critiques et ses glossateurs* (Leipzig and Paris, 1857). Ulybyshev was the patron of Balakirev, whom he introduced to Glinka.

CHAPTER 17

The Missa Solemnis.
Op. 123

In 1818 Beethoven was working on the piano sonata op. 106 instead
of the symphony which he had promised to write for London. The
sonata's first two movements were finished in April of this year, the
last two in the spring of 1819, and this whole period of Beethoven's
life was deeply shadowed by the law-suit over the guardianship of his
nephew. His mind, however, was full of plans for future works, and
during this year he let fall the observation that he wished to compose
'a whole symphony in the old modes'. His increasing occupation with
counterpoint had stimulated this interest in old music and we have
seen him three years earlier, in 1815, dreaming of ending his life as
musical director of a small court chapel, where he could compose and
perform church music.

At some time in the middle of 1818 he received, unofficially, a
piece of information that turned these vague aspirations into a firm
proposition—his royal pupil, the Archduke Rudolf, was to be appointed
Archbishop of Olmütz (Olomouc) in Moravia. This event would
clearly be celebrated in the most magnificent manner, since the
Archduke was brother of the reigning Emperor, and nothing would
be more suitable than that Beethoven should write a large-scale setting
of the Mass for the occasion. The official announcement of the Archduke's appointment, which was given an added importance by the
fact that he had in the meantime been created a cardinal by Pius VII,
was not until 4 June 1819; but in his letter of congratulation, written
the same month, Beethoven refers to 'the day on which a solemn Mass
composed by me will be performed during the ceremonies performed
for Y.I.H.', and the sketch-books make it clear that he had started
to work on the Kyrie of what was to become the Missa Solemnis
by the spring of 1819. (See footnote on p. 39, Part I, ch. 4.) The
sketches of the Gloria were completed in 1819, those of the Credo

in 1820,[1] and the whole Mass existed in draft by the beginning of 1822. The consecration ceremony had meanwhile taken place on 20 March 1820; but the Archduke himself was quite aware that although immediately prompted by this event, the Mass had meanwhile taken on proportions and importance that quite transcended any individual occasion; and he seems to have urged Beethoven not to be in a hurry to publish.[2]

We can certainly believe Schindler when he says that 'from the beginning of his work on the Mass Beethoven's whole personality seemed to take on a different form, as was noticed especially by his older friends. Never before or after have I seen him in such a condition of *Erdenentrücktheit* (oblivion of everything earthly).' It is also perhaps worth noting that it was precisely during this first half of 1819, when he was deep in the composition of the Mass, that Beethoven was most favourably inclined to the scheme of sending his nephew Karl to be educated at Landshut by Father Sailer, whose book *Friedrich Christians Vermächtnis an seine Söhne* ('Frederick Christian's Legacy to his Sons') he also bought at this time. A certain unidentified Father Ignatius was advising him in the conduct of his law-suit, and Zacharias Werner's *Spiritual Exercises for Three Days* is noted in the conversation-books.[3] It would be wholly false to suggest that Beethoven became anything like an orthodox Christian, still less a practising Catholic at this or any other time: there is no evidence or record of his having attended Mass or frequented any of the sacraments. But a comparison of his first Mass (1807) with the Missa Solemnis makes it clear that at fifty he was finding new and very much deeper, more personal significance in the text of the Mass than he had found as a young man. He was no doubt also aware of the assistance that the Church might offer him both in removing his nephew from undesirable influences and in training him morally and intellectually. One of his most frequent visitors of these months, Josef Karl Bernard, whose name recurs perpetually in the conversation-books,

---

[1] The notebook entry in which Beethoven reminds himself of the preparation needed for writing church music is quoted on p. 38. This probably dates from the summer of 1818. Schindler's information that Beethoven was working on the Credo in August 1819, may be true; but we know from the sketch-books that he was certainly working on the 'Gloria' and in Schindler's anecdote (see p. 39) of finding the composer 'singing parts of the fugue in the Credo—singing, howling and stamping', when he visited him at Mödling this month, probably refers in fact to the 'In gloria Dei Patris' of the Gloria. Schindler was certainly wrong when he said that the Credo was complete by October 1819. See Nottebohm, *Zweite Beethoveniana*, p. 148 sqq.

[2] See Beethoven's letter to Franz Brentano, 19 May 1822.

[3] See p. 109.

seems to have combined at least a conventional adherence to Catholicism with liberal opinions surprising in an editor-in-chief of the
Wiener Zeitung under the Metternich régime.

Beethoven never worked on any single composition exclusively,
and the sketch-books show that by the end of 1817, or the beginning
of 1818, he had already done a considerable amount of work on what
were to be the first two movements of the Ninth Symphony. A stray
sheet belonging almost certainly to the second half of 1818 shows
that even at so late a date, when the conception of the Missa
Solemnis might have been expected to be filling his whole mind, he
was planning two new symphonies. During the four and a half years
which elapsed between the first conception of the Mass, in the second
half of 1818, and its final completion in December 1822, we know
that Beethoven conceived and completed the last three piano sonatas
(opp. 109, 110, 111), the Diabelli Variations and the Bagatelles
op. 119; the overture *Die Weihe des Hauses*; and a number of trivial
commissions. In 1822, before finally completing the Mass, he began
the string quartet op. 127 (May) and we know that he resumed work
on the Ninth Symphony in September, though it is impossible to be
sure how much it had been in his mind during the last four years.

If Beethoven's general plan of working may seem to us impossibly
confused and overloaded, it is very different with his ordering of the
different movements of a large work. That the Missa Solemnis[1] was
planned from the outset on a large scale is clear from every circumstance. Although, as wc have seen, no sketches exist for the Kyrie,
an entry in one of the conversation-books (March–May 1819)
contains the note 'Preludium of the Kyrie to be played loud by the
organist and then decrescendo until before the *piano* [before the]
Kyrie'. This presumably refers to bars 18–20 in the score, where a
sudden swell and decrescendo is marked in the organ part. Beethoven
seems to have worked in strict order on the earlier movements of the
Mass. According to Nottebohm (II, pp. 148 ff.) the Gloria was
completely sketched before the opening theme of the Credo was
determined; and while he was working on the Credo, the notebook
entry 'Benedictus in C vno. solo, corno s. fagotto s violoncello', makes
it clear that he had not decided even the key of the Benedictus. The

---

[1] When Beethoven's 'Hohe Messe' is translated as 'High Mass', what is in fact a technical
liturgiological term is being used incorrectly. 'High Mass' (German *Hochamt*) is one celebrated by priest, deacon, and subdeacon and has no particular reference to the character of the
music. At a Solemn Mass (Missa Solemnis) the celebrant may well be assisted by deacon and
subdeacon, but the name describes the general character, rather than defining the liturgical
nature, of the ceremony.

sketches for the Agnus Dei are to be found among those for the Credo, but we can establish no certain chronology for the later movements of the work after the Credo, finished in 1820.

Although no thematic sketches for the Kyrie survive, isolated progressions in the sketch-books seem to show Beethoven having difficulty with the strict rules of syntax proper to an austere choral style. In the eighth bar of the Kyrie there are in fact consecutive octaves between the viola and bass parts, and in an earlier version of the same passage there were parallel octaves between violins and violas; and other similar progressions gave Beethoven trouble.[1] The extreme simplicity of the whole movement is both a measure of the wholeheartedness, or single-mindedness, with which Beethoven approached the text and one cause of the overwhelming effect of the music in performance. Here no intricate questions of theology are involved, only a belief in a personal God and in Christ as a mediator; and the evidence of Beethoven's personal notebooks suggests that the feeling of human insufficiency and dependence on a loving Father were deep instincts that he never found it necessary to examine or justify intellectually. The shape of the Kyrie is as simple as its harmonic scheme—a first section of eighty-five bars never moving far from the tonic D major; a middle section of half that length (forty-two bars) and keeping even more closely to the key of B minor: and finally a return to a variation of the first section (ninety-six bars, including the short coda). The movement carries, beside the marking 'Assai sostenuto. Mit Andacht' (Very sustained. With devotion), Beethoven's personal aspiration—'Von Herzen—möge es wieder zu Herzen gehen!' ('From the heart—may it penetrate to the heart again!') In no other movement of the Missa Solemnis are the four solo voices so closely integrated with the chorus as here, where their function is simply to lead the main body of singers in the prayer for mercy and forgiveness, not to be the mouthpieces of revelation or the heralds of mystery. It is the soloists whose voices enter on the decisive first beat of the bar, like the trumpets and timpani at the very opening of the work. The chorus, like the rest of the orchestra, enter on the third beat, so that there is an implied urgency as the natural emphasis on the first beat of the bar comes to reinforce, like a pulsation, the fading emphasis of the original attack

[1] Nottebohm, II, p.154.

Ex. 1

This is still further enhanced, in the third of the choral 'Kyries', by the combination of tonic and dominant harmony.

The whole of the opening, up to the modulation to the subdominant in bar 45, is shot through with the phrase of three rising notes which Ernest Newman traces[1] as an 'obsession' in Beethoven's slow movements (A in Ex. 1). After the return to D major in bars 49–50 the suspensions pass to the orchestra and the choral entries are on the strong

[1] Newman, *The Unconscious Beethoven* (1927), pp. 79 ff.

first beat of the bar, while the soloists are silent until the next section, the 'Christe eleison', which begins at bar 86. Here the time changes from 4/4 to 3/2, the pace quickens slightly and the relative minor (B) replaces the tonic. Harmonically most noticeable is Beethoven's use of thirds throughout the 'Christe' section. They are heard at once in the woodwind (bars 86–7) and the soloists soon pair off in the euphonious 'companionate' thirds which, as we shall see later in the Credo, seem to have been associated in Beethoven's mind with the idea of Christ as man's friend and helper. This whole section flows smoothly, whereas the movement of the Kyrie suggested successive waves beating with perpetually renewed vigour and 'taking the kingdom of heaven by storm'. In the second Kyrie, the invocation to the third person of the Blessed Trinity, this wave-like movement returns, but the voices enter in the subdominant (G major) instead of the tonic; the soloists appear in a different order; and the music modulates, after the return to the subdominant in bar 160, in a new direction—through E flat major, C minor to what appears, over a six-bar dominant pedal, to be going to be a full close in D major. This is interrupted at the last moment, and the D major cadence postponed for twenty bars, by two final assaults (bars 190–3 and 198–201) each of which rises from a moment's silence and then breaks, wave-like, over the bar-line

Ex. 2

After the second of these two great supplications the words 'Kyrie eleison' grow gradually softer, passing from part to part during the short coda, though the suspensions of the opening are still heard in the woodwind right to the end of the movement.

In the Kyrie, a triple yet unified cry for mercy, there was as little scope for word-painting as for theological speculation. On the other hand, the successive clauses of the Gloria, which follows, admit both. Beethoven's awareness of the immensity and 'otherness', the trans-cendental majesty of the unimaginable Deity, here finds expression in an elaborate movement constructed from strongly contrasting materials, chosen very carefully to illustrate the verbal sense of each clause. Nowhere is his debt to Handel clearer than here—from the dramatically extrovert D major blaze of the opening, the reminiscence of 'Glory to God' in *Messiah* at 'et in terra pax' and the fugato at 'Glorificamus Te' to the great fugue at 'In gloria Dei Patris'. After the repeated opening cries of 'Gloria!' against the tremolando scales of the strings the music comes to a sudden halt on the dominant and a soft, lightly accompanied episode begins at 'et in terra pax'. 'Laudamus Te' returns to the movement and the ascending fifth of the opening, but only for fourteen bars, when 'adoramus Te' brings another halt and quick change of mood. This in its turn lasts only three bars, and the fugato of 'glorificamus Te' which follows from bars 83 to 127 is itself bisected by the sudden dramatic reappearance of the pianissimo 'adoramus Te'. By a sudden and very characteristic harmonic side-step Beethoven deflects the end of the fugato from the G major (or E minor) cadence which the listener expects, to the first of four colossal affirmations of C major which occupy strategic positions in this pre-dominantly D major movement. This lasts ten bars (117–27) for chorus and orchestra and is then reaffirmed for six bars by the orchestra alone.

When the third of the C major triad is flattened in a sudden piano and the woodwind takes over alone, a 'meno allegro cantabile' melody in B flat introduces the first wholly lyrical episode in the Missa Solemnis. Here, in the 'Gratias agimus', the soloists are heard for the first time in the movement, first the tenor and then the soprano taking over the caressing melody announced by the clarinet. The chorus gradually insinuate themselves into this sensuous play of thirds and sixths, until the tempo changes and at 'Domine Deus' the music returns to the mood of the opening of the Gloria. At the word 'omnipotens' in the phrase 'Deus Pater Omnipotens' there is a triple forte climax, where the trombones make their appearance for the first time in the Mass (bar 186), with both orchestra and chorus characteristically anticipating the strong first beat of the bar. The harmony remains for three bars that of the dominant seventh of E flat and then, revealing the fact that this is an augmented 6th on the flat submediant of D,

Ex. 3

expands—the sopranos rising and the basses dropping a semitone to A, and so to a brusque D major cadence. The effect is one of enormous precipitation, dashing the listener from the heights and giving him hardly a moment to recover his balance before he finds himself once again among the 'companionate' thirds of the 'Domine fili unigenite'. After only seventeen bars the brilliant scales of the opening return in 'Domine Deus', which brings the first part of the Gloria to an end, on another fortissimo climax (ten bars) at 'Filius Patris'. This is the second C major burst, harmonically less surprising because it ends a section in F major, not D major, but lent further force by the syncopated rhythm of the inner parts under the sopranos' dominant pedal.

Ex. 4

(continued on p. 230)

This quick succession of violently contrasted tempi, textures and moods in the Gloria, so puzzling at a first hearing, is easily explained by Beethoven's concern with word-painting, his desire to reflect in music every shade of meaning in the text, to leave no single bar neutral or inexpressive. Such occupation with dramatic detail gives the music that kaleidoscopic and restless character which, among other features, makes the Missa Solemnis unsuitable for liturgical performance. The concern certainly did not spring from any lack of conviction in Beethoven, rather the reverse. But the definition of true liturgical music is that it should be secondary to the liturgy of which it is an adornment; and although any congregation can pray the Kyrie with Beethoven, in the Gloria (and some later sections of the Missa Solemnis, as we shall see) he gives his personal reactions to every phrase of the text such vivid, even violent expression that the music claims the whole of the listener's attention, while the text is totally absorbed and disappears from the listener's consciousness.

The second part of the Gloria opens larghetto 2/4 in F major and

the 'Qui tollis', as an invocation of Christ, naturally brings a return to the writing in thirds between the soloists and, in the prayer for mercy, a speaking flexibility of line which communicates itself even to the chorus. Mention of the world's sins ('peccata mundi') brings the vivid suggestion of a shudder in the strings and an anguished chord of the diminished seventh (bars 256–7). Parallel to this is the shudder of awe heard in the strings at the 'qui sedes ad dexteram Patris', a triad fanfare lasting only four bars but taking the sopranos up to the top B flat

Ex. 5

qui   se-des ad dex-te - ram pa - tris,

qui   se-des ad dex-te - ram pa - tris,

qui   se-des ad·dex-te - ram pa - tris,

qui   se-des ad·dex-te - ram pa - tris,

It is very characteristic of the Missa Solemnis, and particularly of the Gloria, that although this first invocation of Christ 'seated at the right hand of the Father' is a fortissimo B flat major fanfare, the prayer for mercy which follows it immediately is a pianissimo D flat major (with what is perhaps an echo of the shuddering figure continuing in the strings) modulating restlessly though smoothly through G flat (F sharp) major to F sharp minor, D major and so to G major in eight bars, before the invocation is repeated. This time the fanfare is reduced to two bars unison tenors and basses (possibly a Gregorian 'fossil')

Ex. 6

with merely a trumpet accompaniment, but the cries of 'miserere nobis!' become increasingly urgent. They reach a climax after a wonderfully effective silence (bar 291), which lasts only a single beat but lends great emphasis to the harsh fortissimo brass and woodwind chord that follows (see Example 7 on opposite page) and to the desolate choral entry on the second inversion of the F sharp minor triad. This whole section of the 'Gloria' reveals unmistakably how deeply Beethoven felt the need of mercy and forgiveness. In the 'Kyrie' he had been voicing, as it were, the need of the whole community, the whole of humanity. Here, however, the pleas for mercy take on a more personal, intimate character which is further intensified in the last ten bars of the section by his addition to the Latin text ('ah!' or 'o, miserere nobis') although this addition was probably made for a musical reason also, so that the petition could start on the strong first beat of the bar. The voices end in C sharp major (dominant of F sharp minor) and their falling fifth is repeated through the orchestra, ending with a pizzicato C sharp, which is taken up *pp* by oboe and

Ex. 7

bassoon and given a new meaning by the soft timpani roll on A. This sudden drop of a major third, throwing the held note into an entirely new light and bringing a modulation to the formality of the flattened sixth, was a favourite device with Beethoven in his last works. We have met it already in the piano sonatas (in op. 101, where the F major scherzo follows immediately on the A major first movement, and in op. 106 at the transition from the Largo to the fugue in the finale) and we shall find it at a climactic place in the finale of the Ninth Symphony. (See p. 332.)[1]

On this occasion it ushers in the 'Quoniam Tu solus sanctus', a strongly rhythmic triadic theme, fanfare-like in rhythm and strongly modal in harmonic character, an archaic succession of perfect consonances (A major, G major, C major, G major, A major, D major) such as Beethoven must have repeatedly noticed in the works of Palestrina and the other sixteenth-century masters whose scores we know he read at this time.

Ex. 8

1. Gloria "Quoniam Tu"   2. "Et resurrexit"

3. "Sanctus"

This deliberate high-lighting, or using for dramatic effect, of a chord-sequence now archaic but once part of the everyday, by no means heightened, language of music has interesting parallels in the other arts of Beethoven's day, as of our own. We find it in the deliberate medievalisms of Keats and Chatterton, for instance; in Grétry's evocation of medieval music in *Richard Cœur de Lion* (which Beethoven probably knew from Bonn, as he wrote piano variations on 'Une fièvre brûlante'); and in the Nazarene school of German painters; while

[1] For a further discussion of this see ch. 7, pp. 426 ff.

the masses of the Munich Palestrina-enthusiasts Kaspar Ett and Johann
Kaspar Aiblinger are evidence of what was later to become a movement of little more than musical pastiche. There is of course no question of anything in the nature of pastiche in the Missa Solemnis, but
we shall have to return to this archaic element in the score when we
discuss the description of the Missa Solemnis as a neo-classical work.

In the great climax at 'Tu solus altissimus' (bars 338–44) Beethoven
intensifies the rhythmic excitement which we have seen (Ex. 4) in a
similar passage at 'Filius Patris'. At 'Filius Patris' the syncopated
rhythms of the inner parts were given to the chorus, doubled by the
woodwind. Here the voices hold the single note (A) while the woodwind, brass, organ, and lower strings enormously increase the tension
by double-dotted rhythms which are tied across the bar lines, giving
the music an ecstatic, stormy character.

Ex. 9

This great acclamation is followed by two others, one of nine and the other of six bars' length; and in both the voices are left sounding while the orchestra is silent (except, in the second case, for the bassoons and horns doubling the voices). On the second syllable of the 'amen' that follows the 'in gloria Dei Patris', the basses of the chorus begin the fugue that occupies the fourth and last part of the 'Gloria'. Although Handelian in outline, the subject is given an unmistakably personal character by the heavy accentuation of the four strong beats in each bar with a sforzando marking. This does not appear in the voice parts or in the trombones, but in the lower strings and the woodwind. The megatherian gait thus communicated to the fugal subject is further emphasized by the rhythmic character of the countersubject— an 'amen' always leaning heavily on to the tied first beat of the bar Developed by the whole orchestra doubling the voices, this four-part fugue parades its full paraphernalia of inversions, augmentations, diminutions, shifted accents, and strettos with a ruthlessness, a single-minded concern with the logical elaboration of an idea, and a disregard for the listener's sensibilities that is magnificent and silences criticism The soloists embark on the stretto proper, soon joined by the chorus which, again doubled by the orchestra, hammers out the fugal subject in augmentation over nineteen bars of dominant pedal (horns, trombones, timpani, organ, and doublebasses)

The tempo then quickens and the soloists introduce the peroration. This includes a passage in which two of the soloists sing the scales of the fugal subject in contrary motion and another where the whole chorus hammers out the fugal subject in unison. This leads to the last of the great affirmations of C major (bars 493–500),

Ex. 10

making the extraordinary effect of a flattened enclave in a D major movement, whose thread is taken up again immediately in 'Amens' antiphonally exchanged between chorus and soloists. There is a similar moment of 'flattened' ecstasy in the coda (bars 554–6) where Beethoven introduces the initial theme of the Gloria at an even faster tempo than before (Presto instead of Allegro vivace). After the sopranos of the choir have risen from A to B flat and from B flat to B natural, the Glorias continue to ring out, homophonically now, like the shouts of a great crowd—in D major, in A major and then, as though the wind had suddenly changed or one part of the crowd had taken a wrong turning, the basses and tenors lead, hurrying ahead of the rest, into C major before plunging into the G major which brings back the final shout in D major—with the voices echoing the orchestra and sounding a bar and a half after the instruments have fallen silent (Ex. 11).

In this whole final section of the 'Gloria' there is an element of that excess, or 'nimiety', already noted in the fugal finale of op. 106. These movements indeed foreshadow the *kolossal* that was to mark the music of Wagner and much else of late nineteenth-century German art and reach its extreme limit in Richard Strauss's *Alpensinfonie* and *Symphonia Domestica*, in Mahler's Eighth Symphony and Schoenberg's *Gurre-lieder*. But what, in Wagner's *Tristan*, only thirty-five years after the Missa Solemnis, was a conscious intention to stun the listener, to bludgeon him into submission,[1] was in Beethoven's case something very different—a vision of power and magnificence to be celebrated with every resource of his art. These resources included, beside a highly personal command of contrapuntal writing, an instinct for the grandiose and the dramatically striking that was characteristic of his age. For it should not be forgotten that Beethoven was a contemporary not only of Cherubini, but of Spontini. A year after finishing the Missa Solemnis he expressed an unexpectedly favourable opinion of Spontini's music to Karl Gottfried Freudenberg. 'There is much good in Spontini', he said. 'He understands theatrical effects and the musical noises of warfare thoroughly.' Perhaps the only work of Beethoven's that really recalls Spontini is the *Battle of Vittoria*; but what was merely grandiose in Spontini, an imposing façade masking a somewhat commonplace personality, was genuine grandeur of character in Beethoven. Those who, sensing the very real element of Napoleonic grandiosity in Beethoven's music, are suspicious of the nature of the musical inspiration itself, will be hard put to it to find any hollow

---

[1] Elliot Zuckerman, *The First Hundred Years of Wagner's 'Tristan'* (1964), p. 21. '*Tristan* is intentionally over-effective. The listener is supposed to be overwhelmed.'

Ex. 11

spots where grandeur of form conceals trivial ideas, as often happens in the case of Spontini.[1] In the 'In gloria Dei Patris' fugue of the Missa Solemnis the element of excess, although liturgically out of place, is so bound up with the composer's personality and so free of any trace of insincerity or effect-seeking that the listener accepts it, if not at once, at least after he has acquired a deeper knowledge and understanding of the work.

So far not even the most sensitive believer could discern any faltering in Beethoven's treatment of the text of the Mass, and certainly no lack of zeal or intensity in the musical expression of his faith—rather the reverse, if anything. Paul Bekker[2] finds the 'Kyrie' and the 'Gloria' the movements of the Mass in which Beethoven is most completely at home—

he not only borrows the words of the Christian rite, he makes use of their imaginative stimulus. Not only as a musician but as a thinker he enters into that crisis . . . where some definite attitude towards the problems of belief is forced upon a man and becomes a condition of further spiritual growth. For Beethoven the crisis results in a joyful, confident yea-saying to the essentials of the Christian faith. As surely as the Missa Solemnis is a most exalted memorial of perfected understanding between a man and his God, so surely does this understanding rest on a Christian philosophy of life.

With the 'Credo' we leave petition and worship and approach the intellectual formulation of belief, a field in which only a philosophically or theologically trained mind will move with ease or certainty. The vast majority of believing Christians are content with an assent that is less intellectual than emotional; their chief concern is with the consecration and strengthening of the will by humble contemplation of truths at which the intellect may grasp but which it can never wholly master. As we have seen in an earlier chapter, it is not possible to discover how orthodox a Christian Beethoven was in his beliefs; but it is perfectly clear that he was not content, like Schubert, to treat any part of the liturgical text in a negative way, to provide a generally appropriate musical setting without penetrating to the real issues involved in each clause. On the other hand it is often the very intensity of his response that, as we have seen, unfits his setting for liturgical

---

[1] The cases of Beethoven and Chopin are similar in that each made use of fashionable forms mostly used by their inferiors for trivial purposes—the grandiose-dramatic in the one case and the salon-charming in the other—to express some of their greatest ideas. Their works in these forms are, no doubt, incidentally grandiose drama and salon music, but they are something much more beside.

[2] Paul Bekker, *Beethoven*, pp. 270–1 (English edition).

performance. Beethoven does not in any sense shirk the issues of the Credo, which is in the first place an affirmation of faith in the existence, omnipotence and fatherhood of God; in the incarnation, death, and resurrection of Christ and its atoning, mediative power; and the existence of the Church as the covenanted instrument through which God communicates grace to men, whom he has destined to an eternal life with Him. This general scheme of faith is filled with a number of details that concern theologians more than ordinary Christians—the exact relationship between the Father and the Son in the earlier part of the creed, and between the Holy Ghost and the two other members of the Trinity in the second; the credentials and precise functions of the Church. These later 'articles' of the creed are not only less inspiring than the general affirmations of the Christian faith; they are also very much less suited to musical setting in Beethoven's dramatic, illustrative manner. It is therefore impossible to argue that a composer who gives less musical importance to, say, 'et in unam sanctam catholicam at apostolicam ecclesiam' than to 'et incarnatus est' or 'et vitam venturi saeculi' is a poor churchman. Beethoven may well have been a poor churchman, but we cannot prove this by the degrees of enthusiasm with which he handled the various clauses of the creed. The composers who in fact treat all clauses with equal enthusiasm (or lack of enthusiasm) are divided into two classes. In the first are those for whom the liturgical text is a sacred formula in the musical setting of which all explicit statements of personality are out of place. This class includes probably the great majority of church music-composers. In the second are those for whom all the clauses are equally meaningless, and these must in the nature of things include composers who have been glad to find a discreet refuge in the ranks of the former class where, by definition, they cannot be identified with any certainty.

In examining the 'Credo' of the Missa Solemnis we shall repeatedly be confronted with the question how far it is legitimate to conclude anything definite about Beethoven's beliefs from his handling of the details of the text. Are we, for instance, to attach any doctrinal significance to the fact that in bars 15–17 the word 'patrem' appears at first with a sforzando on each syllable, and in the next bar marked piano? If, as seems certain, there is none but a purely musical reason to account for this, where do musical reasons end and doctrinal reasons begin? and is there any criterion by which we may distinguish one from the other? All Beethoven's reasons were in the first place musical, of course, but it seems unquestionable that while some were exclusively musical, others were fortified by an extra-musical element. The opening bars of the 'Credo' are a case in point. Is the orchestra's initial leap, which recalls that at the opening of op. 106, a leap of faith? and are the rugged entries of the first theme, with its suspensions and ascents into the void symbolical of Beethoven's battle against doubt? are the suspensions, as it were, suspensions of disbelief? and when the bass line in bar 8 climbs towards an E flat that is in fact sung by the sopranos while the basses break off prematurely, are we to believe that Beethoven dispatched the basses to the heights in search for a God that they never found, and that the sopranos take up the search instead—to discover a God whose omnipotence keeps them, twelve bars later, on a top B flat for the best part of five bars? It is difficult to believe in detailed symbolism of this kind. Although in Beethoven's last works there is no rest, no quaver where we should have expected a crotchet or vice versa, no improbable-seeming dynamic marking that does not prove to be wholly motivated and justified, yet both motivation and justification are always musical rather than literary or visual. Kretzschmar was the first to contradict A. B. Marx's assertion that these opening bars of the 'Credo' represent Beethoven's defiance of doubt and his determination to believe;[1] and the evidence on which he denied this was purely musical—he simply pointed to Mozart's Missa Brevis K.192 in which the 'Credo', he believes, provides a precedent both for the theme and its handling. But in fact, although we may sympathize with Kretzschmar and reject the extreme of Marx's theory, Mozart's 'Credo' is no more than a skilful handling of one of the most familiar fugal subjects, that he was to use again in the finale of the C major symphony K.551 ('Jupiter').

Ex. 12

Mozart. Missa Brevis K.192

Mozart's handling of this idea bears only a very superficial resemblance to Beethoven's handling of his Credo theme. There is no hint of the aggressive accents, the anticipations and suspensions that mark the opening of Beethoven's setting, although the sketch-books

[1] Op. cit., pp. 366–7 and Hermann Kretzschmar, 'Führer durch den Konzertsaal', Abt II, Band 1, p. 218.

show that this aggressiveness was perhaps not part of the original scheme. If there was nothing unusual in the repetition of the word 'credo', Beethoven's deliberately heavy accentuations unquestionably give this affirmation of belief an aggressive character, at least for the first ten bars. After that the texture becomes homophonic, as the chorus mounts to the long held top B flat on 'omnipotentem' (bars 20–4) and drops from that fortissimo climax to the piano 'et invisibilium'. This is, as it were, the first paragraph of the Credo, asserting the existence of God as creator of all things and father of all men; and Beethoven does not go on to the acknowledgement of Christ as God's Son until he has reiterated (bars 34–55) this opening profession of faith. As before, this second clause is homophonic and rises to a climax, this time an A flat unison sung by the whole chorus fortissimo. The repetition of 'et . . . et' was not unusual in the Viennese Masses of Beethoven's day, although he gives here (Ex. 13) an inner intensity of meaning to what was elsewhere often little more than a theatrical formula.

That such a passage as this belongs as much to the theatre as to the church seems to me undeniable, even if we fully grant the splendour of Beethoven's conception. Like Verdi in Italy fifty years later, Beethoven in writing for the Church was faced with the complete decay of the liturgical tradition in his own day and had to supply that deficiency by his imagination. He did this by following Mozart and, more particularly, Haydn in writing a kind of noble and slightly archaic theatre music, as they had done, but giving it an intensely personal, vividly emotional character. It was not by chance that the Concert Spirituel had achieved such popularity in Paris during the eighteenth century or that it had attracted the favourable attention of Mozart on his visit there. Since the liturgy had been reduced to a spectacle, in which the laity could play at best a purely passive part, it was only logical that the Mass and other great ceremonies came to be regarded as little more than a 'spiritual concert'. Haydn's unreflecting *foi de charbonnier* communicated to his last Masses an unmistakably genuine religious character and Beethoven, lacking this unreasoning faith, substituted a dramatic vision and an often desperate-seeming personal quality that are essentially religious without being churchly. Is, for instance, the intense drama of the passage quoted above (Ex. 13) any evidence of Beethoven's profound belief that God the Son was 'born of the Father before all ages'? Surely not. Beethoven's response to the Nicene Creed was, I suspect, similar to his response to Kant's philosophy—an enthusiastic heartfelt assent to those passages which he understood and found relevant to his own condition, and a general sense

Ex. 13

of reverence for the august language of the rest and for the general ideas that inspired it.

In the two-octave leaps and the thirds tossed from voice to voice in 'Deum de Deo' there is a clear parallel to the first movement of op. 106, while in the short fugato (bars 70–86) of the 'Consubstantialem' we find the first strongly Handelian passage of the Credo. The mood of 'Qui propter nos homines' foreshadows the quiet, lyrical centre of the first part of the Credo, but not before Beethoven has skilfully prepared his listener for the infinite condescension of the Incarnation by suggesting the unimaginable splendour of heaven in seven bars of stark leaps, fanfares, and scales (Ex. 14).

The annunciation of the first 'Et incarnatus est' was originally given by Beethoven to the tenors of the chorus, but was later altered so that the tenor soloist and the pianissimo violas should deliver this awe-inspiring and improbable message, with the maximum of clarity and also with that speaking, personal quality that characterizes a single voice and is lost by numbers. Here, at the heart of the Credo, Beethoven turns again to a mode of utterance that was not only archaic but unknown in his day except to musical scholars—the Lydian mode. We know that in January 1820 Beethoven's friend Karl Peters, who was tutor to the two young Lobkowitz princes, looked in the Lobkowitz library for treatises on old music, such as the composer needed during his work on the Mass, and that he found two works—one by Glareanus and the other Zarlino's *Istitutioni armoniche*. In this Zarlino recommends the Lydian mode as 'most suited to tragedies and songs . . . that can move the soul and draw it out of itself'. Perhaps even more remarkable than Beethoven's use of this mode is the instinct which prompted him to recreate something like the dynamic scale and the sonority of a much earlier age. He stipulates 'only a few violins' and 'two violas', 'two violoncellos' and, as the whole passage is marked 'pianissimo dolcissimo' and lies comparatively closely and evenly spaced, the effect is not unlike that of music for viols. Above this, doubling the harmony of voices and strings in repeated staccato semiquavers, are the clarinets and bassoons, while a single flute performs a hestitant fluttering figure that suggests the hovering dove often seen in old pictures of the Annunciation. The delicate detail and exquisitely apt atmosphere of this whole passage can hardly be matched anywhere else in Beethoven's music, any more than we shall find a parallel to the murmured monotone recitative of the chorus in bars 141–2. Other mysteries of the Christian faith inspired Beethoven to make huge demands on his performers and to an expansion of the musical

R

Ex. 14

language; for the Incarnation he humbles even his art, which seems to stammer the language of an earlier age in an access of tenderness. It is almost as though he were contemplating a separate mystery when the tenor soloist's tentative 'et' and the horn's major third carry the music from (Dorian) D minor into the full light of D major, and the word 'homo' is passed with delighted wonderment backwards and forwards between soloist and chorus.

Yet even as Beethoven repeats with amazement the word 'man', the truth seems to dawn on him that synonymous with humanity, with being 'man', is suffering; and he passes without any break into the dramatic 'Adagio espressivo' of the Crucifixus section. Suffering, is, objectively, an evil, because it is the diminution of human potentialities; and no religion has ever succeeded in reconciling intellectually the existence of suffering with that of an all-powerful and all-loving God. Christ himself offered no explanation, but showed instead how suffering could be used, how it could become a means of growth and a glorification of God if it were willingly, and among the heroes even joyfully, accepted, so that the human spirit is not diminished but augmented by the experience. I do not think it fanciful to see in the diminished harmonies of Beethoven's Crucifixus a symbol of that diminishing, narrowing, confining aspect of suffering that is reflected etymologically in the word 'anguish'

Ex. 15

just as the physical tortures of the crucifixion are reflected in the
rudely jolting sforzandos, the shuddering demisemiquaver figures in
the strings and the broken or syncopated rhythms of the woodwind.
Both Handel and Bach provided precedents for this pictorial musical
language in their Passion-music. 'Sub Pontio Pilato' is treated by
Beethoven as an irruption in rudely vigorous unison of Roman power,
monolithic and totally indifferent, upon the contemplation of the
Passion, which is taken up again immediately afterwards by the
soloists. Here there appears in the first violins and bassoons a figure,
at first cramped and anguished but gradually expanding, that enormously
heightens the expressive power of the solo lines and looks both
backward to the 'crucifixion' themes of J. S. Bach and forward to
the great moments of Wagnerian music-drama (cp. *Die Walküre* Act
3, cellos figure at the lento before Wotan's 'Der Augen leuchtendes
Paar'). The importance which Beethoven attached to this figure may
be gauged by the fact that he uses it twice in successive six-bar phrases,
the first simple and the second heightened by syncopation (Ex. 16).
At the words 'sepultus est' the anguished character of the music vanishes
with diminished harmonies, though there is an echo in the last repetition of 'passus est' by the soloists, marvellously re-echoed by the oboe
(Ex. 17) before the music sinks by semitones towards an F minor cadence
that is almost inaudible (*pp più dim. ppp*). The final chord is held, as it

Ex. 16   (1)

were in complete darkness, by the strings and organ and the sopranos
and basses of the chorus. After this long fermata has died away there is a
sudden point of light—a crotchet G sounding forte in the strings and
organ and the tenors, whose tensely expectant 'et . . . ' ushers in the
announcement of the resurrection by the unaccompanied chorus.

This archaic succession of perfect consonances sung by voices alone
(see Ex. 8 (b), p. 234) makes an electrifying effect after the rich
chromatic harmonies and eloquently expressive instrumentation of the
Crucifixus. Subjective feelings are no longer relevant here; for after
the tenors' 'prick of light' at 'et', the risen Christ is an objective presence as real and incontrovertible as that of the sun. The jubilations
of the 'ascendit', homophonic after the first polyphonic scale-entries,
recall those of *Egmont* (also in F major), and the second coming of
Christ ('et iterum venturus est judicare vivos et mortuos') prompts
Beethoven to a magnificent *coup de théâtre*. Schindler tells us that in
the 'Requiem' which was among the many works that he planned to
write, Beethoven did not favour 'noises of the last trump and the
day of judgement'; but it is surely incontrovertible that when, at
bars 220–1, the strings and woodwind descend the scale of D flat
major to arrive with a great sforzando on C flat, the entry of the
trombones does indeed suggest the sound of the 'last trump'. The
harmonic progression between bars 231–2 ('judicare vivos') gave
Beethoven a great deal of trouble, and the final solution (abandoning
the dominant seventh of C flat for the octave unison on the third beat

of bar 231) did not at first satisfy him, as we see him[1] trying a number of different solutions after he has already hit on that which he eventually adopted.

[1] Nottebohm, II, p. 155.

Ex. 18

The excursion into C major on 'vivos'—a very characteristic last-moment screwing-up of the tonality by a semitonal twist—lasts only three bars (cf. the scherzo of op. 106, bars 160 sq.) and the ghostly 'et' in 'et mortuos' is in fact not so much B natural as C flat, leading to the G flat (F sharp) minor cadence in bars 238–9. With 'Cujus regni non est finis' we are back in the *Egmont*-like jubilations, until a twice repeated unison 'non' brings this whole section of the Credo to an end.

The break, and the change of musical atmosphere that follows are not only Beethoven's, but inherent in the text. Hitherto the articles of faith have been proclaimed separately, disjunctly and with the maximum weight and safeguard against misinterpretation or misunderstanding. Having carried the believer from the foundations of Christian theology and christology, through the life, death, resurrection, and ascension of Christ to the hope of the Second Coming, the Nicene Fathers embark on what proves to be a kind of coda, in which the carefully guarded proclamation of central and controversial doctrines makes way for the rehearsal, conjunctly and with less emphasis, of those doctrines which were at the time less controversial. The chief concern of the Council of Nicaea in 325 was to assert the divinity of Christ, in refutation of the Arians; and this had been elaborately safeguarded in the opening and central parts of the Credo. The theologians' dispute over the 'procession' of the Holy Ghost from the

Father and the Son was not yet acute, and the 'coda' of the Credo starts with this doctrine, one over which even the most devout churchman may find it hard to be enthusiastic; and then continues in a gradual crescendo through the assertion of the Church's powers to the final clauses proclaiming the resurrection of the dead and the life of the world to come. There is, in fact, what amounts to a pause for breath, a moment of relaxation, in the Credo itself between the clauses asserting Christ's second coming and the closely related clauses concerning the resurrection of the dead and eternal life. Although this moment of détente was certainly not planned by the Nicene Fathers for any literary, aesthetic reason, it does in fact have the effect of high-lighting these final clauses, so that the Credo gathers speed and ends in an organ-blaze of steadily accumulating clauses, even when recited rather than sung. Beethoven was too conscious an artist not to be aware of this structural character of a text that he was setting with such manifest care, and he makes full use of its dramatic possibilities.

In the first place he marks the break after 'cujus regni non erit finis' by returning to the music of the opening, and the reaffirmation of the word 'Credo', which forms the sole text for the next twenty bars in two of the four parts, exchanged antiphonally first between tenors and basses and then between sopranos and altos. Either above or below this assertion of faith as a principle[1] the various articles are rehearsed rather than proclaimed. None of these articles suggests a visual drama, and it would not have been possible for Beethoven to conjure up for, say, the procession of the Holy Ghost or the unity, holiness, and apostolic nature of the Church the kind of musical image that he conjured up for the omnipotence of God, the incarnation of Christ and His second coming to judge the world. Commentators who speak of these later clauses of the Credo as 'gabbled' (and find in this evidence for Beethoven's lack of interest) have not observed that both the literary structure of the Credo and the content of these later clauses make vivid dramatization impossible and demand formal rehearsal here, rather than jubilant proclamation. The dramatic note recurs with the word 'peccatorum', whose sforzando syllables bring Beethoven to a dominant from which the 'et expecto resurrectionem mortuorum' rises in majestic unison, as it were against the restraining suspensions in the orchestra, to the sopranos' top B flat—and by a *trompe l'oreille* effect beyond, as the lower parts continue their upward climb another fifth.

[1] Cp. Lichtenberg's aphorism 'Erst müssen wir glauben, dann glauben wir' ('First comes the need to believe, then belief').

Ex. 19

The characteristic fall to 'mortuorum' is followed by what, for a moment, seems to be the end of the Credo, when 'et vitam venturi seculi' is concluded uneventfully on an F major cadence. In fact, however, we have only had 300 of the 470 bars of the Credo and Beethoven now embarks on an enormous fugal finale on the words 'et vitam venturi saeculi', an expression of faith in that 'life of the spirit, timeless and endless', which Paul Bekker considers to be 'the alpha of Beethoven's creed, whose omega is to be found later in the Bene-dictus'.[1]

The harmony in the woodwind and horns that ushers in the fugue strikes an immediate chord in the listener's memory—it has been foreshadowed in the Gloria at bar 142, in the 'Gratias agimus' section, also modulating to B flat and also in the woodwind and horns –The two subjects of the double fugue are complementary—the one in descending minims and the other in ascending crotchets.

Ex. 20

[1] Op. cit., p. 270–1.

Beethoven obtains particularly happy effects with the inverted form of the first, and with sequences based on part of the original version, which form a boldly striding bass line in bars 351–7. Very early in the development there is a close stretto between altos and sopranos (bars 327–33), whose top B flat entry (imagined, if not for angels, at least for choirs with a picked commando corps guarding the top line) forestall the great cadence which begins with the stretto in bar 363. This appears to be moving indeflectibly to a monster Handelian cadence in B flat major, but is deflected at the last moment into D minor, through a modal progression G major—A major—D minor (Ex. 21).

The chief characteristics of the 'allegro con moto' stretto that follows (bars 373–407) are the simultaneous appearance of the first fugal subject in diminution and double diminution with itself and the introduction of a short new motive based on the second fugal subject. With inversions and new accentuations that often carry the phrase across the bar line, this is built up by chorus and orchestra into an immense complex of totally organic sound which finally returns at bar 399 to the opening harmony of the movement on an F pedal—only this time it is a dominant minor ninth instead of a dominant seventh. After this pedal, in bars 406–7, the stretto proper finishes and six bars of homophonic jubilation in the style of Handel's great choruses follow. Again the F pedal follows but instead of the E flat major jubilation the whole chorus sings in unison the first phrase of the main fugal subject, rising sequentially. Two interrupted cadences further delay the full close which appears in full Handelian panoply (Grave) after the sopranos have for the last time climbed to their top B flat (Ex. 22, p. 260).

The soloists, who have been silent since 'passus et sepultus est' are the chief actors in the peroration, supported by the choir with held or murmured harmonies. The 'companionate' thirds are heard here again, but soon give way to rising quaver figures passing from voice to voice, and then passing to the strings and woodwind against held chords in all the voices. The enormous space separating the high pianissimo woodwind chords and the string bass produce—by a transference, instinctive in the listener, of the metaphor from space to time —an extraordinarily vivid image of the *vita æterna* in terms of motionless spatial, rather than temporal, infinity and so the Credo ends, with what is perhaps the most superbly telling of all Beethoven's sonorous images.[1]

It has been said that the Missa Solemnis is Handelian in its great

---

[1] The coda of the first movement of op. 106 provides a parallel instance of these B flat major scales as 'distancing' agents.

Ex. 21

Ex. 22

affirmations but leans rather on J. S. Bach in passages of supplication and meditation. The debt to Handel is clear enough, and the Crucifixus was a reminder that Beethoven had quoted the passacaglia bass of the same movement in the B minor Mass in a letter to Breitkopf and Härtel as early as 1810. But neither Handel nor Bach could have provided a model for the music of the Sanctus. The age of the Baroque imagined the Beatific Vision objectively, in *exterior* terms of the theatre and the visual arts of the day, heaven in the likeness of a court beside whose magnificence Versailles would pale. Beethoven's apprehension of the concept of holiness, on the other hand, led him to the expression

s

of a deep *interior* humility, as subjective in character as the representation of an exterior magnificence in the music of the Baroque composers is objective. There is not a single forte marking in all the thirty-three bars of the Sanctus, there are no 'bright seraphim' colours in the orchestra (flutes, oboes, and violins are all silent,[1] as is the chorus) and the music moves with intense reverence and circumspection, indeed with an archaic gait already noticed (cf. Ex. 8, p. 234). The contralto's opening phrase is itself a gesture of the deepest obeisance (falling fifth)

Ex.23

which has absolutely no relation to the purely formal *révérences* of eighteenth-century etiquette but rather to the psalmist's 'bow down thyself, o my soul!' or to the entry in Beethoven's own notebook, 'it is as though every tree in the countryside spoke to me—holy! holy! ecstasy in the woods! who can give expression to all that?'

The short movement is marked 'Adagio, Mit Andacht' (with

---

[1] It seems possible that Beethoven took the idea of writing whole passages without violins (two in the Mass and one in the Ninth Symphony) from Etienne Méhul, whose Ossianic opera *Uthal*, scored without violins, was given in Vienna during January 1810. In February 1823 Beethoven asked Moritz Schlesinger for 'the works of Méhul you mentioned' and thanked him a year later for 'the score of Méhul's which is so worthy of him and makes us mourn his loss even more'. Méhul died in October 1817.

devotion) and it is punctuated by solemn piano trombone chords at
the cadences. At the last of these the voices murmur a 'mezza voce'
'Sanctus', and a slow, rhythmic tremor starts in the lower strings.

Ex. 24

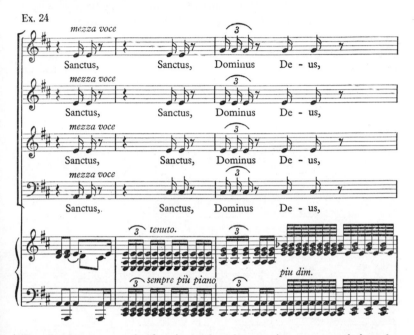

The dominant seventh (first inversion) harmonies are expanded to the
minor ninth by clarinets and violas. The timpani enter and the tremor
quickens in frequency, though the volume of voices and orchestra
decreases to a fermata where voices are silent. This shudder of numi-
nous awe in the contemplation of the Divine Majesty is followed by a
shout of exultation in the 'Pleni sunt coeli' (a short Handelian fugato
'allegro pesante' in D major) and a presto 3/4 Osanna, where the heavy
accentuation in the strings doubles, while the rest of the phrase ornaments, the vocal lines.

In Beethoven's day the short interval between the singing of the
Sanctus and the consecration was normally filled, at solemn Masses,
by an organ improvisation; and it was no doubt in place of this that
Beethoven wrote a *Praeludium* of some thirty bars 'sostenuto ma non
troppo'. The instrumentation is dark, like that of the Sanctus—only
lower strings, organ, flutes, clarinets, and bassoons, which create a
more luminous and tender darkness than the horns and trombones of
the Sanctus. Over a bass that falls, often chromatically, an octave in

eighteen bars, there rises a hymn-like melody in the flutes and violas, while frequent suspensions in the inner parts enrich the harmony. This falls at bar 100 to a low C sharp in the basses—a diminished seventh chord which moves to a dominant minor ninth and then to a tonic (G major) pedal, which only at the last moment drops the added harmony of the dominant. As the music comes to rest on the G major triad (clarinets, bassoons, violas, basses, organ), there sounds more than two octaves above another G major triad (solo violin and flutes) and the movement changes from 3/4 time to 12/8 'Andante molto cantabile e non troppo mosso'.

Ex. 25

This sudden presence of an entirely new element in the orchestral sonority coincides with the act of consecration at the altar; and the slow, hovering descent of the solo violin, encircled by accompanying flutes and greeted with the words 'Benedictus qui venit in nomine Domini' is Beethoven's musical illustration (*Ersinnlichung*) of the Real Presence of Christ, descending to the altar at the words 'Hoc est enim Corpus Meum'. The tenderness and grace of this movement, in which the solo violin has a part comparable to that in the slow movement of a concerto; the pastoral colours and harmonies of the accompanying clarinets and bassoons; the canonic writing for the soloists (recalling 'Mir ist so wunderbar' in Act I of *Fidelio*) and the muted, murmuring acclamations of the chorus—all this creates a complex scene of idyllic rapture. And yet in this movement of the Missa Solemnis more than in any other Beethoven is the child of his age.

For here the liturgy has been replaced not simply by the *concert spirituel* but by the concert-hall, or even the theatre. It is unfortunate that, since Beethoven's day, the combination of solo violin and orchestra, except in the strict symphonic interplay of the concerto, has acquired theatrical, and for the most part voluptuous associations: but the whole conception of symbolizing the Divine presence by a solo instrument that executes trills, leaps, languorous grace-notes, staccato ascents to dizzy heights above the leger-lines, and even unmistakably coquettish triplet ornaments (bars 158 and 198—last bar but two in example 26 below) seems to today's severer taste quite out of place. Indeed, it would hardly be more unsuitable to introduce a ballerina into the sanctuary.

Ex. 26

This objection is fundamentally liturgical and therefore felt, at least in its full strength, only by those who accept the Catholic doctrine of the Mass; but Beethoven's ringing the changes on tonic, dominant, and subdominant harmony and his reiteration of the solo violin's melody almost uninterruptedly for 115 bars of slow 12/8 are open to objection from the purely musical point of view. Is any listener really delighted in bars 222–3, when, after the welcome short diversion of the choral 'Osanna in excelsis', the violinist embarks on yet another statement of the second half of the theme? Was Beethoven in the Benedictus inspired by the example of the Sinfonia Pastorale in which

Handel, in *Messiah*, represents the adoration of the child Christ by
the shepherds? or did he know the corresponding movement in J. S.
Bach's Christmas Oratorio? It is impossible to say.

What we do know, however, is that Beethoven was anxious that
the Missa Solemnis should be presented in Protestant countries as an
oratorio, with a text in the vernacular, such as nineteenth-century
English choirs used when they sang settings of the 'Stabat Mater'.
Removed from its position at the heart of the liturgy, the theatrical
character of the Benedictus would be less marked, but it is difficult to
imagine any text that would find room for the brilliant *coup de théâtre*
of the solo violin's graceful, airy descent on to the stage in the opening
bars.

With the Agnus Dei we return to an austerer world, for the most
part sparely homophonic in character, with the soloists (as in the Kyrie)
leading the chorus in supplication. This is the only movement of the
Mass in the minor mode throughout, and the cries of 'miserere nobis'
have none of the dramatic luxuriance and variety that Beethoven
gave to the corresponding passages in the Gloria. Here both the tempo
(adagio) and the gait of the music (mostly equal crotchets and minims)
suggest the oppression of a heavy weight; and this is further enhanced
by the fact that every smallest rise in the vocal line is followed by a
deeper descent, so that the music seems subject to a strong downward
tow. In the opening entry (bass solo accompanied by bassoons and
horns, with strings joining in threatening unison in bar 9) the vocal
line is, as it were, dragged down to its lowest in contemplating the
world's sins. Here there is a clear reminiscence of *Messiah* ('The
people that walked in darkness') not only in the vocal line but also in
the violin quavers

Ex. 27

pec - ca - ta, pec - ca - ta   mun - - - di,

Another threatening unison (bar 26) in the strings brings a cadence in
E minor, and in this key the second verse opens, with clarinets added
to the original horns and bassoons. The contralto soloist is joined after
two bars by the tenor and Beethoven adds a new urgency to the cries of
'miserere!' by making each of the soloists, and then the chorus,
enunciate the first syllable of this word in close succession, as though in
canon, and also by the striking descending tenor line

Ex. 28

As the contralto soloist is bringing this second verse to a cadence in B minor, the whole orchestra interrupts her by a fortissimo statement of the movement's opening bars. This introduces the fourth of the soloists, the soprano, whose statement of the Agnus Dei theme is joined after only one bar by the other three soloists. Over a nine-bar dominant pedal sempre crescendo Beethoven builds up a powerful climax (bars 60–9) which is followed immediately by a pianissimo excursion into Neapolitan territory (C major in the key of B minor). The desolate scale-figure (quavers) which starts here in the violins continues for the next thirteen bars against the 'misereres' of soloists and chorus and, as these take on a more peaceful and resigned character, the scales become

broken chords, though the even quavers continue right to the end of
the movement in one or other of the orchestral parts.

In these first two of the three petitions of the Agnus Dei there is
not a hint of the tender or the consoling, such as most composers have
introduced at this point in the Mass, influenced perhaps by the gentle
and innocent associations of the word 'lamb'. Beethoven seems to have
concentrated his attention wholly on the weight of the world's sin.
Throughout the Missa Solemnis the word 'peccata' evokes a strong
response. At its very first appearance in the 'Qui tollis' of the Gloria
(bars 239–40) Beethoven gives it prominence by an ornament that
automatically throws additional weight on to the second syllable.

Ex. 29

qui   tol - lis   pec - ca - ta

In bars 250–1 of the same movement all the soloists are given a
melisma on the word 'peccata' and in bar 256 the whole orchestra
shudders on a diminished seventh at the mention of the word. Similarly
in bars 277–9 of the Credo there are heavy sforzando markings over
the three first syllables of 'peccatorum'. Conscious of an unassailable
superiority in his art, Beethoven was deeply aware of failure in his
everyday life, of promptings for which he could give a rational
explanation to others but which he still obscurely felt to be evil. This
is very clear in the 1816 diary entries about his sister-in-law, where we
can pierce for a moment behind the façade of self-righteousness to the
dumb misery of the jealous man who in public gives his jealousy a
different name. In the diary for January or February 1818, for
example, we can trace quite clearly a moment of ambivalence in his
feelings 'I can well imagine that the widow has cared pretty well for
herself, *which I cordially wish her. My duty, O Lord, I have done . . .*'
—an assertion that would have been unnecessary if he were sure that
it was true—

It would have been possible without offending the widow, but that was not
to be and Thou, Almighty One, seest into my heart, knowest that I have
sacrificed the best of my own for the sake of my precious Karl, bless my work,
bless the widow, why cannot I wholly follow my heart's inclinations and
hereafter for the widow . . .

Here the entry ends incoherently, but Beethoven's deep concern with
the justice of his behaviour towards his sister-in-law is very evident.
How unconvinced he was, despite his public declarations, of the

rightness of his behaviour and the purity of his motives, is clear from the agonized outburst that follows—

God, God, my refuge, my rock, my all! Thou seest my inmost heart and knowest how it pains me to be obliged to compel another to suffer by my good labours for my precious Karl!!! O hear me always, Thou Ineffable One, hear me—thy unhappy, most unhappy of all mortals.

It is against that background, that half-awareness of questionable motives underlying acts repeatedly proclaimed as noble and self-sacrificing, that we must understand Beethoven's response to the idea of sin. He was no adept at self-analysis, and neither the psychology nor the casuistry of the day (had he known either) would have helped him very far along the road to understanding his own motives. He was left, therefore, with the burden of an obscure, undifferentiated guilt,[1] and it is the weight of that burden that seems to be dragging down the vocal lines of the Agnus Dei, just as it is a piercing awareness of that guilt that prompts the sudden shocks or shudders which accompany the word 'peccata' elsewhere in the Mass.

It is from this shadowy, because ununderstood, sense of evil and unworthiness that Beethoven now, in the third petition of the Agnus Dei asks for deliverance—the peace of a good conscience as well as from war. This is the meaning of the inscription over the final movement of the Mass—'Bitte um innern und äussern Frieden' ('prayer for peace both inward and outward')—which stands in the sketchbooks as

dona nobis pacem darstellend den innern u. äussern Frieden

Beethoven had therefore in the first place meant the 'Dona nobis pacem' to be a representation (*Darstellung*) of peace, rather than a prayer for it. In fact this pictorial, representational element remained strong in the music of this section, not only in the bugle-calls and martial alarums that echoed Beethoven's memories of the French occupations and the war years in Vienna, but also in the gently rocking rhythms and almost pastoral simplicity of the main body of the music, whose details often seem to look back to the 'representational' Sixth Symphony (semiquaver figures in the strings starting respectively at bars 100 and 107 and again at bars 143 and 200). The 6/8 metre, which seems an integral part of the movement's dominating idea, was in fact an afterthought, since the theme appears first in 2/4 in the sketch-books.

[1] Beethoven's sense of guilt did not of course date from the years of the law-suit. 'Though often darkly led to evil by passion, I returned through penance and purification to the pure fountain—to God and to your [*sic*] art', he wrote in his diary, probably sometime in 1815.

Ex. 30

assai sostenuto

Do - na,   do - na   no - bis   pa - cem

When this appears in its final form, it carries the note 'Stärke der Gesinnungen des innern Friedens über alles. . . . Sieg!' (Strengthening of the mentality of interior peace above all else—victory).

When the first section of the 'Dona nobis' comes to a close on a reiterated A major cadence (bars 160–3) Beethoven makes use once again of the dramatic modulation to the key of the flattened sixth (F major,) and the timpani imitate the roll of a distant martial drum *sempre pianissimo*. The agitation in the strings represents vividly the effect of this alarum on a frightened populace; and when the bugles (trumpets) are added to the drums, the soloists in turn voice the terror of the people over tremolando strings, with the roar of the drums increasing and the bugles blaring no longer in the distance.[1] This realistic military excursion in the Missa Solemnis may seem a descent from the sublime to the trivial, an inexplicable harking-back to the naïver world from which sprang the animal representations of Haydn's *Creation* and Beethoven's own Sixth Symphony; and it was almost certainly suggested to Beethoven by the similar passage in Haydn's C major 'Missa in tempore belli' (sometimes called the 'Paukenmesse') written in 1796 after the French[2] invasion of the Austrian provinces in Northern Italy. The drum-roll in Haydn's 'Agnus Dei' is a characteristically simple figure answered by fanfares in the woodwind.

Ex. 31

Haydn Paukenmesse Agnus Dei

Timpani

W. Wind

W. Wind and Timpani

[1] The sketch-books show (*Zweite Beethoveniana*, p. 150) that Beethoven had planned a full-scale march here.

[2] In 'revolutionary' music of Méhul, Gossec, Catel, and Kreutzer, which had a demonstrable influence on Beethoven's earlier works (*Egmont*, *Leonore* No. 2, etc.), bugle-calls and other military features are common.

Beethoven's sketch-books show that he took great trouble in elaborating the final entry of the timpani just before the end of the 'Dona nobis pacem', trying out so many different versions that his pen finally made a hole in the paper.[1]

The return to the mood of the opening after the first military interruption again recalls the Sixth Symphony ('Joyful thanksgiving after the storm'). The key of D major is not reached for eighteen bars. The soloists' unaccompanied 'dona nobis pacem' (bars 210–15) is followed by a fortissimo entry by the choral basses with a quotation from Handel's 'Hallelujah' chorus, which is made the subject of a powerful fugato. The cries of 'pacem' become increasingly urgent, sforzando chords by the chorus answered with floating melismas by the soloists, when there is a sudden break, and a presto double fugue seems to represent the actual battle from which the singers have prayed to be delivered. The material is extremely sparse, the texture unadorned and there is not one of some sixty bars which does not contain a cell of one of the two subjects (the lower reproducing the figure in bars 107–8).

Ex. 32

This purely instrumental interlude (strings and woodwind), which carries the Missa Solemnis still further outside the boundaries of the liturgy, suggests the ordered activity, the bustle and inhumanity rather than the horror of war, and we are a long way from the realism of *The Battle of Vittoria*. It is only the re-entry of the timpani and the brass that again strikes horror into the singers, and provokes anguished cries of 'Agnus Dei, dona nobis pacem' first from the chorus and then from the soloists. This time the return to the peaceful mood of the opening is made much more easily and in only four bars. This mood is only once again interrupted, by the distant drum-roll that suddenly sounds against the silence in bars 406–9. After that peace is finally established and the movement ends in a jubilant D major.

[1] Nottebohm, II, p. 156.

It is difficult to feel that the Benedictus and the Dona nobis pacem quite sustain the sublime power and simplicity of the earlier movements of the Missa Solemnis. The battle-scenes in the Dona nobis pacem are not on a level of inspiration with the serene magnificence and classical proportions of the 'Kyrie'; and the Benedictus is an exquisite theatrical tableau, a celestial 'Romance' for violin and orchestra on an altogether more primitive level than that of the craggy sublimities and the wonderful human drama of the Gloria and the Credo. Unity of conception, then, is not one of the characteristics that make the Missa Solemnis a supremely great work. That unity is imposed, as it were, from without, by the hallmark of Beethoven's own personality, for there is nothing in the Missa Solemnis that is not manifestly and uniquely his. Perhaps the truth is simply that Beethoven was, as J. W. N. Sullivan says 'not educable . . . not malleable and perhaps hardly aware of the schemes of thought and conduct current at his time . . . utterly faithful to his own experience'[1]—and that experience was of an Old Testament type of religion. Christ as companion and friend, hero and example appears in the 'companionate thirds' of the 'Gratias agimus' and in the deeply felt drama of the 'Et incarnatus' and 'Crucifixus'. These were concepts that, in Sailer's phrase, Beethoven had made his own 'not simply by individual thought, but before all else by an individual experiencing of traditional and revealed truth'. The Real Presence of Christ in the Blessed Sacrament, on the other hand, was not a reality to him in the same way; he may have given or refused the doctrine his casual assent, but in either case it kindled his pictorial imagination rather than any deep devotion of the spirit. And it is for this reason, no doubt, that the music of the 'Benedictus' contains a hint of sentimental complacency beneath its graceful and charming exterior, a streak of pastoral make-believe in its conscious simplicity.

The 'Dona nobis pacem' certainly does not suffer from any similar unreality, any failure to penetrate beneath the surface meaning of the liturgical text. Beethoven had experienced not only the fears and disruptions of war but the more profound disturbances of internal, personal discord—of not being at peace with himself, of repeatedly falling below his own very high standard of personal morality. It is the expansion of Haydn's topical detail, into incidents involving 115 bars out of the movement's 335, that involve a descent from the austere abstractions of the earlier movements, a regression to an earlier and naïver kind of musical expression. The realistic

[1] J. W. N. Sullivan, *Beethoven—his spiritual development*, p. 71.

representation of war and the fear it inspires gives the 'Dona nobis pacem' a touchingly human, personal note, but, in doing so, impairs the unity of the Missa Solemnis. Countless passages in the earlier movements make it clear beyond doubt that Beethoven was capable of expressing the deepest, strongest and most personal feelings in so-called abstract terms, or at least without having recourse to devices whose natural home was the theatre. In the Benedictus and the Dona nobis pacem, on the other hand, the Missa Solemnis suffers from the same mixture of genres or styles that mars *Fidelio*, where French opéra comique and tragédie lyrique, melodrama and oratorio are inextricably confused. Beethoven's personality may easily overcome such objections, but it should not blind us to the facts.

The Missa Solemnis is a personal document without parallel in the history of music. The inequalities of style which we have been discussing are trivial compared with the spiritual energy, the combined strength and tenderness, the magnificence of the general musical conception and the countless felicitous details of the work as a whole. To find a parallel in literature we have to turn not, of course, to the original epics of antiquity but to what C. S. Lewis[1] has called the 'secondary epics'—Virgil's *Aeneid* or Milton's *Paradise Lost*. We have seen Beethoven immersing himself in the study of early models just as Virgil immersed himself in the study of Homer, and Milton in the study of Virgil. We can even find a parallel to the antiquarian taste and the excessive concentration on stylistic details, such as are held against neo-classical architecture, in the archaistic traits and the fragmentariness or looseness of symphonic integration between the different episodes in the 'Gloria' and the 'Credo'. It could be said of both Virgil and Beethoven that learning and enthusiasm, reflection and feeling seem, in the *Aeneid* as in the Missa Solemnis, to take the place of the pure original creative power of the old models and their spontaneous, almost unconscious expressive aspiration. If we read a page of Virgil after a page of Homer, or the Kyrie of the Missa Solemnis after the Kyrie of Palestrina's mass 'Aeterna Christi munera', the most immediately striking of the many differences is the enormous increase in self-consciousness. This increase, inseparable from civilization, has grown steadily right down to our own time, when it forms one of the chief factors in the crisis through which all the arts are passing. In a sense it was a momentary suspension of that self-consciousness, a return to a naïver and more primitive way of feeling, that prompted Beethoven to include the military episodes in the 'Dona nobis pacem'; and he was to follow a similar course on a much larger scale in the Ninth Symphony.

CHAPTER 18

The Ninth Symphony.
Op. 125

In tracing the origin and growth of the Ninth Symphony in Beethoven's imagination a clear distinction must be made between a work that embodied in some way a choral setting of Schiller's *Ode to Joy* and a symphony commissioned in 1816–17 by the Philharmonic Society of London. That Beethoven intended to set Schiller's ode at least as early as 1793 is clear from a letter written by his Bonn friend Ludwig Bartolomäus Fischenich to Charlotte von Schiller, the poet's sister, enclosing a setting by Beethoven of Schiller's 'Feuerfarbe' and continuing 'he also proposes to compose Schiller's 'Freude', and what is more, strophe by strophe. I expect something perfect for, as I know him, he is wholly devoted to the great and the sublime'. In a sketchbook dating probably from the middle of 1811 Beethoven noted 'Freude schöner Götterfunken, Tochter. Work out the overture', and in another place in the same sketch-book 'Freude schöner Götterfunken Tochter aus Elysium. Detached fragments, like princes are beggars,[1] etc., not the whole', and on the same page, 'Detached fragments from Schiller's Freude brought together in a whole.' There is even a sketch marked 'Overture Schiller'. Although found among sketches for the Seventh and Eighth Symphonies, the note 'Sinfonia in D moll—3te Sinf.' is no evidence that Beethoven conceived the choral setting of Schiller's ode as forming the movement of any symphony, at least until the composition of what was eventually the ninth was well under way. The first appearance in the sketch-books of any material that Beethoven eventually used in the symphony was in 1815, when the first three bars of the scherzo (with a different fourth bar added) are found as a fugue-subject, which appears again in 1817 in a slightly different form. (See Nottebohm, II, pp. 157–192.)

[1] This refers to an earlier version of Schiller's ode, which contained the line 'Bettler werden Fürstenbrüder' ('beggars become princes' brothers') instead of 'Alle Menschen werden Brüder' ('all men become brothers').

Ex. 1

The first sketches for what eventually became the first movement of the Ninth Symphony appear on loose leaves belonging to the last months of 1817 and the first months of 1818, when the principal subject was finally fixed. The fugue-theme was to be used in the third movement and there was to be an instrumental finale.

Some time during 1818, however, Beethoven clearly made plans for two symphonies, to appear together like the seventh and eighth. One of these was to be the symphony in D minor, while the other was to contain a choral movement, which Beethoven visualized as

Adagio Cantique
Pious song in a symphony in the ancient modes—Lord God, we praise Thee, alleluia!—either alone or as introduction to a fugue. The whole second symphony might be characterized in this manner, in which case the vocal parts would enter in the last movement or already in the Adagio. The violins, etc., of the orchestra to be increased tenfold (*verzehnfacht*) in the last movement, in which case the vocal parts would enter gradually—in the text of the Adagio Greek myth, *cantique ecclesiastique*—in the Allegro, feast of Bachus [*sic*].

After the early months of 1819 Beethoven, as far as we know, ceased work on the symphony and did not take it up again until 1822. In those intervening three years he completed the Missa Solemnis, the piano sonatas opp. 109, 110, and 111, the greater part of the Diabelli Variations and the overture *Die Weihe des Hauses*. Although considerable progress was made during 1822 on the symphony's first movement, little had been done to the Scherzo and the slow movement did not yet exist. Suddenly, however, we find among the sketches

Ex. 2

Freu - de, schö-ner Göt-ter-fun-ken, Toch-ter aus E - ly - si-um,

That Beethoven was not convinced of the rightness of the choral finale is clear from the note found almost a year later, where he sketches an early version of what he eventually used as the finale of the A minor quartet op. 132 and labelled it 'finale instrumentale'

T

Ex. 3

Not only was Beethoven unsure of whether he should use the setting of Schiller's ode as finale to the D minor symphony: he was also in two minds about the music for it, as we see in the following note

Sinfonie allemand [*sic*.] either with variation after the (?) chorus

Ex. 4

Freu - de, schö - ner Göt - ter - fun - ken, Toch - ter   aus   E - li - si - um

coming in at once or without variation. End of the symphony with Turkish music and full chorus.

Here we have direct allusion to the rhythm of the double fugue in the ninth variation of the finale, and to the Alla Marcia section ('Turkish music'). At about the same time it seems that Beethoven thought of abandoning the idea of the second of the two symphonies in favour of an overture on B–A–C–H 'very fugued with 3' (? subjects). On the other hand he told Rochlitz in the summer of 1822 that he was busy with three works—'two big symphonies, each unlike the other and unlike my other symphonies, and an oratorio' (presumably *Der Sieg des Kreuzes*, which he had not yet definitely abandoned).

Having decided tentatively on the choral finale, Beethoven set to work on the choral parts and the instrumental variations, leaving the crucial transition from purely instrumental to vocal music. The sketches make it plain that he originally planned an instrumental introduction to the fourth movement, using new themes. The first hints of a combined instrumental and vocal bridge from the Adagio to

the *Ode* date from July 1823; but even then the verbal connection
between the two had not suggested itself, for it seems never to have
occurred to Beethoven that a symphony could have a choral finale
without some preliminary explanation, some kind of dramatic *mise
en scène* to orientate the listener. This dramatic framework only
occurred to Beethoven after he had returned from Baden to Vienna,
i.e. after late October 1823. According to Schindler—'one day he
entered the room exclaiming "I have it! I have it!" and showed me
the sketch-book with the words "Let us sing the song of the immortal
Schiller—'Freude'"', whereupon a solo voice immediately begins the
hymn to joy.'

Even so, it is not clear which of the two symphonies that he still
had in mind Beethoven designed for the London commission which
he had accepted in December 1822. Obviously a work whose last
movement consisted of the choral setting of a German text was not
ideally suited for England, and perhaps 'sinfonie allemand' shows that
this symphony was not the one designed for London. In any case it is
quite clear that the Ninth Symphony, as we know it, was a slow and
painful growth, the greater part of which took place during the year
1823. The second movement was completely sketched by August of
that year, the fugue themes of 1815–17 extended and final details
elaborated in the sketch-books. The Adagio followed some two
months later; in fact Beethoven may have prolonged his stay at Baden
until this movement was fully sketched (end of October). The second
of the two themes (Andante moderato D major) appears in the sketch-
books long before the first (B flat Adagio), and was originally conceived in A major with an undistinguished second strain in the
manner of a *Ländler*.

Ex. 5

When it appears in the sketch-books, the B flat major theme undergoes a long process of exploratory amendment until Beethoven finds exactly the right form. The echo-effects at the end of each section, which form one of the most characteristic beauties of the final version, were a comparatively late inspiration. Instead, there was a version in which the wind instruments, instead of echoing the last bars, repeated whole sections of the melody after the strings.

Long after Beethoven had found the final version of the 'Joy' theme and sketched many of the choral episodes in the finale, he was still wrestling with the introduction. This was at first conceived in a conventional instrumental manner as the following quotations from the sketch-books show

Ex. 6 (a)

The first of these is obviously related to the earlier theme, which Beethoven was eventually to use in the string quartet op. 132. The second has equally obvious affinities with the material of the first movement of the symphony. The third seems to belong more to an eighteenth-century divertimento; and a fourth has a nervous, jerky character that would seem more in place in the theatre than introducing the *Ode to Joy*, unless we bear in mind that Beethoven was in fact seeking a dramatic, even theatrical, frame for the ode. The difference in conception between this and the colossal fanfare with which Beethoven finally opened the finale is a measure of how the symphony grew while he was working on it. Every stage of this introduction was hammered out in detail again and again.

Of all the works of Beethoven's last period the Ninth Symphony retains the greatest number of links with the past. At least from opus 106 onwards the piano sonatas explore keyboard territory that had occasionally been divined or hinted at but had never been explored in the earlier piano sonatas; and the same is even more true, of the five string quartets beginning with op. 127. It would be difficult to find any precedent in Beethoven's own music for the great moments of the Missa Solemnis, and it would certainly be useless to look for them in the Mass in C of 1807. But the first three movements of the Ninth Symphony do not so much break new ground as crown the achievements of the other eight. Their conception is deeply rooted in the *Sturm und Drang* of Beethoven's middle period and in the dramatic tradition of the Mannheim symphony; the choral finale owes much to the French Revolutionary composers and the final result is a cross between *sinfonia eroica* and *hymne de la république*. That the work completely transcends its origins is obvious, but for the moment irrelevant; for its origins largely determined its character, though they could not diminish its quality.

First movement. Allegro ma non troppo, un poco maestoso

Of the opening of the first movement Tovey wrote 'of all single works of art, of all passages in a work of art, the first subject of the first movement of Beethoven's ninth symphony has had the deepest and widest influence on later music'.[1] Yet we can see in the sketch-books how the gradual quickening, or coming to life, of the open fifths and their piling up, wave-like, into the colossal descending stride of the D minor triad originated in a purely eighteenth-century idea that would not be remarkable in a symphony by Haydn or Mozart.

[1] Tovey, *Beethoven's Ninth Symphony* (1922), p. 7.

Ex. 7

Under what influences, in exactly what labour of the imagination and the spirit that innocent introductory flourish swelled and burgeoned, like an acorn swelling into an oak tree, it is impossible to say; but it is hard to resist the feeling that the uniquely indeterminate yet pregnant atmosphere of the introductory bars has some extra-musical affinity. We may never know, or even want to know, the exact nature of that hypothetical extra-musical origin, but Beethoven himself gives us a warrant for divining its presence. The London German with whom he got on so famously in 1824, J. A. Stumpff, reported him as saying, 'when I contemplate in wonderment the firmament and the host of luminous bodies which we call worlds and suns, eternally revolving within its boundaries, my spirit soars beyond these stars, many millions of miles away towards the fountain from which all created work springs and from which all new creation must still flow'. Neither astronomy, then, nor astronomical speculation, but the kind of cosmic 'O altitudo' in which, Beethoven, like Sir Thomas Browne, was happy to lose himself. Only Beethoven does anything but lose himself. Tovey observes justly that 'although time-scale and space-scale are gigantic, the broadest and most spacious processes are found side by side with the tersest and most sharply contrasted statements and actions'.[1] Before all else the command of significant, organic detail is greater here even than in the Missa Solemnis, where symphonic thought is repeatedly interrupted by the exigencies of the text. Nowhere is Beethoven's use of anticipation, so characteristic of his last works, more significant than here. Already in bar 15 the anticipation of the tonic by the bassoon (echoed again in bar 49) is like the irresistible attraction of some natural force.

[1] Op. cit., ibid.

Ex. 8

In bars 131–7 the basses and bassoons give a gigantic emphasis to their
staccato leap of a tenth (echoing the oboes third) by a suspension formed
by tying the first semiquaver of every bar to the last quaver of its
predecessor. The sforzando accents off the beat combine with this
frequent tying of the last beat of one bar to the first of the next to give

an impression of extreme tension and even occasionally to destroy for a moment the clear sense of the metre, as in the second strain of the second group of subjects (bars 79 sq).

Ex. 9

Such detail, which enriches the texture and intensifies the significance of the music, by as it were counteracting the broad simplicity of the movement's basic ideas, may be found simply in phrasing or in passage-work that seems at first deliberately dark and confused but proves to be the difficult, as it were groping, ascent to a new idea—as in this approach to the semitone 'sob', overt in the woodwind but in fact doubled by the strings (bars 115–118)

Ex. 10

The actual material of the first movement is enormously rich. In the first group of subjects, beside the unison descending arpeggio we can distinguish the very characteristic tailpiece (also unison) barins

19–20; the three ascending notes[1] in bars 21–2, immediately carried on another three to the *ff* B♭ (bar 24). The descent from the flat sixth to the leading note, over the heavily-accented E♮ bass (bars 25–7) is another thematic cell; and the solemn thirds in the woodwind, over the dotted rhythm in trumpets and timpani (a direct reminiscence of the heroic funeral marches and republican triumphs of the French Revolutionary composers) (see Ex. 11 opposite) leads to the dramatic coups of elided harmony and transferred accent in bars 31–3 and the descending demisemiquaver scale (really a written-out portamento or glissando) in 34–5. Every single one of these features is used later in the movement by Beethoven, and a number of them are developed almost at once in the restatement of the opening theme in B flat major. The tailpiece of bars 19–20, for instance gives rise to the whole passage between bars 55–63; and the descent of bars 25–7, followed by an inversion of the three rising notes of bars 31–2, is developed by Beethoven into the passage between bars 63–71, where first violins and basses are in contrary motion. The E flat so prominent in the bass of bars 24–6 proves to have been the distant forerunner of the second group of subjects, and it is now avoided in the modulating transition bars 71–2, until it prepares the dolce entry of the woodwind thirds which open the first subject of the second group in bar 74.

This second group of material is as rich, and as richly exploited, as the first. The woodwind thirds of bars 74–9 are, as it were, the trio section of the French Revolutionary funeral march of whose main section we heard a moment in bars 27–31 (see Ex. 11). The antiphonal theme whose cross rhythms we have already mentioned (Ex. 9) leads in bars 88–92 to a further snatch of the same march-trio, which returns even more markedly in the dotted rhythms of bars 102–7, in the wind passage (bars 138–47) which is then taken up in the big B♭ tutti fanfare bringing the exposition to an end. Interspersed among this B♭ major march material, and never wholly divorced from it in character, is the Neapolitan incident which starts in bars 108–9, whose augmentation carries the listener into the apparently remote ascent to the semitone 'sob' motif. Here flattened sixth alternates with major sixth, in a manner that we have come to think of as Schubertian, though Schubert may well have been prompted by Beethoven in this,

---

[1] This is no doubt the minor version of the three ascending note-phrases in the major that Newman finds as something approaching mannerism in Beethoven's slow movements. The major version is aspiring, hymn-like (hence no doubt Newman's aversion); the minor version, as here, powerful and minatory.

Ex. 11

as in much else. The semiquaver thirds in flutes and oboes, that seem
to be so much 'filling' or ornament, are in fact preparing the powerful
contrast between falling third (oboes) and rising tenth (basses) in bars
132–7 and the further espressivo motif elaborated by the wood wind
in bars 138–50.

Ex. 12

Ex. 12

It is impossible to find another symphonic exposition in which so much material, so contrasted in character, is presented so tersely and with so much vigour.

When the open fifths of the introduction announce the beginning of the development section, the listener has still never heard the tonic major of the symphony; and when the bassoons and lower strings sound their pianissimo major third in bar 170 it is as though a sudden beam of light pierced the darkness. It is only a momentary gleam, as D major is soon abandoned for G minor, the predominating tonality of the first episode of the development and of the 'refrain' (bars 192–7) by which Beethoven marks the end of each episode in the development section, entrusting it always to the woodwind.

Ex. 13

The second episode is still concerned with the descending arpeggio theme from the first group and is in C minor. The refrain in the same key leads directly into the fugato and this forms the third episode. This is based on the second half of the first theme in the first group (see bars 5–6 in Ex. 7) and is developed in the basses, with a counter-subject in the second violins, while flutes and first violins utter strong sforzando protests off the beat (see Ex. 14).

The episode starts in C minor, and the second entry of the fugato theme is in G minor (flutes and first violins). This is followed un-orthodoxly by two consecutive entries in B flat major, the second a tutti in which the sforzando ties from bar to bar are further emphasized and the leap in the fugato subject is stretched to cover an octave and a fifth. The tension is further increased by the martial punctuations of trumpets and timpani, until in bar 253 'we suddenly step out of the oppressive world of syncopated rhythms, as out of a mêlée, into the open' (Tovey).

It is apparently the refrain that breaks the tension by its sudden

Ex. 14

entry; but the refrain itself is taken up and greatly extended, cantabile indeed but over a bass (dominant in A minor) that threatens to develop the same tensions as before and finally strides, or rather leaps, upwards in bars 268–70 beneath a chatter of repeated woodwind semiquavers that lead to the refrain proper and so into the final episode of the development. This consists of a tranquil return, only in A minor, to the second of the themes in the second group, heard originally in B flat major (see bars 80 ff. in Ex. 9), and a further appearance of the refrain in the full orchestra leads in a big passage of unison semiquavers to the recapitulation.

Here Beethoven does indeed return to the introduction, but in an entirely different light. For whereas he originally approached his main subject through the dominant (A), now he plunges directly into the tonic and, what is even more remarkable, into the major. For eleven bars the bassoons and basses continue to assert their F sharp fortissimo (bars 301–12), only deserting it for the low B flat,

Ex. 15

so that the D minor triad is approached in exactly the same way as the D minor cadence at 'Deus Pater Omnipotens' (bars 185–90) in the 'Gloria' of the Missa Solemnis (see Ex. 3, p. 228). As the theme enters, the basses start an entirely new countersubject, marching upwards to meet the descending D minor arpeggio in the rest of the orchestra, the upper strings and woodwind dialoguing antiphonally, until they start a series of close strettos (bars 327–34) over a heavy tonic pedal in timpani and string basses. This foreshortened reprise of the first group is followed by a full repetition of the second group with many changes in the scoring, which is less continuous and more divided into individual phrases. Thus in the second subject of the second group the violins are given an occasional melodic phrase (bars 349–50) instead of providing only the accompaniment, and the demisemiquavers in bars 401–6 are divided between flutes and violins instead of being given to strings alone as in bars 132–8. Here, too, the oboes answer the upward leap of a tenth in the basses by a downward leap of the same interval, instead of the third as in the earlier passage.

The recapitulation section, only 126 bars to the exposition's 160, is followed by a coda almost as long (121 bars). This opens with twenty-five bars in which a single pattern is pursued. Oboes, horns and middle strings (second violins and violas) have long held chords which provide a stable harmonic pedal. String basses, partnered alternately by clarinets and bassoons, have pizzicato quavers on the weak beats of the bar, while flutes and first violins—partnered by clarinets or bassoons when not otherwise engaged—carry the dotted descending arpeggio theme of the first group through a series of harmonies, most of them diminished sevenths. The effect is at the same time powerful and restless, ruthless yet somehow undecided in direction owing to the versatility or ambiguity of all diminished chords. This is followed by waves of semiquaver scales, in contrary motion and phrased over the bar-line, until at bar 463 we hear the dotted fanfare figures familiar from bars 102 and 369. These come to rest on a single A sounding throughout the orchestra, upon which the horn sounds dolce the major version of what has hitherto been one of the movement's most threatening themes (bars 468–73, Ex. 16)

This is taken up by oboes, bassoons, and flutes and finally sempre piano by all the strings in unison, this time in the original minor. Now the gait is ruthless, as the phrase expands, with a crescendo that grows to a fortissimo when the music veers to the Neapolitan flattened second (key of E flat in D minor) before rising to two more scale-waves that come to rest at bar 505 on a chord of the dominant seventh. One last

Ex. 16

echo of the refrain from the development section contains an interesting pianism in bars 511–12 (see Ex. 17), where the flute echoes the
oboe an octave higher, for all the world like a pianist crossing his
hands in an elegant echo-effect. What follows, however, is much
much more than an echo of what has gone before. A new idea, more
march than ballad, but having something of both, appears in the

Ex. 17

woodwind, imitated by the horns, while in the strings there starts pianissimo, but rising through a long crescendo, a tramping phrase that soon dominates the whole orchestra

Ex. 18

as its chromatic semitone intervals swell to gigantic size reaching all but two-octave spans in bars 531 ff. At the climax of this procession the D minor arpeggio theme appears for the last time in the full orchestra, and the demisemiquaver scale that descended in bars 34–5 now rises to the final unambiguous unison close.

Scherzo. Molto vivace

The scherzo had a long history which goes back, as we have seen, to the year 1815, when the first three bars of the main theme appear in a sketch-book labelled 'Fuge'. Two years later, in 1817, Beethoven was in fact working on a fugal movement with this subject

Ex. 19

At the beginning of 1818 the sketch-books show him meditating a different second movement

Ex. 20

2 tes Stück, 4 Horn 2 in tief und 2 in hoch B

Timp.

and a scherzo with an entirely different trio section, played by the wind alone

Ex. 21

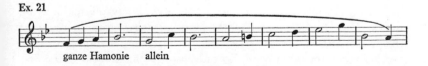

ganze Hamonie   allein

A later sketch, which shows the scherzo theme almost in its final form has the word 'gleich' beneath it, so that we can be sure that the dramatic eight bars introduction were an afterthought. The entry of the solo timpani in the fifth bar of the movement, providing the third in the D minor triad, delighted the audience at the first performance and is indeed one of those rare ideas that delights musicians by its purely musical propriety as much as the naïve listener by its unexpectedness. It is not difficult to trace the thematic connection between this movement and the first, sharing as they do material taken from the D minor arpeggio and scale in their simplest forms.

Ex. 22

The proportions of the movement are remarkable for the great size of the trio, which is only five bars shorter than the exposition of this large-scale though simple sonata movement, in which Beethoven cannot resist the opportunities that the theme offers for contrapuntal ingenuity, yet indulges himself without giving the uninitiated listener more than an occasional hint of what is in fact happening beneath the surface of this apparently carefree dance movement. The five entries of the opening fugato are hardly completed by the strings before small strettos begin to appear, as though by spontaneous generation. These are interrupted, however, by the big tutti statement of the theme, which leads by a singularly natural passage to the dominant of C major (which is now itself the dominant) in bar 77. The appearance of the second subject is thus skilfully delayed and is now prepared by a wonderful eight-bar phrase, which twists, opens and shuts, expands and contracts, swells and dies away with major-minor harmonies (Ex. 23) before the second subject bursts in with its obstreperous, puppy-like gait over the tonic pedal in the basses, who never abandon the original ♩. ♪ ♩ | ♩ rhythm. The second subject keeps as closely to C major as the first kept to D minor, to which the music returns before the repeat of this whole first exposition. When the development section begins after the repeat, on the other hand, Beethoven turns the first bar of the first theme through fifteen keys in seventeen sounding bars, as strings and horns provoke the woodwind to more and more daring excursions away from the tonic D minor, only to find themselves at the end back as near their starting-point as possible—in A major. The unison A dares the strings to screw themselves up to a contradiction, first A♯,

Ex. 23

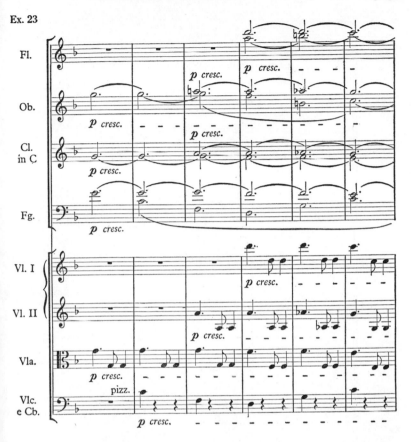

and then (when the woodwind accept the challenge) B♮—and there the game stops on a fermata. The woodwind, accompanied by pizzicato strings, now embark on the main subject of the scherzo in E minor, the metrical scheme changed from four-bar to three-bar groups (*ritmo di tre battute*) so that the fugato entries come even closer together. When the key of A minor has been solidly established, there is a sudden interruption from the timpani (bar 195) with an unmistakable F that jerks the music back to F major in four groups of three, each introduced by the timpani which so delighted the audience at the first performance. When they fall silent, the antiphonal chatter of strings and woodwind is only interrupted by the horns, who try to take the place of the timpani and eventually lead the music back from the three-bar structure to the original four-bar in a long passage (thirty-six bars) which Beethoven repeatedly marks 'sempre pianissimo'. Eight bars

before the end of the pianissimo the strings come to rest on the dominant seventh of E♭ (bar 248), while timpani and horns continue
asserting the ♩. ♪ ♩ rhythm; and it is when this is repeated that a
crescendo first begins, swelling as Beethoven repeats his favourite
Neapolitan approach to D minor through the dominant seventh of the
flattened supertonic (E flat)[1] (see Ex. 24 and cp. Ex. 3, p. 228).

As in the first movement, this ushers in the recapitulation, where the
timpani almost drown the rest of the orchestra by their relentless
insistence, reinforcing the even crotchets of the upper strings and
woodwind against the dotted rhythm of the brass and basses. Example
23 is greatly expanded now, appearing four times instead of two and in
fact engineering the appearance of the second subject in the expected

[1] Cp. Missa Solemnis 'Gloria' bars 185–90 and the recapitulation in the first movement of
the present symphony (bars 312–14), see p. 295.

Ex. 24

key of D major by executing one of those dramatic downward semitonal slips (bars 305–6) which appear so much more rarely than the
corresponding semitonal rise. The recapitulation ends, and the coda
begins, with a pianissimo arpeggio of the dominant seventh (bar 376)
interrupting the antiphonal chatter of strings and woodwind. The
first time we are led almost immediately back to the opening of the

development section, with its round of tonal statements. After the repeat there is an equally short, and now hurried ('stringendo il tempo') dash forward to the trio, which is heralded by a fortissimo trombone note that dies away in a bar and a beat, having projected the theme in the oboes and clarinets, with its equally important countersubject in the bassoons. With this bright D major, pastoral instrumentation, simple three-part writing and innocent melody repeating,[1] Beethoven was in fact anticipating the finale, so that when the great 'Freude' theme finally appears, it strikes a familiar note—as though we had always known that it was there, although it has only been adumbrated in this trio. Anything less like the conventional B flat trio that Beethoven seems originally to have planned

Ex. 25

can hardly be imagined.

The element of repetition in the trio is very strong, and made stronger by the presence of the bagpipe drone beneath the main theme. Nowhere in the whole of Beethoven's music is the pure delight in sound for its own sake (*Klangfreude*) so strong as in the enormous tonic pedal which lasts from bars 491–530 and carries above it a seemingly endless alternation of unadulterated tonic and dominant (occasionally subdominant) harmony. Repetition on this scale is of course deliberately planned, and it is possible that Beethoven was already preparing his listeners for the sounds of a huge popular festivity, such as recur in the finale (bars 747 ff.). The simple harmonies first swelling and then diminishing, against the constant hum of the tonic pedal, easily suggest a great popular gathering in which strains of choral and instrumental music are heard at a distance, the volume of sound varying with the strength of the wind.

[1] Perhaps it was the fact that the theme is said to be Russian that led Schenker (*Beethovens Neunte Symphonie*', pp. 185–6) to compare this trio with the finale of Tchaikovsky's fourth symphony. He speaks of it as 'a little genre picture—how well Beethoven understood the art of realistic presentation in imitating a primitive stage of musical development, though only with methods of the greatest refinement!' If Schenker is right, the trio is a reversion to the world of the Sixth Symphony. To my mind the clear suggestion of choral tone, as well as the actual material, make the whole trio an anticipation of the finale rather than a reminiscence of anything in Beethoven's earlier music.

Ex. 26

w

Was Beethoven present at the huge *Volksfest*, or popular festival, held in the Prater in October 1814 to celebrate the defeat of Napoleon and attended by all the crowned heads who had recently arrived in Vienna for the forthcoming congress? On that occasion, according to Auguste de la Garde,[1] 'veterans of the Austrian army, four thousand in number, had been invited to the festivities. They marched past the tribune occupied by the allied monarchs to the strains of military music and then took their places under the huge tents prepared for them. Games and sports of all kinds followed and occupied the whole day.' This kind of *Männerfest* had become popular during the early years of the Revolution in Paris, and was always accompanied by music specially commissioned for the occasion. It is of an occasion such as this that we must think when examining not only the finale but perhaps also this trio section in the Ninth Symphony.

If the mood of choral jubilation on a huge scale is strong in the second half of the trio, and the similarity to the choral sections of the finale therefore most marked there, it is in the second strain (bars 422–38)

Ex. 27

that those who already know the finale will recognize an anticipation of the first and second instrumental variations (bars 116 sqq). The chronology of the symphony's composition does not allow of any certainty in the establishment of priorities. According to Nottebohm (*Zweite Beethoveniana*, p. 170) the scherzo and trio were completely sketched 'approximately in August 1823'. The same source informs us (p. 183) that in July of the same year Beethoven was still undecided on the second half of the 'Freude' theme so that it seems most unlikely that the instrumental variations on that theme were written before the trio section of the scherzo. If that is the case, and Beethoven had completed the scherzo and trio before he had finally determined the central melody of the finale, he was himself harking back to the trio when he wrote the finale.

When the scherzo is repeated, the second ending (bars 388–95) leads to a dramatic fermata on the dominant, from which the music plunges straight into the short coda—a mere sixteen bars of crescendo and stringendo from pianissimo to presto fortissimo, when the main scherzo theme is wrenched apart into two bars of unison common time; seven bars reminiscence of the trio, introduced by the fortissimo note on the trombone and executed by the woodwind over a tonic pedal in the whole string body; a bar's pause—and the movement flashes out with the final unison assertion of D without the third, major or minor.

Slow movement. Adagio molto e cantabile

Bearing in mind the key-sequence in op. 101 (A major first movement followed by F major scherzo) and the climactic switch from A major to F major that introduces the final fugue in op. 106, we are not surprised to find Beethoven's Adagio, following a D major-minor movement, in the key of B flat. That it is in variation form is even less surprising if we think of opp. 109 and 111, and of the Diabelli Variations on which he was working more or less simultaneously with the Ninth Symphony. Unlike the Diabelli Variations, however, those in this Adagio movement remain for the most part singularly close to the theme, always clearly identifiable through the veil of decoration that Beethoven casts over it. We are, in fact, on our way from the regions of outer space—Lucretius's *flammantia moenia mundi* devoid of all human inhabitants, where we found ourselves in the first movement—to the glorified *Volksfest* of the finale. The scherzo was a whirlwind still largely impersonal, though carrying the listener forward with an unmistakable purpose; and in the trio we suddenly came upon human warmth for the first time—we had sighted the familiar earth, even if we had not yet got our feet firmly planted on its soil. The Adagio is perhaps the most tenderly, compassionately human of all the movements that Beethoven wrote during the last ten years of his life, at least until the Cavatina of op. 130; and like that movement it opens with a 'curtain' that is gradually drawn back to allow us to hear (or overhear) a melody so simple yet so consoling that it seems to have been trying to find embodiment in sound, ever since man discovered this almost magical property of music. To Schenker[1] the bassoons and clarinets that slowly build up the opening chord call up the picture of 'human arms stretched in longing towards an object so nearly within their reach' yet unattainable, like Virgil's dead on the banks of the Styx stretching out their arms *ripae ulterioris amore* —in longing for the further shore (see Ex. 28).

We shall meet the outstretched, questing seventh again and again throughout the movement, recurring as a refrain. For although this Adagio is immediate in its appeal (and has even offended some commentators as much by the sensuousness of its lyricism as by its atmosphere of unashamed moral elevation) in structure it is as firm, as rigorously organic as that of Beethoven's most austere contrapuntal

---

[1] Heinrich Schenker, op. cit., p. 195.

Ex. 28

essays. If, as Bekker believes, the 'impulse towards abstraction' was really the driving force behind Beethoven's later works, then this Adagio (and the Cavatina of op. 130, which Beethoven himself valued as highly as anything that he ever wrote) are moments of regression. But in fact this image of a Beethoven increasingly concerned with Kantian metaphysics, or even with ethical absolutes in a philosophical sense, is false.[1] A severely practical musician, he had

[1] How far Bekker goes can be seen from the following passage (op. cit., p. 339). 'The religion of Beethoven's day was the ethical system of Kant. This ethical system is at the back of Beethoven's music, and it was the effort to express the philosophic concepts involved which carried his music so far into the region of abstraction.' Even if an ethical system could ever be a religion, Kant's was certainly not the inspiration of the Missa Solemnis or the Adagio of the Ninth Symphony, let alone of the ejaculations of 'holy! holy!' and the agonized prayers to a Heavenly Father, such as we find in the note books.

little interest in aesthetic theories and wholly lacked the intellectual training (and perhaps the natural powers, though that is less certain) needed to appreciate the ideas of Kant or any other philosopher, except as symbols of some vague and noble ideal.

We have seen that the idea of echo-effects in connection with this B flat major theme had occurred to Beethoven comparatively early. At first the winds were to repeat each strain as it was announced by the strings. Then came the idea of the winds echoing the last bar of each strain. These, apart from their own charm, also obviated the full close which, in early versions of the theme, formed an ugly break at bar 8. For a long time there was a turn in bar 4, thus

Ex. 29

and the same entry shows another trait of the final version—the syncopated dominant pedal which the violas provide in the first two strains. This gives the theme its gently urgent character, the very slight forward motion that saves it from the four-squareness of a hymn, just as the strong contrary motion between the melody and its bass save it from the suspicion of being simply a melody with accompaniment. Already in bar 6 the inner strings introduce the wind echo by the 'reaching-out' seventh that we noticed in the introduction, and this is echoed in the next bar by the clarinets and bassoons. After the two following strains the wind echoes are independent and not attached to the strings as in bars 6–7

Ex. 30

Now however, as the melody gains force and height, stretching in its turn towards the upper B♭ and the tension of dominant seventh harmony, the other strings do in fact assume the part of accompanists, their repeated and then harped chords reinforced by the horns, whose unexpected crescendo figure in bar 15 contains, as it were, a promise of much more important things to come later (bars 96 and 111).

The theme has come to rest on a dominant seventh in the tonic and moves easily, though unexpectedly, thence on to a pianissimo D major triad, first inversion. The 'Andante moderato' which follows is not a second theme of equal importance, but a subsidiary theme forming a kind of interlude. All its sixteen bars develop over a dominant pedal (cellos) reinforced by the rocking bass provided by the bassoons and double-basses. The gently swaying rhythm of the melody itself and its narrow span suggest a lullaby, and this impression is not contradicted by the syncopated character lent by the heavy leaning across the bar-line and the tied notes in melody and accompaniment.

Ex. 31

Of the original, rather conventional middle-section, Beethoven wisely preserved only the eight bars that were plainly the kernel of his idea; when these are completed he merely repeats them in a different orchestration and adds an exquisitely simple and appropriate counter-melody in the first violins. The contrast between the severe lines and hymn-like rhythm of the theme and the caressing (Beethoven marks 'espressivo' and even 'morendo')[1] swaying melody of this interlude, where second violins and violas in unison are answered by oboes, is as complete as Beethoven could make it. He himself was troubled by having lit upon two such admirable yet apparently incompatible ideas for his Adagio; and that he was unwilling to abandon either, yet puzzled how to combine them, is suggested by his nephew Karl's remark in a

---

[1] An unusual marking, but one that Beethoven had used as early as 1795 in the third of his op. 1 trios and again in the quartets op. 59, no. 1 and op. 74, always at cadences, as here.

conversation-book belonging to the autumn of 1823—'I am only delighted that you have brought in the beautiful Andante.' After its short sixteen bars are over, Beethoven glides, unostentatiously this time, over his favourite modulation—back from D major to B♭ major and the first variation. For the first sixteen bars of this clarinets play the skeleton of the melody, harmonized by the horns and pizzicato basses, with the violas retaining as closely as possible their dominant pedal. Above and beneath this firm web of sound the first violins execute a flowing ornamental arabesque, surrounding the notes of the theme with playful or tender semiquaver figures that never obscure its contours. The winds still retain the echo-phrases at cadences (the bassoons 'reaching-out' seventh in bar 47 is doubled by the second violins, who for that bar abandon their pizzicato accompaniment), and after the fourth cadence the variation ceases and the last strain of the theme is repeated exactly as it was heard on the first occasion. Only, where the B flat of the theme modulated into the D major of the Andante interlude, there is now a modulation to G major; and it is in that key that the Andante is heard a second time—not so much varied as adorned with a new countermelody and new instrumentation (including a swaying internal horn-pedal) that enhance the combination of innocence and sensuous allure that proved irresistible to a later generation of composers.[1]

In the second variation, which follows the Andante immediately, the dance and the lullaby are followed by a chorale. During this whole variation in E flat major[2] the strings play pizzicato, pointing or breaking the mostly three-part harmony of the clarinets and bassoons, whose churchly meditation on the theme is shorn of all echo effects, though carefully marked 'dolce'. This marking is even extended to the fourth horn part, which is in fact a kind of obbligato, answering the clarinets statement of the theme two bars later (bars 85–6) and then, when the theme moves into the minor and thence into C♭ major, assuming a major role. First the horn doubles the flute, which has taken over the top line of the melody, at the octave; and then, as the pizzicato strings transform themselves into harps at bar 95, with broken chords in triplets,

---

[1] Particularly Gustav Mahler, whose ländler movements surely owe something to this passage.
[2] When Mozart writes solemn wind music in this key, we are told that it is 'masonic'. This variation suggests that the theme of E♭ for wind music has as purely technical, practical an explanation as the choice of D or A major for violin music.

Ex. 32

embarks on a perilously high-lying solo scale passage which returns to
the dominant of C♭ major and so—by Beethoven's favourite Neapolitan modulation—to the original key of B♭ and the next, third,
variation.

  Hitherto there has been a marked contrast between the sober 4/4 of
the theme and the more relaxed 3/4 of the intermezzo. In the first
variation the theme in the woodwind was merely decorated by the
play of the strings; its rhythm was not altered or in any way disguised,
while in the second variation its angularity was stressed by the woodwind and only slightly relieved by the pizzicato strings. Now, however,
Beethoven allows the theme to expand into a flowing 12/8 in which
the whole orchestra takes part. The woodwind, as before, play the
melody almost unaltered, accompanied by the lower strings pizzicato.
The horns are divided, the first and second horns playing with the
woodwind and the fourth filling in the rhythmic accompaniment
figure of the lower strings. Weaving their way in and out of this

firmly compact web of sound, the first violins execute an exquisite and often brilliant embroidery far more ambitious and extensive than that which they provided in the first variation. There their part adhered closely to the melodic line of the theme and did not spread itself in widely spaced figuration or any variety of note values, only evenly flowing semi-quavers. In this third variation, on the other hand, the first violin part resembles rather that of the soloist in a concerto. Starting with a leap of two octaves, the even flow of the line is soon interrupted by triplet figuration, by dotted semiquavers and trills,

while the wide spacing of the figuration moves freely backwards and forwards over a two-octave span, imparting to the music a lightness and an airy motion that it would otherwise lack. Not content with this enhancing of the purely sensuous attractions inherent in the theme, Beethoven expends a wealth of detail on the cadence-echoes, which were always an important part of his scheme. At the first two of these the flutes echo the clarinets, while at the third cadence the fourth horn exercises a prodigious falling arpeggio (bars 111–12) as though to rival the first violins for a moment; and this is repeated in bar 117, before the horns join the rest of the wind in the rise to the B♭ which is the last high point of the theme. The violin semiquavers have now been replaced by harped chords, as the variation dies down, against a diminuendo sobbing figure in the horn (bars 118–20) and we pass with an unsuspected flourish into the coda.

This starts with a series of fanfares and what seems (bars 123–4) to be going to develop into a stretto that belongs to the chorale world of the second variation. These four bars, however, never get any further, for the sensuous swaying rhythm and the violins' semiquaver embroideries return, while the theme is echoed again from instrument to instrument (in augmentation in horns and bassoons bars 127–9). Once again the fanfares of the coda interrupt this reverie-like atmos-

phere; and this time it seems that the fanfares will indeed lead somewhere, when in bar 133 what is always for Beethoven the most
dramatically significant modulation (to the key of the flattened sixth)
carries the music into D flat major

Ex. 34

But this in its turn covers hardly four bars of shifting harmonies, and then the theme returns again, dolce. This time it is for good, and the rest of the movement is an unrestrained revelling in the delights of a B♭ major cadence prolonged over a period, and even in a manner, that seems to recall the murmuring of the brook in the Sixth Symphony.

Finale

The last movement of the Ninth Symphony, like the last scene of *Fidelio*, is a cantata. Beethoven had certainly not originally planned it so, and it seems as though it was only when he dropped the idea of a tenth symphony that he decided to incorporate in the symphony destined for London that setting of Schiller's *Ode to Joy* that he had been planning for some thirty years. We have already seen that, after he had finally determined the 'Joy' theme and written much of the vocal part of the movement, he was still contemplating an instrumental production on new themes; and that even when he had abandoned that idea, the text introducing the ode gave him great trouble. It was only after the end of October 1823, when he had found this, that he could go straight on to complete the symphony, which he did in February 1824. We have not yet considered the source of Beethoven's inspiration for the cantata and the models, if any, that guided him. It is conceivable that the great Volksfest in the Prater, given in October 1814 to celebrate the defeat of Napoleon and the end of a twenty years' war, may have given him general inspiration; but that was an occasion on which music played a subordinate part. To find a precedent for music intimately associated with a great popular festivity, both national and in the broadest sense religious, it is necessary to turn to France in the early days of the Revolution.

Christianity was not at first rejected by the leaders of the Revolution. As the Goncourts wittily expressed it, 'le bon Dieu eut aux premiers jours de la Révolution la popularité de Louis XVI', while a certain Abbé Fauchet spoke of Jesus Christ as 'la divinité concitoyenne du genre humain'. The Fête de la Fédération on 14 July 1790 was the first great ceremony held outside a church and even that was a Mass, with a Te Deum specially written by Gossec, who also provided the Marche lugubre for Mirabeau's funeral nine months later. It was not until the Fête de l'Etre Suprême given on 8 June 1794 that we find anything that could remotely have inspired Beethoven, had he known of it.

At the Tuileries Robespierre made a speech which he interrupted in order to set fire to a monster representing Atheism, whose smoking remains collapsed at the feet of the statue of Wisdom. . . . 2,400 voices then sang the 'Hymn to the Supreme Being' to music by Gossec and Desorgues.

Later there was a kind of community singing—

Old men and boys sang the first verse to the tune of the Marseillaise, and all the men at the gathering sang the refrain in chorus. Mothers and daughters sang the second verse, whose refrain was taken up by all the women at the meeting. The third, and last, verse was sung by all those on the Montagne [the top benches of the Convention] and the refrain was taken up by the whole crowd.[1]

[1] See Lavignac, *Histoire de la Musique* (Paris, 1913) Part I, p. 1586.

The music of the *Hymn to the Supreme Being* is a larghetto 6/8 in C
major marked 'très gracieux et religieux'—in fact a sentimental *opéra
comique* melody that represented, no doubt, the highest common
musical factor of the Parisian proletariat in 1794. Gossec himself,
however, was no mean musician. If his march for Mirabeau's funeral
is clearly derived from Gluck, his *Triomphe de la République* (1795)
anticipates the finale of Beethoven's Seventh Symphony. We have
already said something of Beethoven's enthusiasm for another of these
French Revolutionary composers, Méhul, whose wind overture
Musique à l'usage des fêtes nationales was not without its influence on
Beethoven's *Egmont*. A third, Rodolphe Kreutzer, became a personal
friend of Beethoven's during his stay at the French Embassy in Vienna
during 1798. We know that Beethoven was much at the Embassy
and greatly influenced by the enthusiasms of the ambassador, Count
Bernadotte, and by the cosmopolitan revolutionaries whom he met
there. It was certainly at this time and in this company that he
conceived his admiration for Napoleon, which led to the dedication
of the Third Symphony, and for the music of Méhul and of Cherubini,
which led indirectly to the composition of *Fidelio*. There is nothing
more likely than that Kreutzer should have described to him, and even
shown him the music of these revolutionary festivals. In this connection it is perhaps even significant that the first ideas that seem to have
occurred to Beethoven for the 'Joy' theme were French (see Ex. 4,
where the 3/8 is a very characteristic *opéra comique* rhythm) rather
than German, and certainly seem to suggest an entirely different
conception from that of the final version, in which the foursquare
German folk-song contributes so strong an element.

If the exact character of the finale is difficult to decide simply by
seeking its origins and precedents, the form of the movement is even
more puzzling. In fact Beethoven was here exploring new territory,
and no precedents will really help us to grasp his meaning. The attempt
by Otto Baensch[1] to fit the whole movement into a system of archaic
Stollen and *Abgesang*, though interesting and ingenious, comes hope-
lessly to grief in details, even if we can accept either of the equally
improbable premises—that Beethoven was acquainted with these
forms or that he invented them unwittingly. For example bars 192–202
are duly labelled by Baensch 'Abgesang' following two Stollen; but
unfortunately he has to admit that bars 192–8 are in fact the

[1] Otto Baensch, *Aufbau und Sinn des Chorfinales in Beethoven's neunter Symphonie*, 1930. This
is an application to Beethoven's music of the findings of A. Lorenz in his *Das Geheimnis der
Form bei Richard Wagner* (1924–6).

continuation of the Stollen, and he therefore weakly labels bars 199–202 as 'Schluss'. His essay, though full of interesting detail, fails to carry conviction; and it is characteristic that it includes the sketch of a scenario for a proposed stage performance of the finale, which he conceives as an *Erziehungsdrama* (educational drama) in the spirit of *The Magic Flute*. It is probably wise, and certainly safer, to accept Heinrich Schenker's division of the movement into three parts:[1]

Part 1   from the beginning to bar 594, i.e. to the end of the eighth variation

Part 2   bars 594–653 Andante maestoso 'Seid Umschlungen'

Part 3   bars 654–end, i.e. the ninth variation (double fugue) choral recitative and coda.

Although this may be arbitrary, it at least recognizes the Andante maestoso as the kernel of the movement, and the affinity between the double-fugue here and those at 'in Gloria Dei Patis' and 'Et vitam venturi saeculi' in the Missa Solemnis—all three great fugues which form both climax and end of a movement.

We have seen (Ex. 6) how Beethoven first imagined the instrumental opening of the finale, and how far that was from what he eventually wrote. The 'horror-fanfare' (*Schreckensfanfare*) of the first seven bars, repeated in bars 17–24, announces unmistakably the opening of a movement designed not only to contrast strongly with the brook-like murmurings with which the Adagio ends, but also to form a worthy conclusion to the craggy magnificence of the first movement. It is almost as though Beethoven himself felt that in the coda of the Adagio he had wandered a little too far from the strenuous mountain air of the first two movements and needed to concentrate his forces again. The Adagio's calm yet persistent assertion of the tonality of B♭ major is characteristically contradicted in the fanfare, where B flat is combined with an unambiguous D minor triad over a dominant (A) roll in the timpani. The recitatives that follow are six in number, and all are given to the bass strings, whom Beethoven instructed to play strictly in tempo. Without the verbal 'key' that Beethoven is to produce later, the unprepared listener must be puzzled, although in retrospect he can piece together the meaning of the two apparent outbursts of rage and the three quotations from the earlier movements of the symphony, just as he grasps that bars 77–80 are a kind of 'trailer' of the music that is to come. But the situation is a little too like a musical quiz or conundrum for the beginning of a great symphonic movement.

[1] Schenker, *Beethoven's Neunte Sinfonie*, pp. 244 sq.

It is certainly not improved when the *Schreckensfanfare* and the recitatives (this time with words attached) reappear long after the listener
has received the impression of being well advanced into the movement,
having already heard the 'Joy' theme announced with three full-scale
variations. Musicians and music-lovers have mostly come to accept
this unsatisfactory opening to the finale not simply because it represents
a comparatively small blot on a very great work, but because that very
blot is so completely characteristic of the composer. This is the kind of
miscalculation that may endear rather than alienate, though it has
alienated many great musicians, including Verdi, and continues to do so
today. Nobody, however, has been able to deny the 'Joy' theme in its
final form an almost unique note of simple exultation, physical as well
as emotional, and a popular character that no subsequent composer
has ever quite achieved, without either deliberate condescension or
unconscious compromise. We may explain this in a general sense by
the fact that Beethoven himself remained, certainly physically and in
many ways emotionally, an unsophisticated man of the people who
knew by instinct the stimulus to which simple listeners respond.
Nevertheless, the sketch-books reveal the pains which he took to
achieve the final version of the theme. His chief concern seems to have
been to balance unity (even exact repetition) with variety in an easily
memorable form. What appears to be an almost laughably simple
melody shows a number of subtleties in its construction. This follows
the scheme a1, a2, b, a2, b, a2—in which a2 differs from a1 only in
the final bar

Ex. 35

The appearance of quavers only in the b section carries this, as it were unconsciously forward, at a slightly faster tempo; and the very characteristic anticipation in bar 13, which might seem a sophistication, proves in practice one of the most easily memorable features of the whole melody.

Announced at first piano and unaccompanied, by cellos and basses, the theme is harmonized first by lower strings and bassoons, which provide a countermelody. When the violins are added for the second variation, the music is marked by an increasing warmth (dolce) and excitement, which reach their first climax in the third variation. Here the theme is heard for the first time forte, announced in clear thirds and fifths ('hunting harmony') by the winds punctuated, as it were, by the applause of the strings, whose double stopped chords mark the rhythm. In the coda to this variation (bars 187–207) the strings have non legato semiquaver scales and broken chord figures. These lead to a strong and repeated assertion of A major (bars 201–2), which is taken up again in bars 206–7 and leads straight into the next, choral section of the movement. Before that, however, in bars 203–5 Beethoven playfully changes his mind—slackens the tempo (poco ritenente) and reduces the volume to piano while flute and upper strings take, as it were, another look at the so confidently proclaimed A major—trying the cadential phrase first in B minor and then in D♯ (E♭) minor before returning to the unequivocal A major and the original tempo (see Ex. 36).

This naïvely humorous spirit of contradiction, which shows itself on many occasions in Beethoven's music after a particularly uncompromising statement, holds back the impetus of the music only to draw greater attention to the flood that is once again unloosed, as the *Schreckensfanfare* is heard in the full orchestra and this time with the additional 'frightfulness'—for we can really speak here of a policy of *Grässlichkeit* on Beethoven's part—of diminished seventh harmonies to the tonic, i.e. a dissonant C♯, E and G added to the B flat which gave the fundamental D minor triad harmonies their cutting edge in the first two fanfares. The opening of the baritone soloist's first recitative provides the words that were missing from the first of the instrumental recitatives at the beginning of the movement, and his final phrase (bars 230–6) harks back to the sixth of the instrumental recitatives. As the 'trailer' that we first heard in bars 77–80 is repeated in bars 237–40, the baritone's first cry of 'Freude' (joy) is taken up by the basses of the chorus, but it is the soloist whose voice first announces the theme complete, doubled by the string basses. The

violins meanwhile provide an internal dominant pedal, while above them oboe and clarinet indulge in a game, the one following the contours of the theme while the other provides a skittish counter-melody. The chorus repeat the soloist's last lines, doubled by the strings in unison and against a full-scale wind harmonization, which continues in a small codetta after the voices fall silent (bars 265–8). The final cadence of this is perhaps an unconscious borrowing from *The Magic Flute* (ritornello of Papageno's first aria Act I, Scene 2)

Ex. 37 (a)
  Mozart "Die Zauberflöte" Act 1 sc. 2

(b)

as though Beethoven here turned instinctively to what was already the classical expression of Viennese popular participation in fundamentally serious musical matters. There were certainly a great many Papagenos at the Volksfest in the Prater in October 1814, and no doubt Beethoven welcomed their potential presence in the chorus of his Ninth Symphony.

The fifth variation belongs to the soloists, who are only joined by the chorus for the last lines of the verse. Here the orchestral accompaniment is very light, the cellos answered by flutes and bassoons two octaves apart (could this be another reminiscence of the *Magic Flute*, where the same disposition is prominent in the overture?). Once again a codetta ending with Papageno's cadence rounds off this fifth variation and introduces the next, in which the music becomes increasingly florid. The tenor and baritone soloists lead off in sixths, doubled an octave above by oboe and clarinet. They are joined first by the contralto and then the soprano soloists, while the steady repeated crotchets of the horns form a kind of tom-tom pedal, taken over by the timpani when the harmony demands a dominant pedal. The excitement is further whipped up by the strings which, at first singly and then in alternating couples, punctuate the voices with a gadfly figure on the weak beats of the bar. The music becomes even more lively when the chorus takes up the soloists' words

Küsse gab sie uns und Reben,
einen Freund geprüft im Tod:
Wollust ward dem Wurm gegeben
Und der Cherub steht vor Gott

(Joy gave us kisses and wine,
a friend tried to the uttermost;
even the worm was granted pleasure
and the cherub stands before God)

It was inevitable that the last line, which destroys the unfortunate impression made by the penultimate, should catch Beethoven's imagination, and he repeats it to form the coda (bars 321–30) of this sixth variation—a solid climb in minims by the chorus, from A up to D and then (characteristically poised on the D which the contraltos take over from the sopranos) up to G♯ and A on the words 'vor Gott'. The strings hail this arrival before the heavenly throne with a battery of descending semiquavers, repeated as the chorus repeat in ecstasy 'vor Gott' and once again, with the modulation to the flattened sixth of the scale (D major in F major) used here at its most dramatic, repeating the threefold salutation of the Deity with a long tenuto—'vor Gott'.

Ex. 38

In order to realize quite how strange and unorthodox Beethoven's next step must have seemed to his contemporaries we must go back for a moment to the sketch-books of the summer-autumn 1822 where we found after the projected 'sinfonie allemand' the note, 'Ende der Symphonie mit türkischer Musik und Singchor.' 'Turkish music' refers to the percussion instruments used by the Turkish corps of Janissaries and borrowed with increasing frequency by European armies during the eighteenth century. Poland led the way during the 1720s, under Augustus II, soon followed by the Russian Empress Anne and then by other European sovereigns including Prussia, Austria, and England. The instruments—'jingling Johnny', kettle-drum, side drum, bass drum, cymbals, and triangle—were at first played by Turks, except in England, where negroes were generally employed; but it was not long before serious composers became interested in the possibilities of bass drum, cymbals, and triangle to lend an exotic note to their works. Gluck introduced them in *La Rencontre Imprévue* (known in German as 'Die Pilger von Mekka') in 1764, and again in *Iphigénie en Tauride* (1777). He was followed by Mozart in *Entführung* (1781) and, obliquely, in the Rondo alla Turca for pianoforte K. 331, and by Haydn in the so-called 'Military' symphony (1794), while Beethoven himself had used this combination in his music for *The Ruins of Athens* (1812) and *The Battle of Vittoria* (1813). That such sonorities, with their military and popular associa-tions, might well be suitable at the end of a big movement depicting communal rejoicing is plain;[1] but to introduce them when the text speaks of the angelic host mustered around the throne of God and the music itself has fallen, as it were, into an 'O altitudo!' seems almost perverse. This, however, is exactly what Beethoven does after the third of the chorus's shouts of 'vor Gott' have carried the music into F major. From the extreme distance, as it were, but drawing rapidly nearer come the sounds of a military march—bass drum, bassoon, and double-bassoon marking the rhythm, joined first by clarinets and horns, and then the march itself in piccolo (in place of fifes), clarinets, and horns, with triangle and cymbals added to the percussion. This turns out to be the seventh variation of the 'Joy' theme, with a completely changed rhythm—6/8 and starting in the middle of the bar, so that the accents fall differently

---

[1] There was certainly 'Turkish music' to be heard at the march past of the veterans during the Prater Volksfest in October 1814. The approach of a regimental band from the distance, which is the effect of this section of the finale, may well have struck Beethoven on this occasion, if he was present.

Ex. 39

In all this the strings only take the subordinate part of a chorus, and in fact their echoing of the cadences in bars 358 and 374 is really a convenience in order to give the wind band time to breathe and also, in the second case, to introduce the tenor soloist. It is only after his entry that Beethoven slowly relaxes his pianissimo markings, reaching più forte as the chorus join the soloist and fortissimo as the variation ends. The tenor soloist's music is a countermelody to the original theme, out-of-doors if not specifically military in character and ingeniously modelled on the contours of the original. 'Glad as his suns that hurtle through the vast abyss of space, brothers, run your race, joyful, as a hero who marches to victory.' As the chorus sings 'victory' and the soloist rises twice in triumph to his top B♭, the strings, who have played a completely subordinate role in this seventh variation, join the woodwind in introducing the purely instrumental interlude which separates the seventh from the eighth variation. This is a fugato, whose subject and countersubject appear together

The rhythm of the main subject is taken from the preceding variation, and the restless countersubject—whose persistent quavers never cease from bars 432 to 516, gives this whole interlude a character of 'wrestling and struggling', something between the Presto section

Ex. 40

Fag. & Bassi

of the 'Dona nobis pacem' in the Missa Solemnis and the Grosse Fuge of op. 130, that still lay in the future. Although this countersubject is never absent, and Beethoven makes use of its obvious suitability for sequential treatment and extension to carry the music forward (bars 477–91), the subject is never heard without it until in bar 517 the long passage in B minor ends in the whole orchestra with a fortissimo F♯ unison. This is hurled to and fro through the orchestra for eight bars fortissimo[1] and then continued for another sixteen (diminuendo to pianissimo) in the horns. Distant woodwind thirds, at first in B major, then in B minor and finally (as the bass sinks to A) in D major form an intensely dramatic return to the 'Joy' theme; and we then realize that this whole instrumental interlude has been a battle, a struggle to reach D major from B flat major not by any short cut or *coup de théâtre* (such as Beethoven is quite willing to use on other occasions) but by deliberately plodding 'the long way round'—from B flat major to B flat minor (bars 432–62) through F major, G major, C minor and E flat major—and facing and rebutting, even on the last stage of the journey (B minor), every possible objection before claiming final victory.

When this arrives in variation 8, the woodwind double the simple primary harmonies of the chorus (return to verse 1 'Freude schöner Götterfunken, Tochter aus Elysium'), but the strings embark on a triumphant version of the ostinato quaver rhythm which pervaded the whole of the instrumental interlude—a wonderful inspiration that links the sections and emphasizes the continuation of activity even after victory is assured.

The final rocketing D major arpeggio of the strings in bars 590–1 is followed by an unexpected turn to G major and a fermata: we have reached the heart of the movement, the declaration of the fatherhood of God as the truth on which the brotherhood of man rests. The bass trombone, supported by the string basses, rings out like the ritual *shofar* anticipating and giving the note to the choral tenors and basses

---

[1] Brahms surely had this at the back of his mind in bars 119–28 of the first movement of the Second Symphony, and perhaps in the second subject of the violin concerto's first movement.

Ex. 41

This all-embracing love is something quite different from the theory of universal benevolence proclaimed by the eighteenth-century rationalists. It is difficult for us, who have the theory of humanitarian idealism bred into our bones, to understand the novelty and the inspiration of this revelation. Walt Whitman has since familiarized us with the idea of embracing millions and imprinting a kiss on the face of the world; but when Beethoven was a young man and read this passage in Schiller's ode, such things were not dreamed of and they made an impression that never left him, although it took him thirty years to give it expression.

As in the Missa Solemnis, Beethoven turns to the simplest means for his most solemn moments. Perhaps it is chiefly the dislocation of the rhythm (and consequent harmonic clashes) caused by the characteristic anticipations—the leap of the ninth in bar 596 and the strange forward leaps in bars 604, 606, and 608—that reveal the enormous emotional tension beneath this apparently simple choral passage. This is enhanced by the *tripudium*, or stamping-dance of ecstasy, executed by the basses beneath the sforzando hammering of the violas in example 41. The harmonic progression in bars 609–10 (C major–D major) is already archaic, and the unison bars for trombones and the basses of strings and chorus (bars 611–18) seem to be nothing less than a Gregorian fossil, such as we found in the Gloria of the Missa Solemnis (see Ex. 6, p. 232).

Ex. 42

Beethoven's instinctive turn from the brotherhood of man to the fatherhood of God, as its natural corollary, explains this change of mood from ecstatic optimism to awe-stricken awareness of the creator and, in musical terms, to a certain archaism of expression. As the whole chorus and orchestra take up the words intoned by the male chorus[1] the anticipations are found again in the choral writing, but the *tripudium* in the basses has become much more restrained, with octave leaps replaced by the interval of a single tone, though the violas have the same hammering sforzando that maintains the interior tension of the passage. The double versicle and response are now concluded in a half close in C major, and with a brusque anticipatory chord of G minor the 'Adagio ma non troppo, ma divoto' begins.

Here, as in the Sanctus of the Missa Solemnis, Beethoven dispenses entirely with the upper strings, which are replaced by the violas playing in three or four parts, doubled by flutes and clarinets, while bassoons double the string bass. As there, too, his harmony is modal (cp. also bars 369–71 of the Credo, Ex. 21, p. 259).

> Ihr stürzt nieder, Millionen?
> Ahnest du den Schöpfer, Welt?
> Such' ihn überm Sternenzelt!
> Ueber Sternen muss er wohnen

Humanity's instinctive fall to its knees is depicted by the telling fall of the vocal line a seventh, from G minor through G major to C major;

[1] The whole form of this Andante maestoso section is quasi-liturgical—first versicle (bars 595–602) and response (603–10): second versicle (611–18) and response (619–26); hymn (627–53).

and the slow raising of man's eyes from the dust of his own nothingness to the 'starry tent' imagined as hiding the Creator, is suggested by the corresponding rise back through G minor and B flat major to the C major of 'Welt'. Then the ear, as it were, follows the eye upwards, through F major to D major and finally—by Beethoven's favourite device of screwing up the music a semitone—to the E flat, which finds the basses at the very top of their range and so imparting a strong tension to the lower of the two thirds into which Beethoven divides the choral parts. As though to add particular solemnity and point to the words of this hymnic utterance, Beethoven anticipates each half line of the chorus by a strong orchestral anticipation of the changing harmony. This reaches its climax in bar 637, where the archaic juxtaposition of triads of B♭ and C major is enormously emphasized:

Ex. 43

The great E♭ major affirmation of bars 643–6 ('Über Sternen muss er wohnen') ends in half a bar's silence.[1] In that moment Beethoven, as

---

[1] Those who look for an unmistakable indication of Beethoven's beliefs in his handling of words meet here the same difficulty as they met in the Credo of the Missa Solemnis. In bar

it were, quietly redirects the intention of his music, passing from religious contemplation to visual description. No longer trying to pierce
beyond the visible majesty of the night sky to its creator and his purposes, Beethoven contents himself with the beauty of the scene itself.
As the pianissimo diminished seventh in the strings is gradually
taken up, first by the woodwind and then the voices, and turned to the
prolonged expectancy of the dominant seventh of D major (bars
647–53), we have the sensation of being poised at an infinite space
above the earth, bathed in starlight and on the brink of some great
revelation.

The revelation is not slow in coming, and it takes the form of the
last and most powerful of all the statements of the 'Joy' theme in a
double fugue. The words 'Freude, schöner Götterfunken' sung by the
sopranos are countered by the altos with the second or countersubject of 'Seid umschlungen, Millionen!'

Ex. 44

614 he accented 'muss ein lieber Vater wohnen', but in 645 the emphasis is 'muss er wohnen'.
Does the first express the will to believe, rather than belief itself, and the second a joyful
recognition of a presence already believed in ? Is it the difference between the searcher who
says in despair 'He must live there' and the worshipper who says 'He must live there' ? or is it
entirely a matter of musical consideration ? In either case, of course the Sternenzelt is Kant's
'starry heavens' rather than the 'up above the bright blue sky' of the old hymn.

The anticipatory lead by the altos is strengthened by the trumpet
(cf. the trombone at the opening of this section and in the scherzo),
The winds double the voices throughout the whole variation, while the
strings alternate between doubling the voices and providing a swirling

quaver accompaniment, which is sometimes doubled by the bassoons. There are six entries of the two themes—the first by sopranos (A) and altos (B), the second by tenors (B) and Basses (A), the third by tenors (A) and basses (B), the fourth by sopranos (B) and altos (A), the fifth by sopranos (A) and altos (B). The sixth entry follows an episode in which the rhythms of both subjects persist uninterrupted and lead in bars 717–18 to a triple top A for the sopranos, who then hold this note while beneath them altos (A) and basses (B) sing the two themes and the tenors first support the sopranos and then fill in the harmony. The fugue ends suddenly, its huge momentum exhausted but reverberating in the alto part, half a bar after the other voices, which ends (as it began) half a bar before them.

Without a moment's pause Beethoven continues the text to which he had returned in 'Seid umschlungen!' In an accompanied choral recitative, deliberately angular in line and jerky in rhythm, basses ask 'Ihr stürzt nieder, Millionen?' and tenors continue 'Ahnest du den Schöpfer, Welt?' Altos follow the same pattern with 'Such ihn überm

Ex. 45

Sternenzelt' and this is repeated by the whole chorus rising to a single A. The combination of tonic and dominant harmony over a tonic (A) pedal during the next dozen bars (745–57) immediately carries the listener back to the trio section of the scherzo (bars 495–530, see Ex. 27) and once again we have the impression of the singing of a crowd so vast that its harmonies become confused, as one section gets ahead of another without realizing it, so great is the space between them. This section ends with the whole orchestra and chorus on a chord of G major, and it is in this key that the strings lead into the final 'Allegro ma non tanto'.

This coda of 180 bars is in the form of an increasingly excited jubilation three times checked, but only to break out again with an impetus that finally carries all before it. When the strings have led from G major to D major, the male soloists in thirds, followed by the female soloists in sixths, lead off like couples at a dance, over a pedal first tonic and then dominant. This dominant pedal is still sounding when the voices follow each other in a series of canonic entries which eventually bring in the chorus in octave unison. In bars 801–3 this unison invades the orchestra as well as the chorus, leaving only timpani and brass sustaining the dominant pedal. The instruments carry the mounting unison phrase a bar and a half higher, whereupon the chorus re-enters fortissimo with five repetitions of the words 'alle Menschen', as though intoxicated with the idea of universal brotherhood; and the movement only receives its first sudden check in bar 810, where a sudden reduction of the tempo (poco adagio) and expressive falling figures in the strings mark a moment of serious meditation in the excitement. This breaks out again in bar 814, only to be checked this time more seriously by the soloists. They 'screw up' the tonality from E minor to E major and embark on a florid cadenza-like passage (bars 832–42) only very lightly accompanied by the orchestra. The element of display proper to the cadenza is not absent, for the bass line spans almost two octaves (from low F sharp to top E) in two bars and the soprano rises to a top B, which is repeated (on the two difficult syllables of 'Flügel') with a diminuendo, as the harmony changes through B major to B minor and so back to the D major in which the movement is to end.

Ex. 46

This cadenza is the last serious interruption of the festivities, into
which the strings return us at a tempo that does not cease mounting
until in bar 851 we reach Beethoven's marking 'prestissimo'. Here
again we meet the 'Turkish music' which assists in whipping
up the excitement for the rest of the symphony. The soloists are silent,
leaving the rest of the entertainment to the crowd, rather as the allied
sovereigns and plenipotentiaries retired from the Volksfest in
October 1814 to dine and dance, leaving the Prater to the populace.
Beethoven, however, keeps a tight hold over the musical proceedings
and does not allow the music to deteriorate. The tension in the choral
writings is preserved by the high-lying bass line, which at one point
joins the tenor on a top F natural, and by the indefatigable rhythmic
invention. There is one last interruption at bars 915–20—a solemn
final apostrophe of

Tochter aus Elysium, Freude schöner Götterfunken

The voices and the winds have solemn dotted rhythms, to which the
strings add lustre and pomp by demisemiquaver staccato scale passages
in the baroque manner of a Handel chorus. After this, and the return
to prestissimo, the crowd's voices are only heard at intervals, and
always in unison, above the riotous D major din of the orchestra. The

symphony which opened with a D minor arpeggio ends with a D major scale, triplets in the winds rising to an unambiguous final drop of a fifth in plain crotchets.

Beethoven's only other large orchestral work during these last years was the overture *Die Weihe des Hauses* (The Consecration of the House), written during the late summer of 1822, which he spent at Baden. The commission was for music to be played at the opening of the new Josefstadt Theatre at the beginning of October and, at such short notice, Beethoven could only supply a new overture and adapt the music which he had written in 1812 for Kotzebue's play *Die Ruinen von Athen* on the occasion of the opening of another theatre, in Budapest. Karl Meissl made the necessary alterations in Kotzebue's text, and Beethoven supplied a new chorus of dervishes, as well as the overture, which is based on two strongly contrasted ideas. The first is a solemn march, opening in the winds with pizzicato accompaniment, and then a big Handelian fugue. These two parts are connected by a transitional passage in which dramatic tension is slowly augmented in a manner that owes a good deal to Rossini.

After five solemn opening chords in C major, fortissimo and sforzato, the march theme is heard pianissimo in the winds. The bare modulation, the relative minor of the dominant (E minor) enhances the austere solemnity of the theme, which is then taken up by the whole orchestra. Trumpet calls, drum taps, and a running semiquaver figure in the bassoons now punctuate widespread chords in the strings, as the pace mounts; but this proves a false alarm, and when the pace slackens again, we hear instead the following passage for strings and woodwind, over an open fifth in the horns:

Ex. 47

Despite the canonic imitations, the light stamping tread of the accompaniment is unmistakably Rossinian, and so is the subsequent unison mounting passage in the strings, semiquavers over a long dominant pedal. The sforzando markings off the beat and the suspensions in the woodwind, however, make this whole passage unambiguously Beethoven's rather than an imitation of the notorious 'Rossini crescendo'. When this passage arrives at a dominant cadence, the music comes to a complete standstill, and from this point of rest the last stage of the transition is built up by short pianissimo string phrases, echoed immediately by the winds. Finally the strings embark on the rising unison figure which, 'crescendo e poco stringendo il tempo', finally leads to the statement of the fugue subject allegro con brio, with countersubject

Ex. 48

In 1822 this must have sounded not so much archaic as ecclesiastical, since in church music there was a recognized, even consecrated, time-lag. There was certainly nothing archaic in Beethoven's handling of his two subjects. He relishes, and often deliberately accents, the harmonic clashes produced by the suspensions of the countersubject; and, since this was an occasional piece for a theatrical occasion, he allows a great deal of brilliant semiquaver passage-work, including frequent repeated notes which greatly enhance the simplicity of the tonal scheme and the dynamic contrasts, while the foursquareness of the phrases unmistakably recall the baroque, and especially Handel. That Beethoven should have conceived music so solemn and so little popular for the opening ceremony of a theatre is yet another proof of how deeply ingrained in him were the principles of the eighteenth-century Enlightenment. The very use of the word 'Weihe'—consecration—suggests that for him the theatre was not so much a place of entertainment as an institution for the moral education of the public. We do not meet this attitude again until Wagner's *Bühnenweihfestspiel*, *Parsifal*.

CHAPTER 19

The String Quartets. Opp.
127, 130, 131, 132, and 135

A performance of Beethoven's C sharp minor string quartet op.
131 some eighty years ago prompted Bernard Shaw to speak of
'the simple, unpretentious, perfectly intelligible posthumous quartets'.
This was a characteristically provocative phrase, for Beethoven's last
quartets were still often considered unintelligible and shapeless, un-
finished torsos by a partially deranged genius; and although we can now
see that they are the purest stuff of music, exquisitely and logically
constructed and finished to the highest degree, to say that they are
simple and unpretentious is misleading. The claim to understand them
perfectly is a bold claim to personal as well as musical maturity; and
honest puzzlement, or Platonic ἀπορία, at least reveals a clear
instinctive understanding of the music's quality. These works are
indeed self-communings, in the sense that Beethoven no longer goes
out of his way to make clear to the listener either the logic or the
emotional consequence of his thoughts; but they were not written, like
J. S. Bach's *Art of Fugue*, without a view to performance. In fact how
much importance Beethoven attached to their performance can be
gauged by the letter to the players written on the eve of the first
performance of op. 127, quoted in Part 1, p. 66.

Opus 127
    This, the first of the three quartets written to Prince Galitsin's
commission was begun perhaps as early as May 1822, interrupted by
work on the Ninth Symphony, but taken up again in the summer of
1824 and finished. The first performance was in any case on 6 March
1825.
    This is the only one of the last five quartets, except the last, op. 135,
to observe the traditional four-movement scheme, and even so there
is enormous variety within movements. The first is an Allegro with
a slow (maestoso) six-bar introduction that recurs twice: at the

beginning of the development section and again, in a foreshortened form, in the middle of that section, long before the start of the recapitulation, where it might have been expected. The character of this introduction is anything but prefatory in the sense of being tentative, and looks back to the slow introductions of Haydn's symphonies rather than forward to the atmospheric, improvisatory introductions of Liszt and the other Romantics. Tonic is followed by dominant harmony, in rich, hymn-like lay-out, cloudless E flat major only propelled by the heavy sforzandos off the beat. These are, as it were, echoed in the suspensions and anticipations noticeable in the two inner parts during the even flow of the Allegro theme,

Ex. 1

There is a parallel between the opening of this quartet and that of the piano sonata op. 81ᵃ, where a slow introduction in E flat leads to a statement of the main theme in the subdominant region, as here. But nothing could emphasize more clearly than a comparison between the two passages the change in the concentration and, as it were, the tempo of Beethoven's thought-process in these last years. Whereas in the sonata there is still a large degree of symmetry, repetition and extended, song-like melody, all this has now been refined to a minimum; and the rhetorical element has entirely disappeared. If such a pruned, chastened style is characteristic of advancing age, it does not denote a falling-off so much as a redirection of creative energy, an interiorization and concentration of the powers that were previously directed instinctively outwards to charm, persuade, or convince a hypothetical listener. The last quartets are addressed to that inward ear which, like Wordsworth's inward eye, may well be called the 'bliss of solitude'.

The simple four-part writing at the opening of the Allegro is interrupted by the second of the first group of subjects, when the two inner voices have repeated chords in accompaniment; but it returns again in the transitional passage leading to the second subject, and throughout that subject itself. This is in the unexpected key of G minor, which persists unbroken throughout the rest of the exposition and is heavily reaffirmed in the last ten cadential bars; so that it is not surprising to find the development section opening with the theme of the Introduction in G major, and continuing in that key. Almost exactly half the development is taken up with the first two bars of example 1, and their rhythmic shape persists in one part or another even when new ideas are introduced—first diminished harmonies, which lead to a restatement of the Introduction in C major, and then twenty bars in which Beethoven takes up a slightly different version of bar 3

Ex. 2

instead of

When the recapitulation comes, it is as though by stealth, and so varied and ornamented with new figures and interchange of instrumental parts that it is almost a new experience, comparable to meeting a friend, whom one has known as reserved and reflective, after a glass of wine that has released energies and prompted fancies previously dormant. The cello, in particular, indulges in fanciful embroideries and during the second subject, which duly appears in the tonic E flat major, makes an excursion into its higher register. The second subject's long cadential passage is made still longer by the addition of a forty-two-bar coda proper, based entirely on example 1, which in one way or another occupies nine-tenths of the whole movement.

The second movement ('Adagio, ma non troppo e molto cantabile') is a theme and five variations. The theme cost Beethoven endless trouble, as the sketch-books show.[1] Only the opening seems to have been an initial 'inspiration' or *Einfall*—what Paul Valéry called a 'vers donné'. All the rest was the result of repeated experiment.

[1] See Nottebohm, II, pp. 210 ff.

Beethoven tried, as usual, a number of different keys and rhythms; and a phrase from an idea eventually rejected in one place often occurs somewhere else later in the theme. The situation seems to have been complicated by the fact that two entirely different works seem to have been maturing together in Beethoven's mind at this time—this slow movement in A flat major and an entirely different movement, which was never completed, in C major and bearing the title 'La gaieté'. The first sketch for this appears thus

Ex. 3

Although Beethoven assured Schlösser (see pp. 129–30) that 'he sometimes worked on several things at the same time but could still depend on not confusing one with another,' there seems no doubt that this harmless and unbuttoned C major piece did somehow first hinder the final shaping of the A flat major melody that we know.

Ex. 4   Adagio, ma non troppo

Each of the four-bar strains of the theme is first played by the first violin, then repeated by the cello, with the other two instruments providing the harmony or a strand of counterpoint.

    In the first variation this antiphonal structure is even more marked, the instruments pairing off and then rejoining each other as in a dance. The contrapuntal texture is unusually close-knit; there is not an otiose, unaccounted note anywhere and the cadence of one phrase is inextricably tied to the opening of the next, as so often in Beethoven's last works (bar 25).

Ex. 5

For eighteen of the twenty-three bars of the second variation the first and second violins execute an elaborate duo, either answering each other antiphonally, imitating each other's figuration, or providing a countersubject to each other's melody. The two lower instruments meanwhile provide harmonic and rhythmic support as simple and constant as the violins' duo is elaborate (trills, suspensions, syncopations, etc.) and mercurial in character. This exquisite chatter comes to a sudden end in A flat major (first inversion) and with hardly a moment's pause the whole character, mood, tempo, and tonality of the music changes, from a playful and elegant conversational exchange to an Adagio molto espressivo, one of Beethoven's hymn-like slow movements. The transition is particularly worth noticing as it is effected by a single 'step' which recalls immediately the bar added as an afterthought to the Adagio of op. 106 (see p. 164).[1]

Ex. 6

Ex. 7

The prevalence of the flattened sixth (C natural in the key of E major) throughout the harmony of these seventeen bars is very striking (there is a parallel in the theme of the finale in op. 109, another E major movement) and the combination of this feature with anticipation and a swift return to diatonic harmony are very characteristic of Beethoven's last works, and particularly the quartets, where he often refers to, or hints at rather than states a modulation. Typical, too, is the sudden swell from forte to piano in a single beat, already shown in the multiple markings of example 5.

Ex. 8

In the fourth variation Beethoven returns to the tonality (A flat) and the metre (12/8) of the theme. Here it is the outer instruments that conduct a duet, while the inner support the harmony and maintain a steady rhythmic flow of even quavers. The first violin and the cello divide the theme between them, as at its first appearance, and alternate this with widely spaced broken-chord figures liberally sprinkled with trills and in the cello part (bar 82), a double-shake that we shall meet again in op. 131. The effect is that of an ethereally voluptuous nocturne, sensuous music without a trace of sensuality.

The intermezzo that separates this fourth variation from the fifth starts *sotto voce* and has a spare, solemn recollected quality that we find again in a similar episode of Chopin's Barcarolle (bars 34 sq.), and the late Barcarolles of Fauré. The semiquaver ornamentation of the theme that is passed from instrument to instrument in the fifth variation, against a syncopated accompaniment, clearly recalls the third variation in the Ninth Symphony's slow movement. The eight bars of the coda have as a middle point an exquisite enharmonic pun, in which the A flat major tonality of the movement is finally affirmed by being held up for a moment (bars 125–6), against the light of E (or rather F flat) major, exactly as Beethoven had done in the first movement and in the Adagio of op. 110.

The sketch-books show that Beethoven had almost as much trouble in hammering out the final version of the scherzo's main theme as he had with the theme of the Adagio. The dotted rhythm, which is one of its most salient features, does not appear in the first sketches; but the melodic scheme—four bars of ascending three-note phrases answered by four descending—was an integral part of Beethoven's conception. What puzzled him most was on which step of the scale to start:

Ex. 9

It would hardly be an exaggeration to say that the two basic ideas (1) and (2) between them account for the whole of the scherzo, with the exception of a strongly contrasted idea whose rhythmic peculiarity Beethoven emphasizes by marking it *ritmo di tre battute* (as in the scherzo of the Ninth Symphony):

Ex. 10

(ritmo di tre battute)

If the scherzo itself is given over exclusively to dotted rhythms and quirks such as these, the trio on the other hand is in evenly flowing crotchets (E flat minor *presto*), except for the popular-sounding dance-melody, with its heavily accentuated rhythms and drone bass, in the second half:

Ex. 11

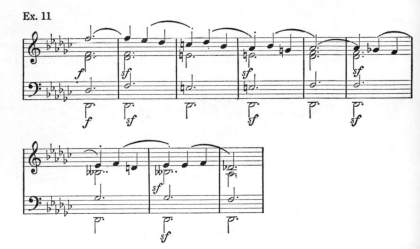

The coda is provided by an extension of the transition passage from the scherzo to the trio, which seems (as often in Beethoven) to be about to begin again, but is cut short after eleven bars.

The finale opens with four bars unison introduction which, as it were, raise the curtain on what seems at first to be a thoroughly Haydnish, good-humoured idea. The sketch-books show that in fact Beethoven did have in mind at one time an unmistakably rustic idea for this movement.

Ex. 12

Instead of this however, the physical good humour or euphoria of the movement is disturbed in the second group of subjects. The first of these starts conventionally enough, but gathers momentum and even a touch of savagery in the descending scale passage, every other note ornamented by an aggressive grace-note that leads to the second of the two (bars 61-6). This also starts light-heartedly

Ex. 13

but soon develops a violent, mordant character emphasized by harmonic clashes, repetitions, very thick string-writing, and stamping rhythms:

Ex. 14

If this can be called rustic, it is nearer to Bartók's stylized realism than to the idealized village scenes of Beethoven's own Sixth Symphony.

Most of the short development section is taken up with the broken chord figure of the first group of subjects, so that when this same figure leads off the recapitulation in A flat instead of the tonic E flat, and with the accents changed, the listener is taken by surprise. But that surprise is small compared with what Beethoven holds in reserve for the coda. The recapitulation has ended, with the stamping rhythms of the second subject group not only dying away, but coming almost to a standstill on a C major triad. Suddenly the whole mood changes—4/4 gives place to 6/8, an allegro comodo ('con moto' in some sources) marking suggests the relaxation of tension, and the two violins start trilling. Pianissimo semi-quaver triplets pass from one instrument to another while first in C major then in A flat then in E major and finally back to the tonic E flat major, we hear the triad theme (Ex. 15a) transfigured into a mysterious, beckoning bird-call. A long crescendo

Ex. 15

brings the music back into the light of common day; and the rustling semiquaver triplets gradually yield to conventional cadential figures, only to return, once again pianissimo and in trill form, twice before the movement ends.

Opus 132

The second of the Galitsin quartets was not the next in order of opus number (op. 130) but op. 132, finished in May 1825, after the work had been interrupted by the serious illness during which his doctor gave Beethoven a severe warning about looking after himself and avoiding spirits. The sketch-books show that, as often, Beethoven worked on op. 127 and 132 at the same time; but it seems that the night work, which Schindler and the doctor considered so prejudicial to his health, was probably done on op. 132. The composer himself headed the slow movement 'Song of thanksgiving offered to the Divinity by a convalescent, in the Lydian mode'; and on the strength of this A. B. Marx tried to fit a sickroom programme to the first movement, imagining the slow opening bars as Beethoven stretching himself uncomfortably, and seeing bursts of physical irritation in the changes of tempo and mood.[1] This movement has, it is true, a number

[1] A. B. Marx, *Ludwig van Beethoven, Leben und Schaffen*, (5th edition, 1901), Vol. 2, pp. 440 sq.

of unusual traits; but they are not to be explained by such naïve methods as these.

The eight pianissimo bars introduction, 'assai sostenuto', are a contrapuntal working of a two-bar theme closely related to one already used by Beethoven years earlier, in his overture to *Egmont*

Ex. 16

This theme also looks forward to the Grosse Fuge of op. 130; and, since the viola part opens with the notes A, G sharp, C, B, we may perhaps also associate the theme with the overture on the name BACH (B flat, A, C, B or, transposed A, G sharp, B, A sharp) which the composer was planning at this time. In any case, these bars create a mysterious and impressive atmosphere which is rudely interrupted at bar 9 by the first violin's semiquaver passage leading into the statement of the first of the main movement's themes (*Allegro*). The rhythmic articulation of this theme gave Beethoven great trouble, and we can follow in the sketch-books the steps (1) and (2) by which he approached the final solution (3) Nottebohm II, p. 547.

Ex. 17

A feature of this theme, which finds an important echo in the main subject of the second group, is the chromatic alteration of the interval of the third shown in example 18. No. 1 shows the contracting of the minor third in the first theme; no. 2 (a) the first form and no. 2 (b) the contracted answer in the second subject theme

Ex. 18

A further, clearly related trait of this first theme is to be found in the B flat major bars (18–19), felt either as a passage of Neapolitan harmony in the movement's tonic, A minor, or as a continuation of the D minor from which the music is clearly moving in bars 17–18. In favour of the Neapolitan solution is the appearance immediately afterwards of a single expansive bar of unclouded A minor (adagio), before the scurrying violin figure from bar 9 reintroduces the first theme, this time with the theme of the introduction (inverted) as a counterpoint.

The second theme of the first group is a strongly rhythmical one which Beethoven treats canonically for four bars and then embarks on a furious mounting crescendo (bars 44–7).

Ex. 19

This fiery incident which seems to look forward to the love-duet in *Tristan*, leads straight into the blissful lyrical interlude of the second subject (Ex. 18 (2)). The motif of chromatically altered thirds returns once again in two bars of dotted, heavily accented rhythm just before the end of the exposition, and the development section opens with the theme of the introduction sounding pianissimo in the cello part.

The development takes up a mere thirty-six bars in this enormous movement, but the recapitulation is unusually long—in fact it may be considered a double recapitulation (bars 111 and 193). The restless movement of the coda ceases for a moment at the pianissimo morendo passage (fourteen bars before the end.) This is no more than a written out ritardando; but it returns immediately afterwards, where it is interesting to observe the idea of interval-alteration (expansion here, rather than contraction) making its last appearance in a movement which it can almost have been said to have dominated.

The whole of the scherzo which follows ('Allegro ma non tanto') is constructed from the two ideas announced by the violins in bars 5 and 6

Ex. 20

The mood is serene, almost playful, as relaxed as that of the first movement was tense and often distraught. The clash of thirds moving in contrary motion has none of the emotional emphasis that Beethoven had given it in the first movement of op. 106, but appears as a natural result of the contrapuntal play. This play element, though not in its contrapuntal form, is even stronger in the trio section, where the first violin executes a kind of popular song[1] over an open A string pedal, which produces the effect of a drone. This is followed by a moto perpetuo in which the viola has the chief part, followed by the first violin. Beethoven carefully marks 'sempre staccato' for the quavers and their accompanying chords, and the playful mood is only interrupted for a moment before the return of the Savoyardlied. This interruption takes the unexpected form of what seems an intrusion from the future op. 131, in the same C sharp minor tonality.

Ex. 21 L'istesso tempo

Whether this is a private joke or a reference to some relationship between the two quartets, only intelligible to the composer himself, it appears like a momentary cloud or a stormy gust of wind disturbing the serene relaxation of the movement.

[1] This so-called 'Savoyardlied' may well have been a song that Beethoven heard in the street or, more probably, the courtyard of the house in which he lodged—the courtyard is the normal choice of street-singers in Vienna to the present day.

Serenity in a far more positive and august sense is the hallmark of the Molto adagio which now follows. The form of this slow movement recalls that of the Adagio in the Ninth Symphony, in that it consists of variations on two strongly contrasted themes; but its character is unique. Beethoven marks the movement 'Heiliger Dankgesang eines Genesenen an die Gottheit, in der lydischen Tonart' ('holy song of thanksgiving of a convalescent to the divinity, in the Lydian mode') but only the first of the two themes is hymn-like in character; the second is a solemn dance, whose wide leaps, profuse ornamentation, and rhythmic variety do indeed suggest a return to physical and mental well-being and even something like the ecstasy of recaptured youth.

The first, hymn-like theme is the clearest reflection that we possess of Beethoven's interest in the modes, which prompted a number of passages in both the Missa Solemnis and the Ninth Symphony. Here, however, he does not use modal harmony as a spice, to give a few bars a specifically different colouring. He contrasts a complete archaic, ecclesiastical-sounding hymn—in fact a chorale in five strains, separated by short contrapuntal ritornellos—with a completely modern, secular dance-like movement. It is as though Beethoven were aware of two aspects of his recovery; the feeling of objective gratitude, which he found it natural to express in a hymn to the God whom he always instinctively envisaged as a father, and the subjective physical and emotional sensations of a *retour à la vie*. In the first statement of the chorale theme there is an austere, hieratic note, a solemnity that could quite as well be funereal as gratificatory

Ex. 22

The mode is plagal hypolydian (F major with B natural instead of flat) and it is scrupulously observed by Beethoven. The narrow span of the melody, its rhythmic simplicity, the predominance of step-wise motion and the frequent crossing of the parts combine with harmonic austerity to create the strongest possible impression of remote, other-worldly solemnity. The framework of two-bar, imitative counterpoint provided by the ritornellos[1] enhances the archaic character of the whole conception, and with it the sense of entering literally a new world when, the chorale having modulated to A major, the second theme (D major 3/8 replacing the modal 4/4 and andante succeeding molto adagio) appears with Beethoven's marking 'Neue Kraft fühlend' (with the feeling of a new strength)

Ex. 23

[1] Did this design furnish Wagner, consciously or unconsciously, with the model for the opening scene of *Die Meistersinger*?

Here the heavy accents, the wide leaps, the unusual rhythm and the trill (as so often in these last works, a sign of intense inner vitality rising to ecstatic self-abandonment) bring the movement in a single bar out of church into the sun, from the stillness of a devout recollection into the tingling activity of the dance, but David's solemn dance of thanksgiving before the Ark. The profuse ornamentation of grace-notes and trills are the spontaneous, gratuitous burgeonings of the new life, and sometimes even suggest half-coquettish forms of ballet steps (compare the solo violin part in the Benedictus of the Missa Solemnis, Ex. 26, p. 265).

Ex. 24

There is perhaps also a parallel here with the Tempo di Menuetto which forms variation 33 of the Diabelli Variations. There too Beethoven transfigured the formal, artificial world of the eighteenth-century dance, setting its order, or *kosmos*, in the sharpest possible contrast to the controlled *chaos* of the preceding fugue, as he contrasts it here with the severe monotony of the chorale-theme. By the side of these many dance elements in this D major section is a strong, lyrical expressiveness, to which Beethoven carefully draws attention (cantabile espressivo).

In the return of the first theme (molto adagio) the first violin is given the chorale, while the other three instruments elaborate contrapuntally the motif of the ritornello.

Ex. 25

This (a) appears in a slightly altered form (b), and the gentle movement of the parts combined with much syncopation and frequent octave intervals provides a full yet transparent tide on which the chorale floats without effort or disturbance. The following variation of the D major theme is entirely ornamental, with re-orchestration (i.e. redistribution of ideas among the four instruments) and still further rhythmic subdivision.

What appears to be a second variation of the chorale is in fact a long coda, based entirely on material from the chorale and its ritornello, which now appears in a third rhythmic shape (Ex. 25 (c)). Only the first five notes of the chorale are used; but Beethoven, who marks the section' Mit innigster Empfindung' (with the deepest, most intimate feeling) communicates an extraordinary feeling of space, of an immobility that is nevertheless intensely active and alive. This may be compared to the activity of the *vita contemplativa* as Dante describes it in the *Paradiso*.[1] The sudden quivering of the sforzandos and the oscillation of the semiquaver (Ex. 26–x) convey that same contemplative ecstasy which Beethoven expressed in the last variations of opp. 109 and 111. Whereas the percussive, non-sustaining pianoforte needed myriads of notes, the strings need a minimum; but in each case the principle of repetition is important. In every art the mystical, i.e. non-intellectual experience of reality has always found expression in this repetition of formulae that represents the last stage before the silence of consummation. The 'Om mani padme hum' of the Buddhists,

---

[1] Dante, *Paradiso*, xxvii, ll. 7–10:

O gioia! o ineffabile allegrezza!
O vita intera d'amore e di pace!
O senza brama sicura ricchezza!

the Jesus-prayer of the Orthodox Philokalia and the 'Deus meus et omnia' of the Catholic mystic are all simple methods to keep the mechanism of the conscious, 'lower' mind unobtrusively in play, thereby freeing the contemplative faculty. The long trills and repeated murmuring of the same rhythmic or melodic shape in opp. 109 and 111 (see pp. 185 and 203) perform the same function; and here, as the extension of the music decreases and we seem to be moving towards silence, so the intention becomes correspondingly greater, as *multum in parvo* gradually approaches the great silence of *omnia in nihilo*, the *nada* of the Spanish mystics—

From the timelessness of this contemplative ecstasy Beethoven turns—like Teresa of Avila to her administrative and kitchen duties—to a baldly factual, neatly rhythmic march movement. Everything about this twenty-four-bar episode is regular: the cadences and their modulations fall where we should expect them, the canonic entries and points of imitation are symmetrically planned. There is no hint of introspection or arrière-pensée; this is most emphatically not one of the mysterious nocturnal marches such as Tchaikovsky and Mahler were to favour, but as functional as the march that accompanies the changing of the guard between Scenes 4 and 5 in Act I of *Fidelio*.[1] There is even the hint of a side-drum in the semiquaver figures (Ex. 27, bar 3).

Ex. 27

The clean A major cadence with which the march ends is followed immediately ('attacca subito') by a quickening of tempo and a change to the minor. Eight short chords introduce a quiet but agitated recitative in the first violin, accompanied by tremolando chords in the other strings, surely as plain a reference to the opera as the similar passage in the slow movement of op. 110. But what Beethoven in fact quotes is one of the recitatives from the Ninth Symphony (finale bars 56–8)

[1] The sketch-books (Nottebohm, II, p. 549) suggest, however, that Beethoven did originally imagine something different here. There is the beginning of a 'marcia serioso [*sic*] pathet' that appears among the sketches for this quartet.

Ex. 28

This would surely not have had the character clearly intended by Beethoven when he marked the Alla marcia *assai vivace*, which puts pathos out of court.

Ex. 29

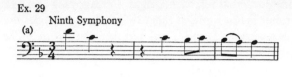

(a) Ninth Symphony

(b) Op. 132

The recitative mounts, becomes faster and more short-breathed and ends on a first inversion of the dominant seventh of A—a fermata from which the first violin descends in a two-octave scale-passage presto, to usher in the allegro appassionato which forms the last movement.

The theme for this movement was originally intended for the Ninth Symphony (see p. 278, Ex. 3), but Beethoven's presentation with accented cross-rhythms in the accompaniment give it a true chamber-music character, intimate and closely knit in spite of its restlessness

Ex. 30   *espress.*

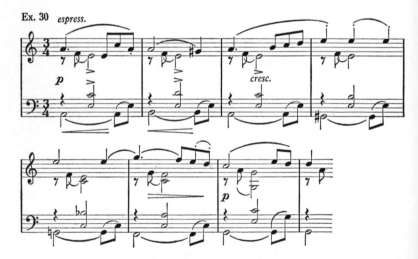

The form of the finale is a sonata-rondo, and the second episode brings a subdivision of the bar (2 × 3 instead of 3 × 2) such as Beethoven had used in the no. 18 of the Diabelli Variations (bars 64–7). The return from this episode to the main theme is very characteristically brought about through the subdominant (D minor), in which the theme appears for four bars before settling into the tonic A (bar 176)

Ex. 31

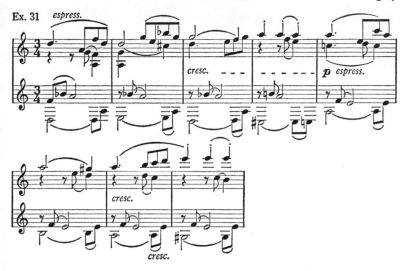

The short third episode introduces an oblique reference to the motto theme of the first movement (Ex. 16), which has been absent as a formally recognizable entity from the intervening movements. The reference here to its inverted shape, and its severely contrapuntal treatment pianissimo form a strong link in the chain that binds the whole work into a unity (bar 234)

Ex. 32

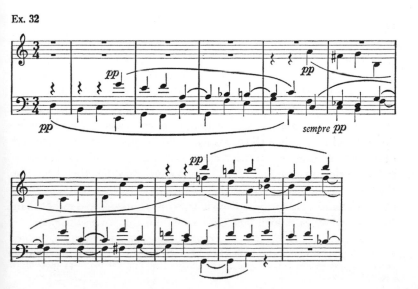

We hear the movement's main theme once again, this time presto, before the music moves into the major and the coda begins. Here, in the 'non ligato' quaver figures, the high tessitura and the rhythm of the melody the listener is aware of a reference to an earlier experience —the second half of the trio, where the *Savoyardlied* gave way to the moto perpetuo dance-like figures. Again, as in example 21, there is a sudden break—an aposiopesis followed by a brusque unison passage that ushers in the final bars.

Ex. 33

Opus 130

If the A minor quartet was largely composed during illness or convalescence, the third of the Galitsin quartets—op. 130 in B flat major—was written during a period, if not of health (for at this time of his life Beethoven was so sick a man that individual illnesses were only more marked episodes in a general physical deterioration) at least of comparative physical and mental well-being, between August and November 1825. As we should expect, the general mood of op. 130 is sunnier and more extrovert. The brusque alterations of tempo in the music and character are as numerous, but they have not the same character of nervous excitement, or even irritability, as those of op. 132 and seem to come from a happy plethora of ideas rather than from a restlessness which welcomes change for its own sake.[1]

[1] This is borne out by a note written by Beethoven to Holz in the autumn of 1825, when he was working on op. 130. 'Dear friend, I have had another inspiration, but that will have to be for the next quartet but one [op. 131], the next [op. 130] has too many movements already.'

The 'Adagio ma non troppo' with which the quartet opens is on a notably larger scale than the slow introductions to opp. 127 and 132. The first four bars, question and answer, seem to propound the subject for the whole vast work

Ex. 34

We shall find the chromatically descending first four notes of the theme (x) and their combination with harmonies or figuration involving contrary motion as constantly recurring features under different disguises.

The matter of the argument once propounded, the music seems to stretch itself towards the light, and at bar 7 there emerges from the dominant cadence a quiet theme in the cello.

Ex. 35

Taken up by each of the four instruments in turn, this leads to the dominant seventh fermata from which the Allegro springs, like a jet of water suddenly released

Ex. 36

This contrapuntal combination of a rapid descending figure with a boldly rising motif like a trumpet-call forms the first of the first group of subjects. It has hardly run the first lap of its course before it is interrupted by four bars of the opening Adagio. Released again, it hurtles forward with irrepressible momentum until it rises to a climax

and at once burgeons (bar 37) into a new idea (A 2) based on the cello
theme from the introduction (Ex. 35). This leads to a hectic passage
first of contrary motion semiquavers and then of heavily accented
unison quavers, and so to the second subject, in G flat major (bar 53).
Note the presence of (x) in bars 3–4 below.

Ex. 37

The cello's semiquaver figure (cp. A 1 in Ex. 36) is immediately
taken up in a series of pianissimo ben marcato unison comments by all
four instruments. These develop into a return of the semiquaver figure
in example 37, passed from one instrument to the other, and the
exposition ends with a strong unison passage leading back to the
introductory Adagio the first time, and the second time into the
development section.

This, as in other works of Beethoven's last period is remarkably
short; for when the exposition contains so much organic growth and
inter-relationship as it does in these sonata movements, the distinction
between exposition and development becomes tenuous. Beethoven
no longer devotes one section to formal statement and another to
formal development of what he has stated, but telescopes the two
processes into a single growth, as organic as the structure of a plant or an
animal. It was this elliptical trait in the late works that puzzled musicians educated in the formal, architectural tradition of the eighteenth
century. And it is in this, and not in any philosophical or metaphysical
sense, that these works could be said to have moved outside the province
of music proper—if by music was understood the arrangement or 'composition' of sounds according to fixed, symmetrical patterns which must
serve as moulds for the composer's ideas. Beethoven's last works take
little account of such moulds. It was second nature to him, after some
forty years, to follow the general schemes that he had inherited from the
eighteenth century; but he expanded, contracted or otherwise reshaped
such schemes to suit the natural growth of his ideas, their relationship
by association, their sometimes wayward character and their common
inclination to protean transformations. The development section of

this movement is an excellent instance. Beethoven starts with a
tentative pianissimo reference to A 1 (Ex. 36) in F sharp (G flat)
minor. This gives way to a memory of x from the introduction,
ending with a falling fifth (the inversion of the rising fourth of A 1
shown below, bars 1–3) and this and the harmonic suspension accompanying it provide him with a new rhythmic idea which permeates the
whole development (bars 98–107)

Ex. 38

Did Beethoven know Schubert's song 'Geheimes'? The accompaniment figure there and here has exactly the same rhythm
but it was not until the last month of his life
that Beethoven was shown a collection of sixty of Schubert's songs,
and those that he picked out according to Schindler did not include
'Geheimes', written in 1823. This does not mean, of course, that
Beethoven might not have known the song.
   The melodic fragment which is shown in the last two bars of

example 38 is as new as the Schubertian rhythm which accompanied it, and the Schubertian freeness of tonality, which for all its apparently spontaneous character soon brings the music back to the tonic B flat, in which the recapitulation appears. There is no reference to the introduction now until the coda, where the first four bars appear in a different lay-out and with slightly different harmony. A I appears three times, starting a tone higher on each occasion, and after this dramatic gesture the movement dies away sempre pianissimo.

In complete contrast to this opening, spacious, and sunny movement is the Presto which follows—a whispering, half sinister scherzo in B flat minor.

Ex. 39   Presto

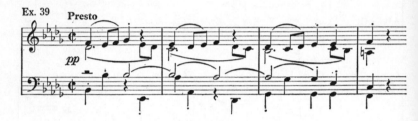

The trio section is a complete contrast in the major, with an energetic 6/4 in which the fourth beat of each bar is heavily accented. The transition from the trio to the repeat of the scherzo is effected by what amounts to three written out, slow motion glissando scales in the 6/4 of the trio alternating with bars of the scherzo's 4/4, which finally gets the upper hand

Ex. 40   L'istesso tempo

The return of the scherzo is the occasion for a number of playful
ornaments, octave-leaps and trills which add to the tension and, in the
higher register where the music is now heard, largely efface the note of
sinister whispering, which however returns in the short pianissimo
coda.

The 'Andante con moto, ma non troppo' carries this playfulness
into a rather different field. The first two bars (poco scherzando),
where x is again hinted at, leave the listener in doubt as to whether
the movement is to be in B flat minor or D flat major; and when Beethoven moves unambiguously into D flat major, it is not at all in the
solemn, Klopstockian mood (as he called it himself) with which he had
earlier associated this key. Instead, this resembles a slow scherzo
rather than a conventional song-like slow movement, and the detailed
filigree writing, closely woven texture and rococo richness of ornamentation recall the second variation in the Adagio of op. 127. Affinities
with the motto theme x, and with earlier movements in general, are
deeply woven into the material, if present at all. Rudolph Reti, with
his unfailing ingenuity,[1] calls attention to the second violin part in
bars 2–5, as evidence of Beethoven's conscious employment of x as
ground-material throughout the whole quartet

Ex. 41

There can be no doubt that an obsession with a certain pattern of
notes is one of the fundamental characteristics of all composition.

---

[1] Rudolph Reti, *The Thematic Process in Music* (1951), p. 237.

To the trained musician this pattern will also include the inversion and reversal of the original sequence, and a number of more complex variations of the original pattern; so that there forms in his mind a network of note-patterns or sequences identical in their component parts but not in their significance,[1] which are the raw material whose arrangement and development we aptly name composition. How conscious such cross-references are between themes and cells, rhythmic fragments and harmonic colours, will depend on the degree of self-consciousness of the individual. We may safely say that twentieth-century composers are more self-analytical, and therefore more conscious of the processes by which they create, than those of any previous age; and that in this sense music has, at one extreme, seemed to be returning to the purely intellectual discipline that it was for the Greek philosophers, while at the other extreme inclining to purely sonorous experiment. Beethoven talked only in guarded and general terms about his methods of composition; and we have no means of knowing exactly how consciously he manipulated his material or established that extraordinary unity of conception that is one of the most remarkable features of his music, particularly in its lastest phase. It is perhaps presuming too much to say, as Deryck Cooke does in an interesting attempt to prove the close thematic connection of these last quartets,[2] that 'Beethoven himself obviously took all the principles (i.e. inversion, retrograde motion, retrograde inversion, octave transposition and interversion) for granted, and worked them persistently in the late quartets, in the conscious sense of thematic development.' The sketch-books fail to substantiate this, and it is precisely in these that we should expect to find, if not clear evidence, at least repeated hints.

The plodding yet delicate gait of this first subject (for this is, rather unusually, a slow movement in sonata form) is emphasized by the staccato semiquavers in the bass; and these staccato semiquavers appear again in the second group of subjects, which is introduced by a semi-comical modulation (bars 10–11), more consequential for being played pizzicato, from the tonic to the dominant. The combination of pawky humour with extreme fineness of texture, which is characteristic of this whole movement, can be seen in these three bars that usher in the development section (bars 17–19)

---

[1] Parallels may be found in numbers (e.g. 7, 321, which has the same components as $73\frac{1}{2}$, but not the same significance): or words (e.g. 'dog' and 'god').
  Article in *Music Review* (1963), p. 34.

Ex. 42

The grace-notes, the wide leaps, the sudden halt, the contrast between legato and staccato and the crescendo on to the single D flat in the last bar—which leads into the recapitulation in the key of C major piano —all these together form a portrait that is in every trait Beethoven's, though perhaps not in his most familiar mood. In the development section Beethoven follows his common practice of introducing an entirely new melodic idea, a dolce cantabile that he presents with a series, as it were, of fluttering caresses (bars 27–8)

Ex. 43

Demisemiquaver scale passages staccato play an increasingly important part both here and in the coda, which also contains string writing of a delicacy and sophistication (if such a word can ever be used of Beethoven) that had no precedent anywhere, except in Spohr (bars 69–70)

Ex. 44

To the intense, 'indoor' cultivation of this writing, with its exquisite refinement, succeeds a popular dance movement of extreme simplicity and serenity—the 'Alla danza tedesca' originally planned (in A major instead of G major) as part of op. 132. In form this is another scherzo movement, with two trios; but Beethoven at this period of his life was as careless of convention in the character as in the form of his movements. Coming as it does between the elaborate Biedermeier *niello*-work, or inlay, of the Andante con moto and the Cavatina, this Allegro assai makes almost the effect of a folk-song, so devoid of a chromatic sophistication is the harmony, so regular and uncomplex the rhythm. Only the careful dynamic markings and the strange effect of a catch in the breath at the end of alternate bars reveal the order of the feeling contained in so simple a vessel. The return of the scherzo brings widely-spaced figuration varying the melody in the first violin, and there is a moment of humour in the cancrizans episode of the coda (bars 129 ff.)

Ex. 45

The Cavatina ('Adagio molto espressivo') which follows had an immediate success with the first audience of the quartet, who asked for it to be repeated. During the summer of 1825, when this movement was written, Beethoven's relationship with his nephew Karl was particularly painful. Holz declared that 'the Cavatina was composed amid tears of grief; never had his music reached such a pitch of expressiveness, and the very memory of this piece used to bring tears to his eyes'. This movement is in fact the *locus classicus* of 'la musique que l'on écoute la tête dans les mains', admired increasingly during the nineteenth century and then, in a predictable revulsion, dismissed as an instance of the confusion of art with emotional self-indulgence. The example of its grief-laden cantabile and of the almost physical poignancy of its chromatic harmony and sob-broken melody was not lost on the later Romantics; but neither Wolf nor Mahler nor Berg possessed the instinctive reserve, the interior *tenue* which was a legacy from Beethoven's unsentimental eighteenth-century upbringing and

saved him even here, though sometimes only just, from indulging in
self-pity. Perhaps we may find the background to this music in a note
to Karl written during these months:

Not a word more. Only come to my arms, you won't hear a single word
[of reproach]. For God's sake don't abandon yourself to misery. . . . Si vous
ne viendres pas, vous me tueres surement.

   The Cavatina is short, only sixty-six bars, but most highly organized.
It opens with three beats introduction *sotto voce*, plunging the listener
so immediately into a highly-charged emotional atmosphere that he
has the sensation (as at the opening of the A major piano sonata op
101) of having suddenly opened a door and intruded on a scene not
meant for his ears. This impression is enhanced by the affecting change
of chromatically rising harmony in the bass as early as the second beat
of the movement

Ex. 46

These chromatic alterations—there is another in bar 3—greatly
emphasize the pathos of what would otherwise be no more than
another example of Beethoven's familiar hymn-like adagios, with which
it already shares the three-note rising figure (bars 5–6) noticed by
Newman as a characteristic finger-print. The sob-like foreshortening
of the melody on the first beat of bar 3 is another feature that makes
this not so much a hymn as an aria, as the operatic title 'cavatina'
suggests.

   When the first strain of the melody comes to an end in bar 9, the
final phrase is echoed in a repetition exactly like those which form so

marked a feature of the first theme in the Adagio of the Ninth
Symphony. This echo-bar runs straight into the introductory bar
(bar 1 in Ex. 46) and the second strain of the melody. This begins
like the first (only without the sob in bar 3), but soon comes to a halt
in C minor. Once again a painful echo or repetition occurs, before the
melody continues, with rising thirds answering falling sixths

Ex. 47

A further repetition or echo of the last three beats of example 47
introduces the third strain of the melody *sotto voce*. Here, within the
melody itself, the third and fourth of the eight bars are a variation of
of the first and second. At the cadence the last phrase is echoed, as at
the end of the first and second strains, and the fourth strain is
simply a variation of the third, with the same phrase appearing in four
different forms in the two strains, as though this single idea represented
both a grief and a consolation from which the composer cannot bear
to separate himself, a bitter-sweet enigma that he must contemplate
from every angle—as we saw him doing in the introduction to the first
movement of the piano sonata in C minor, op. 111 (see Ex. 45, p. 197)

Ex. 48

In the short, eight-bar middle section of the movement the vocal element that we noticed in bar 3 of example 46 is predominant. Over an accompaniment of repeated triplets provided by the three other instruments, the first violin stammers a recitative far more broken even than that in the Adagio of the piano sonata in A flat op. 110 (see Ex. 43, p. 192). The line here is so fragmentary as to be almost non-existent, and Beethoven's marking *beklemmt* (oppressed, or 'with a feeling of oppression') has led some commentators to believe that this is, as it were, a transcription of the action of a diseased heart, such as his may well at this time have been[1]

Ex. 49

There was of course nothing new in the principle of instrumental recitative; it was indeed, a not uncommon device of Beethoven's during his last years. But its position in this already highly charged movement and the dramatically remote tonality (that of the familiar flattened sixth, C flat in E flat major) combine with Beethoven's mysterious *beklemmt* marking to give this passage a uniquely 'speaking' character; so that it is almost with a feeling of relief that we return to the final statement of the theme, where grief is no longer naked and physically distressing, but distanced and mastered by being given formal expression. In the short coda (bar 58) Beethoven uses the original introductory figure (Ex. 46, bar 1) which emphasizes the movement's unity, and in the very last bar we hear once again the sobbing, foreshortened phrase (Ex. 46, bar 3) as the music swells for a moment and then diminishes to pianissimo.

The Grosse Fuge, which Beethoven wrote as the finale of this immense quartet, follows at once, over 700 bars of a rhythmic violence and often ruthless density of thought and texture that quite defeated his first listeners and still make huge demands on an audience, as well as on the performers. Beethoven was aware of this and accepted M. Artaria's immediate offer to publish the fugue as a separate work, if Beethoven would write another finale. That finale was written during the following autumn (1826) and was probably the last work that the composer completed. We shall consider it later; but priority must be given to Beethoven's original (and beyond all doubt deeply considered)

---

[1] See Charles Niemark, 'Herzschlag und Rhythmus', *Die Musik*, VII (1908), pp. 20–5.

design, the fugue whose main theme echoes the basic motif (see Ex. 16) in op. 132 but whose introduction is largely lost unless the work follows immediately the hushed close of the Cavatina.

The contrasts in this quartet have already reached what might have seemed a point beyond which they could hardly go further. But Beethoven characteristically forces that barrier with this uniquely shaped movement, in which two fugues are intimately welded together by sharing a common subject that is secondary in the first and primary in the second. From the unison, leaping G which rises like a rocket out of the darkness and silence in which the Cavatina ends, there springs this theme (A)

Ex. 50
(a)

Beethoven presents this in the three main rhythmic shapes in which it will be heard complete, thus producing the effect of a cinematic trailer of coming events comparable to the review of past experiences that we find at the beginning of the last movement of the Ninth Symphony. After this oddly named 'Overtura', which perhaps the composer did conceive as a kind of Italian for this sketch of a forthcoming programme, the first fugue opens with the pianissimo statement of A, which is not its subject but its countersubject. The subject (B) is an inimitably aggressive, leaping theme whose characteristically jerky rhythm, seems according to the sketch-books, to have been an afterthought (Nottebohm, II, pp. 5–6)

Ex. 51
(b)

The B flat major tonality and the interval of the third (or tenth) immediately suggest at least a cousinship with the fugal finale of the piano sonata op. 106; and this resemblance is confirmed by the scale of the movement, its ruthless rhythmic drive and the thorough-going adaptation of contrapuntal resources to the purposes of that drama which is the dominant characteristic of the whole movement in which fugue and variation-form are combined. For even though it may be true that Beethoven's interest in fugue during the last ten years of his life sprang from a dissatisfaction with so-called sonata form and a wish to replace it by something more highly unified in character, yet nothing could alter the fact that the whole stamp of Beethoven's musical personality was dramatic, that is to say founded on the exploitation of contrasts. Hence the quiet D major episode in the finale of op. 106 and the intimate G flat major fugato which follows the first three episodes or variations of this B flat major fugue. Nor, we may imagine, if Beethoven was really in search of the kind of monolithic unity that can be achieved in the fugal examination of a single idea, but never (by definition) in a sonata movement, would he have chosen such strongly and dramatically contrasted subjects and countersubjects as we find here. In a sense no passages in his music are more dramatic than those in which he seems to be consciously avoiding drama, as in the 'Heiliger Dankgesang' in op. 132, where the deliberate austerity and monotony of the chorale only serve to enhance the bright colours and rich ornamentation of the D major sections. It was very rare for Beethoven to write a serious and extended movement that did not also reflect an intense inner drama.[1]

The triplets which, after the statutory four entries (bars 30–50), provide the first relief from the hammering and jerking rhythms of B, form a variation which lasts from bars 58 to 94. They are followed after a transitional episode by a figure which recalls Ex. 35

Ex. 52

(a) 1st movement (cf. Ex. 35 bar 2) (b) Grosse Fuge

[1] No doubt it is this deeply 'Dionysian' character that Stravinsky, with his strongly 'Apollonian' theories of art, finds unsatisfactory, or at least unsympathetic, in Beethoven's music. His high praise of the Grosse Fuge ('pure interval music') is made less impressive by an exaggeration that is almost meaningless ('absolutely contemporary music that will be contemporary for ever').

This figure dominates the music from bar 111 to bar 128, and ten bars later the triplets return in a more specifically thematic form (var. 3)

Ex. 53

This third variation lasts until bars 157–8, where the music takes a sudden flatward turn and changes completely in character. The key signature turns from B flat to G flat, the wide intervals and jerking rhythms make way for smoothly flowing semiquavers, either repeated notes or closely adjacent. So marked is the change that Vincent d'Indy[1] regards this as the beginning of the second fugue rather than as a fugato episode, based on the countersubject and still belonging to the first. Certainly we can connect the new countersubject against which (A) appears with the G flat semiquaver passage that occupies the last twenty-three bars of the exposition in the first movement (bars 70 ff.)

Ex. 54

The four entries of (A), with the new countersubject do indeed suggest that this is the beginning of a new fugue. Joseph Kerman says

[1] Vincent d'Indy, 'Beethoven' in *Cobbett's Cyclopedic Survey of Chamber Music* (2nd ed., 1963).

that 'at the risk of some oversimplification it might be said that the B flat fugue, the G flat fugato, and the A flat fugue concentrate respectively on rhythmic, harmonic, and melodic potentialities of the basic theme.'[1] This section lasts some seventy bars (159–232) and is followed by a return to B flat major 'allegro molto e con brio' and a light-hearted, dance-like version of the basic theme, exactly as the listener heard it in the 'Overtura' (bars 11–16). D'Indy regards this as the first episode or variation of the second fugue (233–72) and the fortissimo (A) flat in the cello in bar 272, which Kerman takes as the opening of the second fugue, as the beginning of the second of these episodes. However we regard the form, two important elements now enter the music for the first time—the inverted version of the first phrase of (A) and the trill, which can be seen in bar 10 of Example 50 but has not appeared again until bar 238 ff., where its function is still largely ornamental. The combination of close imitation with wide-spacing, of flowing 6/8 with important entries off the beat and the intense rhythmic accentuation inseparable from trills, forms a sound-complex that is very characteristic of Beethoven's last years (bars 310–20)

Ex. 55

The variation starting at bar 340 and lasting to bar 403 is dominated by a figure based on (A) in diminution combined with long trills, often in succession and passing from one instrument to the other, while canonic entries are brought ever closer together. From bar 372, where it makes its first appearance in the second violin part, this section is dominated by a figure (Ex. 56 (a)) thrown up by the fierce seas of

[1] Joseph Kerman, *The Beethoven Quartets*, 1967, p. 288.

thematic inversion in which (A) has become increasingly deformed; and this figure in a slightly new form (Ex. 56 (b)) is combined with the return of (B) in the development of both fugues (bars 404–522)

Ex. 56 (a)

This E flat episode repeatedly veers towards the subdominant, and it is in A flat that the whole following section is cast, from bar 442–500, where there is a formal A flat major cadence. The first part of this section treats the first three notes of (A) (often inverted), while the leaps of (B) grow to gigantic proportions, often spreading over two octaves. In the second part (bars 483–500) the 'meno mosso e moderato' and the smooth-moving semiquavers of the former G flat major section return; but this time they are combined with frequent, though unaccented two-octave leaps, most prominently in the viola part.

After the A flat major cadence in bar 500 there are six three-bar chordal statements, each based on a trill in the cello and diminishing dynamically as they gradually gather speed. These prepare the way back to B flat major and the 'allegro molto e con brio' which followed the G flat major fugato in the first place (cp. bars 237–69 and 523–55). This exact repetition of thirty-two bars does indeed seem to make what Kerman well calls an 'almost glib recapitulatory effect'; but although it marks the first notable détente which prepares the end of the movement, there is still far more to come than is normally contained in any coda. In fact the greater part of the next ninety-two bars (565–657) is taken up with a new rhythm and an entirely new texture, all four instruments very close together and the cello often in the highest register, sometimes above the viola as in bars 573 ff.

Ex. 57

The instruments pair off and move in contrary motion (another trait recalling the first movement), until in bar 599, pianissimo and on an unexpected suspension, (A) appears in soft remote-sounding chords, veering to A minor but steered back in a very characteristic 'screwing-up' of the bass from E natural to F, into a B flat major cadence that seems for a moment final. It leads, however, to another twenty bars of the close writing and single rhythm of example 57, after which the coda proper begins in bar 647.

Here Beethoven, with more humour than wit, re-presents the 'Overtura', giving us the constituent parts in retrospect and in a different order (647–92). The paired, trilling cadential bars that follow closely resemble those in the coda of the finale of op. 106, but there is nothing there to match the extraordinary last appearance of the two themes that have prompted this giant movement (bars 708 ff.)

Ex. 58

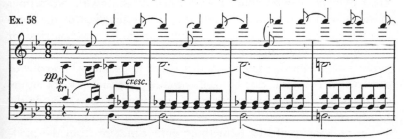

When this has run its full course, there are nothing left but ten bars of cadential figures, in which, nevertheless, the leaps still bear witness to Beethoven's persistent thematic instinct.

The Grosse Fuge is unique. The contrapuntal ingenuity of the music, which might suggest an affinity with J. S. Bach's *Kunst der Fuge*, is in reality secondary. What grips the listener is the dramatic experience of forcing—for there is frequently a sense of violence in this mastery—two themes which have, by nature, nothing in common, to breed and produce a race of giants, episodes or variations that have no parallel in musical history. Later composers, like Busoni, who have attempted to follow Beethoven, have not worked within similar restrictions of language; and it is Beethoven's struggle with these restrictions that provides one of the mainsprings of the work. The element of excess or 'nimiety', already noticed in parts of the Missa Solemnis and the 'Hammerklavier' sonata, is strong here and has prompted the invention of programmes for the Grosse Fuge which are not so much wrong-headed as irrelevant. To envisage theme A as representing Necessity and theme B as Free-Will,[1] and their inextricable contrapuntal involvement as an image of human destiny, is certainly not alien to Beethoven's own mentality; but it tells us nothing whatever of importance about the music. He might well have used such imagery himself to an inquirer puzzled by the work's character, in an attempt to explain the order of the ideas involved and the nature of their engagement; but it would have been as an after-thought, in exactly the same way as he 'explained' the opening of his Fifth Symphony with 'thus Fate knocks at the door'. No serious musician will believe that the *conscious* labour involved in the composition of the Grosse Fuge was philosophical or psychological or anything but purely musical. This is indeed, as Stravinsky says, 'the purest interval-music'; but to say that is not to exclude philosophy or psychology. It is clear that the ability to conceive such a work argues certain definite psychological traits—a huge fund of aggression, in the first place, and an instinctive resentment of restriction in any form—and a 'philosophy of life' (something quite different from the intellectual systems of professional philosophers, for which Beethoven had little or no understanding) based on the struggle for self-development on the one hand and self-mastery on the other. In this sense the Grosse Fuge is one of the most personally revealing of Beethoven's works; but, as always, he reveals himself in purely musical terms and it is almost as though his 'personality', which determined the form and

[1] As e.g. Sullivan, op. cit., p. 129.

moulded the details, can be withdrawn from the finished work, just as the wooden mould can be withdrawn from the completed arch.

The movement which Beethoven wrote in the following year to replace the Grosse Fuge as the finale of op. 130, was as different as it is possible to imagine. It seems most probable that the composer, although resentful of his hearers' failure to accept the Grosse Fuge as a finale, was himself obscurely aware that it was somehow out of place where it stood. The prospect of having the fugue published (and paid for) separately, and seeing it in a four-handed piano arrangement, mollified him no doubt; but there is no other instance of Beethoven making such a modification in his original plans for a major work at the instance of others. When he came to write the new finale, he had already finished the F major quartet op. 135, in which he had returned in a kind of transfigured sense to the world of Haydn; and it is to that same world that the new finale of op. 130 belongs. Kerman has put very succinctly the dilemma which faced the composer and still, in a sense, faces us in choosing between the two movements as finales of op. 130. 'The fugue runs the danger of trivializing the experience of the other movements, but the new finale runs the danger of seeming trivial itself.'[1]

The practice of concluding a deeply serious work with a light-hearted finale was a return to Mozart (B flat major piano concerto K.595 and G minor string quintet K.516) and to an earlier, pre-romantic aesthetic. It should not be forgotten that in 1826 Beethoven, at fifty-six, would already seem to himself and to others an old man even if he had not been prematurely aged by ill health. His deliberate turning away from the piano and the opera, both favourite genres with the younger generation of composers, and his declared intention to devote himself to orchestral music and to oratorio or church music were signs of an increasing inclination to return to the forms and aesthetic of his youth, even though he would doubtless have rethought, refashioned, and ultimately wholly transcended both. This is exactly what we find in op. 135 and, in a subtly different way, in the second finale of op. 130; and it may well be that what we consider a characteristically late, even terminal, style would have proved, had he lived, nothing more than the style of a certain period—the period of the ten years' perturbation and emotional distress associated with the upbringing of his nephew. If Beethoven had surmounted those years and lived to seventy, it seems very possible that the works he would have

---

[1] Op. cit., p. 374.

BI

written might have been nearer in character to op. 135 or to the new finale of op. 130 than to the Grosse Fuge.

As it is, there is something almost cynical-sounding in the opening of the new finale, as the staccato notes of the viola break in on the tense emotional silence at the end of the Cavatina. The quirk of starting a movement on the dominant seventh of the supertonic and the whole gait of the music, easy-going despite the allegro marking, suggest a mood of self-conscious relaxation. The contrapuntal writing, too, is as plain sailing here as it was rough in the Grosse Fuge, the texture almost too transparent, while the moments of agitation are no more than clouds momentarily obscuring a sun that is still manifestly shining. Is this the 'tutto nel mondo è burla' with which Verdi concluded his *Falstaff*? The opening quip and the deliberate contradiction in the second subject (bars 69–70)

Ex. 59

seem to suggest that it is; but *Falstaff* is a comedy, and whatever the B flat major quartet may have included in its ample folds, it cannot be described as comic. We are faced, then, with a dilemma. On the one hand the Grosse Fuge, coming at the end of the quartet, almost annihilates not only the listener, but his experience of what has gone before. On the other hand the new finale seems to have been written by a composer so different from the man who wrote the foregoing movements that it leaves a sense of inconsequence and almost of deprivation. Mozart might conclude even his most serious meditations with a flight or dance of rococo angels; but Beethoven has placed, at the end of his gallery of masterpieces as it were, a well-turned and comfortably upholstered Biedermeier chair into which the listener can sink. Beethoven's tribute to the domestic, middle-class spirit of the Biedermeier age, which was just beginning, was by no means negligible, but it is mostly confined to his lesser, occasional works—songs, arrangements, isolated piano pieces. Certainly this movement and the Andante con moto of op. 127 are the only examples of Biedermeier art among the last quartets. As a replacement for the Cyclopean masonry of the Grosse Fuge the effect is as incongruous as that of a Baroque chapel attached to a Romanesque cathedral.

Opus 131

The next and perhaps, as Beethoven himself believed, the greatest of the last five quartets was composed between November 1825 and July 1826. To Holz's question, which was the greatest of the quartets, 'Each in its own way' he answered. 'Art demands of us that we do not stand still. . . . You will find a new kind of part-writing, and thank God there is less lack of imagination (*Phantasie*) than ever before.' The work is in seven movements which the composer numbered and clearly wished to be played without any substantial break between them. Add to this the fact that the first movement is a fugue, and even the least musical can hear at once that this is a new kind of string quartet. The composer characteristically labelled the work 'put together from various pilferings' ('zusammengestohlen aus verschiedenem diesem und jenem') which was no doubt meant to make his publishers nervous, and did so until they heard this wholly original and novel music.

Original and novel the C sharp minor quartet most certainly is, in every detail as well as in general conception, but quite without the 'nimiety' and the sense of strain that could be felt in the Grosse Fuge of op. 130 and even, perhaps, in a different sense in the deliberate austerity of the 'Heiliger Dankgesang' in op. 132. The fugal movement with which it begins is as unmistakably the first scene of a drama as the Grosse Fuge is the last. It has no countersubject, so that all contrast must be sought within the potentialities of the theme itself

Ex. 60

The basic ideas here are (a) the augmented third rising to the tonic, and the heavily accented sixth note of the scale (A); and (b) the smooth scalar descent and ascent of three adjacent notes. The similarity between the first half of this theme and that of the C sharp minor fugue in the first book of J. S. Bach's '48' (Ex. 60 (2)) can hardly be fortuitous, particularly in view of the extreme rarity of the key of C sharp minor in Beethoven's music. Apart from the piano sonata op. 27 no. 2 (the so-called 'Moonlight' sonata) we only know that among the plans which Beethoven left unexecuted at his death was one for a Requiem in C sharp minor. Whether this opening fugue was at any time or in any way associated with that scheme we do not know. Wagner, writing in 1870,[1] called 'the lengthy opening Adagio surely the saddest thing ever expressed in notes'; but this is a confusion that the later composer of *Parsifal* would not perhaps have made, between the austere but life-enhancing beauty of contemplative art and the absence of animal high spirits, the 'sadness' occasioned by the transience of beauty or the mutability of everything human—such as we often find in Schubert, and not least in such major-mode pieces as 'Das Wirtshaus' in *Die Winterreise* and the Adagio of the string quintet. There is, to me at least, no hint of this, or indeed any other kind of 'sadness' in this opening fugue. The subdominant harmony arising from the heavily accented A of the theme does indeed seem to give the music a certain downward gravitation; but as Kerman points out,[2] the composer seems aware of this and anxious to counteract it, since he harmonizes this fourth note of the theme in no less than twenty different ways during the movement's 120 bars. The second and fourth (second violin and cello) entries of the theme a fifth below the first statement introduce a new and important Neapolitan element with the heavily accented D natural

Ex. 61

This again, which Wagner perhaps regarded as in some sense 'sad', is no more than a streak of sombre colour that runs through much (though by no means all) of the movement without ever dominating it entirely. In fact the last and most emphatic insistence on this element, in bars 112–15, is immediately resolved, like the memory of a grief or doubt, in the radiant C sharp major affirmation with which the fugue ends (Ex. 63 below).

Beethoven's ready and always imaginative use of stretto, which begins as early as bars 22 ff. and is hardly ever absent from some detail or other for the rest of the movement, is not contentious here, as in most of the fugues of these last works. He is no longer reconciling, or even demonstrating the irreconcilability of, opposing ideas but rather contemplating, like the Creator himself, the principle of order or *kosmos* inherent in the theme that he has chosen, drawing it out and revealing it with a kind of awe, that sense of wonder that he shares with the great poets and mystics and never lost to the end of his life.

[1] Richard Wagner, *Gesammelte Werke*, IX.   [2] Op. cit., p. 296.

After the E flat minor stretto in bars 45 ff. close stepwise motion or narrow intervals give way for the first time to octave intervals, the hitherto ubiquitous crotchets are replaced by quavers (diminution of b), while the cello rises first chromatically and then diatonically over two octaves and a half, in a crescendo whose final mounting sequences are surely nothing less than quietly triumphant (bar 57)

Ex. 62

The ethereally high-lying passage that follows this climax is marked 'dolce' and its crescendo (bars 63–5) leads straight, with a sudden piano, into the two-part A major canonic episode based on the smooth-flowing crotchets of (b), exchanged first between the two violins and then between viola and cello (dolce again, and in the high register). After the quiet exultation of example 62 we are once again in a region beyond simple, identifiable pleasure or pain, rapt in the contemplation of reality—a solemn progression, or interrelation, of sounds whose significance is indeed primarily musical, but may also be felt (and was perhaps obscurely so felt by the composer himself)[1] as symbolic of that 'order' which distinguishes *kosmos* from *chaos* in the widest, 'cosmic', sense but also in human life. Here Beethoven's music loses completely its Dionysian character and becomes for a moment wholly Apollonian.

In the last section of the fugue, where (b) in diminution plays a large part, the last grand-scale stretto brings in the theme in augmentation in the cello, and from there onwards (bars 99–120) the bass line has a quite special importance. The cello sinks to its lowest register, while above it the texture becomes increasingly more open, the intervals wider, until the climax is reached in bars 110–16

---

[1] This whole movement is quite satisfying enough when regarded simply as 'significant form'. But just as in the controversy over that concept of Roger Fry's in the plastic arts, those who refuse to see anything more than a purely abstract 'aesthetic' beauty may be missing other significances that can greatly enrich their experience. Is the difference between a fugue by Cherubini and a fugue by Beethoven really an exclusively aesthetic matter? A quality is not absent or negligible simply because it cannot be satisfactorily defined or described in words.

Ex. 63

The final chord of C sharp major is held (*cresc. dim. p. più p*) for seven beats in its complete fullness (seven parts) and then begins to thin out from the bass upwards, leaving eventually a rising C sharp octave interval in first violin and viola to end the first and set the stage, in a single gesture, for the second movement, which follows immediately.

In so completely organic a work as this quartet perhaps it is not fanciful to see in the D major tonality of the Allegro molto vivace a reference to the Neapolitan aspect of the fugue's C sharp minor tonality. Or is the octave D–D which follows immediately the C sharp–C sharp octave which ended the fugue, simply another example of Beethoven's favourite practice of 'screwing-up' a phrase, repeating it a tone or a semitone higher and then either playing with the contradiction, as in the scherzo of op. 106, or making it the starting point for an entirely new idea, as here? Perhaps it is both. In any case the swift movement, fleeting 6/8 and wide spacing make the greatest possible contrast with what has gone before. Everything about this movement is elusive, including its form. To describe this as a highly compressed sonata form with no development is not really very enlightening, and the material suggests rather a scherzo or a rondo-finale

Ex. 64   Allegro molto vivace

This seems something to be hummed under the breath with a
secret, interior delight emphasized by the moment of unexpected
hesitancy in the last bars which suggests a smile of complicity. Restless
quavers accompany its repetition, and in bar 24 we meet a new melodic
idea, which still maintains the same rhythm

Ex. 65

This proves to be no more than a bridge passage, however important,
and still the modulation to the dominant is delayed. In fact no sooner
is there an unambiguous moment of A major than the reprise starts
in D major (bar 84). Ex. 65 does not appear here, where its place
is taken by an episode built on part of the main theme; but it does
reappear (bars 175–85) in the coda, ten bars of unison climbing and
descending, that strangely recall a passage in *Fidelio*.[1] The coda ends
with two fortissimo bursts each followed by a pause on the dominant
seventh; and the movement closes 'mezza voce pianissimo'.

The allegro moderato which follows is marked by Beethoven as a
third movement, but it is only eleven bars long. Six of these are
conversational exchanges between the instruments, nothing so formal
as recitative but rather pawky comments. When the tempo changes to
Adagio in bar 7 the first violin executes an elaborate cadenza-like
gesture leading to E major and thence to the A major of the fourth
movement.

This is the last but one of Beethoven's great variation movements.
We can follow the line from the two piano sonatas, opp. 109 and 111,

[1] See *Fidelio* Act 2, Scene 2, Trio in A major—at 'o mehr als ich ertragen kann'.

through the Diabelli Variations and the Adagio of the Ninth Symphony, to the Adagio movements of opp. 127 and 132. In the Ninth Symphony and op. 132 Beethoven alternated between two very distinct themes, which in themselves provided all the contrast needed. The Diabelli Variations offer, with J. S. Bach's Goldberg set, the supreme instances of *multum in parvo*, the exploitation of every conceivable potentiality of a single, simple theme. In op. 109 and 127 Beethoven circumscribes his fancy by keeping generally close to the character of the original theme but, within that, embroidering and subdividing, altering the lighting and the gait, the texture and the rhythm. In op. 111 the theme is manifestly omnipresent throughout, its metamorphoses mathematical and spatial, matters of the microscope's augmentations and diminutions until the final change of scene to the stratosphere. In op. 131 Beethoven adopts a slightly different scheme, a combination of purely melodic (vars. 1 and 7) metamorphosis and the more searching harmonic variation. The A major tonality and the smiling, relaxed mood of the original theme never disappear; and its strongly antiphonal build is easily traceable in the first four variations, at least vestigial in the texture of all.

Ex. 66

In variation 1 the theme's tender, almost willowy gracefulness and flexibility are mutated into a stiff little double-dotted rhythm, maintained by the inner instruments while violin and cello punctuate and comment. But in bars 37–9 there is a perfect example of that indescribable and inimitable impression of elevation (is it 'aesthetic' or ethical as well as physical, or is this simply association of ideas?)

that Beethoven and Schubert communicate to the octave leap combined with close-lying harmony in the upper ranges.

Ex. 67

Variation 2 Piu mosso maintains the antiphonal game between
first violin and cello against the rhythmic pattern that Rossini was so
fond of providing as a background for his voices. ♪ᵧ ♪ᵧ ♪ᵧ ♪ᵧ |

♪ᵧ ♪ᵧ ♪ᵧ ♪ᵧ | Kerman[1] discovers a rustic note in this varia-
tion, hearing perhaps the thump of hob-nailed boots in the rhythmic
accompaniment; but what is more certain is the plain echo in bars 86–9
and 94–6 of the mounting figure (Ex. 65) whose grand unisons played
such an important part in the coda of the second movement.

Variation 3, marked 'Andante moderato e lusinghiero', is a kind
of mock contrapuntal exercise. Here the theme's antiphonal character
is very marked, as pairs of instruments execute canons at the second
and trills, which sound pedantically precise at first, eventually serve
to accentuate the dissonances resulting from the uninhibited progression of the counterpoint. 'Lusinghiero' means flattering, coaxing, or
caressing and the first canon is marked 'dolce' on each occasion. What
effect did Beethoven wish to obtain? perhaps a schoolroom precision
and correctness seen, after nearly half a century, in an affectionate,
wistful light?

With variation 4 Adagio we leave for the first time the theme's
duple metre for a flowing 6/8. The movement is both solemn and
graceful, the alternation of arco and pizzicato giving a new dimension to the four instruments' sonority. Antiphony remains in the
fragmentation of the theme. How much Brahms learned from a
passage such as the following (bars 142–5)!

[1] Op. cit., p. 335.

Ex. 68

Variation 5 Allegretto might belong to the Diabelli set. Everything is here pared down to the bone, and we are given a blueprint of the theme with the perspective drastically foreshortened. As in variation 3 the dolce marking insists that this economy has nothing to do with austerity. If brevity is the soul of this elegant puzzle, nothing can be too expansive for the 'Adagio, ma non troppo e semplice' of Variation 6. The first three notes of two phrases of the theme (see Ex. 66) are expanded by repetition into eight crotchets in a bar of 9/4; and the gently oscillating motion, 'sotto voce' and 'cantabile' markings make this more a nocturne than a hymn, despite the almost Mendelssohnian suavity of bars 7–8 and 15–16. Is Beethoven's marking 'semplice' a warning against any hint of exaggerated soulfulness in performance? He marked the Arietta in op. 111 'adagio molto semplice e cantabile', which suggests a relationship; but here he reserves his 'cantabile' marking for the first of the two cadences mentioned above. An unexpected and, despite the marking 'non troppo marcato', rude interruption of this dream-like euphoria appears first in bar 9 and completely dominates the movement between bars 25–33. This is a small gesture at first, hardly more than a fidgeting movement, in the cello

Ex. 69

Is there any significance in the fact that this figure appears for a moment in the last bar of the exposition in the first movement of op.

127 and again in bar 3 of the fourth variation in the Adagio, each time
in the cello? The floating movement of equal, detached crotchets
continues unchecked even when this interruption is continuous, and
the two cease together at bar 220. Here the movement dissolves into a
series of cadenza-like passages for each of the instruments, followed
by a long trill flattening from C sharp to C natural and so leading to
the 'allegretto p. dolce' reappearance of the theme in C major. At the
theme's fourth phrase, however, this characteristically peters out, as
Beethoven quickens the pace and then converts a slow trill (with which
we may compare example 69) into the full-blown ornament that
introduces and pervades the seventh and final variation. Here the effect
is not of a string quartet but rather of a string orchestra, with percussion
furnished by the cello phrase (see below Ex. 70). It is foolish as well as
impudent to speak of a direct miscalculation at this period in Beethoven's life. He knew exactly what he wanted, and his deafness offers
no explanation for a texture that any student could criticize on sight.

Ex. 70   (Andante)

If the texture here sounds laboured and thick, we may be sure that it
is because Beethoven meant it to sound so, and it lasts a mere seven
bars. A fragmentary cadenza, all broken chords and trills makes the
airiest of contrasts and reintroduces the allegretto version of the theme,
this time in F major instead of C major. But as before, it peters out at
the fourth phrase and a plunging and soaring passage in the first violin
carries us to the theme's final cadence and, after two broken repetitions,
the four final bars of the variation. There are no fewer than fifteen
separate versions of these four bars in the sketch-books,[1] and the
differences between them are often infinitesimal—the repetition of a
pizzicato note in an inner part at the same pitch or at an octave
distance, the harmony provided by a quaver chord or two semiquavers,
the exact disposition of rests, etc. Such attention to details of texture
and presentation makes it quite unthinkable to attribute anything that
seems puzzling in these last works either to miscalculation or to some

[1] See Nottebohm, II, pp. 54–9.

aural peculiarity due to advanced deafness. Did Milton's blindness seriously affect his vision of the external world as presented in his later poems?

Under the last two notes of the four gossamer bars which end this movement Beethoven wrote the word 'semplice'—once again the warning against affectation of any kind, any hint of emotional pretentiousness. We may perhaps compare the rare marking 'innocente' or 'innocentemente' in the last of the op. 119 Bagatelles and the eleventh of the Diabelli Variations.

The contrast that is to be furnished by the next, fifth movement (Presto) is immediately suggested by the cello's comic anticipation of the first bar of the theme, and the theme when it comes is deliberately simple to the point of grotesque

Ex. 71

Not only is the theme simple, but it is treated comically, in a series of quips of which the cello's anticipation of the first bar is characteristic. Five times in the course of the movement the mechanism is halted in Beethoven's favourite manner—by suddenly repeating a phrase and interrupting the course of his thought to go off on a digression that only returns, it seems, by chance to the original matter

Ex. 72

Similarly both returns of the scherzo (for the trio section is repeated) are introduced by each of the four instruments contributing a single pizzicato note to the opening figure of the theme (bars 161–8 and 327 sq.). The theme of the trio itself, marked 'piacevole', is pleasant, easy-going and very adaptable; and the tonal scheme of what is quite a long movement is unusually simple—E major, G sharp minor, A major, with moments of E minor and B minor quickly rectified. For the coda Beethoven returns to the main theme, which is whispered 'pianissimo sul ponticello' in the top register (bars 470 ff.).

After the E major cadence, a two-octave leap on G sharp followed by a short pause leads straight into the sixth movement—'Adagio quasi un poco andante'. This is a mere twenty-eight bars based on a theme whose connection with the fugal subject of the first movement is manifest

Ex. 73   (Adagio)

Any comparisons between this movement and the Cavatina of op. 130 are surely irrelevant, for the scope, character and function of the two movements are entirely different, only their placing in each quartet (between a light-hearted scherzo-like movement and a big finale) is similar. There is no emotional effusion here, no hint of that major-mode luxuriance of grief that made the Cavatina such a popular and dangerous model to later composers. This Adagio is a transitional piece, an introduction to the tragic finale but still restrained, almost hymn-like and concise in form, whereas the operatic Cavatina foreshadows *unendliche Melodie*. The Neapolitan element that characterized the opening fugue begins to appear again here (A naturals in bars 9, 17, 25–6) and in the last five bars this promotes the modulation to C sharp minor, the key of the final Allegro as of the opening fugue.

How Beethoven first envisaged the grim, tragic theme of this movement can be seen from the sketch-books,[1] where it appears in a mild 6/8

[1] See further Schindler, op. cit., pp. 711 ff.

form, starting in F sharp minor, the form in which it reappears at the end of the exposition. A comparison between this and the final version shows once again how Beethoven could conceive the shape of an idea without associating it immediately with the rhythm from which it eventually seems inseparable

Ex. 74 (a)

(b)

The stamping rhythm over which this develops immediately recalls the finale of the second Razumovsky quartet op. 59, no. 2, but there is nothing there to compare with either the wide-leaping second subject or the furious contrapuntal activity of the development section here. The second of the first group of subjects (Ex. 75 (b)) makes an even clearer reference to the opening fugue's theme (Ex. 75 (a))

Ex. 75 (a)

(b)

But is there any parallel in any of Beethoven's works for the long descending scale and ecstatic leap of the second subject?

Ex. 76 Allegro

The smooth-flowing quavers form the strongest possible contrast to the persistent jerking rhythm that has so far dominated the movement, while the leap to the equally even flow of soaring minims seems deliberately to counterbalance the tonal or semitonal jerks by which the first subject progresses.

The development opens with a fugato (bar 93), with each instrument contributing its angry rising figure of four or seven notes, twisting the music to B minor. From bars 124–48 a moto perpetuo of *non ligato* quavers is combined with the questioning first phrase from the first subject (Ex. 74 (b) bar 2). These quavers eventually subside into a slow written-out trill (cf. the mysterious figure of example 69, that interrupted the sixth variation in the fourth movement) and this provides a dramatic background for the opening of the recapitulation. Here the second subject (Ex. 76) is allowed more scope, the leaps in particular being brought close together in an espressivo (bars 248 ff.) that carries a unique note of exultation. This, like the Grosse Fuge, is the Dionysian obverse of such great moments of Apollonian contemplation as the finale of op. 111, the 'Heiliger Dankgesang' of op. 132, or the opening fugue of the present work. The full violence of this affirmation of life through struggle is only revealed in the coda, where the fugato of the development is inverted and descends as crushingly and inexorably as it there thrust upwards. The end is held back by two extraordinary D major scales (bars 329–36), each terminating with the Neapolitan twist to C sharp that explains their organic connection with the music, though leaving their exact aesthetic significance still debatable. If they hark back, to the second (D major) movement, the remainder of the coda is given over to asserting the link with the first movement, which we saw in example 75 (b). We speak of 'thrashing out' an issue or a argument, and no term could be better suited to the activity of this finale.

Opus 135

Beethoven finished the C sharp minor quartet in July 1826, hardly more than a matter of days before his nephew Karl's attempt at suicide, It was during the next two months that he wrote most of the last string quartet, op. 135, when Karl was in hospital. It was finished very soon after Beethoven arrived at Gneixendorf, early in October, and was thus the last completed work, except for the substitute finale of op. 130. There is, as we have already noticed a considerable resemblance between the eighteenth-century good humour and good manners, and even the slightly self-conscious touch of Biedermeir-domesticity, that we found in the new finale of op. 130 and the neo-Haydn exterior of the first movement and the final Allegro of op. 135.

It is not merely a matter of appearances. In both these works Beethoven seems to have exorcised the angels and the demons, pity and terror, to have momentarily finished with supramundane contemplation and the Dionysian assertion of the significance of life's struggles and contradictions. He is now content to cultivative his garden, to smile and to remember, to mock a little perhaps at his own dramatization of cosmic problems and to exercise his incomparable gift for sheer musical invention, the instinctive grasp and unfolding of a single melodic cell's potentialities.

The opening Allegretto often suggests Haydn in its humour and deliberate unexpectedness; Mozart in its formal symmetry and freedom from all those mercurial changes of mood and direction that have marked the quartets since op. 127. Beethoven's return to his own past and to his own former models is so clear that we feel that it must have been conscious and deliberate; but he no more ceases to be Beethoven than Stravinsky ceased to be Stravinsky when he wrote *Pulcinella*.

The opening ten bars of the movement proved one of the happiest of hunting-grounds for Rudolph Reti in his scrupulous panning for the gold of Beethoven's thematic construction and motivation (op. cit., pp. 206 sqq). His findings are certainly worth following. Example 77 (1) shows the first two bars of the movement, with two interlinked ideas, marked (a) and (b). Example 77 (2) shows the inversion of b over a dominant pedal, in bars 4–5; and (3) shows (a) twice and (b) once unaltered, and a + b with intercalary connecting notes filling the skeleton pattern. In bars 10–13 (Ex. 77 no. 4) the thematic material is again demonstrably present, giving the complete outline of a + b, with 'intercalary' notes in brackets; but here these intercalary notes are much more important, and begin to reveal the hazards of a game which can be played too seriously and may result in the distorting of a musical idea to fit a preconceived notion. The fact that Beethoven phrases the crotchets in example 77 (4) across the bar-line easily conceals the connection between this idea and the original, which is perhaps clearer in the build of the bridge passage which introduces the second subject (Ex. 77 no. 5).

Ex. 77

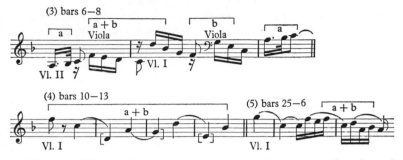

(3) bars 6—8

(4) bars 10—13

(5) bars 25—6

The chief idea in the second group is an alternation of tonic and dominant bars, with rocketing semiquaver triplets in attendance, such as we should expect to find in one of the op. 18 quartets (the resemblance between the Allegro finale of op. 18 no. 1 and this movement makes comparison most instructive). At the opening of the development section (bars 62–80) these semiquaver triplets punctuate and relieve the quasi-solemn contrapuntal combination of the original subject (a + b) with the crotchet-derivation shown in example 77 (4). In the end the triplets get the upper hand (cp. finale of op. 18, no. 1) and the texture of bars 89–100 seems almost to glance at the con brio repeated notes of Rossini.[1] This marks the stretto with which the recapitulation opens, over a hammered D flat in the cello, harking back to bar 1,

Ex. 78

The chromatically altered version of example 77 (4) in the recapitulation is as playful as this stretto. All through this movement Beethoven seems, in fact, to be making good-humoured fun of the counterpoint that he had been using so recently for the most austere purposes, laughing at its crabbedness, the angularity of line and disregard of merely aural pleasure that he had been turning to such magnificent purposes in the works immediately preceding this. The humour, mockery even, is never anything but affectionate, and draws its whole

[1] Cp. Schubert D minor string quartet. Final variation of the theme in the Andante con moto.

quality from the fact that it is based on an affection or a belief so strong
that they can be taken for granted. Counterpoint was such an integral
part of Beethoven's musical thinking that he could afford to make fun
of it, and his mockery always implies an identification with what he
mocks, a close family tie.[1] Just how light-hearted this movement is
can be seen from the two bars (176–7) introducing the coda, where
each of seven successive quavers in each instrument is prefixed by two
grace-notes.

The humour of the scherzo is, as we should expect, much rougher.
Whereas the first movement is an extension of the witty chamber music
addressed to an audience of connoisseurs, the second belongs to Beethoven's stylized out-of-door scenes, like the corresponding movement
in the Sixth Symphony. All the elements are simple to the point of
banality, their amalgamation subtle to the point of sophistication.
Rhythm is preponderant in the two upper instruments, with their
different cross accents—the melody in the first violin, a dominant
pedal in the second. The two lower instruments execute a hobbledehoy
dance

Ex. 79

The rhythmic dislocation, already the strongest feature here,
becomes even more marked in the second half of the scherzo, which
opens with an apparently invincible stammer

Ex. 80

---

[1] A comparison with Berlioz's mockery of counterpoint (the 'Amen' chorus in *La Damnation
de Faust*) is telling on the onehand, with Verdi's 'Tutto nel mondo è burla' fugue in *Falstaff* on
the other. Verdi's art was still rooted in the eighteenth-century world, with its strongly
contrapuntal premisses. Berlioz was a real 'modern' of his day, proud yet somehow astonished
if a moment of counterpoint served his purpose (cf. the childlike 'réunion des deux thèmes'
in *Roméo et Juliette*, Part 2, bars 120 ff.).

These two elements (Exs. 79 and 80) occasion between them a contrapuntal display quite in the manner, though not at all in the spirit, of
the preceding quartets. Several commentators[1] find ominous under-
tones in the scherzo, and one even believes the trio section to be 'more
extreme in its fury than the Great Fugue'. The trio section is certainly
a whirlwind movement in whose 134 bars the same phrase recurs
seventy-seven times, sixty of these in all three lower instruments while
the first violin executes a wildly leaping dance above

Ex. 81

The figure x in fact opens the trio, still in F major, and combines
with evenly repeated crotchets to form the accompaniment to a
rising-scale melody, which moves stepwise until the leaps in its last
two bars. This is heard first in F major and in G major, before taking
the A major shape shown above.

I am not convinced that either scherzo or trio is really sinister,
except in the sense that the first violin part in the A major section
of the trio suggests the not very seriously 'daemonic' figure of the
'demon fiddler'. With Beethoven at this stage in his career we are
often reminded of Tacitus's *omne ignotum pro magnifico*—every feature
that is not immediately intelligible is interpreted in a sense as august
and transcendental as possible. There is no doubt that this seventy-
seven-fold repetition of a single phrase is an example of Beethoven's

[1] Joseph Kerman (op. cit., p. 359). Philip Radcliffe (*Beethoven's String Quartets*, 1965,
p. 168) speaks of 'nightmarish obsession' and compares a similar passage in the third movement of Elgar's Second Symphony.

natural tendency to excess, the 'nimiety' that we have noticed in the
finale of op. 106, in the Gloria and Credo of the Missa Solemnis and
in the Grosse Fuge. He had, as we know, in life as in his art, moments
of regardlessness when he felt an interior prompting to break every
barrier, to let himself run completely wild. This trio is one of these
moments; but is it not a wild, rampaging cosmic humour rather than
anything sinister or on the shadow-side? Of course even humour on
such a scale, or indeed any instinct so untrammelled as this, has
something daemonic about it that shocks the ordinary listener.
Beethoven himself, however, might have been amused by his admirers'
awe and a little contemptuous, perhaps, of their superstitious inter-
pretations. On the other hand if this is indeed laughter, then it is on
the Homeric scale, such laughter as shook the Olympian gods at the
spectacle of Ares and Aphrodite caught making love and netted by her
jealous husband.

After the outburst of rhythmic energy that marked the scherzo
Beethoven moves to the opposite extreme. In the 'Lento assai, cantante
e tranquillo' the movement of the music is as smooth and even as
possible, almost imperceptible at moments or confined to a single
voice, as in the opening strain of the theme. This is the last and simplest of the great variation-movements that star these years, formally
a combination of song (ABA) and variations and as unified in its rapt
lyricism as any slow movement that Beethoven ever wrote. The
key is D flat major, the significant flattened sixth above the F major
of the two first movements; but it is neither the Klopstockian D flat
major about which Beethoven joked, nor the jeweller's or cabinet-
maker's D flat major of the Andante in op. 130. 'Süsser Ruhegesang'—
a tender lullaby—is what the composer called it; and once again, as
in the slow movements of opp. 106 and 127, and the Ninth Symphony,
a curtain is slowly drawn back before the melody emerges (bars 1-2).
The 'sotto voce' marking, the immobility of the dominant pedal in the
second violin and cello and the rocking tenths in viola and cello do

Ex. 82   **Lento assai**

indeed suggest a cradle-song, or the motion of 'such a tide as, moving, seems asleep'. In the second strain the melody raises itself (bars 7 and 8), through B flat minor and E flat minor, to the sixth above the tonic only to fall again to the low A flat; and it is only in the repetition of the final phrase in the higher octave that it reaches to the F, a tenth above the initial D flat. There is no sense of either effort or fatigue here, only one of grateful well-being in repose. Variation 1 is hardly more than a continuation of the melody, given a note of greater animation by the close-lying harmony in the higher register of the instruments and by the chromatic alterations and rinforzando markings in the two bars corresponding to the B flat minor and E flat minor bars of the theme. It is as though the dream had shifted from darkness into light. In the second variation (Più lento, C sharp minor) the temperature is lowered. Now the music moves in jerks instead of flowing, and all extraneous material has been removed from the theme's skeleton. In bars 27–8, centres of movement in the theme and of a disturbance, however minimal in variation 1, the diminished harmonies introduce the only threatening note in the whole movement. But in fact these are hardly more than the formal climax in the Grave section of a Baroque overture, which this variation recalls, if only by its dotted rhythm

Ex. 83

In variation 3 Beethoven returns to tempo primo and the major mode, and a canonic treatment of the theme between first violin and cello, while the viola moves in thirds with the cello or the second violin. This constitutes a return to the close texture of variation 1 after the wider spacing of variation 2, and it is followed in the final variation by a rhythmic and melodic fragmentation of the theme set out in an exquisite pattern such as was later favoured by Schumann.

Ex. 84

The marking 'semplice' warns, as always, against any underlining or exaggeration of the purely sensuous aspect of this variation, whose exquisite D flat major transparency, swaying rhythm and occasional chromatic colouring again seem to anticipate Chopin's Berceuse, written only twenty years later.

'Der schwer gefasste Entschluss' is Beethoven's title for the finale, and a motto stands at the head

Ex. 85

What the decision was, and who found it so difficult to make has been discussed earlier (see ch. 9, p. 73). But whatever the factual origin of the joke, the music suggests that Beethoven was laughing at the connection between a trivial instance of the great metaphysical problem of Freedom and Necessity, so distantly involved. The later nineteenth century caught the metaphysical allusion, but not the joke.[1] Kerman[2] suggests that the operatic mannerisms of the first twelve bars may be a parody of the opening questions and reflections of the Ninth Symphony's finale, a joke very much in Beethoven's vein; or, with much less probability, an allusion to his own operatic plans for the future. The circumstantial evidence suggests, as in the case of the scherzo and trio in this quartet, that the more portentous interpretation is likely to be wrong. In op. 135 Beethoven has, at least for the time being, washed his hands of metaphysical problems. He is concerned with the *diesseits*, not the *jenseits*, and even the Lento assai is innocent of any note of the moral elevation so common in Beethoven's slow

[1] The slow introduction to the first movement of César Franck's symphony might well have delighted Beethoven as an elaboration of his own joke—until he discovered that it was in deadly earnest.

[2] Op. cit., p. 363.

movements. Certainly the F major Allegro which follows the questionings of the Grave is one of the most transparent and light-hearted
movements in all the quartets. Its first theme (Ex. 85) besides being a
major inversion of the questioning 'muss es sein?' is easily related
to that of the opening movement; and its second theme is based on the
same interval of the fourth and closely related to the theme of the
Lento assai

Ex. 86

This finale contains in fact a multitude of ingenuities and unusual
traits. In the first place the tonality immediately becomes that of the
subdominant (B flat major) in which we hear a six-note phrase already
familiar from the theme of the fugue in op. 131 and constituting an
invitation to the canonic treatment which is not long in appearing
(bar 17)

Ex. 87

Then, after a sly reference to the sevenths in the first movement (Ex.
77 no. 4), we find ourselves in the improbable key of A major—the
tonality of the two-part canonic episode in the first movement of op.
131 (bars 66 sq.)—and Beethoven once again puts this theme (Ex. 87)
through its canonic paces as a way of introducing the second subject
(Ex. 86 no. 2), all in a cloudless A major, in which the exposition ends.
For its repetition Beethoven enjoys wrenching the A major version
of example 86 no. 1 through F sharp minor, by a characteristic
flattening or 'screwing-down', to F major. When he wishes to start
his development, on the other hand, he takes a leaf straight out of
Mozart's book, the opening of the development section in the finale
of the symphony in G minor K.550.

Ex. 88 (a)

(b)

After this mock explosion Beethoven weaves Ex. 86, no. 1 (bars 89–111) with the infinitely adaptable Ex. 87 in innocent contrapuntal blessedness and even involves the second subject, which appears in D major, in the same sport. A turn flat-ward, followed by a change of key to F minor (bar 135), momentarily clouds the sky, and grumbling trills foretell the storm which breaks when the recapitulation starts (bar 163), with a mock orchestral version of the original 'question' of the motto. But the storm passes as quickly as it came. If the 'question' is not a joke, then the answer is insufferably frivolous; but the very solemnity of the question, exaggerated now so that no one can miss the parody, gives the joke away—and we find ourselves in a pastoral world as sunny as anything in Haydn. Once again example 87 is more prominent and ubiquitous than the true second subject, and Beethoven is so content and relaxed that he suggests repeating the whole second part, but does not insist ('si ripete la seconda parte al suo piacere'). In the coda, as we might have foreseen, he reverses the roles and presents the 'answer' in the interrogative form of the 'question' (bar 243)

The second subject makes a last appearance, heard 'pianissimo pizzicato' as though on the musical glasses; and as each of the players returns to his bow, the 'answer' theme comes tripping down the scale, still pianissimo, until a sudden fortissimo unison brings the movement to a speedy end in four bars.

The difference between this last movement and the new finale which Beethoven wrote at much the same time for op. 130 is perhaps the difference between the eighteenth century, with its wit and individualism, reviewed in the perspective of 1826—and the new spirit of the Biedermeier age, when paternalist conservatism was reducing the arts in Austria to a high form of domestic entertainment or an adornment of public life and official institutions. Beethoven never lived to endure the 'interior emigration' that was forced upon his friend Grillparzer, reducing a man who should have been a poet of European stature to a merely regional eminence and eventually extinguishing his creative impulse by enclosing it in a dusty vacuum. Beethoven, who discussed the Viennese situation with Grillparzer, was of quite different metal and had not been brought up, like Grillparzer, in Metternich's Vienna; nor, if he had lived, can we imagine him ever reducing his art to Biedermeier proportions. Nevertheless, a mental climate is insidious in its effect on even the strongest personalities, and no forces of persuasion are as strong as those that are unseen, unavowed and directed below the conscious level. Perhaps only a comparison with op. 135, which it superficially resembles in many ways, will reveal how close Beethoven came in the op. 130 finale to the contracted scope and vision of Biedermeier art. If the first and last movements of op. 135 do indeed represent a contraction of scope and a reduction of visionary power compared with the preceding quartets, they still retain potency of a different kind. The harmless, gelded quality that is characteristic of Biedermeier art is hardly found even in Beethoven's occasional compositions; but an occasional composition is exactly what the finale of op. 130 proved to be.

CHAPTER 20

Characteristics of the
late style

It is not difficult to find links between all the main works composed by Beethoven during the last ten years of his life. No music is more individual than this, if only in its combination of apparently contradictory features, of which the most immediately remarkable are complexity of texture and simplicity of intention, archaism and innovation. In order, however, to establish the existence of a specific 'third period' style we must be sure that the works of these last ten years share characteristics that are either absent from earlier works or present in a much lower proportion. Our examination of Beethoven's life and character (including, as a most important factor, his health) during this period would lead us to expect a change in his music, a reflection of the sufferings and anxieties: the waning of popularity and the increasing interior loneliness and self-sufficiency imposed by his deafness. The fact that we can trace such a progressive interiorization and recollection in the music of Gabriel Fauré, whose deafness also eventually became all but complete, naturally strengthens this expectation; and it is further confirmed by the general consensus among musicians as to where this 'last period' may be said to start, i.e. in the two violoncello sonatas of op. 102. Very few of the characteristics of these later works are new, in the sense that there is absolutely no example of them in any of Beethoven's works prior to op. 102 (1816). The chief instance is the use of the modes, suggested to Beethoven by his preliminary study of old church music before writing the Missa Solemnis and appearing most strikingly there and in the string quartet op. 132. For the rest, what distinguishes Beethoven's late from his early and middle styles is the frequent appearance in conjunction of a comparatively few features—melodic, harmonic, rhythmic, and textural—all of which can be paralleled in isolation in his earlier works. Thus, to take the most obvious instance, there are plenty of instances of contrapuntal writing, and not a few of formal fugue or at least fugato passages, before 1816; but after that date counterpoint seems to have taken on a new importance to Beethoven, while his interest in canon is shown by the many occasional pieces that he wrote for his friends in these last years, and the importance that he attached to fugue is shown by his strategic placing of fugal movements at climactic points in his most ambitious works—initial in op. 131, final in op. 106 and op. 110, in the 'Gloria' and 'Credo' of the Missa Solemnis and the Ninth Symphony, both central and final in the Diabelli Variations.

Nothing was further from Beethoven's whole attitude to his art than a conscious search for originality, the deliberate adoption of a 'new style', such as we find in Monteverdi, in Wagner, in the nationalist composers of the later nineteenth century and in all the conscious innovators of our own time. 'What is new and original appears of its own accord (*gebiert sich selbst*)', he said, 'without one thinking about it.' His interest in the music of the past was not surprising in early middle age, when the tide of the creative impulse is on the turn in even the most richly endowed artists. Both Mozart and Mendelssohn showed the same interest, and at an earlier age. Certainly there was in Beethoven's case no suggestion of the uncertainty or despair expressed by the ageing Verdi's 'torniamo all'antico e sarà un progresso'. Beethoven was not instinctively attracted by the music of his younger contemporaries: he found Spohr's chromatic writing monotonous, dismissed Marschner and only came round to Weber after a struggle. But he never seems to have been in any doubt about the future of the art in general or of his own personal contribution to it. Unlike most composers, he wrote by instinct music that was far more original, even revolutionary, than his expressed opinions, professing his supreme admiration for Handel among his predecessors and Cherubini among his contemporaries, while he himself was moving instinctively into the worlds of opp. 106 and 111 and the last string quartets. He was confident that his was the music of the future, in the sense that it would only be fully appreciated by later generations; but it never occurred to him to adopt the role of a conscious pioneer in this or any other matter.

The works of his last decade sprang, like those of his early and middle years, from the promptings of an inner compulsion; and they reflect, not the conscious, intellectually determined search for originality or novelty, but the gradual reorientation of a complete, mature personality. It is not possible to describe this reorientation simply, in terms of the deaf man's enforced retreat into a private world. Such a description, which might conceivably account for some of the slow movements of the late sonatas and quartets and the opening fugue of op. 131, is reduced to nonsense by such virtuoso movements as the finale of op. 106 and the opening Allegro of op. 111, by the superb dramatic rhetoric of the Grosse Fuge and the speaking, intimate, thoroughly sociable character of op. 135. These are no self-communings but 'communications' of the highest and most intense kind. What they communicate is evidence of an inner life of almost unparalleled reality and intensity, a sense of fulfilment and plenitude that wholly transcends not only the mental and physical sufferings which we know Beethoven to have experienced while engaged on their composition, but even the moods of interior abandonment and the sense of dereliction that find expression in the Adagio of op. 106, the cavatina of op. 130 or the opening fugue of op. 131. Does any listener in fact feel melancholy, sad, depressed or afflicted by vague nostalgia after hearing these movements, as he may feel after listening to many works by Schubert, Schumann, Chopin and their followers in the late nineteenth and early twentieth century? Is not the overwhelming impression one of heightened awareness and vitality, of having vicariously faced and conquered the tragedy that is at the heart of every human existence and received an absolute, though strictly speaking ineffable assurance that behind, beyond, or beneath that very real tragedy there is a far more real, more lasting, infinitely more important joy?[1] In this literal sense the old jibe about the 'metaphysical' quality of Beethoven's last works is indeed true; for they do seem to furnish evidence of the reality of an order which lies behind, beneath, 'after' (and, it often seems, in blatant contradiction to) the everyday world of phenomena as perceived by our senses and interpreted by our intellects.

Is it possible to discover any organic connection between what this music communicates and its physical, technical characteristics? or are we confronted with the familiar dilemma of the indivisibility of form and content?

> O chestnut-tree, great-rooted blossomer,
> Are you the leaf, the blossom or the bole?
> O body swayed to music, O brightening glance,
> how can we tell the dancer from the dance?

[1] For this reason Deryck Cooke's division of the last quartets (op. cit., p. 32) into those 'basically concerned with pleasurable emotions' (opp. 127 and 135), the chiefly tragic opp. 131 and 132, and op. 130 ('compounded of a tremendous positive depth and power to which it is difficult to give a name') seems altogether too simple-minded; as does the suggestion that the last quartets are 'about' death.

This is a problem in all music, but perhaps nowhere more acute than in these last works of Beethoven's. Let us see whether the clues that we possess will take us any further, and start with the plainest of all: the markedly contrapuntal character of these works.

The beauty—in the mathematical sense—of good counterpoint is that it excludes everything fortuitous or otiose, furnishing the composer with a strict discipline by which every detail of a work can be made organic. This is not in itself any guarantee of musical quality and a good contrapuntist, if he is a dull composer, will write good counterpoint but dull music (Cherubini, Taneiev, Reger and, on occasion, even J. S. Bach). But if a composer of Beethoven's power and originality can submit his musical thinking to this discipline, his works will have an organic unity, a density of concentration and a specific gravity such as can be obtained by no other means. They may well lack, as Beethoven's contrapuntal movements do, the bland progressions and smooth flow that he himself admired in Palestrina and Cherubini, and they will not have the apparently effortless, instinctive 'second nature' quality that we admire in J. S. Bach. Beethoven had to fight for his contrapuntal mastery, and his counterpoint is full of evidence of the struggle. Jagged, angular lines, harsh suspensions, crude pitch-contrasts and frequent rhythmic and melodic overlaps mark all his greatest fugal movements. They form part of the very essence of the finale of op. 106 and the Grosse Fuge, and of the fugues in the Gloria and Credo of the Missa Solemnis. In the finale of the D major cello sonata op. 102, no. 2 we may suspect that some of the asperities are due to lack of experience in what was, for Beethoven, still a comparatively unfamiliar medium of expression; and the finale of the piano sonata in A major op. 101 has a similar aggressive quality that gives the movement an unexpectedly youthful character. There is an entirely new mastery of fugue as an expressive medium in the finale of the piano sonata in A flat op. 110, where the asperities and knotty points in the contrapuntal writing are strategically planned to create points of tension, whose relaxation carries the listener steadily forward from climax to climax. But the supreme example is the fugue with which the C sharp minor quartet op. 131 opens. Here Beethoven achieves a natural flow and mastery of transition comparable to that of J. S. Bach, without for a moment sacrificing the personal note, the suggestion of implicit, controlled interior drama that becomes explicit at nodal points in the design. A similar ease and recollectedness mark the fughetta (variation 24) that forms the quite unexpected point of rest in the Diabelli Varations.

In all these instrumental fugues we are reminded of Beethoven's reputation as an interpreter of the '48' while still a young man at Bonn. The vocal fugues in the Missa Solemnis and the Ninth Symphony, on the other hand, reflect his enthusiasm in middle and later life for Handel. In these mass is as important as line, and the dramatic element is so strong that we are aware of an almost visual, spectacular quality whose only counterpart in the instrumental fugal movements is in the great virtuoso displays of op. 106 and the Grosse Fuge, and to a lesser degree in the fugue of variation 32 of the Diabelli Variations. This spectacular element is found in the often cruel tessitura of the vocal fugues and in the crude contrasts of pitch and dynamics and the sheer technical difficulty of op. 106 and the Grosse Fuge.

The principle of unity in diversity that finds its most dramatic expression in fugue permeates almost every movement in these last works, persistently though often unobtrusively, in the form of canonic, or more loosely imitative writing. We saw an example of this at an unexpected moment in the Adagio of op. 106 (see Ex. 20, p. 169) but the instances are countless. In the Diabelli Variations particularly this imitative writing seems to have become second nature; and we know in fact that the writing of canons was at this time one of Beethoven's amusements, extending to his relations with his doctors ('Doktor, sperrt das Tor dem Tod' and 'Ich war hier, Doktor') as well as his friends ('Falstafferl, lass dich sehen', 'Sankt Petrus war ein Fels, Bernardus war ein Sankt', 'O Tobias', 'Alles Gute, alles Schöne', 'Edel sei der Mensch', 'Das Schöne zum Guten' or the uncomplimentary 'Bester Herr Graf, Sie sind ein Schaf') and chance acquaintances ('Kühl, nicht lau', 'Schwenke dich ohne Schwänke', 'Wähner ist kein Wahn', 'Hoffmann, sei ja kein Hofmann', 'Brauchle, Linke', all containing puns on proper names). These, and many other similar occasional canons, thrown off in a moment of affection, irritation, or convivial good-humour reveal Beethoven's persistent underlying concern at this time with the manipulation of sound in one of its purest forms, a discipline which became first a pleasurable activity or game and finally second nature. In the same way a writer might invent acrostics, and Beethoven's own delight in puns was no doubt an extension of this instinct to the verbal sphere. We should certainly expect to find evidence of this concern in such a writer's or composer's finished works—a heightened awareness of the hidden relations between sounds in the one case and words in the other, a consequent precision and economy of language and a gnomic or epigrammatic conciseness of style. In fact we do find instances of these traits in

Beethoven's later works, and particularly in the variations which form such a large proportion of these movements. Obvious instances are to be found in the Diabelli Variations (nos. 20 and 22), in variation 5 of the fourth movement in op. 131 and the fugal (also fifth) variation in the finale of op. 109. The elliptical suppression of all inessentials and the taking for granted of intermediate steps in a musical argument, both characteristics of the epigrammatic style, account for many of the harshest and apparently most arbitrary passages in the finale of op. 106 and the Grosse Fuge, and long formed one of the barriers to the general appreciation of the late quartets.

I do not think it fanciful to see in this search for unity in diversity and *multum in parvo* a reflection of Beethoven's growing awareness of a unity lying behind the diversity of the phenomena of human existence. Or shall we say that, if the uniquely bracing and life-enhancing character of Beethoven's last works is due to the witness which they bear to such a unity, these are exactly the means that we should expect him to employ? If we find a prevalence of variation-form to be another equally prominent feature of these works, and also another means of expressing unity in diversity, our supposition will be strengthened, though we shall still have no evidence of Beethoven's conscious intention. Our only reliable evidence of Beethoven's interior life during these last ten years is to be found in the music itself; and all our knowledge of the man would lead us to suppose that his apprehensions of philosophical or religious truth were then, as always, immediate and instinctive rather than conceptual, formulated directly in musical terms without ever being verbalized.

Variation-forms are certainly ubiquitous, even entering fugal and sonata-movements, as in the Adagio of op. 106 and the Grosse Fuge. Moreover Beethoven, who in his middle period had largely abandoned the melodic or purely decorative form of variation for the more intellectual harmonic variety, now found a use for both species. On the one hand there are the Diabelli Variations, where the trivial theme is soon concealed by the wealth of allusion that it suggests, and the Adagio of the quartet op. 127; on the other we find the simply ornamented version of the arioso in the finale of op. 110, the astonishingly close variations of the Arietta in op. 111 and the Adagio and finale of the Ninth Symphony, where the contours of the original theme hardly for a moment cease to show through the surrounding tracery, however luxuriant. Even in the Andante ma non troppo of the C sharp minor string quartet op. 131 harmonic variations alternate with melodic, so that the most casual listener remains aware of the original melody. In these last works Beethoven uses a third kind of variation, in which melodic and structural links with the theme are less important than the elaboration of a psychological mood prompted by some individual trait or some particular aspect of the theme. Such are nos. 20, 22, and 24 of the Diabelli Variations and no. 5 (Allegretto) in the Andante ma non troppo of op. 131. It seems mistaken, therefore, to speak of a progressive intellectualization in Beethoven's music. If contrapuntal forms and variations play a greater role in these last works than the sonata-form that had so dominated his earlier music, this was rather an instinctive movement away from the dramatic principle of contrast, with its implicit idea of struggle. In its place we find a unified vision where music borrows nothing from the theatre, which had played so important a part in late eighteenth-century musical aesthetics, and aspires to its own unique condition.[1] We have seen that in the sonata-movements of these last piano works and string quartets the development sections are quite surprisingly short: in op. 111, for instance, there are only twenty bars development in a movement of 158 bars, in op. 132 only thirty-six bars in a movement of 264 bars. Instead we meet movements like the 'Allegro ma non tanto' (scherzo) of op. 132 which are all but monothematic and once again seem to reflect, like the fugal and variation movements, Beethoven's instinctive search for unification or, if our interpretation is right, his new apprehension of a single reality behind the diversity of the phenomenal world. We may observe this on the very largest scale in op. 106, where the interval of the major third permeates almost every bar of four movements, whose scope is so wide that they seem to cover the whole of human experience.

When Beethoven does employ contrast in these works, it is simple and striking in the extreme. The flowing 3/4 D major theme that alternates with the hymn-like 4/4 B flat major theme of the Adagio of the Ninth Symphony is as completely antithetical as the dancing D major 3/8 ('Neue Kraft fühlend') that alternates with the austere modal chorale in the 'Heiliger Dankgesang' of op. 132. But in both cases the listener feels that what he is experiencing is not so much a dramatic contrast between opposing forces as a change in the composer's angle of vision. The landscape, as it were, remains the same; but his view, which was directed at first towards the mountain range

---

[1] We might compare the case of Dante's *Divina Commedia*, in which the 'Purgatorio' and 'Inferno' present the human drama seen by a spectator from above, or at least outside, while in the 'Paradiso' contemplation and affirmation take the place of comment, invective and partisan spirit, and the poet finds himself drawn irresistibly upwards (Beethoven's *Blick nach oben*, as it were) to the source of all Being.

that determines the general character of the landscape, now moves to the green and smiling valley at his feet. Without the mountains, which provide shelter and water, the valley would be neither green nor smiling, and to shift our view from one to the other is simply to pass from cause to effect. In the same way the A major variations complement the opening fugue in op. 131 and the finale of the Ninth Symphony centres round the G major section 'Seid umschlungen', where Beethoven proclaims the fatherhood of God as the truth which alone justifies the complementary truth of the brotherhood of man. These contrasts, then, appear as different facets of a single whole, rather than as antagonistic ideas.

This complementary principle explains another marked feature of Beethoven's last works—the frequent use of ornament. As we should expect, this is most noticeable in the variation movements such as the finales of opp. 109 and 111 and the Adagio ma non troppo of op. 127, where a profusely ornamental style of writing forms the natural climax in a set of melodic variations. Less frequently, as in the Andante con moto which forms the third movement of op. 130, Beethoven writes a complete movement in a style whose elaboration of texture, juxtaposition of colour and miniature precision of detail recalls the inlaid work of rococo cabinetmakers (see Ex. 42, p. 377); and indeed the effect is somehow old-fashioned and grandfatherly in its extreme precision[1] of gait and delicacy of texture, neither of them typical of Beethoven at this or any other period.

Even more puzzling are the movements or episodes in which the combination of a broken, highly ornamented surface with dance-like rhythms suggests something approaching ballet music. In the final Tempo di menuetto of the Diabelli Variations Beethoven's title shows his conscious intention of writing a transfigured dance-movement. In the D major ('Neue Kraft fühlend') section of the 'Heiliger Dankgesang' of op. 132, on the other hand, there is no overt allusion to the dance, but the music irresistibly suggests ballet steps of the most formal kind (cp. Ex. 24, p. 364). The solo violin part in the 'Benedictus' of the Missa Solemnis, with its trills, leaps, and gestures, and the rather similar decoration by the first violins of the theme in the third variation in the Adagio of the Ninth Symphony[2] are two other striking instances of plastic suggestion in these late works, where ornamentation is almost as prominent a feature as the strict contra-

---

[1] Joseph Kerman, op. cit. (p. 317) describes it, in spite of Beethoven's marking 'poco scherzando' as 'somehow above joking, even in a curious way above humour'.
[2] See Ex. 26, p. 265 and Ex. 33, p. 320.

puntal writing of which it is the complement. This profusion of ornament and these dancing rhythms are the exterior, physical expression of that boundless sense of elation whose interior, spiritual counterpart is to be found in the chorale of the 'Heiliger Dankgesang', the 'Sanctus' of the Missa Solemnis, 'Ihr stürzt nieder' in the finale of the Ninth Symphony and the Arietta of op. 111.

There is one feature common to all these late works, but most noticeable in the piano sonatas, and that is the frequency of the trill. Although in essence ornamental, this is so frequent in these late works and so integral to the conception of each passage in which it occurs, that we may almost regard it as organic.

The trill's normal function is to accent the note on which it occurs, to lend it melodic prominence and to provide rhythmic propulsion. We find countless instances of this use of the trill in all Beethoven's music, and there are very many occasions in the late quartets where its use is entirely normal, even if rather more frequent than in the earlier quartets. In the piano sonatas the trills that introduce the finales of op. 101 and 106 and the Allegro con brio in the first movement of op. 111 belong to this conventional category. But in the finale of op. 106 and the Grosse Fuge we find this traditional use of the trill raised to an altogether higher power. In op. 106 the sforzato trill on the second (weak) beat of the 3/4 bar is one of the most marked characteristics of the fugal subject, and for the listener an easy means of identifying the return of the theme even when otherwise disguised. But it soon becomes clear that the trill in this movement is not simply a means of rhythmic propulsion or melodic accentuation, another and stronger form of the sforzando markings that occur so frequently throughout the whole movement. Already at the end of the G flat major scherzando grazioso episode (bars 85–93) we find a left-hand trill which has the tension-producing character of the initial trills introducing this movement, as they introduce the finale of op. 101 and the main section of the opening Allegro in op. 111. And in fact this trill (bars 94–5) is initial in character, providing the pressure, as it were, which sets in motion the following section (treatment of the theme by augmentation bars 97–110). In the stretto by augmentation and inversion, which follows in bars 111–124, explosive, 'pressure' trills of this kind are brought closer and closer together (see Ex. 23, p. 173) so that for a short time the whole landscape of the music consists of nothing but these small erupting volcanoes.[1] The fact that the trills are passed from hand to hand and explode on the weak third beat of the

[1] Cf. also bars 243–6 in the same movement.

bar completely disrupts the rhythmic flow of the music, which is only restored when the quavers begin to flow evenly in the left hand (bar 126), although the right hand is still occupied with the last of the trills. There is a similar effect in the Grosse Fuge. Here trills are entirely absent from the whole of the first fugue and only appear from bar 238 onwards, i.e. in the variations of the second fugue. In variation 1 the trills are normal and not particularly remarkable; but they begin to play an organic part in variation 2, as they appear closer together and invade and dominate the whole scene in variation 3. From bars 357 to 400 trills are never absent from one of the four parts, either thematic or else forming (bars 360 ff.) a background of excitement against which the unornamented sforzando dotted minims of the subject stand out all the more powerfully.

These two passages in op. 106 and the Grosse Fuge are climactic and resemble crises in a drama. Although in fact the thread of the argument is never interrupted (i.e. the trills are mostly organic, not ornamental) the listener has the impression that Beethoven is on the verge of being overcome by the violence of his own creative energy and of lapsing into incoherence. The trills in the last variations of the finales in the piano sonatas opp. 109 and 111 are entirely different in character; they are not dynamic but static, not explosions resulting from inner tension but the formalized expression of motionlessness. For the most part they are on pedal notes which provide the platforms or bases from which Beethoven conducts his explorations of the theme. In the finale of op. 109 the dominant pedal which sounds throughout the whole of variation 6 starts in simple crotchets, moves to quavers and so to quaver triplets; and then begins to oscillate in slow semi-quavers, which finally become a demisemiquaver trill, first in both hands and then in the left hand only (eight bars) and the right hand only (eleven). We saw an example of this static, slowly oscillating but not forward-moving music in the last section of the 'Heiliger Dank-gesang' of op. 132 (see p. 366, Ex. 26) and associated it then with the motionless ecstasy and incantatory repetitions of the contemplative. In variation 4 of the finale in op. 111 this same incantatory effect is achieved not only by the dominant pedal trill, under and over which the arietta makes its final appearance, but by the obsessive reiteration of figures built either from broken chords or from appoggiaturas that are in essence ornamentations of a single note (bars 74 ff.). The close-lying interrelation of the two hands pianissimo in the treble clef also produces something like an hypnotic effect, so that the return to the full range of the keyboard in bars 81 sq. gives the listener the feeling of a descent to earth. The long trill on D, which starts as the supertonic of C and ends as the leading note of E flat major, forms the transition from the world of impersonal contemplation to that of human espressivo and can thus be regarded as a Janus, both final and initial (bars 106–14), while the mounting crescendo in which each note is trilled (bars 114–16) is simply an extreme example of the trill as a form of melodic and rhythmic emphasis. In variation 5 the treble oscillations, broken chord and appoggiatura figures of variation 4 are transferred to the bass of the keyboard, where the left hand's wide wave-like figuration replaces the close-lying, glittering triplets executed by the right hand in the preceding variation.

If the long pedal-trills in the piano sonatas represent the principle of minimum motion (and are incidentally a method of compensating for the instrument's inability to sustain a single note) the opposite principle of maximum motion is to be found in the wide-leaping melodic intervals and the violent pitch-contrasts that form an equally noticeable characteristic of Beethoven's last works. Some of the most extreme examples are to be found in both movements of op. 111 (bars 48–9 of the first movement, where Beethoven leaps the whole length of the keyboard of the day, and bars 116–19 in variation 4 of the finale, where the player's two hands move remorselessly away from each other to similar extremes). To speak of such passages as miscalculations, and to relate them to the composer's deafness, is to disregard the fact that in these works Beethoven was plainly aiming at an extension of the sound-world of his day. It cannot seriously be suggested that he had forgotten the quality of the sound produced by combining the top and bottom registers of the piano with no intermediate filling, any more than he had forgotten the practical difficulty for choral sopranos of sustaining a high B flat, as in the Credo of the Missa Solemnis. Even if we were to suppose that such forgetfulness were in theory possible, the quartets contain innumerable examples of the most detailed and precisely calculated instrumentation, which shows that Beethoven still knew exactly the quality of the sound which he wished to produce and how to produce it. Extremes of pitch, and the leaps from one to the other, are particularly common in the piano sonatas opp. 106 and 111 and in the Grosse Fuge where, like the trills already discussed, they are evidences of tension. We find them again in the coda to the finale of op. 110 and the stormier numbers of the Diabelli Variations (variations 10 and 21, for example). In the trio of the string quartet op. 135 the leaps in the first violin part have a similarly wild, tense, obsessive character, demonic whether we regard it as sinister or humorous and in either case different in character from the superficially similar leaps in the trio of op. 132, which are manifestly playful.

If we are to look for evidence of miscalculation owing to deafness in these last works (and the idea seems to be altogether too simple-minded) it would be rather in certain apparently clumsy harmonic progressions, which have already been noticed in the discussion of the first movements of the D major cello sonata op. 102 and the piano sonatas op. 109 and op. 110.[1] These are not deliberate enharmonic puns, such as appear in the scherzo of op. 106 and no. 22 of the Diabelli Variations, although they consist of a similar semitonal slip. They are rather lyrical than humorous in intention, but still after forty years close acquaintance strike me afresh at every hearing as blemishes on the movements in which they occur, a weak joint or unnatural transition in the argument. I am well aware that the arguments that I have used against those who interpret other features of these works in terms of miscalculation apply equally here; but honesty compels me to register my inability to find these passages convincing. On the other hand where Beethoven prepares abrupt changes or shifts of this kind—as in the shift from C sharp major to G major in bars 13–14 of the Adagio in op. 106[2] or the rather different transformation scene that takes place when the first subject is transfigured in the finale of the string quartet op. 127—the effect is unforgettable and wholly convincing.

The late works contain a number of instances of Beethoven producing transformation scenes of this kind by a single stroke, or rather by a single modulation to the key of the flattened sixth in the scale of the tonic. This relationship is frequently found between separate movements in a work (e.g. the F major Marcia following the A major opening Allegretto in op. 101, the E flat major Cavatina following the G major Alla danza tedesca in op. 130, and the D flat major lento assai following the F major Scherzo in op. 135), but even more often at dramatic points within a single movement. The most striking of these are in the Ninth Symphony at bar 133 in the coda of the Adagio and at the end of the coda in the sixth variation in the finale. Here the chorus repeat the words 'vor Gott' (before God), and at the third time the A major cadence is replaced by F major, with the effect of a sudden intensely dramatic change of scene (see Ex. 38, p. 331). Only slightly less dramatic are instances of this same modulation in the 'Gloria' of the Missa Solemnis. The first of these is at bar 270, where the fanfare F that follows 'qui sedes at dexteram Patris' melts into the

[1] See p. 178, Ex. 28 and p. 189, Ex. 40.   [2] See p. 165, Ex. 16.

D flat major of 'miserere nobis' and the modulation suggests the psychological transition from the proclamation of God's majesty to the supplication for His mercy.[1] The second instance appears at the end of this section and represents, with equal aptness, the return from supplication to praise and adoration (bars 309–10, modulation from C sharp major to A major introducing the 'Quoniam Tu solus sanctus'). There is a similar passage in the Credo at the transition from 'homo factus est' to 'crucifixus' (D major to a transitional B flat major at bars 155–6).

In the instrumental works the most dramatic use of this modulation is at the transition from the introduction to the fugue in the finale of op. 106 (Prestissimo A major to allegro risoluto F major, leading to B flat major). The relationship between the first and second group of subjects in the Adagio of the same sonata is similar (F sharp minor and D major). But the fact that Beethoven spreads the modulation over nine bars (bars 36–45) and devotes a bar or more to each intermediate tonality (F sharp major—B major—E major—A major—D major) greatly modifies its effect, which is a function of its suddenness. In op. 110, for instance, the E major section in the recapitulation of the first movement has only to be thought of as F flat to give us the same relationship with the A flat tonic of the movement; but here again the intermediary steps are so carefully worked through that we are less aware of the relationship.

A most unusual example, where this modulation is neither carefully prepared nor quite executed at a single stroke, is the transition from variation 2 to variation 3 in the Adagio of the string quartet op. 127. Variation 2 comes to a close on the first inversion of the A flat major triad and appears to move at once towards the minor of the subdominant (D flat). Instead of this the Adagio molto espressivo of variation 3 is in E (or F flat) major.[2] There is an exquisite reminiscence of this modulation 5 bars before the end of the coda.

Another example occurs at the opening of the development section in the first movement of the string quartet op. 130, where G flat (F sharp) major allegro is immediately answered by D major adagio— a good instance of the elliptical thinking which puzzled listeners in the quartets, where the transparency of the medium automatically magnifies all such effects. Here too, however, there are cases where

[1] This modulation may be regarded as a further instance of that 'change of perspective' discussed above (see pp. 421–2; and thus of the fundamental unity, beneath apparent diversity, that is characteristic of all Beethoven's later works.
[2] See Exs. 6 and 7 on pp. 353–4.

Beethoven so thoroughly prepares the listener that the slow progression towards the flattened sixth is hardly noticeable (op. 131 transition from the A major of variation 7 in the Andante to the F major of the Allegretto in bars 250–4, and op. 135 final Allegro, where the exposition ends in A major and the tonic F major is not reached until the sixth bar of the development section).

Can Beethoven's frequent and dramatic use in his last works of this modulation to the key of the flattened sixth be usefully related to any other characteristic of this music as well as to the general principle of 'changed perspective'? There is, I believe, another feature comparable to these transformation scenes in which the whole landscape of the music seems suddenly to dissolve and change its character and the listener is presented with what often seems an entirely new prospect. That is the use of what has been described as a 'curtain' or 'pedestal', a short passage in which Beethoven either draws back a veil to reveal a new idea or raises that idea on to a level above that of the foregoing passage or movement. The most obvious instances of the raising of a curtain or withdrawing of a veil are the opening bars of the Adagios of the Ninth Symphony and the string quartet op. 127, and the Lento assai of the string quartet op. 135, where the actual instrumentation has a plastic suggestion, as each instrument moves into place for the act of revelation. The 'Et incarnatus' in the 'Credo' of the Missa Solemnis is prepared in a similar way, whereas the solo violin and the flutes that introduce the 'Benedictus' are suddenly present, like a point of light piercing the darkness in which the 'Praeludium' ends.

The image of the pedestal is suggested in the first place by the mysterious introductory bar which Beethoven added at the beginning of the Adagio of op. 106. Wilhelm von Lenz[1] was the first to analyse this introductory bar rationally, as an easing of the transition from the B flat major tonality of the Scherzo to the F sharp minor (G flat minor) of the Adagio. He regards the opening A as still the leading-note of B flat and the C sharp as marking the first unmistakable move into the new F sharp minor territory (and he compares the progressions F sharp–A in bar 69 of the same movement and D–F sharp in bar 154). The fifteen B naturals at the end of the Scherzo he regards as 'heralds' of the new sharpward turn of the music.

The same rising third, combined with the modulation to the key of the flattened sixth, raises the Adagio molto espressivo of the variation 3 in the Adagio of op. 127 above the exquisite inlay-work of variation 2.

[1] W. von Lenz, *Beethoven—eine Kunststudie* (1855–60), IV, pp. 41–4.

Here again, however, it is not so much a new prospect that is presented to the listener as the old prospect in a new light; so that we are in fact witnessing another example of that fundamental unity of experience that seems to be the secret of Beethoven's last works. Beethoven's use of such humble material as folk-melodies (scherzo of op. 110 and 'Danza tedesca' of op. 131) hurdy-gurdy tunes (trio of second movement in op. 132) or the Piacevole theme at bar 69 in the Presto section no. 5 of op. 131 and the A major theme at bar 53 in the finale of op. 135, side by side with passages or movements of great emotional intensity and intellectual concentration, perhaps furnishes another instance of this unity of vision. It is certainly an indication of that instinctive humanity which increasingly marks Beethoven's last works; and the fact that we find a similar concern with 'little' music in Mozart, Schubert, Mahler, and even Berg (violin concerto) suggests that it may be an Austrian trait.

From what has already been said in this chapter about the distinguishing characteristics of these works it will be clear that the piano sonatas and variations and the string quartets provide slightly different evidence from that of the Missa Solemnis and the Ninth Symphony. The reason for this is obvious. Both the Mass and the symphony were designed for large audiences and must belong, by their very nature, to the order of public music-making. In the piano works and string quartets, on the other hand, Beethoven was writing either for himself or for a small body of connoisseurs. If the virtuoso sonatas opp. 106 and 111 still retain clear indications of having been conceived for concert performance, they are still 'private' works compared with the Mass and the symphony. It is improbable that Beethoven thought consciously in such terms, or evolved any theory of *prima* and *seconda prattica* such as Monteverdi's in the seventeenth century and Shostakovich's today. He was simply too well founded and trained in the clear categories of the later eighteenth century ever to confuse public and private music-making. He never condescends in the Mass or the symphony, as he had consciously condescended in the *Battle of Vittoria* and *Der glorreiche Augenblick*; the days for such things were long over and his pot-boiling folk-song arrangements for Thomson or his refurbishing of his own old works were kept in a quite separate compartment from his serious composition. But the Mass and the symphony contain, by the side of much that was wholly new in Beethoven's art, innumerable ties with the past, with what was familiar not only from his own earlier music but from the works of earlier writers of Masses and symphonies. As we have seen, this is particularly true of the Ninth

Symphony, where we are reminded of Mannheim symphonists and French Revolutionary composers. What distinguishes most clearly the more familiar language of the Mass and the symphony from the exploratory and often elliptical language of the quartets and much of the piano music is the persistence of the strong rhetorical element which played so important a part in the works of Beethoven's middle years.

Rhetoric is the art of persuasion by words, and the transference of the term to any other art but that of public speaking is a metaphor. In Greece during the fourth century B.C., and again in the last days of the Roman republic and the early days of the Empire, the study of rhetoric resembled the study of law in our own time: it was essential to a public career, whether this was in law itself or in politcs. The good rhetorician could make a fortune in either sphere, very much as a good legal training is often the foundation of a successful career in business or politics today. But, unlike law today, rhetoric in the ancient world was also the basic training for philosophers and writers; and it was this aspect that passed into the *trivium* of medieval educational theory, and even persists today in the classification of studies in Jesuit schools. It is the rhetorical element in Greek and Latin literature that is most alien to modern ways of thinking and has probably made Demosthenes and Cicero the most hated authors to generations of schoolboys. The whole elaborate theory of rhetoric, classically expounded by Quintilian in the first century A.D., suggests to the modern mind a cross between a skilled lawyer's chicanery— the art of making a good case out of a bad cause—and the magniloquent platitudes of the old-fashioned preacher. Rhetoric in all but the greatest artists seems to us today as so much wind, or worse. Yet it is impossible to deny the strong rhetorical element in the art of the Greek dramatists, in Lucretius, Virgil, Seneca, and indeed all the playwrights and most of the poets of the ancient world except the pure lyricists. Rhetoric as the conscious art of public persuasion never wholly died in Western Europe until our own times, when Winston Churchill was one of its last political practitioners. It flourished in literature during the seventeenth and eighteenth centuries, manifestly in the sermons of Bossuet and Massillon, the writings of Edmund Burke, only slightly disguised in the poetry of Milton and Pope, and in French classical tragedy. The fundamentally didactic character of these men's writings is thought by many today to contradict the very nature of art as such, to constitute a wholly unwarrantable intrusion of the conceptual thinking proper to public debate into the instinctive, private world of aesthetic experience. Perhaps this reaction against what seem to us to be a confusion of the moral and the aesthetic, inherent in the very idea of rhetoric as an art of persuasion, lies at the root of the decay of classical studies at the present time.

It was the early opera-composers' conscious intention of recreating Greek tragedy that introduced rhetoric into Western European music. For although that intention was never successfully carried out, the exposition of the drama in the dialogue or recitative narration, and in the 'set pieces' represented by the formal aria, corresponds fairly closely to the demands of traditional rhetorical practice.[1] We can see this most clearly not in the works of Monteverdi, but in the next generation and particularly in Lully's operas, consciously modelled on French classical tragedy. In Italy the form of the *opera seria*, as we know it in Handel's operas, owed much to the poet Metastasio's classical training and represents the fullest flowering of a fundamentally didactic text wedded to a rhetorical music, in which the formal classification of the different types of aria closely recalls Quintilian's classification of the tropes and figures at the rhetorician's disposal. It was from the opera, and its alternative the oratorio, that this 'oratorical' or rhetorical character passed into instrumental music during the second half of the eighteenth century.[2] We find clear traces of it in the *Affektenlehre*, or language of the emotions, elaborated by Mattheson and popularized in the sentimental and moralistic world of the years immediately before the outbreak of the French Revolution. After 1789 this same rhetoric, far from disappearing, was given a new stimulus by the powerful new ideals which were everywhere current and easily lent themselves to rhetorical expression.

Beethoven had grown up in a centre of this pre-revolutionary idealism at Bonn and had encountered in Neefe a teacher in the direct line of the North German sentimentalists, or followers of the *Affektenlehre*. Whereas Haydn and Mozart were only indirectly or superficially touched, in each case towards the end of their lives, by the irruption of this conscious moral idealism into their music, the young Beethoven's conscious partisanship and adherence to the new humanitarian order is already implicit in his early works. Two circumstances in his life greatly enhanced this initial inclination to moral fervour. The first was his acquaintance with the French ambassador in Vienna,

---

[1] Cp. Quintilian's *Institutio Oratoria*, Lib. III, 3, where he enumerates the five parts of a speech as *inventio, dispositio, elocutio, memoria* and *pronuntiatio*.
[2] So-called 'sonata form' itself is not unlike the dramatic pattern elaborated and classified by the rhetoricians.

Bernadotte, and the enthusiasm for Napoleon Bonaparte which he imbibed at the French Embassy; and the second was his incipient deafness, which began to make itself noticeable very soon after. His enthusiasm for Napoleon proved, as we know, too naïve and ended in disappointment, but a disappointment which itself showed how deep Beethoven's republican idealism went at this time. His deafness, increasing catastrophically over the next fifteen years, forced him to come to terms with disaster, to find some solution that would satisfy him emotionally as well as intellectually, and to abandon his first, instinctive attitude of defiant stoicism for a more mature and far-seeing attitude that was religious in character.

It was these moral and emotional influences that largely determined the increase in the works of Beethoven's middle period, of the rhetorical element. Old-fashioned rationalists like Edward Dent and Ernest Newman find here[1] a note of conscious moral elevation distasteful to them; and critics of a later generation have complained more generally of Beethoven's tendency to rant and to preach, to force the tone of his music like an actor over-acting a tragic role.

If we are to accept these criticisms as in any way justified—and I think that, although often grossly exaggerated, they do contain more than a grain of truth—how far do they apply to the works of Beethoven's last years? Since rhetoric is concerned with convincing a listener, its use implies an acute awareness of the effect of an 'oration' (whether verbal or musical) on an audience, whose emotions the orator is consciously concerned with swaying. In three of the last five piano sonatas (opp. 101, 109, and 110), in the Diabelli Variations and all the last five string quartets this consciousness of the listener is reduced to a minimum. Beethoven has not indeed abandoned communication, which would, to him, have meant abandoning music altogether; but the listener is a friend whose interest and understanding can be taken for granted, rather than an audience to be captured, dazzled, touched, or excited. In these works, therefore, the rhetorical element is virtually non-existent. In what Schindler called the two 'virtuoso' piano sonatas, on the other hand, we should expect to find traces of the old rhetorical style, virtuosity being itself a form of rhetoric (Quintilian's *pronuntiatio*); and in fact both opp. 106 and 111 do show these traces. In op. 106 they are manifest in the first and last movements, present in a modified form in the quasi-operatic sections of the Adagio. The opening gesture of op. 111 is unthinkable without an audience, impos-

---

[1] In the slow movements of the C minor violin sonata, or the E flat major piano concerto; and perhaps the slow movement of the C minor concerto is an early instance.

sible to imagine in one of the quartets, for instance; and the whole introduction suggests a dramatic scene.[1] The Arietta and variations, on the other hand, are as free from rhetorical appeal or display as any movement in the quartets.

The very scale and intention of the Missa Solemnis and the Ninth Symphony invite, even presuppose a certain display of rhetoric. Both works are addressed to large audiences, employ large forces and can only be performed in buildings whose proportions demand a certain exaggeration of gesture. They are essentially public, as the string quartets are essentially private music, and Beethoven had no scruples about using every resource to make them effective—the military music in the Agnus Dei of the Mass and the finale of the symphony, the quasi-ballet music of the Benedictus executed by a soloist, the *Schreckensfanfare* that opens the symphony's finale and the popular junketings with which it ends. The actual language of both works, particularly the symphony, differs very little in harmonic or melodic character from that of the works of Beethoven's middle period, though the language may be put to new uses.

There is, however, one very noticeable rhythmic feature of both works which, though not wholly novel, is a new extension of a familiar trait in the works of the early and middle periods. Sudden sforzandos, frequently on the weak beat of a bar, are so much a part of Beethoven's style that we hardly feel any need to account for them. And yet this sudden insistence on a single note or chord is in fact a kind of rhetorical device, all the more if it is unexpected. It is as though a speaker were suddenly to raise his voice or to emphasize a point by striking the palm of one hand with the fist of the other. Beethoven often uses such points of emphasis or, if they fall on a weak beat, dislocations of rhythm in his scherzos, where their effect is comic or grotesque; but they are a characteristic and important feature of his high tragic (as in the funeral march of the Third Symphony) and even of his lyrical style (Florestan's aria 'In des Lebens Frühlingstagen' *Fidelio* Act 2). In these cases the sudden sforzando still corresponds to the gesture of a speaker or an actor, but in order to convey the depth of his own emotion, or its sudden access to his consciousness, rather than to shock his audience into attention. It is the counterpart of the open hand laid on the heart, or pointed dramatically upwards, rather than of fist striking palm.

When Beethoven began to prefer strict contrapuntal textures and forms to the essentially more dramatic form of the sonata, this sforzando

---

[1] The Adagio of op. 110 represents the nearest approach to rhetoric in that sonata, but it is a transfigured and interiorized drama that is enacted.

element in his style took on a slightly different and more organic
character. The suspensions or anticipations, which form an integral
part of contrapuntal writing, produce the harmonic friction or tension
which forms one of the chief interests of contrapuntal music, however
swiftly and smoothly it may be resolved. Beethoven particularly
relished this aspect of contrapuntal texture and often insists on a
dramatic underlining of the tension. This he does by sforzando markings, as in example 23, p. 173, taken from the finale of op. 106. The
short fugue that forms variation 5 in the finale of op. 109 is an excellent example of Beethoven's delight in the harmonic clashes produced
by suspension

Ex. 1

Allegro, ma non troppo

The fugues in variation 32 of the Diabelli Variations, in the 'Gloria'
and the 'Credo' of the Missa Solemnis provide many examples of this
dramatic insistence on the harmonic asperities that contrapuntal
tradition preferred to gloss over as quickly as possible. But the dramatic
use of such suspensions and anticipations—particularly anticipations—
is nowhere more marked than in the Ninth Symphony, where it
almost amounts to a mannerism. Examples have been already quoted
(see p. 292) from the first movement and they are everywhere in the
finale. In the 'Adagio ma non troppo, ma divoto' of the finale each of the
four first phrases of the chorus's 'Ihr stürzt nieder, Millionen' (bars
630–8) is anticipated and this continues throughout the section (cp.
Ex. 43, p. 339). There is a typical instance of anticipation on the 'Joy'
theme itself, which gives a kind of excited stumble to the last four bars,
and communicates itself to all the variations.

Are we to regard this as a new and extended form of sforzando, a kind of pre-echo technique instinctively evolved by Beethoven, to lend additional weight and importance to an idea? If so, it was probably suggested to him by his contrapuntal studies and transferred from purely contrapuntal movements to those in which polyphony alternates with homophony. Certainly the jolting, dislocated rhythms characteristic of Beethoven's sforzato style in all its forms are much less frequent in the last quartets, with the obvious exception of the Grosse Fuge and the scherzo of the last quartet, op. 135. In the Diabelli Variations no. 28 is an obvious example, but otherwise heavy accentuation is most frequent in the canonic variations. So that we may speak in general of a marked diminution in sforzando markings—that is to say, rhetorical emphasis—in the last years of Beethoven's life. It is as though he gradually ceased to feel the need to emphasize the dramatic element in his music as the prompting of that music became increasingly interior and the influence of immediately personal, everyday events paled in the light of the ideal world which bathes all these works.

The name that we give to this world is not very important. One of the most impressive guarantees of the genuineness of Beethoven's vision is the fact that it has been accepted as authentic by thinkers of every complexion, who find in it the perfect embodiment of their own most intimate hopes, longings, fears, and aspirations. Of those who are accessible to music as a language in this sense—those who, in old-fashioned parlance, are truly 'musical' personalities—only the incurably trivial-minded or superficial are deaf to its appeal. For Schindler, so often wrong-headed and lacking in perspicacity, was right when he insisted that these works make unique demands on both performer and listener: they come from the depths of a singularly profound and mature human personality and can only be fully appreciated, understood, and 'enjoyed' by those who are themselves profound and mature enough human beings to enter this world. Bernard Shaw's easy assumption of the universal accessibility of the last quartets constitutes, in fact, a large claim, and one not to be made lightly by anyone who understands its full implications. Myra Hess's remark, that when she played the last sonatas she felt like 'a little Jew', suggests a far deeper insight into the true nature of this music, whose quality humbles those who understand it. Musicians can analyse its structure and demonstrate Beethoven's skill and originality as a composer; but neither they nor anyone else can explain the overwhelming sense of joy that it communicates, the plenitude of being and the nourishment of the whole person that it never fails to impart. In attempting an

explanation the religious-minded will use one language, the philosophers or humanists another, but the experience is the same. For here
we all share Beethoven's experience in handling words, which are
simply inadequate for the task, the wrong set of tools to break the
cipher. In the case of Beethoven, as elsewhere, the mid-twentieth
century prefers (reasonably but unheroically) technical analysis, which
is a craft aspiring to the status of a science and admits demonstration
on its own level, to the bandying of vague philosophical and religious
generalities which are, by their very nature, incapable of clear proof
and indeed of any finally compelling conclusions whatever. Every
light that can be shed on this music is of course welcome; but it should
never be forgotten that a technical analysis of Beethoven's language in
these works achieves no more—perhaps rather less, music being the
non-conceptual art that it is—than a similar analysis of Shakespeare's
language in *King Lear*. Analysis brings us nearer to understanding
how they are constructed and the means by which such and such an
effect is achieved; but the essence of the work still eludes us, as thoroughly as the 'soul' eluded the scientist who complained that he found
no trace of it when dissecting a corpse. The day to which Ernest
Newman, with the touching optimism of the nineteenth-century
rationalist, confidently looked forward, when the science of musicology
would be able to demonstrate the essential nature and quality of a
work, still seems as far off as ever.

To review the influence of Beethoven's last works on the development of music would be to write a history of the art during the
nineteenth century and the first decade of the twentieth, perhaps even
later. Before his death even the works of Beethoven's middle years had
begun to serve as models and to stimulate composers (Schubert in
particular) to new forms and methods of writing. In the new generation Schumann, Wagner, and Berlioz were ardent admirers and
deeply influenced, while Brahms was to be long withheld from writing
his first symphony by the awe which Beethoven's nine inspired in
him. But the works of Beethoven's last years took far longer to make
their full impression. Schumann and Wagner were the first of the
great composers who not only understood the full stature of the Missa
Solemnis and the Ninth Symphony but knew and admired the last
quartets, which enjoyed a reputation of being in some way esoteric or
problematical down to living memory, as Edward Dent's words show.[1]
Liszt, a pioneer here as so often elsewhere, not only knew, admired,
and performed the last piano sonatas but was influenced by them in his

[1] See p. 12.

own writing for the keyboard. Not surprisingly it was the string quartets that came into favour when the inevitable reaction against Beethoven's domination of the musical scene set in, and the symphonies in particular were dismissed for their naïve rhetoric and idealism. Bartók's quartets are not only unthinkable without a deep knowledge and understanding of Beethoven's last five, but form the only remotely comparable body of quartet music by any subsequent composer. Even today, when music has moved into a world which Beethoven himself would hardly recognize as having anything in common with that in which he worked, the reputation of the late works, and particularly the last quartets, is hardly dimmed. Our attitude to them has changed, of course, from that of the nineteenth century, just as our attitude has changed to the music of Bach and Mozart. 'Late Beethoven' conjured up to the nineteenth century the image of a music of extreme intellectual complexity and philosophical profundity, a world closed to all but the few. This was *la musique qu'on écoute la tête dans les mains*, the music of intellectual pretension and emotional agonizing against which the whole modern movement in France at the end of the 1914–18 war was a protest. Stravinsky himself was the mouthpiece, and incomparably the most gifted composer, of that reaction, which resembled the normal spirited adolescent's instinctive rejection of his parents' gods. But when the crisis of that adolescence passed and the adolescents themselves grew to maturity, when the smoke cleared from the battle-field and the dead were counted, Beethoven was not among them. Today we see his music more clearly in its historical perspective, identify his debts to his eighteenth-century forerunners and the movements of his own day and distinguish the different quality of individual works and movements within them. The music of his last years no longer presents us with technical, linguistic, idiomatic problems, nor is it the fashion to listen to these works in the pose of Rodin's 'Thinker', *la tête dans les mains*. But its quality remains unique and unassailed.

If we ask ourselves how this has come to be so, I believe we are thrown back on the personality of the composer, on the unique quality of Beethoven the man. We no longer accept any account of him even remotely like that of Schindler's touched-up portrait or the Promethean genius of late nineteenth-century biographers. But we have to admit that his personality dominates and informs all his music, and particularly the works of his last years, in a way that is absolutely unique. Neither Dante nor Shakespeare nor Goethe nor Tolstoy, let alone Bach or Mozart, is quite so unmistakably omnipresent in all his works, such a living and speaking human being. And the quality of that humanity is perhaps summed up best in the naïve comment of the innkeeper who, after commenting on Beethoven's liking for fish, observed as an afterthought to Moritz Schlesinger 'Der Beethoven ist ein wunderlicher Kerl, aber gut ist er'—'He's a strange chap, Beethoven, but he's good.'

APPENDIX A

Beethoven's Medical History

by EDWARD LARKIN

Introduction

Beethoven attributed his deafness and his bad health to abdominal disorder. His lifelong friend Wegeler,[1] Professor of Medicine and Dean of the University of Bonn, agreed. In fact, he suffered from a group of disorders into which research is fairly recent. Hitherto it was not possible to correlate his formidable list of symptoms: colitis, rheumatism, rheumatic fever, skin disorder, abscesses, endless infections, ophthalmia, and inflammatory degeneration of arteries. They culminated in a chronic active hepatitis, a cirrhosis of the liver, after an acute jaundice which he contracted at the age of fifty. It was fatal in seven years, a termination consistent with the peculiar susceptibility of the connective tissue[2] which seems the principal common factor in his group of disorders. Beethoven suffered wretchedly all his adult life, so much so that it is necessary to know his medical background to appreciate his personality. He was certainly a difficult man, to whom much must be forgiven, but he suffered much. As a patient he can only be admired, even though few doctors would have cared to treat him. His real testimonial is to be found in the degree to which he was loved and respected, and in the fidelity that he inspired.

An account of the development of his condition will be given and will have to include explanatory matter to clarify the medical concepts of his day in order to forestall the anachronisms which largely vitiate the existing literature. The questions of alcoholism and of syphilis will be examined, and this will be followed by a discussion of his mental health and psychiatric status generally. Fortunately, the religious

[1] 'In my friend's sick abdomen already in 1796 lay the foundation of his evils, of his hardness of hearing and of his final fatal dropsy.' (Wegeler and Ries, 1838; Wegeler, 1845.)

[2] The matrix in which the body cells are sustained. Bone, tendon, joints, blood-vessels are almost entirely connective tissue. All tissues contain substantial amounts either as fibrous tissue or as a kind of web. Muscle is innumerable parcels of cells in connective tissue, parcel within parcel down to individual cells, the outer wrapping conjoining into tendons attaching the muscles to bones, etc.

phase (in Comte's sense) of mythopoetic psychiatry is behind us, so that a humourless reconstruction of his soul will not be looked for; novelists *manqués* can find all they want in the wholly conjectural if earnest *jeu d'esprit* of the Sterbas (1954).

Deafness

Beethoven's deafness is clearly of such importance that it should be described first. It started somewhere about his twenty-eighth year, when he had already written the first symphony, the first two piano concertos, and the sonatas up to op. 13, and had done most of the work on the string quartets of op. 18. He first admitted to it in his thirty-first year, i.e. about the end of his 'first period'.[1] It was progressive but with periods of standstill. It was accompanied by incessant noises, ringing, whistling and rushing. There were ear-aches and head-aches for the rest of his life, the ear-aches being particularly troublesome every February, the depth of winter. The upper tones were lost first and loud jarring noises were very painful. 'Sometimes I can scarcely hear a person who speaks softly; I can hear sounds, it is true, but cannot make out the words. But if anyone shouts, I can't bear it.' (1801).During the bombardment of Vienna (1809) he went to the cellar and covered his ears with cushions: even in his fifties he sometimes had to have cotton wool in his ears in noisy surroundings. The progress of his deafness was such that by his thirty-fifth year (1805) wind instruments were lost in orchestral tutti (ABL). According to Czerny (TF), between 1812 and 1816 visitors had to shout to be understood, and by 1817 he could not hear music. He last played in public in 1814 (the Archduke Trio). The conversation books date from 1817. There is some evidence that he could perhaps hear a little sometimes for the next ten years, but for all practical purposes he was quite deaf. He was therefore very deaf only during the 'third period'. He would have heard, for instance, the Razumovsky Quartets, op. 5 (1807), and the fifth symphony, op. 67 (1810), quite reasonably well.

There have been many papers by otologists whose total opinion massively in favour of a form of otosclerosis, 'mixed type with degeneration of the auditory nerve', the degeneration being aggravated by the state of his general health. The two greatest authorities are Heinrich Neumann (1927), Professor of Otology, University of Vienna, and G. Bilancioni (1921). A very able and accessible authority is Sorsby (1930) whose paper is ample and very readable. Schweisheim

[1] This information is contained in his letters. ABL, TF, and S indicate letters. Thayer, Forbes and Schindler as elsewhere. Other references to the bibliography are by author and date.

(1922) is thorough and readable. Otosclerosis is due to a constitutional tendency, usually hereditary, for the cartilage rim of the opening to the inner ear to turn into bone thus immobilizing the ossicle (stapes) whose base fits in the opening and transmits the sound waves. It is by no means a rare condition.[1]

General View of Health, Sources, etc.

He was stocky and short, like many energetic and effective men, just under 5′ 6″, Napoleon's height. He was ugly (*hässlich*) with a severely blemished skin but brilliant eyes, and the portraits show the keen upward glance[2] of the deaf (Asherson, 1965). We know a good deal about his health from numerous contemporary sources, from his own letters and, in particular, from three memoirs by eminent doctors who were his personal friends, Wegeler, Weissenbach, von Breuning.[3] There are the entries in the conversation books and diaries, and there is an account of his last illness by the physician in attendance, Dr. Wawruch.[4] A post-mortem examination was made by Professor Wagner of the University of Vienna and a copy of the report survives. Wagner was assisted by a student doing his first post mortem, Rokitansky, who was later to become the father of modern morbid anatomy (von Breuning, 1874). All the above are readily accessible. There has grown up a large medical literature, which is thoroughly reviewed by Forster (1956), who includes the post-mortem report and a comprehensive bibliography.

Beethoven's first recorded severe illness was the feverish attack

---

[1] The other possible diagnoses are otitis media (middle ear disease as in ear abscesses): labyrinthitis (disease of the actual receptor-analyser, the 'inner ear'): and auditory nerve degeneration. Sorsby says that most cases show all four by middle age. In Beethoven's case, the relevant parts were removed at the autopsy for detailed study, but no record survives. The parts were displayed for many years in the Vienna anatomy museum, but have disappeared without trace. For completeness the diagnosis of Paget's Disease (from the thickness and shape of the skull), which can be complicated by otosclerosis, may be mentioned but onset at age twenty-eight would be very young (Asherson, 1965).

[2] His well-known 'Blick nach oben'.

[3] Franz Gerhard Wegeler, 1765–1848. Professor of Medicine and Dean, University of Bonn. Lifelong friend in Bonn and Vienna.

Aloys Weissenbach, 1766–1821, sometime military surgeon, later Professor of Surgery, Salzburg. He wrote the libretto of Beethoven's cantata, *Der Glorreiche Augenblick*, op. 136, and was himself deaf.

Gerhard von Breuning, 1813–92. Eminent physician, who as a boy had been close to Beethoven during the last two years of his life. Gerhard's father had been an intimate friend from boyhood and shared a lodging with Beethoven, 1804–5. Gerhard von Breuning published his very informative memoir in 1874.

[4] Andreas Johann Wawruch, 1772–1842. Ex-seminarian, Professor of Special Pathology and Head of Medical Services, Surgical Department, General Hospital, Vienna.

with asthma, followed by melancholia, when he was sixteen, at the time of his mother's death. He moved to Vienna when he was twenty-one and already was suffering from the *Kolik* and diarrhoea[1] that were to be with him for the rest of his life; continually so, according to Schindler. There was a severe illness in 1797, 'A terrible typhus',[2] according to Weissenbach, and after this illness the deafness is thought to have begun, very insidiously. The fever was said to have been produced by a thorough chilling due to sitting down immediately to work when overheated from a long walk during which he had been caught in the rain (TF). From now on there are numerous colds and *Katharrhen* (bronchitis) for the rest of his life. In 1804, there was

[1] Letter to Wegeler 1801: 'That jealous demon my ill-health has put a nasty spoke in my wheel ... for the last three years my hearing has become weaker and weaker. The trouble is supposed to have been caused by the condition of my abdomen which, as you know, was wretched even before I left Bonn but has become worse in Vienna, where I have been constantly afflicted with diarrhoea and have been suffering in consequence from an extraordinary debility. [Dr. Frank's] treatment had no effect; then my deafness became even worse and my abdomen continued in the same state as before. Then a medical asinus advised me to take cold baths ... a more sensible doctor prescribed the usual tepid baths ... the result was miraculous and my inside improved ... during this last winter I was truly wretched for I had dreadful attacks of *Kolik* and again relapsed completely ... and thus I remained until four weeks ago.' Wegeler gives a first-hand account of an attack of continual diarrhoea whilst writing the last movement of the B Flat Concerto the day before the concert (1795): 'I gave him what simple remedies I could.'

[2] In contemporary medical parlance 'typhus' meant a fever in which there was clouding of the mind, as distinct from a 'synocha' (e.g. influenza, scarlet fever) in which there was not. It included our typhoid, typhus, bubonic plague, meningitis, encephalitis, as well as the terminal stages of wound fever (i.e. septicaemia), peritonitis, certain cancers, to name a few. Nowadays the word *Typhus* in German means 'typhoid': to increase the confusion, the terminal state of many feverish illnesses is still called the 'typhoid state' in English. The derivation is from the Greek Τῦφος (clouding). Germs were not discovered until very many years after Beethoven's death; indeed the germ theory of disease was not generally taught until the 1870s. Clearly there was no possibility of scientific classification and study of the fevers; and although the clinical (i.e. bedside) acumen shown was often brilliant, the ordering of their knowledge was so confused that today it requires considerable effort and reflection to penetrate their writings. Cullen's *Textbook*, in English; Pinel's *System*, in French; Busch, Hecker in German and the *Encyclopaedia* of Busch, Grafe, and Horn have all been found useful exponents of the medicine of that era. A short quotation from Busch's *Handbook* may be illustrative: 'Braüne, Angina, throat disease is in general every inflammation of the fauces (tonsils), mouth cavity, tongue, uvula, throat and larynx including the neighbouring glands.' There follow several pages of description indicating that the habit of thought was to consider angina a genus, of which the individual varieties were species. The description of the illness, which, of course, might remit at any stage, ends: 'Death follows if the wind-pipe becomes so narrowed that the patient can no more draw breath; this death is terrible in that the patient must undergo the death agony for quite long. In other cases there sometimes supervenes, if suppuration becomes established and pus falls into the respiratory apparatus; terminally also through destruction and gangrene of the throat; in such cases, the patients die with manifestations of typhus.'

'Typhus is often the result of another illness, such as serous and mucous profluvia of every type, prolonged intermittent fever (malaria), gout, a variety of skin diseases, mental diseases, all types of convulsions, continuous type fevers, inflammations, etc., of which many continue into a typhus.' (Busch, op. cit.)

another severe fever (TF), of which very little is known; in 1807 an abscess nearly cost him a finger (Wegeler, op. cit.). In 1808 he had an abscess of the jaw. In 1813 a septic foot (February to April), gave him 'such a fever that I was quite without sense'.

His brother Karl died in 1815, and from this time Beethoven was a sick man who was never to recover his health. That winter he was laid up with 'severe *Kolik* going on to a terrible rheumatic attack' plus 'severe catarrhal inflammation [lungs]' (ABL). By this time he had suffered a great deal and the effect can be followed in his portraits. Hippius's (1816) shows a sick, old man; and already in 1812 the life-mask shows how much he had aged from Mähler's alert, vital, young man of only seven years previously. The portraits, some fifty or more, are reproduced in the volumes of *Die Musik*, 1902–??. There is also an adequate, well-produced collection in Robert Bory's *L. van Beethoven, His Life and Work in Pictures* (1966).

1817. At the beginning of the year Beethoven had not recovered from 'inflammatory catarrh' and a 'terrible rheumatic seizure' that had attacked him again in the previous October. Finally he quarrelled with Dr. Malfatti[1] who, with his assistant Dr. Bertolini, had looked after him since 1808; and in July Dr. Staudenheim diagnosed 'disease of the lungs'. His hearing had got worse and he was warned that he would be ill for a long time (ABL). He was now attempting to make a home for his nephew, so that the letters are preoccupied with house-keeping. There are references to further bad colds in the autumn and winter.

1818–19. Remarks about 'my continuous ill-health', 'I am never in good health', 'lying in bed with a violent cold'. He was informed that his heart was fatigued. Anxieties about Karl's guardianship and school-ing dominate the letters, whose style and content indicate that he was close to a breakdown.

1820. A bad year for health, ending with six weeks in bed. 'Rheu-matic Fever. All friends of Art feared for him', according to the *All-gemeine Musikalische Zeitung* of 10 January 1821.

1821. A severe illness culminating in prolonged jaundice.

1822. Ear-aches 'my usual trouble at this time' (February). 'Thor-acic Gout' for many months with six weeks in bed. Numerous symp-toms recur throughout the year.

1823. Sick, irritable; ill with a painful eye condition (April until the following January) severe enough to require a darkened room and a bandage over his eyes at night.

[1] 'A genius all right, but a muddle-head (ein confuser Kerl)', Malfatti said of Beethoven.

1824. At the first performance of the Ninth Symphony, the contralto soloist (Caroline Unger) turns him round to see the applause. Confined indoors in November with another chill. Frequent noisy rows with Karl, now eighteen.

1825. A severe painful illness, April and May. Dr. Staudenheim, who had had difficulty in managing him, declined to attend. Dr. Braunhofer, Professor of Biology in the University and a commanding figure, put him on a strict diet, repeating Staudenheim's veto on all wine, coffee, spirits, and spices of any kind. He expressed relief when the fever lessened—'you are very liable to inflammatory attacks and were close to a real inflammation of the bowels; the tendency is still in your body', 'if you take a drink of spirits you will be prostrated in a few hours'. Beethoven was kept indoors until the weather grew warm, and then sent to Baden where he wrote to Braunhofer that he was 'still weak . . . belching, etc, . . . my catarrhal condition is as follows: I spit up rather a lot of blood, apparently only from the windpipe. But often it streams out of my nose, as happened frequently last winter as well. There is no doubt that my stomach has become terribly weak.' Braunhofer had evidently explained his condition to Beethoven, who writes in mock dialogue, 'Doctor: I will alternate Brown's and Stoll's treatments.' The medical atmosphere is clearly still that of the eighteenth century. Brown died in 1788; his treatment was to cure by opposites, weakness by stimulation, stoppage of the bowels by purgation, etc. His methods had great vogue and are credited with killing more people than the Napoleonic wars.[1] Stoll (d. 1787) represented what has been mainstream medicine since Hippocrates, i.e. to rely on and try to supplement the *vis medicatrix naturae*, a homely example of which is applying foments to an inflammation. Braunhofer's warning about inflammation of the bowels is more grave than it sounds. 'Inflammation' was a sickness-process which overtook the vital principle in the same way as the fever-process, to which it could change: medicine was still 'vitalistic', that is to say, it postulated *a priori* a 'vital principle' (i.e. soul), and derived disease reactions, from affections of this principle, by chains of arguments similar to those in scholastic philosophy (as in Comte's second or 'philosophical' stage in the evolution of knowledge). There was no medical science as we know it: no microscopes, no laboratories, no bacteriology, no chemical tests. The clinical thermometer was invented but not in use. The cell-structure of the body was not known, it was many years before the discovery of even

[1] Dr. Braunhofer wrote in the conversation book, 'you would be a second Brown if you had studied Medicine'.

the basic principle *omnis cellula e cellula*. The relating of disease-processes to post-mortem findings had barely begun and was far from generally accepted; and consequently there was no knowledge of pathology, or what actually happens in disease. Beethoven's doctors, though they were all very eminent, were trained in the eighteenth century, and their ideas were little advanced from those of medieval medicine. For example, our appendicitis-peritonitis-septicaemia-death sequence would have been described as *Kolik*[1] developing into inflammation of the bowels developing into a fatal typhus. As a person with an 'inflammatory tendency' Beethoven would likewise be in danger of progressing from a catarrh to an inflammatory catarrh to inflammation of the lungs to fever, which might progress from a synechdocha to a fatal 'typhus'. This digression is necessary in order to explain the grave view taken of Beethoven's illness and the alarm his many previous attacks must have caused him and his friends. During 1825 he suddenly looked much older and his complexion became permanently sallow.

1826. At the time of his matriculation examination in July, Karl attempted suicide. Beethoven visited him regularly in hospital, where he was mistaken for a shabby old peasant. He eventually took Karl to his brother's estate at Gneixendorf, where his swollen belly and feet were commented on. Again he was mistaken for an old peasant

[1] Not our 'colic' (which was *Magenkrämpfe* or *Grimmen* . . . gripes). *Kolik* was an inclusive term for abdominal disorders characterized by pain and which did not fit into the classification of either 'fever' or 'inflammation'. The descriptions show that it included what we now recognize as ulcerative colitis, gastric and duodenal ulcers, intestinal obstruction, visceral perforations, inflammation of the gall bladder, gallstones, kidney stones, lead and other poisonings, food poisoning, etc. 'In severe cases the abdomen is stiff and too painful to touch, there are convulsive tremors in the muscles and about the mouth, the testicles are retracted. . . . As a rule, *Kolik* is certainly a very painful but not a life-endangering illness . . . and only readily becomes so if organic lesions are present in the viscera, and if it has lasted so long that the processes of digestion suffer and nourishment goes wrong, whereby finally a consumption develops. It may well become fatal also if during its course inflammation of an important organ ensues.' (Busch, op. cit.) It could occur 'not infrequently through metaschematization from gout, rheumatism, cramp in the limbs, suddenly suppressed bloody flux and diarrhoea and suppressed sweating of the feet, but more usually through disturbance of the abdominal organs from diet, chills, fatty food, poisoning, inspissation of faeces', and 'deprivation of brandy and wine'.

Wawruch in the description of Beethoven's last illness calls his chronic abdominal disorder 'Haemorrhoidalleiden'. . . . 'Already by his thirtieth year there were "Haemorrhoidalleiden" ' of which the correct translation is 'haemorrhagic complaints' with the implication that the haemorrhage is via the rectum (but *haemorrhois* was still used in certain contexts for bleeding from lungs, nose, stomach, as well as bowels).

(Cp. The Emperor, it was given out, had died of a 'haemorrhoidal Colic' in reference to the probable murder of Catherine the Great's husband.—Horace Walpole, *Hieroglyphic Tales*, London, 1785.)

Beethoven's *Kolik* and diarrhoea, therefore, were ulcerative colitis (*vide* Busch, et al. 1837).

because of his shabbiness and self-effacing demeanour. Although it is evident that he was now a broken man, nevertheless at Gneixendorf he wrote the new finale for the B Flat Major Quartet, op. 130, and completed the F Major Quartet, op. 135. On 1 December he left for Vienna, a two-day journey, in an open farm cart. The weather was suddenly very cold and he passed the night in a wayside inn, in an unshuttered, unheated room. On arriving home he took to his bed; the history of the next few days is uncertain but a doctor was called after three days, on 5 December. Braunhofer excused himself because of the distance and a stranger, Dr. Wawruch, was called. At this stage Beethoven in a letter to his friend Holz describes himself as *unpässlich* ('unfit'). Wawruch's questions survive in Karl's handwriting: '*Ob du an Hämorrhoiden leidest? Hast du Kopfschmerz? Wann war die letzte Offnüng? Du sollst lang Athem holen. Seit Wann der Bauch so gespannt? Häufig Urin? und ohne Beschwerden? Die Füsse waren nicht geschwollen? Ist nie Blut beim Mastdarm gesehen worden?*' This sequence is exactly what would pass between doctor and patient today at a first examination in a case of ascites (dropsy). 'Do you suffer from haemorrhoids? have you a head-ache? when was the last opening (bowels)? Take a deep breath. Since when is the abdomen so swollen? Frequent urine? No difficulty? The feet were not swollen? Blood never been seen from the rectum?' The 'take a deep breath' shows that Beethoven did not have pneumonia, and the rest of the questions show that Wawruch started on the right track; when dropsy is due to liver disease, the intestinal and rectal veins become distended and usually bleed. The 'have you never seen blood from the rectum?' indicates that Beethoven's answer to the first question must have been 'No.' Wawruch concluded it was a lung inflammation (Gerhard von Breuning pours scorn on the idea).

We can continue in Warwruch's own words. 'On the seventh day the patient felt reasonably well so that he was able to get up, walk about, read and write. Then on the eighth day I had quite a shock. At the morning visit I found him in great distress [physical distress, *verstört*], jaundiced over his whole body; a terrible vomiting and diarrhoea [*Brechdurchfall*, mistranslated in Thayer as 'choleric attack'] had threatened him for the whole night with death. A violent rage, a deep hurt from ingratitude suffered and undeserved insult induced the powerful explosion. Shivering and trembling, he writhed with pains which raged in the liver and the bowels, and his hitherto only moderately bloated feet were massively swollen.' These last two sentences are fair, if rather extreme, samples of the style throughout the paper, which could not possibly have been written for medical readers, an important point which will be returned to. 'From this point on developed the dropsy, the urinary output became diminished, the liver presented distinctly signs of hard knots, the jaundice increased.' Evidently the hard knots became palpable only now, so that the liver had swollen quickly, which points to an acute inflammation. The dropsy was massive and had to be tapped four times in as many weeks, and a great total of fluid was removed. Although the nursing conditions were incredibly primitive,[1] and much of the medical management pedantic and unimaginative, nevertheless Beethoven transacted business, writing some letters himself and dictating others. He received many visitors, including Schubert. Some manuscript sketches for a tenth symphony survive written clearly and firmly 'ten to twelve days before his death' (S).

He received the last sacraments, fully aware and quite tranquil, on the morning of 24 March. Schott, the Mainz publishers, had sent him a case of Rüdesheimer Berg '06 in response to a medical prescription. It was delivered in the early afternoon and he recognized it ('Pity, pity, too late') but shortly afterwards he became unconscious. He was in coma for two days and died on the 26th. The terminal illness had lasted four months.

The autopsy was performed the next day; the report is thorough by the standards of the day and compares well with, for instance, the English and French reports on Napoleon (1821). The liver was 'shrunk to half its volume, leathery and greenish blue, beset with nodules the size of a bean on its tuberculated surface and throughout its substance.' This is macro-nodular cirrhosis, i.e. post-hepatitic, not the micronodular cirrhosis proverbially associated with alcoholism.[2] In fact Beethoven's was a long-term hepatitis, as the history from 1821 shows, which had flared up after the exposure during the journey from Gneixendorf. Such a chronic active hepatitis associated with colitis,

[1] Conversation books 25 to 28 February. Young Gerhard von Breuning: 'I heard today that the bugs wake you every moment. Sleep is good for you. I'll get something for the bugs. When you see one, catch it with a needle, you'll soon get rid of them.'

Schindler: 'The maid will put a wooden vessel under the bed so that the water cannot run over the room. No more straw in the house to fill the other mattress. The straw is all fouled. This evening the other will be filled and you can have it this day.'

Stephan von Breuning (Gerhard's father): 'You must cheer up, poor spirits stop you getting better.'

[2] The latter is tawny-orange in colour, hence the name 'cirrhosis' from the Greek name of that colour. Cirrhosis has come to be used for any fibrosis, i.e. hardening, of the liver probably because it sounds like a derivative of 'scirrhus', pronounced 'cirrus', a common pathological term meaning hard.

rheumatism, repeated catarrhs, abscesses, cryopathy (attacks pre-cipitated by chilling), the ophthalmia and the skin disorder soon to be described are extremely suggestive of connective tissue immunopathy: such a diagnosis explains all his numerous[1] illnesses. Manifestly an in-fallible diagnosis cannot be made after so long a time and in the ab-sence of anything remotely resembling a modern clinical history; but the hypothesis is advanced with considerable confidence.[2]

At the post mortem 'the facial nerves were of considerable thickness, the auditory nerves on the other hand shrivelled and marrowless (*die Hörnerven dagegen zusammengeschrumpft und marklos*), the accompanying auditory arteries were dilated to more than a crow's quill and like cartilage.' Arterial disease is constant in immunopathy; indeed one manifestation, polyarteritis nodosa, now known to be a relatively common disorder of varying severity, has been reported as having deafness as its presenting symptom in a number of cases (Peiter-sen, 1966). The atrophy of the auditory nerves could be due to arterial disease (Vieille, 1905, Niemack-Charles, 1907 . . . the idea is not new) aggravated possibly by the chronic diarrhoea interfering with the absorption of vitamins and proteins. Disease of the auditory arter-ies explains an extraordinary story related by Beethoven himself. At a rehearsal as a young man he lost his temper with a tenor and was thrown ('threw myself' literally, but in German a reflexive supplants a passive construction in such a context) to the ground. 'When I rose, I was deaf.' This would describe an attack of vertigo, 'labyrinthine apoplexy', from interference with the blood supply to or bleeding in the auditory region. An attack might well be precipitated by increased blood pressure during one of Beethoven's spectacular rages.

Weissenbach who, as has been said, was deaf himself, often dis-

[1] How numerous will be sadly familiar to readers of Beethoven's letters. We classified them on forty-two separate cards, many with multiple entries, before experiencing the rather rueful excitement of discovering Forster's monograph. However, we were at least in a position to appreciate his thoroughness. Another rueful occasion occurred at the Beethovenhaus when Professor Schmidt-Görg produced Piroth's (1959) paper. We had arrived independently at his conclusion that the cirrhosis was hepatitic after searching the medical museums of London and finding two livers like Beethoven's (both their owners had had very relevant histories).

[2] It is now possible to amplify the statement in the opening paragraphs, since the reader is aware of the broad picture. The group of diseases under discussion are usually, at present (1969), referred to as 'auto-immune disease': the 'collagen' (i.e. connective tissue) diseases such as rheumatoid arthritis are a sub-group and are generally considered to be manifestations of auto-immunity, often to proteins altered by chilling of all, or part, of the body. Other syndromes such as the well-known colitis with arthritis and inflammation of the eyes, although immunopathic, have not yet been securely proven to be *auto*-immune although the probability is high. As a group, they respond to cortisone, a fact which may orientate the reader. The word allergy has become debased but represents broadly the idea of immunopathy: auto-immunity, then, is allergy to one's own proteins.

cussed Beethoven's deafness with him and writes (1820), 'He once had a terrible typhus, from this time on dated the ruin (*Verfall*) of his nervous system and probably the ruin of his hearing, so calamitous in his case.' If this was so, Beethoven may well have had the specific form of immunopathic disease known as Systemic Lupus Erythematosus, which typically commences in early adult life with a fever which is typically accompanied by mental confusion. It becomes chronic, with periods of intermission and with phases of emotional instability. Typical symptoms are destructive rash ('lupus') and redness ('erythema') of the butterfly area of the face,[1] rheumatoid arthritis, special susceptibility to arterial disease and liver disease,[2] tendency to haemorrhage, to catarrhal infections, to inflammations of the eyes, to abscesses. Any of the immunopathic disorders may occur, notably colitis (Dubois, 1966). Precipitation of the attacks by cold is common, as in one of Osler's original cases (Osler, 1897).

Syphilis
Previously the evident likelihood that his troubles derived from a common constitutional cause led to the consideration of syphilis, the

[1] Beethoven's facial rash was so disfiguring that his ugliness was often commented on; one memoir speaks of 'the terrifying countenance of a leper'. The excellent life-mask of 1812 (though not, of course, the rather worn casts in music studios) shows marked lumpiness and induration of the skin at the root of the nose, on the cheeks and around the mouth and chin. In the middle of the forehead at the root of the nose, in a large area measuring 5 cm. from side to side and 2 cm. vertically and extending for a further 2 cm. down the nose, there are eight deep punched-out scars. Five of these are circular and from 0·75 to 0·5 cm. in diameter; three are elongated and measure 2 cm. by 0·4 cm.; and the rest are of varying shapes and smaller size. The thickened skin of the cheeks is similarly, though not so deeply, scarred and there is much similar disfigurement about the mouth and chin. The right side of the nose shows an elongated (1·5 by 0·5 cm.) atrophic scar particularly suggestive of lupus. The portraits clearly show flushing of the cheek-bones and nose ('butterfly area') and pallor of the eye sockets. Beethoven's high colour was frequently commented on and may have aroused suspicions of heavy drinking. The frontal hairs are broken in the portraits by Schimon (1818), Hippius (1816), and Klöber (1818). The fact that they are not shown in the more idealized portraits indicates that they were a blemish and not a hairstyle. Beethoven was described as pockmarked, but there is no record of his having had smallpox; and although some of the scars, both discrete and confluent, could be due to smallpox, the larger lesions and indurations are not anything like it. The death mask by Danhauser, 27 March 1827, shows the large deep scars very well.

[2] Medical readers will be interested that at the post mortem the pancreas was indurated and the spleen more than doubled in size and very firm. The kidneys were 'pale and teased-out in substance, invested by a web-like membrane an inch thick', every calyx being occupied by a chalky concretion the size of a split pea. As regards family history, his mother and brother both died of consumption in their forties and his nephew Karl of liver disease, which was called cancer, at fifty-two; but in view of the date (1858) and the rural situation it may well have been a misdiagnosis of a hepatitic condition. This type of family history is not unusual in immunopathy.

general medical scapegoat from 1906 (Wassermann test) to 1945 (penicillin). The grounds for this diagnosis in Beethoven's case are, in view of its wide currency, surprisingly slight. It is not favoured by any of the medical writers of substance with the exception of one who, although he did not ascribe the deafness to it, was led to believe in it on being assured that there was documentary proof (Jacobssohn, 1910, 1927); the evidence was shown to be worthless by the Director of the Beethoven Archiv (Schiedermair, 1927). The mid-twenties controversy, medical and lay, is typical of the unfortunate level of much of the medical and paramedical literature that Beethoven has prompted. Professor Schultze (1928) writes with some irony, 'now there are to hand prescriptions, as Dr. Prieger [E. Prieger, a well-known Beethoven enthusiast in Bonn] communicated to me personally "as leaving the presence of this disease in no doubt. These prescriptions the renowned otologist Politzer had had in his hands." His son-in-law, a famous writer on music, personally assured Prieger that "of this there can be no doubt". Prieger was informed by "close friends of the first biographer of Beethoven, Thayer, that as a direct consequence of this knowledge the English author became disinclined to carry on his work".' Schultze goes on to ask how the prescription could prove anything; presumably it must have contained mercury, but that was a panacea in those days and Beethoven tried everything.

Mercury was proverbially the treatment for syphilis until the First World War; but as Schultze says, in Beethoven's day it was a panacea; but more particularly it was the recognized treatment for *Kolik*, dysentery, rheumatism, and ophthalmia and Beethoven would certainly have been given it at some time for these (Hecker, 1806; Busch, 1812; Wardrop, 1830). Schultze himself is inaccurate: his own remarks about Thayer (who was of course an American, not English, but apparently such hypocrisy could only be English) are careless; Thayer was not the first biographer: Schindler, Schindler-Moscheles, Lenz, Marx, Nohl, vol. 1, were all published before Thayer (vol. 1, 1866). Indeed already in 1852 Ulybyshev was commenting on the flood of biographies and memorials that were appearing. This carelessness in checking sources is only one of the faults of much of the medical writing. It is true that Thayer completed the biography only up to 1817, and the reason given for his stopping at that point makes a good story and sounds in character; but the real reason was a breakdown which left him with chronic head-aches. Even so the necessary research and annotations were completed by him so that Deiter's part in finishing the work was almost entirely editorial.

Grove seems actually the first to write about syphilis (1879). 'The whole of these appearances (post mortem) are most probably the result of syphilitic affections at an early period of his life,' and in a footnote, 'This diagnosis, which I owe to the kindness of my friend Dr. Lauder Brunton, is confirmed by the existence of two prescriptions, of which, since the text was written, I have been told by Mr. Thayer who heard of them from Dr. Bartolini [sic].'

We will return to Dr. Bertolini, but first it is necessary to question some of the arguments[1] that have been advanced. Beethoven, for instance, used a 'volatile salve', said to be mercurial. But in fact 'volatile salve' is a pretentious transliteration of the usual German for liniment. Forster, by the elementary tactic of consulting a contemporary formulary, has shown that it was a simple ammonia rub, not containing mercury. Moreover, the reference is in a letter written by Beethoven in 1817, when he was being treated for a severe abdominal illness, to Countess Erdödy, hardly a person to whom he would have described an anti-venereal treatment.[2]

Dr. Bertolini, whom Grove quotes Thayer as quoting, was Dr. Malfatti's assistant and Beethoven became their patient in 1808 when he had been ill for more than ten years. He remained in their care until he had the disagreement with Malfatti. (In 1810 he had been a suitor of Malfatti's niece, and surely very few syphilitics court the niece of the doctor treating them. Beethoven actually went so far as to make preliminary arrangement for the marriage.) If Beethoven's deafness had been syphilitic, the infection must have dated from 1797 at the latest. Bertolini, therefore, would not have seen the attack himself. It is possible that he was shown prescriptions that Beethoven had previously been given for '*Lustseuche*' or '*Lues*'. Both terms were in use and can easily cause misunderstanding because today both mean syphilis; the former is the normal German vernacular, the latter the specific technical term in English-speaking countries. In Beethoven's

[1] That he showed interest in a French book on venereal disease in 1819 proves nothing: he could easily have been preparing himself to tell Karl what a young man should know. It is not impossible that an attack of one of the manifestations of auto-immunity, Reiter's non-specific urethritis with rheumatism, first described at this time (Gardner, 1965), was the cause of his interest.

[2] Contemporary treatment of 'inflammation of the bowels: liquid stimulating mixtures, especially opium and mercury tend to heal the inflammation . . . especially in the haemorrhoidal cases strong blistering plasters to the abdomen . . . stimulating fomentations and embrocations of the abdomen, even with mercury ointment, should not be omitted' (Hecker, 1806). If Beethoven's threatened inflammation of the bowels had been just a little more refractory, he might have had mercury inunctions (the standard treatment for syphilis 1850 to 1908) which would invincibly have convinced those who suspected syphilis.

day they meant simply 'venereal disease', and the venereal diseases (distinguished today as gonorrhoea, syphilis, soft sore, non-specific urethritis) were thought to be one. They were not distinguished until Ricord had made his intensive study (1835–8) by inoculating 2,500 Paris prostitutes with gonorrhoeal pus. ('The Voltaire of pelvic literature . . . who would have . . . ordered a course of mercury pills for the Vestal Virgins', says Oliver Wendell Holmes). To quote from a textbook of military medicine of 1812, '*Lustseuche* (*Lues Venerea*) is a cachexia which has its incidence on the genitals and thence through the whole body . . . usually starts as a clap (urethritis) and at the height of the illness bone pains supervene and many other accompaniments such as generalized rash, ulcers etc. . . . . If it is not cured at the outset, the venereal poison is resorbed and further to the local affections of the genitals, such as clap, chancre, phimosis, buboes, there arise small, white hard ulcers in the throat, palate and inner surfaces of the cavity of the mouth, similar to the chancres on the genitals' (Busch, 1812). He goes on to describe what is predominantly secondary syphilis, but with some features of early tertiary (the word syphilis was not yet in use) confused with those of soft sore such as suppurating buboes. Clap (i.e. gonorrhoea), which Boswell caught so often, was practically inevitable for all but the very chaste and remained so until the recent drug revolution. The most, therefore, that Bertolini could have said to Thayer was that he had seen prescriptions for '*Lustseuche*', and by the time Thayer passed the information on the word had changed its meaning to syphilis. What induced Bertolini, a very discreet man, to speak to Thayer? One of the alleged proofs of Beethoven's syphilis (verity usually varies inversely with the number of proofs) was that Bertolini, when dangerously ill with cholera in 1830, had ordered his letters and documents to be destroyed; it was presumed that they must have recorded syphilis. In fact there are many other more likely medical reasons (for after all no doctor takes much notice of a 'dose') especially in connection with so inelegant a disorder as diarrhoea; and there may even have been political reasons. Beethoven was outrageously indiscreet in his letters and in 1830 Austria was a police state. Beethoven was friendly with many of the aristocracy who comprised Malfatti's very smart practice, and Beethoven was very politically minded. It would be natural for this deaf man to write gossip which people normally reserve for conversations, and in fact such gossip probably accounts for Schindler's destruction of a large number of conversation-books alluded to later. On the other hand Beethoven may have been abusive of Malfatti, or Bertolini, for at the time of the rupture, in the same letter to Countess Erdödy already cited, he wrote, 'I changed my doctors, because my own doctor, a wily Italian, had powerful secondary motives where I was concerned and lacked both honesty and intelligence.' Perhaps Thayer provoked Bertolini by his inquiries about Beethoven's sexuality, which could possibly have elicited 'of course he had women, I've actually seen prescriptions for V.D.' This would be neatly consistent with Thayer's 'he did not always escape the usual consequences of these departures from strict purity'.

It is likely that Beethoven, like everybody else, caught gonorrhoea but there is no evidence that either his lifelong illnesses or his deafness were syphilitic, and the substantial medical writers make other diagnoses.

Alcoholism

The charge of alcoholism is likewise unsubstantiated. Thayer is quite firm that he was temperate, as is Wegeler. Schindler says he took little alcohol and that his favourite drink was fresh spring water.[1] People seem to have jumped to the conclusion that since he died of cirrhosis he must have been an alcoholic, prejudiced, perhaps, by his facial erythema. Schindler fancied that Dr. Wawruch implied that Beethoven was too fond of spirits, and he is quite circumstantial and convincing in rebutting the charge. Wawruch's account, which he would not have wished to see published, was among his effects and was sold on behalf of his widow by Aloys Fuchs to the editor of a daily paper (*Wiener Zeitschrift*, 13 April 1842). As already stated, it is not written in the style of a medical communication of the period, but rather in that still affected by doctors with a cultured reputation in medical circles and a medical reputation in cultured circles, when presenting a causerie on a favourite topic. Wawruch, who looked like Mr. Pickwick, had been a theological student; he played the cello; the first words he wrote in Beethoven's conversation-book were 'One who reveres your name will do everything possible for you, Professor Wawruch.' Beethoven loathed him. His account has all the marks of an occasional piece, and if Wawruch himself had intended to publish it, he would have done so. The relevant passages are: 'From about the same time (i.e. as his deafness started) Beethoven began to suffer with his digestion; disturbed appetite brought indigestion, severe belching, sometimes stubborn constipation, sometimes frequent

---

[1] Plain town water could be dangerous. His really favourite drink was coffee 'exactly sixty beans to the cup'.

diarrhoea. Never accustomed to think much of medical advice, he began to favour spirits to waken his lost appetite, and to help somewhat the weakness of the stomach with strong punch and ices taken in excess and with long exhausting excursions on foot. This change of habits brought him about seven years ago to the brink of the grave. He developed a violent inflammation of the bowels which, it is true, yielded to art [i.e. medical art] but left as a result frequent bowel disorders and *Kolik* pains, which would also have contributed a part to his final fatal illness.' (Wawruch's chronology is wrong, *vide supra*.) He describes the final phases—'the appetite diminished daily and the strength must have declined markedly through the repeated gross loss of body fluids [from the tappings]. At this point Dr. Malfatti came and from now on he supported me with his advice. As a friend of many years' standing he understood Beethoven's predominant inclination to value spirits, and in the event he advised frozen punch.[1] I must concede that for at least a couple of days the prescription worked excellently. Beethoven was so mightily refreshed by the alcoholic ice that he slept peacefully through the first night and began to sweat mightily. . . . However his joy did not last long as could be foreseen. He began to abuse the prescription and to do stout justice to the punch. The spirits originated a strong rush of blood to the head, he became soporous and stertorous like a person in deep drunkenness.' The jocosity of 'do stout justice' (*'sprach dem Punsch wacker zu'*) is, like the impressionistic dating already cited, quite certainly in the style of the informal causerie. All that Wawruch is saying is that Beethoven used spirits for his appetite and digestion, in the way most of the public still do. Strong wine and spirits were recognized treatments for *Kolik* and weakness of the bowels (Busch, 1812; Hecker, 1806) and their use does not prove an alcoholic tendency. Schindler accuses Wawruch of reporting *'sedebat et bibebat'* (he sat and drank) but it cannot be found in Wawruch's writings. In a speech he might easily have followed up the laugh for *'wacker zu'* with an impromptu phrase in seminarian's Latin.[2] This could have been relayed to Schindler who seems to have imagined an imputation of alcoholism where none was intended; he says himself that he had been asked in Paris whether it was true that Beethoven drank, and this may well have made him oversensitive. As Forbes points out, Schindler has himself provided the smoke that has led people to suspect a fire.

[1] *'Punschgefrorenes'*. It was flamed and heated with fruit juice before freezing. This would have reduced the alcohol to about the strength of our mild beer, poor stuff for a real drinker.
[2] In Conversation Book, 20–27 February in Gerhard von Breuning's handwriting: 'Professor. He passed his exams in Theology before doing Medicine.'

Beethoven was never able to compose if he had taken anything to drink (an alcoholic on the other hand cannot work without a drink) and he was such a prodigious worker that he cannot have had many opportunities. None of the numerous autographs, some to within a week or two of his death, show any sign of tremor. When entertaining 'Sir Smart' (Sir George Smart of the London Philharmonic) in 1824, Beethoven was heard to say, 'Let's see how much the Englishman can drink.' 'But,' writes Sir George, 'he had the worse of the encounter.' They had to rise hurriedly from this liberal meal to catch the coach and Beethoven 'wrote me the following droll canon as fast as his pen could write in about two minutes of time as I stood at the door' (TF). The autograph survives and the firm notes and staves show that he could not have been even slightly drunk after what he regarded as a drinking match. He seems rather to have been what he called 'a devil of a fellow' and what we might ironically call a 'real devil', in fact an innocent; and indeed his innocence and simplicity are repeatedly mentioned by his contemporaries. We can afford to accept the evidence of the people who knew him well that he was not a drinker. We might concluded this exploration of his physical health by referring to Schultze's paper again. After showing up the fatuousness of much of the so-called evidence, he points out the inelegance of doctors' discussing a man's mishaps before the general public, who are not trained in the merciful acceptance of the misfortunes of others and who may, in their innocence, react with censoriousness when nothing but compassion is called for. Paul Bekker, who as a critic would have no vested interest in compassion, finds the medical discussion of Beethoven childish and irrelevant (Bekker, 1922); and it is impossible not to agree with him that the only Beethoven that matters is the one who speaks out in the music. Nevertheless one cannot help being glad that Nature has sufficient sense of style not to have loaded one of humanity's really firm heroes with two such equivocal disorders.

Mental Health

Drink might well have been the guess of anyone who saw this red-faced man striding furiously around Vienna, hat on the back of his head, coat-tails flying and sagging with the weight of books crammed into the pockets, and singing (described as roaring) at the top of his voice. This was his daily habit in his later years and he did much of his composing on these walks. His behaviour could be very embarrassing. Rochlitz who describes him in 1822 striding up and down the fashionable promenade, the Helenenthal, from ten in the morning to six at night with his coat hanging on a stick over his shoulder, making the Emperor, the Empress, and the Court stand aside for him; 'uncommonly gay, amusing, all that was in his mind had to come out . . . his barking tirades . . . his talk and his actions all formed a chain of eccentricities, in part most peculiar' (TF).

Karl Zelter, a self-made man and a first-class musical administrator reported to Goethe on 16 August 1819, 'Beethoven is intolerably *maussade* [peevish, sullen] and some say he is mad' (TF). Was he mad? In 1820 he was locked up one night as a vagrant (TF). 'I am Beethoven.' *'Warum nicht gar. Ein Lump sind sie.* [Sez you. You're a bum.]' In 1826 when he went to Karl in hospital he was so diffident and unkempt that he was taken for 'an old peasant': the same mistake was made in a solicitor's office later in the year. He bellowed and gesticulated so grotesquely on his walks at Gneixendorf that he actually caused the cattle to stampede; the herdsman advanced on him, but when he saw him stood uproariously laughing at the obvious lunatic (TF). For the previous ten years there had been various incidents of being jeered at by street urchins, notably on one occasion when he stood composing by an open window without noticing that he had not put on his trousers.[1] One of the prima donnas at Bonn had been courted by him 'but he was too ugly, besides he was crazy' (TF). But although his behaviour was very eccentric, there is no evidence that he was ever insane, even temporarily. His nerves were very bad, to adopt a well understood locution less misleading than unprepared technicalities. Weissenbach (op. cit.) writes *'sein Nervensystem ist reizbar im höchsten Grade und kränkelnd sogar'*, (his nervous system is highly-strung in the highest degree and sick (disordered) even) and dates the *'Verfall seines Nervensystems'*, (decay, ruin of his nervous system), from the previously mentioned *'furchtbarer Typhus'*; but Beethoven (ABL) indicates that it began earlier. Just after his mother's death, he wrote, 'Since my return to Bonn (two months) I have as yet enjoyed very few happy hours. For the whole time I have been plagued with asthma, and I am inclined to fear that this malady may even turn to consumption. Furthermore I have been suffering from melancholia, which in my case is almost as great a torture as my illness.' This was September 1787, when he was sixteen. The next recorded bout of 'melancholia' was in connection with the realization of his deafness (in letters to Wegeler and Amenda in 1801). 'Melancholia', in modern terms de-

---

[1] Recounted by Per Atterbom, the Swedish poet, who visited him in 1819. Atterbom describes his habitual facial expression 'a countenance bearing not a trace of happiness'. (Nohl, op. cit.)

pression, and its obverse, pathological emotional excitement, though inherent are often activated by grief. Excessive emotional reactions, 'an accentuated emotionality in all the experiences of life' (Mayer-Gross et al. 1954) plus a constitutional 'increased disposition to sad and cheerful moods' (Bumke, 1924) are characteristic of Affective Disorder, or Manic-Depressive Disorder as it is usually called. (The latter term is more appropriately confined to cases in which the judgement and behaviour are so utterly at the mercy of the affects ('emotions') that custody becomes advisable.)

To avoid oversimplifying the account of Beethoven a certain diffuseness will be inevitable from now on. The intention is to proceed with an account of his nervous disorder. But nervous disorder, character disorder, character traits, temperament are an inseparable complex, not neat compartments.

After the death of his brother Karl (15 November 1815) there seems to have been a severe reaction in his general health; and in addition his judgement seems to have become dominated by his emotions to a pathological degree. Like many consumptives, Karl looked deceptively well and his death was unexpected. Beethoven insisted on an autopsy, on the grounds that his wife Johanna might have poisoned him. Since he was satisfied by the pathologist's report and never raised the question again, the idea was not a delusion in the psychiatric sense; that is to say, not an unjustifiable false belief unamenable to proof of its falsity. Was it sufficiently wild to be 'paranoid'? Beethoven says that her lover was staying in the house during the husband's illness, and certainly she subsequently had an illegitimate child by him. On two occasions previously she had been in the hands of the police for dishonesty, actually charged by her husband in one case. Beethoven called the widow 'Queen of the Night' and wrote that she took money for her favours (ABL). Since he was writing to his lawyer, to whom the facts were readily accessible, and since there are no other examples of indecent abuse in his letters, it is highly likely that her character laid her open to this sort of accusation. Thayer covers the whole question very well and Johanna van Beethoven does seem to have been of pretty poor character. There is perhaps not really adequate evidence strictly to label Beethoven paranoid in this connection. The son, also called Karl, was nine and the father had asked in his will that Beethoven should take charge of him; but during his last few hours, he was induced to sign a codicil including the wife in the guardianship. Beethoven contested it immediately, and the child was taken from the mother. She appealed. The Estates Court on finding that Beethoven was not of the nobility, as had been assumed because of his 'van', referred the affair to the Municipal Court who reinstated the mother. On further appeal, Beethoven finally had her excluded. The whole affair lasted five years. It is surely impossible that the boy would have been taken from his mother if she had been in any way respectable; it is also certain that in family matters Beethoven was very firm and rigorous. He had had his father declared incompetent for alcoholism and at eighteen had taken over responsibility as head of the family. He had gone to extreme lengths to stop his other brother, Johann, from marrying a-woman who had had an illegitimate child and was now Johann's mistress; he refused to know people in his own, aristocratic, circle known to be living in adultery; he objected to the moral laxity of Mozart's 'Don Giovanni'. His sense of family responsibility is shown by bringing his brothers to Vienna and setting them both up in life.

Beethoven was a violent man. He would come to blows with his brother Karl when both were in their forties; he attacked Prince Lichnowsky with a chair for insisting on his playing for some French officers, packed his bags and went back to Vienna, very determined behaviour considering that Lichnowsky was supporting him financially. There are other incidents of which one is worth quoting as an example of an impulsiveness and insensitiveness approaching the psychotic. He threw a badly cooked lung-stew over the waiter in an eating house and stood roaring with laughter at him, the waiter's retaliation having been interrupted by an involuntary licking of the gravy from around his mouth. He violently destroyed the dedication of his third symphony to Napoleon for calling himself Emperor, and his political opinions were so violently expressed that Schindler thought it advisable to destroy large parts of the conversation-books.

It is possible that his self-will, aggressiveness, self-righteous Catholic dogmatism in family affairs might be character-traits rather than symptoms; but even so his handling of the guardianship was pathologically emotional, the anxiety state of a depressive under stress. It is revealed in the memoranda to the Court and his attorney in their content, presentation, and handwriting;[1] in the changes of plan for schooling and domiciling young Karl, where his crazy attempts at housekeeping and fastening on to trifles demonstrate classical displacement of anxiety. Evidently he had reacted to his brother's death, as to his mother's and to his deafness, with a depression, expressed largely

---

[1] That to the Court of Appeal has been published in facsimile by the Beethovenhaus, Bonn, edited with transcription and notes by Dagmar Weise (1954).

in anxiety-thinking and somatic illness. Such 'anxiety-depression', one of the very common forms of affective disorder, is treacherously apt to induce unwise decisions and imprudent planning. With his various publishers he made false moves which, if fully deliberate, would have been crassly dishonest. For although both Schindler and Thayer emphasize the fact that Beethoven had an unbelievably bad memory, this does not provide sufficient explanation; nor does it explain his silly lack of common sense (i.e. judgement) in, e.g. sending three very minor old works in place of the three major new works commissioned and paid for by the London Philharmonic (1816). His continued relationships with publishers, the London Philharmonic, and the world in general show that he was regarded not as crooked but as muddled.

The somatic repercussions of affective disorder require perhaps a little exposition. Nervousness produces different somatic symptoms in different people. Heart, digestion, breathing, bowels, bladder, 'brain', are some of the targets; head-aches, migraine, asthma, peptic ulcer, 'blood-pressure', colitis, fibrositis are some of the disorders likely to have nervous components. There is also a general, if imprecise, association of temperament-type with target-organ. Now Beethoven's continual washing, his obsessional attention to the cleanliness of his linen, his perfectionism and his incessant cerebral activity are congruous with bowel fixation, so that we should expect a vicious circle of worry . . . *Kolik* . . . worry . . . *Kolik*, when his nerves were bad. This is not to say that Beethoven's illnesses were simply neurotic even though, like any other obsessive-depressive he would be rather 'neurotic' (hypochondriac) about them. Mitigating anxiety by unconscious conversion of it into physical symptoms is a valuable mental economy; and Beethoven, for instance, would be able to work with less difficulty during an attack of *Kolik* than during one of mental agitation. 'He cherishes the hypochondriac fancy that everybody here persecutes and despises him. His peevishness may indeed have repelled many of the good-natured, easy-going Viennese . . . I was often deeply grieved to see the honest excellent man gloomy and suffering, but I am convinced that his best and most original work can only be produced during these wayward despondent moods', wrote Reichardt in 1808 (Nohl, 1877). He was trying to arrange for Beethoven to succeed him as Court Composer to the King of Westphalia (Jerome Buonaparte), and this was impossible if Beethoven was either insane or crooked. In 1816 Dr. Karl von Bursy wrote, 'He is full of wormwood and gall, dissatisfied and defiant, pouring out curses against

Austria and especially Vienna. He speaks quickly and with great vivacity . . . he is not reserved, for he soon adverted to his personal affairs and told me a great deal about himself and his circumstances. This is exactly the *signum diagnosticum* of hypochondria.' ' "One can trust nobody" . . . he seems very anxious about money . . . when he is silent, his brow contracts and his gloomy appearance might inspire fear.' Bursy had a distinguished medical career and his account is valuable. In 1814, the most successful and exciting year in Beethoven's life, Tomaschek gives a pen-picture of his apartment: 'anything but luxuriously furnished and as untidy as his hair . . . conversation equally confused . . . left out many verbs . . . spoke disjointedly and rather rhapsodically.' He reports some of the conversation direct and repeatedly inserts Beethoven's loud inconsequent Ha-ha-has. Tomaschek was a great admirer, a leading musician with a legal and philosophical training and an author of sound reputation, a valuable witness. He is evidently describing one of Beethoven's hypomanic (i.e. excited) phases, like that in the Helenenthal.

The picture then is of persistent ill-health, of a prevailing mood of depression, a highly strung, suspicious, 'persecuted' man, unstable under stress, hypomanic at times.[1] impulsive to the point of violence, perfectionist, deaf, irritable. Nevertheless, he had enormous charm, and although he might one day drive a visitor away with brutal discourtesy, he would put himself out to be attentive on another occasion. Here is a man who tried to make up for his failings in temperament, breeding, and education, whose tremendous achievements were in spite of cruel handicaps and who did not flounder in self-pity, though not above occasionally being pathetic in letters to women.

An engrossing occupation ('getting your mind off yourself') is the best possible weapon against depression, but motivation is always the difficulty. Motivation ('will-power' in common parlance) is the resultant of the various drives and inhibitions, the positive and negative forces, in the personality ('in the Unconscious'). It would be fascinating to attempt to deduce the operation of these, and of the safety valves, in Beethoven's case. Psycho-analysis, however, requires the physical presence and co-operation of the patient. Conjectural, analysis-type fortune-telling ('houseman's Freud' or 'novelist's analysis'), is detested by psycho-analysts not only because it is unscientific

---

[1] In these phases the mind accelerates so that everything seems too slow, the reverse in depression. Beethoven's metronome markings would be affected; experience would have taught him to choose tranquil periods for fixing, or at least revising them, but even then any undue pressure could cause uncertainty and impatience with some fallible results.

(and usually inartistic), but because it gives an air of slickness and speciousness to what is in fact a rigorous and most self-critical discipline. The guesses are usually promulgated in the sensational *UrFreud* terminology most calculated to titillate, no matter how inopportune the connotations nor how outmoded the terms, and with no realization of the fact that it is hazardous to deduce from thousands of couched neurotics all the laws applicable to normal men and women, much less to geniuses.

Sexuality

Certain analytic hypotheses of general application can be applied to Beethoven. He evidently had a great abundance of creative energy ('libido'), a certain amount of which was consumed or had an outlet in irritability, tenseness, and somatic symptoms, e.g. his disorderly bowel function. With this last went, as might be expected, an obsessional habit of mind, shown in his minute repeated reworking of his musical ideas, his spotless linen, his incessant washing, his stubbornness, his financial preoccupations, his scribbling arithmetic everywhere (they even used to sell his shutters for souvenirs) his rigid habits of work. But so much energy is sublimated in his immense artistic accomplishment (hard work this, he was more like a sculptor than a singer), that there was little left for ordinary 'sexuality' (i.e. gratification plus courtship plus marriage plus nest building plus fatherhood plus food-getting plus launching the children plus becoming a patriarch) even though his successes with women,[1] his strong family feelings, and his devastating love for his nephew show that he had all the requisites except the will. He was in fact as committed to his music as a saint to his God, one whose will is no longer free once he has had a glimpse of the Beatific Vision.

It is unrealistic to try to explain Beethoven, though some writers have made elaborate constructions based on the usual generalizations, e.g. that the poet is communicating to the lost mother to whom he is fixated, that the hero is fulfilling the phantasy of 'rescuing the beloved (mother)'. Little is known of Beethoven's mother. She had been in domestic service as a cook, she had been married previously, she had taken him at eleven on a tour of the Low Countries as an infant prodigy; she died of consumption when he was sixteen. There is no evidence that he was abnormally attached to her. He writes naturally

---

[1] 'In Vienna, at least as long as I was there, Beethoven was perpetually engrossed in a love affair, and among his conquests were some that most lovers would have found extremely difficult, if not impossible' (Wegeler).

about her and with tenderness soon after her death. In 1825, in answer to a letter from Wegeler, he asks him to kill the rumour published in editions 5 to 7 of Brockhaus's *Conversations-Lexikon* that he was the illegitimate son of Frederick William II of Prussia 'to make known my parent's integrity, especially my mother's'. These are the only two references to her, so that any ideas about their relationship must clearly be surmises only. Another otiose surmise is that he ought really to have been homosexual in spite of his never having written one seductive, languid, or voluptuous tune. That he could have been an actual homosexual would hardly suggest itself to any unbiased reader of the biographies and letters; moreover, Stephan von Breuning, attorney, State Councillor, part author of *Fidelio*, who had known him all his life and had shared a lodging with Beethoven for a couple of years from 1804, let his young son Gerhard play in and out of Beethoven's house for the last two years of his life. The boy was in his fourteenth year and Beethoven's cronies were visiting constantly: the von Breunings would never have allowed the boy to be free of the house if homosexuality was in the air.

Nephew Karl

Stephan von Breuning in his obituary notice[1] says, 'While possessing lofty musical genius, a great and cultured mind and rare depth of soul, Beethoven was from a boy perfectly helpless in all economic and financial matters.' This unpracticality is shown in the matter of his nephew Karl, who dominates the whole of the third period. Karl seems to have been a likeable young man. He was described as good-looking, well brought up, pleasing, clever, and perceptive. The conversation books exhibit his fundamental dutifulness and goodness of heart. They also show that he tried to stand up to Beethoven quite manfully but he had no more chance of success than anybody else. Some of Beethoven's scores, notably the Ninth Symphony, have additions in Karl's hand which show that he not only helped but also had enough knowledge and skill (and patience) to help intelligently.[2] Beethoven had an immense love for him. He does not appear to have been suppressive or possessive except in his stubborn determination to keep him away from his mother's influence (there are, by the way, several instances of Beethoven's making sacrifices to spare her feelings,

[1] In *Augsburg Allgemeine Zeitung*, 4 April 1827.
[2] 'The delicate feeling for music which the nephew displayed on this occasion induced the uncle in after years to consult him about his new themes and melodies.' Starke, Karl's music teacher, quoted by Nohl (op. cit.).

and her finances, which do not usually get recognition) but he made some bad mistakes. Within a year of the boy's father's death, and when he had effectively lost his mother, Beethoven had him operated on for hernia. Karl was ten and there were no anaesthetics. It would be hard to imagine a more traumatic timing for a terrifying operation which the boy would regard as on his genitals. Beethoven tried to make him a musician, then a philologist, then a financier, and he seems to have been blind to the fact that the boy had no talent for these things and no academic aptitude. Beethoven made a fetish of trivial details of truthfulness and economy, meddled in his schooling, changed schools, tried a boarding-school, then tried to have him at home with servants, then tried to send him to his friend Weissenbach in Salzburg and to Father Sailer at Landshut and finally boarded him out at a kind of crammer's. In the summer of 1826 at the age of twenty Karl attempted suicide by blowing his brains out. Thereafter Beethoven was a broken man, he was dead within a year; it was tragedy, a noble protagonist led inevitably to catastrophe by his own nature.

Karl told the magistrates, 'I have become worse because my uncle insisted on making me better.' Holz reported, 'It is not hatred but quite another feeling which irritates him against you. He gives no other reason but imprisonment at your house, the existence under your surveillance', and Breuning told him, 'He stated at the police station that it was your constant worrying him which had driven him to the deed.' These reproaches are almost intolerably sad; but Beethoven's rare depth of soul included the humility to accept reality, and he behaved with great address, stood by the boy, found a suitable spiritual adviser for him[1] and then took him away to Gneixendorf. He helped him in his ambition to join a regiment where he did well enough to prove that Beethoven had not made too utter a failure of rearing him.[2]

Conclusion

Medical reports list disorders. What is not mentioned is what is healthy. In actual medical practice, however, the patient's strength and his reserves of health are in the long run more important than the current disease. In a psychiatric condition, what is occurring in the patient's consciousness is fallacious and misleading; the real man lies deeper and

[1] Suicides were detained until they showed a genuine, firm change of attitude. Psychotherapy was still in the hands of priests and it was a half a century before Freud began his work at the same hospital.

[2] Karl inherited from both his uncles and was able to live as a country gentleman with three daughters and a seat on the local council.

can be deduced only from his 'style' and from his pre-verbal ideas (the 'phantasies' of psychoanalysis, the 'species' of the Schools) as projected for instance in his dreams. In these not only are his nature and his experiences inherent, but his intentions (not as yet conscious to himself) and his orientation towards his future foreshadowed. Now works of art are phantasies realized, and since music is the most immediately pre-verbal of the arts and the least distorted by literalness, Beethoven's third period works reveal him in his maturity directly, almost without mediation. At a simple level we perceive how the mature works integrate the whole of his musical experience. His interest in fugue derives from his early immersion in the Forty-Eight. In the last movement of the Ninth Symphony he finally achieved the setting he had looked for in early manhood for the Ode to Joy, and even incorporated a tune from his middle period. The religious experience of a lifetime is summed up in the Missa Solemnis. Beethoven's mind was integrating more and more; at his core he was becoming fulfilled and there is the air of serenity during his final illness that is so often the outward sign of completeness. After what turned out to be the last bedside consultation of his doctors, though he did not know it, his comment as they withdrew[1] was: '*Plaudite, amici, commoedia finita est.*' He never did think much of us; perhaps we should leave him in peace.

BIBLIOGRAPHY TO APPENDIX A

Asherson, N., *Beethoven's Deafness and the Saga of the Stapes*, Presidential Address, Hunterian Society, London, 1965.

Beethoven, *Letters*. Edited Emily Anderson, London, 1961

Bekker, Paul, *Beethoven*, Stuttgart, 1922.

Bilancioni, G., *La Sordità di Beethoven*, Rome, 1921.

Breuning, Gerhard von, *Aus dem Schwarzspanierhaus*, Vienna, 1874.

Brodie, B. C., *Pathological and Surgical Observations on Diseases of the Joints*, London, 1818. (Cited by Gardner, below.)

Bumke, O., *Textbook of Mental Diseases*, Munich, 1924.

Busch, Wilhelm, *Anleitung die Krankheiten der Feldhospitäler zu erkennen und zu heilen*. Marburg, 1812.

Busch, Gräf and Horn, *Encyclopaediasches Wörterbuch*, 30 vols., Berlin, 1837.

---

[1] Gerhard von Breuning, op. cit.

Cullen, William, *A Practice of Physic*, 4th ed., Edinburgh, 1784.

Dubois, Edmund, *Lupus Erythematosus*, McGraw-Hill, New York, 1966.

Forster, Walther, *Beethovens Krankheiten und ihre Beurteilung*, Wiesbaden, 1956.

Gardner, D. L., *Pathology of the Connective Tissue Diseases*, London, 1965.

Grove, Geo., *Dictionary of Music and Musicians*, London, 1879.

Hecker, A., *Taschenbuch für Feldärzte*, Berlin, 1806.

Jacobsohn, Leo, 'Beethovens Gehörleiden', *Deutsche Medizinische Wochenschritt*, 34, 1910.

Jacobsohn, Leo, 'Beethovens Gehörleiden und letzte Krankheit', *Deutsche Medizinische Wochenschritt*, 43, 1927.

Ley, Stephan, 'An Beethovens letzten Krankenlager', *Medizinische Welt*, 10, ii, 1936.

Mayer-Gross, Slater and Roth, *Clinical Psychiatry*, London, 1954.

Muir, Robert, Article, 'Bacteriology', *Encyclopaedia Britannica*, 1911.

Neumann, Heinrich, 'Beethovens Gehörleiden', *Wiener Medizinische Wochenschritt*, 76, 1927.

Nohl, Karl Ludwig, *Beethoven nach seinen Zeitgenossen*, Berlin, 1877.

Osler, Wm., 'On the Visceral Complications of Erythema Exudativum Multiforme', *New Sydenham Soc.*, London, 1897.

Peitersen and Carlsen, 'Hearing Impairment as the Initial Sign of Polyarteritis Nodosa', *Acta Otorhinolaryngologica*, Stockholm, 61, 1966.

Piroth, M., 'Beethovens letzte Krankheit auf Grund der zeitgenössischen Quellen (Beethoven's last illness based on contemporary sources), *Beethoven Jahrbuch*, Bonn, 1959–60.

Schiedermair, 'Ludwig Beethovens Krankheiten', *Kölnische Zeitung*, 29 Sep. 1927.

Schindler, A., *Beethoven as I knew Him*, editor MacArdle, London, 1966.

Schweisheimer, Waldemar, *Beethovens Leiden*, Munich, 1922.

Schultze, F., 'Die Krankheiten Beethovens', *Münchener Medizinische Wochenschritt*, 75, 1928.

Sorsby, M., 'Beethoven's Deafness', *Journal of Laryngology and Otology*, 45, 1930.

Sterba, R. and E., *Beethoven and his Nephew*, trans. Trask, London, 1957.

Thayer, A. *Life of Beethoven*, editor Forbes, Princeton, 1964.

Wardrop, J., 'Rheumatic Inflammations of the Eyes', *Abhandlungen zum Gebrauche praktischer Aertzte*, 15, Leipzig, 1830.

Wawruch, Quoted in Nohl, complete. See above.

Wegeler, F. G., *Nachtrag zu den Biographischen Notizen*, Coblenz, 1838.

Wegeler and Ries, *Biographische Notizen über L. v. Beethoven*, Coblenz, 1838.

Frimmel is not mentioned in this list because of his medical status, particularly misleading owing to his medical degree. He was curator of an art museum and had already begun that work before the end of his medical student days, which were pre-Pasteur. He did not practise, but writes with great assurance. Squires whose paper looks as if he would have to be a medical man was not.

A Note on Beethoven's Metronome Markings

Much detailed work has been done on this complex, and in the last resort unrewarding subject, most notably and recently by Peter Stadlen, the first part of whose findings are embodied in an article 'Beethoven and the Metronome' published in *Music and Letters* (October 1967, vol. 48, no. 4). The whole position with regard to Beethoven's metronome markings has been bedevilled by the composer himself, the shortcomings of whose mathematics made it hard for him in the first place to express his wishes with regard to tempo in the mechanical-numerical formulae devised by Maelzel. As Stadlen shows, at the session on 27 September 1826, when uncle and nephew were trying to establish correct metronome markings in the presentation copy of the Ninth Symphony for the King of Prussia, there was considerable confusion over the units in question. Such passages, in Karl's handwriting, as 'twice 80 would make . . .', and then '80 = 𝅝', later corrected to '♩ = 80'; or '132 is the same tempo, only in half notes (in two beats) which would be better' reveals a state of affairs which has been perpetuated with almost incredible wantonness by copyists and printers. In the Eulenburg scores alone, for example, Stadlen has no difficulty in finding two crass instances from op. 74 (♩ = 100 instead of 𝅝 = 100 for the 'Più presto quasi prestissimo' and ♩ = 72 instead of ♪ = 72 for the Adagio) and the story of stems cavalierly added to semibreves, blocked-in minims, tails added to crotchets and dots sprinkled apparently *ad libitum* continues almost to our own day. Beethoven himself seems to have passed, in good health, the marking 𝅗𝅥 = 144 instead of ♩ = 144 in the proofs of the finale of op. 106; and Schindler's 'so I am to mark the second movement of the A major symphony 𝅗𝅥 = 80' (instead of ♩ = 80) in a conversation book of 1823 passes unremarked, not only by Beethoven himself but even by the twentieth-century editor of the notebooks (cf. George Schünemann, *Beethovens Konversationshefte*, iii, p. 12).

A further source of error originating in the composer himself is suggested by another of Karl's entries in the conversation book of 27 September 1826. 'You are taking it faster then 126. 132. This is how we had it this morning.' Like any other composer and perhaps more than most others, Beethoven plainly felt the 'right' tempo for his music slightly differently at different times. In his case particularly we cannot ignore the part played by the physical-psychological element in his determination of tempi. A man of his temperament and in his physical condition might very well feel in a mood of physical exhaustion and depression that the tempi which he had decided upon in good health and high spirits were too fast, and vice versa. Schindler's acid comment on the conversation-book concerned—'this proves the unreliability of Beethoven's own metronome markings'—is not wholly unjustified; but it does not absolve us from trying to determine, first the markings that Beethoven himself intended, and second the correct interpretation of those markings.

Select Bibliography

German

Baensch, Otto, *Aufbau und Sinn des Chorfinales in Beethovens Neunter Sinfonie* (Berlin, 1930).

Bekker, Paul, *Beethoven* (Berlin 1911, English translation London, 1925).

Breuning, Gerhard von, *Aus dem Schwarzspanierhaus* (1874).

Brühl, Moriz, *J. M. Sailer, systematische Anthologie und Lebensbild* (1885).

Bülow, Hans von, *Briefe und Schriften*, (Leipzig, 1895–1908), 8 vols

Cassirer, Fritz, *Beethoven und die Gestalt* (Berlin and Leipzig, 1925).

Fournier, August, *Die Geheimpolizei auf dem Wiener Kongress* (1913).

Frimmel, Theodor, *Beethoven Handbuch* (Leipzig, 1926), 2 vols.

——*Beethoven Studien* (Munich and Leipzig, 1905–6), 2 vols.

Hankamer, Paul, *Zacharias Werner* (1920).

Innerkofler, Adolf, *Ein oesterreichischer Reformator—Clemens Maria Hofbauer* (Regensburg and Rome, 1910).

Kinsky, Georg, *Das Werk Beethovens Thematisch-bibliographisches Verzeichnis seiner sämtlichen vollendeten Kompositionen* (1955).

Langer, Rudolf, *Missa Solemnis—über das theologische Problem in Beethovens Musik* (1962).

Leisching, E., *Der Wiener Congress*, (Wiener Congress Ausstellung, 1896).

Leitzmann, Albert, *Beethovens Persönliche Aufzeichnungen* (n.d.).

——*Beethovens Persönlichkeit* (1914), 2 vols.

Lenz, Wilhelm von, *Beethoven—eine Kunststudie* (Hamburg, 1855–60).

Marx, A. B., *Ludwig van Beethoven—Leben und Schaffen* (1859; 5th ed. 1901).

Metternich, Clemens Graf von, *Denkwürdigkeiten* (1844), 4 vols.

Nohl, Ludwig, *Beethoven nach den Schilderungen seiner Zeit* (Stuttgart, 1877).

Nohl, Walter, *L. van Beethovens Konversationshefte* (Munich, 1923).

Nottebohm, Gustav, *Beethoveniana* (1872).

——*Zweite Beethoveniana* (1887).

Orel, Alfred, *Ein Wiener Beethovenbuch* (Vienna, 1921) (includes Karl Wagner's 'Beethovens Beziehungen zur zeitgenössischen Literatur und Presse').

Pichler, Caroline, *Denkwürdigkeiten aus meinem Leben* (Vienna 1844).

Reti, Rudolph, *The Thematic Process in Music* (London 1951).

Ries F., *see* Wegeler.

Schenker, Heinrich, *Beethovens Neunte Sinfonie* (Vienna 1912).

——*Die letzten fünf Sonaten von Beethoven* (Vienna, 1914).

Schiedermair, Ludwig, *Der junge Beethoven* (1925; 2nd ed. Leipzig, 1951).
——*Die Gestaltung weltanschaulicher Ideen in der Vokalmusik Beethovens* (Leipzig, 1934).
Schindler, Anton, *Biographie von Ludwig van Beethoven* (Münster, 1840, English translation London, 1966).
Schmitz, Arnold, *Das romantische Beethovenbild* (Berlin, 1927).
Schünemann, Georg, *Konversationshefte*, i–iii (1941).
——*Musikerhandschriften* (1936).
Stadtlaender, Chris, Beethoven zieht um—eine heitere Dokumentation (1962).
Till, Rudolf, *Hofbauer und sein Kreis* (Vienna, 1951).
Unger, Max, *Beethoven und seine Verleger* (Berlin and Vienna, 1921).
Wagner, Richard, 'Beethoven' in *Gesammelte Schriften*, ix.
Wegeler, F. G. and Ries, F., *Biographische Notizen über Ludwig van Beethoven* (Coblenz, 1838).
Wolfsgruber, C., *Hohenwart* (1912).
Zuckerkandl, Victor, *Die Wirklichkeit der Musik* (Zurich, 1963).

English

Cockshoot, John V., *The Fugue in Beethoven's Piano Music* (London, 1959).
Dru, Alick, *The Contribution of German Catholicism* (London, 1963).
Kerman, Joseph *The Beethoven Quartets*, (New York and London, 1967).
Mies, Paul, *Beethoven's Sketches* trans. Doris Mackinnon, 1929.
Newman, Ernest, *The Unconscious Beethoven* (London, 1927).
Sullivan, J. W. N., *Beethoven—his spiritual development* (London, 1927).
Thayer, A. W. *Life of Beethoven* ed. Forbes (1964).
Tovey, Donald *Beethoven's Ninth Symphony* (1927).
——*A Companion to Beethoven's Pianoforte Sonatas* (1931).
Tyson, Alan, *The Authentic English Editions of Beethoven* (London, 1963).

French

Prod'homme, J.-G., *Les Cahiers de conversation de Beethoven* (Paris, 1946).
Lenz, W, von *Beethoven et ses trois styles* (St. Petersburg, 1852 and Paris, 1855).

Italian

Magnani, Luigi, *I Quaderni di conversazione di Beethoven* (Milan, 1962).

General Index

Index of works by Beethoven discussed in the text